THE HEALTH CARE SYSTEM

ISSN 1543-2556

THE HEALTH CARE SYSTEM

Barbara Wexler

INFORMATION PLUS® REFERENCE SERIES
Formerly Published by Information Plus, Wylie, Texas

GALE
CENGAGE Learning·

Farmington Hills, Mich • San Francisco • New York • Waterville, Maine
Meriden, Conn • Mason, Ohio • Chicago

The Health Care System

Barbara Wexler

Kepos Media, Inc.: Steven Long and
Janice Jorgensen, Series Editors

Project Editors: Tracie Moy, Laura Avery

Rights Acquisition and Management: Ashley M.
Maynard

Composition: Evi Abou-El-Seoud, Mary Beth
Trimper

Manufacturing: Rita Wimberley

Cover photograph: ©Lighthunter/Shutterstock.com.

Gale
27500 Drake Rd.
Farmington Hills, MI 48331-3535

ISBN-13: 978-0-7876-5103-9 (set)
ISBN-13: 978-1-57302-644-4

ISSN 1543-2556

This title is also available as an e-book.
ISBN-13: 978-1-57302-676-5 (set)
Contact your Gale sales representative for ordering information.

Printed in the United States of America
1 2 3 4 5   19 18 17 16 15

TABLE OF CONTENTS

PREFACE

The Health Care System is part of the *Information Plus Reference Series*. The purpose of each volume of the series is to present the latest facts on a topic of pressing concern in modern American life. These topics include the most controversial and studied social issues of the 21st century: abortion, capital punishment, care for older adults, child abuse, crime, the economy, energy, gambling, national security, race and ethnicity, social welfare, youth, and many more. Although this series is written especially for high school and undergraduate students, it is an excellent resource for anyone in need of factual information on current affairs.

By presenting the facts, it is the intention of Gale, Cengage Learning, to provide its readers with everything they need to reach an informed opinion on current issues. To that end, there is a particular emphasis in this series on the presentation of scientific studies, surveys, and statistics. These data are generally presented in the form of tables, charts, and other graphics placed within the text of each book. Every graphic is directly referred to and carefully explained in the text. The source of each graphic is presented within the graphic itself. The data used in these graphics are drawn from the most reputable and reliable sources, such as from the various branches of the U.S. government and from private organizations and associations. Every effort has been made to secure the most recent information available. Readers should bear in mind that many major studies take years to conduct and that additional years often pass before the data from these studies are made available to the public. Therefore, in many cases the most recent information available in 2015 is dated from 2012 or 2013. Older statistics are sometimes presented as well, if they are landmark studies or of particular interest and no more-recent information exists.

Although statistics are a major focus of the *Information Plus Reference Series*, they are by no means its only content. Each book also presents the widely held positions and important ideas that shape how the book's subject is discussed in the United States. These positions are explained in detail and, where possible, in the words of their proponents. Some of the other material to be found in these books includes historical background, descriptions of major events related to the subject, relevant laws and court cases, and examples of how these issues play out in American life. Some books also feature primary documents or have pro and con debate sections that provide the words and opinions of prominent Americans on both sides of a controversial topic. All material is presented in an evenhanded and unbiased manner; readers will never be encouraged to accept one view of an issue over another.

HOW TO USE THIS BOOK

The U.S. health care system is multifaceted and consists of health care providers, patients, and treatment facilities, just to name a few components. This book examines the state of the nation's health care system, the education and training of health care providers, and the various types of health care institutions. Implementation of the landmark health care reform legislation, efforts to control the cost of health care, prevalence of insurance, mental health care, and a comparison of health care throughout the world are also covered.

The Health Care System consists of nine chapters and three appendixes. Each chapter is devoted to a particular aspect of the health care system in the United States. For a summary of the information that is covered in each chapter, please see the synopses that are provided in the Table of Contents. Chapters generally begin with an overview of the basic facts and background information on the chapter's topic, then proceed to examine subtopics of particular interest. For example, Chapter 2: Health Care Practitioners begins by describing the roles of physicians and their training as well as conventional and newer medical specialties. Next, the chapter considers the education, responsibilities, and supply of nurses and the expanding roles of advanced practice nurses and physician assistants. This is followed by a discussion of dentists and allied health care providers, including physical and occupational therapists, pharmacists, and mental health professionals. The chapter also describes practitioners of complementary and alternative medicine, including homeopathy, naturopathic medicine, traditional Chinese medicine, acupuncture, and chiropractic. It concludes with a discussion of how and why health care employment is increasing and the impact of the Affordable Care Act on the demand for health professionals. Readers can find their way through a chapter by looking for the section and subsection headings, which are clearly set off from the text. They can also refer to the book's extensive Index if they already know what they are looking for.

Statistical Information

The tables and figures featured throughout *The Health Care System* will be of particular use to readers in learning about this issue. These tables and figures represent an extensive collection of the most recent and important statistics on the health care system, as well as related issues—for example, graphics cover the rate of supply and demand for registered nurses, the number of emergency department visits, the national health expenditure amounts, the percentage of people without health insurance, and the percentage of Americans that are familiar and unfamiliar with the Affordable Care Act. Gale, Cengage Learning, believes that making this information available to readers is the most important way to fulfill the goal of this book: to help readers understand the issues and controversies surrounding the health care system in the United States and reach their own conclusions.

Each table or figure has a unique identifier appearing above it, for ease of identification and reference. Titles for the tables and figures explain their purpose. At the end of each table or figure, the original source of the data is provided.

To help readers understand these often complicated statistics, all tables and figures are explained in the text. References in the text direct readers to the relevant statistics. Furthermore, the contents of all tables and figures are fully indexed. Please see the opening section of the Index at the back of this volume for a description of how to find tables and figures within it.

Appendixes

Besides the main body text and images, *The Health Care System* has three appendixes. The first is the Important Names and Addresses directory. Here, readers will find contact information for a number of government and private organizations that can provide further information on aspects of the health care system. The second appendix is the Resources section, which can also assist readers in conducting their own research. In this section, the author and editors of *The Health Care System* describe some of the sources that were most useful during the compilation of this book. The final appendix is the Index. It has been greatly expanded from previous editions and should make it even easier to find specific topics in this book.

COMMENTS AND SUGGESTIONS

The editors of the *Information Plus Reference Series* welcome your feedback on *The Health Care System*. Please direct all correspondence to:

Editors
Information Plus Reference Series
27500 Drake Rd.
Farmington Hills, MI 48331-3535

CHAPTER 1
THE U.S. HEALTH CARE SYSTEM

When asked to describe the U.S. health care system, most Americans would probably offer a description of just a single facet of a huge, complex interaction of people, institutions, and technology. Like snapshots, each account offers an image, frozen in time, of one of the many health care providers and the settings in which medical care is delivered. Examples of these include:

- Physician offices: for many Americans, health care may be described as the interaction between a primary care physician and a patient to address minor and urgent medical problems, such as colds, allergies, or back pain. A primary care physician (usually a general practitioner, family practitioner, internist, or pediatrician) is the frontline caregiver—the first practitioner to evaluate and treat the patient. Routine physical examinations, prevention management actions such as immunization and health screening to detect disease, and treatment of acute and chronic diseases commonly take place in physicians' offices.

- Medical clinics: these settings provide primary care services comparable to those provided in physicians' offices and may be organized to deliver specialized support such as prenatal care for expectant mothers, well-baby care for infants, or treatment for specific medical conditions such as hypertension (high blood pressure), diabetes, or asthma.

- Hospitals: these institutions contain laboratories, imaging centers (also known as radiology departments, where x-rays and other imaging studies are performed), and other equipment for diagnosis and treatment, as well as emergency departments, operating rooms, and highly specialized personnel.

Medical care is also provided through many other venues, including outpatient surgical centers, school health programs, pharmacies, urgent care and worksite clinics, and voluntary health agencies such as Planned Parenthood, the American Red Cross, and the American Lung Association.

IS THE U.S. HEALTH CARE SYSTEM AILING?

Although medical care in the United States is often considered to be the best available, some observers feel the system that delivers it is fragmented and in serious disarray. This section offers some of the many opinions about the challenges of the present health care system and how to improve it. For example, in "Four Years after Passage of Obamacare, Health Care System Remains in Crisis" (STLToday.com, December 29, 2013), Jim Doyle describes the nation's health care system as being "in desperate straits." He notes that the cost of health care in the United States is significantly higher than it is in other industrialized nations, yet Americans are "among the unhealthiest populations in the Western world." Doyle observes that "efforts to streamline the delivery of health care have been hobbled by fights over politics and money."

In *The Quality Cure: How Focusing on Health Care Quality Can Save Your Life and Lower Spending Too* (2014), David Cutler, a health care economist, Harvard professor, and former adviser to President Barack Obama (1961–) identifies cost, access, and quality as the key issues in the U.S. health care system. He observes that the Patient Protection and Affordable Care Act (ACA, sometimes called Obamacare), was designed to address these issues. Cutler asserts that there are many ways to simultaneously improve the quality and lower the cost of health care. Among them are the use of information technology, such as electronic health records; changing how providers are paid; creating incentives to coordinate care and lower costs, and; improving efficiencies and limiting wasteful spending."

Robert Pearl, a physician and industry observer, believes that the U.S. health care system can make better use of its resources. In "What's the First Step in Transforming American Health Care?" (Forbes.com, February 20, 2014), he observes that the United States ranks first in the world in the proportion of specialists to primary care physicians. He argues that specialists are more expensive than primary care physicians, but have not yielded better outcomes, and suggests rebalancing the ratio in favor of primary care providers and using nonphysician providers such as nurses and pharmacists to help care for patients. Like Cutler, Pearl believes that increasing use of health technologies such as video consultations and mobile services will also serve to improve quality, expand access to care and reduce costs.

In another article, "Malcolm Gladwell on American Health Care: An Interview" (Forbes.com, March 6, 2014), Pearl and commentator Malcolm Gladwell offer a number of suggestions to improve quality and reduce costs, including:

- Financial incentives to motivate health care providers to use electronic health records.

- Increased payments for health plans that offer prevention programs above and beyond those required by the ACA.

- Reducing payments to hospitals with high rates of patient complications attributable to medical errors.

- Incentives to encourage hospitals and physicians to work together to better coordinate care and to implement proven measures to improve the efficiency of patient care.

- Reduce the unnecessary costs that are associated with end-of-life care.

In "On Breaking One's Neck" (NYBooks.com, February 6, 2014), Arnold Relman, professor emeritus of medicine at Harvard Medical School and former editor of the *New England Journal of Medicine*, decries the lack of coordination and integration of health care services from his perspective as a patient as well as a physician. Relman attributes the fragmentation, duplication, and lack of coordination of care to the growing national shortage of primary care physicians. He also expresses concern about an over-reliance on technology—such as monitors, images, and devices—that fill electronic health records with data but sharply reduce bedside care or interaction with physicians.

The previously described ideas are just a few of the wide variety of ways in which people have proposed improvements to the existing health care system in the United States. Besides individual ideas, large-scale reforms have been proposed by presidential administrations, such as by the Clinton administration during the early 1990s and the sweeping health care reform legislation signed into law by President Obama in 2010. The

ACA contains numerous health-related provisions that began taking effect in 2010 and were phased in through 2015. Despite its problematic rollout—most notably the botched launch of HealthCare.gov, the technically flawed and often inoperable federal online marketplace—the ACA aimed to extend coverage to millions of uninsured Americans, institute measures designed to control health care costs and improve system efficiency, and eliminate denial of health care coverage based on preexisting conditions.

Reforming the U.S. Health Care System

Derek Bok of Harvard University observes in "The Great Health Care Debate of 1993–94" (1998, http://www.upenn.edu/pnc/ptbok.html) that in 1993 it appeared that President Bill Clinton (1946–) might successfully enact sweeping reform of the health care system, but that by September 1994 the legislation his administration had championed was dead. Bok attributes the demise of the legislation to divisive special interest groups and to inadequate efforts to educate the public. This resulted in confusion and misunderstanding of the provisions of the legislation, and opposition to it. Bok asserts that because many Americans mistakenly assumed that eliminating excess health care costs generated by fraud and waste would not free up enough money to provide coverage for all of the uninsured, they opposed the Clinton initiative, which they deemed too costly. Bok also recounts that even as public sentiment appeared to be opposed to the Clinton plan, a poll asking respondents to evaluate various health plans without disclosing their sponsors found that 76% of respondents favored the Clinton initiative.

Health care reform was a key issue during the 2008 presidential election. Shortly after taking office, President Obama announced his intention to make his campaign resolve—to fix health care by expanding coverage of the uninsured and helping Americans afford coverage and care—a reality. After a year of bitter partisan (adhering to one party) conflict, the ACA was signed by President Obama and became law on March 23, 2010. A few days later this act was amended by the Health Care and Education Reconciliation Act, which became law on March 30, 2010. They are generally referred to together as the ACA.

The aim of the ACA was to expand coverage, contain health care costs, and improve the health care delivery system. More specifically, the ACA requires most U.S. citizens and legal residents to have health insurance, and it created health insurance exchanges and other mechanisms to enable people with low incomes and small businesses to purchase insurance coverage. Beginning in 2016, all employers with 50 or more full-time employees are required to offer coverage; failing to do so will result in penalties as high as $3,000 per employee. The ACA expands Medicaid (a state and federal health insurance program for low-income people) and the Children's Health Insurance Program (CHIP) to ensure that these public programs cover eligible people. It also strengthens Medicare (a federal health insurance program for people aged 65 years and older and people with disabilities) prescription drug benefits. Furthermore, it eliminates lifetime and annual limits on insurance coverage.

Opposition to the ACA continued after it was passed. The ACA's opponents argued that some or all of the law was unconstitutional. Some challenged the individual mandate, arguing that the federal government could not legally require people to purchase health care. Michael Cooper observes in "Conservatives Sowed Idea of Health Care Mandate, Only to Spurn It Later" (NYTimes.com, February 14, 2012) that, although the mandate had at one time been favored by conservatives, in 2012 it was "Republicans and conservatives who oppose the individual mandate, arguing that it is unconstitutional, while Democrats, who were long resistant to it, are its biggest defenders." There were also challenges to the idea that the ACA could require states to expand their Medicaid programs. In "Health Care Ruling, Vast Implications for Medicaid" (NYTimes.com, June 15, 2012), Robert Pear indicates that more than half the states challenged the constitutionality of this aspect of the ACA.

The U.S. Supreme Court was called on to consider these issues. On June 28, 2012, in *National Federation of Independent Business v. Sebelius, Secretary of Health and Human Services* (No. 11-393), the Supreme Court voted 5–4 to uphold the core components of the ACA. Chief Justice John G. Roberts (1955–) wrote the majority opinion. In it, Roberts reasoned that requiring individuals who choose to forgo health insurance to pay a penalty is not unlike a tax, and thus was a constitutional exercise of Congress's powers. However, the court did limit the ACA's requirement that the states expand Medicaid coverage, rejecting the plan to deny federal payments to states that failed to do so.

While supporters of the ACA celebrated the Supreme Court decision, its detractors, many of whom were Republican, vowed to continue their efforts to repeal it. John Parkinson explains in "House Gears Up to Repeal Obamacare (Again)" (ABCnews.com, July 10, 2012) that although there were insufficient votes in the U.S. Senate to repeal the ACA in July 2012, the U.S. House of Representatives had voted 32 times to "defund, dismantle and repeal" it, and that it would continue to oppose the legislation despite the dwindling odds of successful repeal.

By May 2014 more than 8 million Americans had signed up for coverage under the ACA, but efforts by Republicans in the House to repeal or weaken the legislation continued. For example, in April 2014, the House made its 52nd attempt to modify the legislation, voting to change the definition of full-time work from 30 hours a week to 40 hours a week. Supporters of the change argued that it reflected the traditional conception of full-time work, and would help businesses suffering from increased costs caused by ACA's requirement that they provide full-time workers with health benefits or pay a penalty. Opponents of the measure argued that the 30-hours-a-week standard was necessary to prevent employers from skirting the law by reducing full-time hours to 39 hours a week. As with other changes passed by the Republican-led House in 2014, there was no prospect of the Democrat-led Senate passing the bill into law.

THE COMPONENTS OF THE HEALTH CARE SYSTEM

The health care system consists of all personal medical care services—prevention, diagnosis, treatment, and rehabilitation (services to restore function and independence)—plus the institutions and personnel that provide these services and the government, public, and private organizations and agencies that finance service delivery.

The health care system may be viewed as a complex consisting of three interrelated components: health care consumers (people in need of health care services), health care providers (people who deliver health care services—the professionals and practitioners), and the institutions and organizations of the health care system (the public and private agencies that organize, plan, regulate, finance, and coordinate services) that provide the systematic arrangements for delivering health care. The institutional component includes: hospitals, clinics, and home-health agencies; the insurance companies and programs that pay for services (such as Blue Cross/Blue Shield), managed care plans (such as health maintenance organizations), and preferred provider organizations; and entitlement programs such as Medicare and Medicaid. Other institutions are the professional schools that train students for careers in medical, public health, dental, and allied health professions, such as nursing and laboratory technology. Also included are agencies and associations that research and monitor the quality of health care services; license and accreditation providers and institutions; local, state, and national professional societies; and the companies that produce medical technology, equipment, and pharmaceuticals.

Much of the interaction among the three components of the health care system occurs directly between individual health care consumers and providers. Other interactions are indirect, such as immunization programs or screenings to detect disease, which are performed by public health agencies for whole populations. All health care delivery relies on interactions among the three components. The ability to benefit from health care depends on an individual's or group's ability to gain entry to the health care system. The process of gaining entry to the health care system is referred to as access, and many factors can affect access to health care. This chapter provides an overview of how Americans access the health care system.

ACCESS TO THE HEALTH CARE SYSTEM

In the 21st century, access to health care services is a key measure of the overall health and prosperity of a nation or a population, but access and availability were not always linked to good health status. In fact, many medical historians assert that until the beginning of the 20th century a visit with a physician was as likely to be harmful as it was helpful. Only since the early 20th century has medical care been considered to be a positive influence on health and longevity.

There are three aspects of accessibility: consumer access, comprehensive availability of services, and supply of services adequate to meet community demand. Quality health care services must be accessible to health care consumers when and where they are needed. The health care provider must have access to a full range of facilities, equipment, drugs, and services provided by other practitioners. The institutional component of health care delivery—the hospitals, clinics, and payers—must have timely access to information to enable them to plan an adequate supply of appropriate services for their communities.

Consumer Access to Care

Access to health care services is influenced by a variety of factors. Characteristics of health care consumers strongly affect when, where, and how they access services. Differences in age, educational attainment, economic status, race, ethnicity, cultural heritage, and geographic location determine when consumers seek health care services, where they go to receive them, their expectations of treatment, and the extent to which they wish to participate in decisions about their own medical care.

People have different reasons for seeking access to health care services. Their personal beliefs about health and illness, motivations to obtain care, expectations of the care they will receive, and knowledge about how and where to receive care vary. For an individual to have access to quality care, there must be appropriately defined points of entry into the health care system. For many consumers, a primary care physician is their portal to the health care system. Besides evaluating and addressing the patient's immediate health care need, the primary care physician also directs the consumer to other providers of care such as physician specialists or mental health professionals.

Some consumers access the health care system by seeking care from a clinic or hospital outpatient department, where teams of health professionals are available at one location. Others gain entry by way of a public health nurse, school nurse, social worker, or pharmacist, who refers them to an appropriate source, site, or health care practitioner.

Comprehensive Availability of Health Care Services

Historically, the physician was the exclusive provider of all medical services. Until the 20th century the family doctor served as physician, surgeon, pharmacist, therapist, adviser, and dentist. He carried all the tools of his trade in a small bag and could easily offer state-of-the-art medical care in the patient's home, because hospitals had little more to offer in the way of equipment or facilities. In the 21st century it is neither practical nor desirable to ask one practitioner to serve in all these roles. It would be impossible for one professional to perform the full range of health care services, from primary prevention of disease and diagnosis to treatment and rehabilitation. Modern physicians and other health care practitioners must have access to a comprehensive array of trained personnel, facilities, and equipment so that they can, in turn, make them accessible to their patients.

Although many medical problems are effectively treated in a single office visit with a physician, even simple diagnosis and treatment relies on a variety of ancillary (supplementary) services and personnel. To make the diagnosis, the physician may order an imaging study, such as an x-ray that is performed by a radiology technician and interpreted by a radiologist (a physician specialized in imaging techniques). Laboratory tests may be performed by technicians and analyzed by pathologists (physicians specialized in microscopic analysis and diagnosis). More complicated medical problems involve teams of surgeons and high-tech surgical suites that are equipped with robotic assistants, and rehabilitation programs in which physical and occupational therapists assist patients to regain function and independence.

Some health care services are more effectively, efficiently, and economically provided to groups rather than to individuals. Immunization to prevent communicable diseases and screening to detect diseases in their earliest and most treatable stages are examples of preventive services best performed as cooperative efforts of voluntary health organizations, medical and other professional societies, hospitals, and public health departments.

Access Requires Enough Health Care Services to Meet Community Needs

For all members of a community to have access to the full range of health care services, careful planning is required to ensure both the adequate supply and distribution of needed services. To evaluate community needs and effectively allocate health care resources, communities must gather demographic data and information about the social and economic characteristics of the population. They must also monitor the spread of disease and the frequency of specific medical conditions over time. All these population data must be considered in relation to available resources, including health care personnel; the distribution of facilities, equipment, and human resources (the available health care workforce); and advances in medicine and technology.

For example, a predicted shortage of nurses may prompt increased spending on nursing education; reviews of nurses' salary, benefits, and working conditions; and the cultivation of non-nursing personnel to perform specific responsibilities that were previously assigned to nurses. Similarly, when ongoing surveillance anticipates an especially virulent influenza (flu) season, public health officials, agencies, and practitioners intensify efforts to provide timely immunization to vulnerable populations such as older adults. Government agencies such as the Centers for Disease Control and Prevention (CDC), the National Institutes of Health, state and local health departments, professional societies, voluntary health agencies, and universities work together to research, analyze, and forecast health care needs. Their recommendations allow health care planners, policy makers, and legislators to allocate resources so that supply keeps pace with demand and to ensure

that new services and strategies are developed to address existing and emerging health care concerns.

A Regular Source of Health Care Improves Access

According to the CDC, whether or not an individual has a regular source of health care (i.e., a regular provider or site) is a powerful predictor of access to health care services. Generally, people without regular sources have less access or access to fewer services, including key preventive medical services such as prenatal care, routine immunization, and health screening. Many factors have been found that contribute to keeping individuals from having regular sources of medical care, with income level being the best predictor of unmet medical needs or problems gaining access to health care services.

The National Health Interview Survey (NHIS) is an annual nationwide survey about American's health. The National Center for Health Statistics (NCHS) analyzes the 2013 NHIS in *Early Release of Selected Estimates Based on Data from the January–September 2013 National Health Interview Survey* (March 2014, http://www .cdc.gov/nchs/data/nhis/earlyrelease/earlyrelease201403 .pdf). The NCHS finds that between 1997 and September 2013 the percentage of people of all ages with a usual source of medical care did not substantially vary—ranging from a high of 88% in 2001 to a low of 85.4% in 2010. (See Figure 1.1.)

FIGURE 1.1

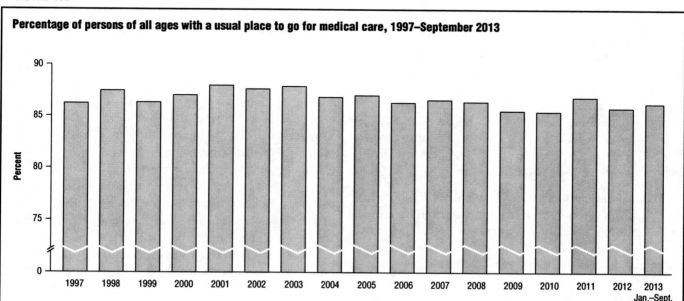

Percentage of persons of all ages with a usual place to go for medical care, 1997–September 2013

Notes: Data are based on household interviews of a sample of the civilian noninstitutionalized population. The usual place to go for medical care does not include a hospital emergency room. The analyses excluded persons with an unknown usual place to go for medical care (about 1.5% of respondents each year).

SOURCE: B. W. Ward, J. S. Schiller, and G. Freeman, "Figure 2.1. Percentage of Persons of All Ages with a Usual Place to Go for Medical Care: United States, 1997–September 2013," in *Early Release of Selected Estimates Based on Data from the January–September 2013 National Health Interview Survey*, National Center for Health Statistics, March 2014, http://www.cdc.gov/nchs/data/nhis/earlyrelease/earlyrelease201403.pdf (accessed April 4, 2014)

FIGURE 1.2

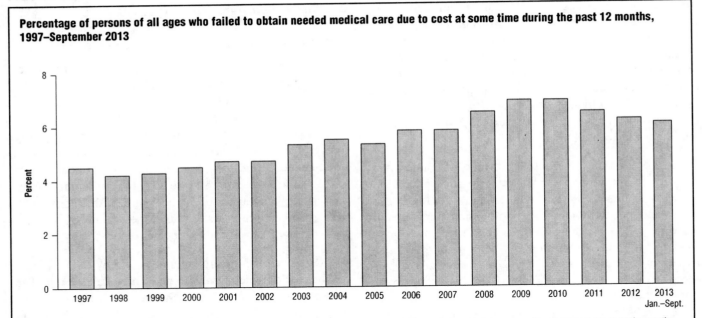

Percentage of persons of all ages who failed to obtain needed medical care due to cost at some time during the past 12 months, 1997–September 2013

Notes: Data are based on household interviews of a sample of the civilian noninstitutionalized population. The analyses excluded persons with unknown responses to the question on failure to obtain needed medical care due to cost (about 0.2% of respondents each year).

SOURCE: B. W. Ward, J. S. Schiller, and G. Freeman, "Figure 3.1. Percentage of Persons of All Ages Who Failed to Obtain Needed Medical Care Due to Cost at Some Time during the Past 12 Months: United States, 1997–September 2013," in *Early Release of Selected Estimates Based on Data from the January–September 2013 National Health Interview Survey*, National Center for Health Statistics, March 2014, http://www.cdc.gov/nchs/data/nhis/earlyrelease/earlyrelease201403.pdf (accessed April 4, 2014)

Still, between 1998 and September 2013 the percentage of people who needed medical care but did not obtain it because of financial barriers to access increased fairly steadily until 2010, when it peaked at 6.9%. (See Figure 1.2.) It subsequently decreased to 6.1% by 2013.

The NHIS finds that people aged 18 to 24 years were the least likely to have a regular source of care, but the likelihood of having a regular source of medical care increased among people aged 25 years and older. (See Figure 1.3.) Children under the age of 18 years were more likely than adults aged 18 to 64 years to have a usual place to go for medical care. Among adults (aged 18 to 64 years), women were more likely than men to have a usual place to seek medical care.

The National Association of Community Health Centers (NACHC) is a nonprofit organization that represents the interests of federally supported and other federally qualified health centers. It serves as an information source about health care for poor and medically underserved populations in the United States. The NACHC reports in *Access Is the Answer* (March 2014, http://www.nachc.com/client/PIBrief14.pdf) that, in 2014, 62 million Americans of all income levels, race, and ethnicity were "medically disenfranchised." That is, they were at risk of inadequate access to basic medical services and "without a regular and continuous source of primary care" because of an inadequate supply of primary care

physicians. The NACHC asserts that low-income populations (43%) and ethnic/racial minorities (38%) are disproportionately affected, as are persons living in rural areas (28%).

Race, Ethnicity, and Regular Sources of Medical Care

According to the NHIS, Hispanic adults continue to be less likely to have a regular source for medical care than non-Hispanic white and non-Hispanic African American adults. After adjusting for age and sex, 79.2% of Hispanics had a usual source of medical care in 2013, compared with 88.2% of non-Hispanic whites and 84.2% of non-Hispanic African Americans. (See Figure 1.4.) Hispanics and non-Hispanic African Americans were more likely than non-Hispanic whites to suffer financial barriers to access. After adjusting for age and sex, 7.4% of Hispanics and 7.5% of non-Hispanic African Americans were unable to obtain needed medical care because of financial barriers, compared with 5.5% of non-Hispanic whites. (See Figure 1.5.) Health educators speculate that language barriers and the lack of information about the availability of health care services may serve to widen this gap.

Women Face Additional Obstacles

In *Health Reform: Implications for Women's Access to Coverage and Care* (August 2013, http://kaiserfamily

FIGURE 1.3

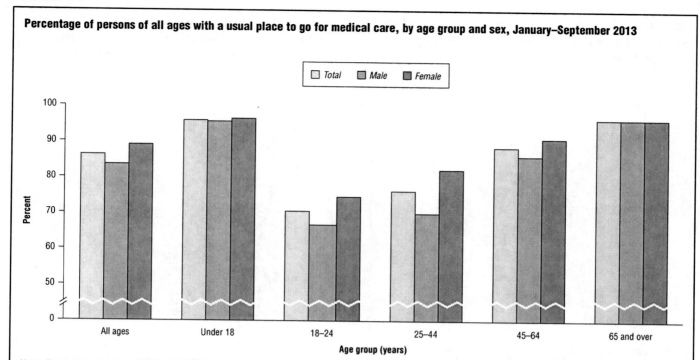

Percentage of persons of all ages with a usual place to go for medical care, by age group and sex, January–September 2013

Notes: Data are based on household interviews of a sample of the civilian noninstitutionalized population. The usual place to go for medical care does not include a hospital emergency room. The analyses excluded the 0.4% of persons with an unknown usual place to go for medical care.

SOURCE: B. W. Ward, J. S. Schiller, and G. Freeman, "Figure 2.2. Percentage of Persons of All Ages with a Usual Place to Go for Medical Care, by Age Group and Sex: United States, January–September 2013," in *Early Release of Selected Estimates Based on Data from the January–September 2013 National Health Interview Survey*, National Center for Health Statistics, March 2014, http://www.cdc.gov/nchs/data/nhis/earlyrelease/earlyrelease201403 .pdf (accessed April 4, 2014).

foundation.files.wordpress.com/2012/03/7987-03-health-reform-implications-for-women_s-access-to-coverage-and-care.pdf), the Kaiser Family Foundation (KFF) writes that women fare worse than men in terms of access to health care services, because they are more likely to be covered as dependents on their spouses's plans and are at greater risk of losing their coverage should they divorce or if their spouse becomes unemployed or dies.

The NHIS also document gender-based disparities in access. Women aged 18 to 64 years and those aged 65 years and older were more likely than men to have failed to obtain needed medical care because of financial barriers to access. (See Figure 1.6.)

The KFF observes that the ACA improves access to care and coverage for women by instituting insurance system reforms, lowering out-of-pocket costs, and mandating comprehensive benefits packages to meet the health service needs of women of all ages. As of 2013, more than one million young women had gained health insurance as a result of the ACA provision that extended dependent coverage through age 26. KFF anticipated that an additional 13 million women would gain insurance coverage by 2016, as the law's expansion actions are implemented.

Children Need Better Access to Health Care, Too

Barbara Bloom, Lindsey I. Jones, and Gulnar Freeman of the NCHS analyzed data from the 2012 NHIS to look at selected health measures, including children's access to care, and compiled their findings in *Summary Health Statistics for U.S. Children: National Health Interview Survey, 2012* (December 2013, http://www.cdc.gov/nchs/data/series/sr_10/sr10_258.pdf). Among other factors, the researchers' analysis focuses on the unmet health care needs of children under the age of 18 years, poverty status, insurance coverage, and usual place of medical care.

Bloom, Jones, and Freeman note that in 2012, just 3.8% of children in the United States did not have a regular source of medical care. (See Table 1.1.) Non-Hispanic white children (97.1%) and non-Hispanic African American children (96.7%) were more likely to have a regular source of care, compared with Hispanic children (94.1%). The researchers also find a relationship between not having a usual source of medical care and family structure, family income, poverty status, and health insurance coverage. The likelihood of lacking a regular source of care was higher among poor and near-poor families of all races and ethnic groups.

FIGURE 1.4

FIGURE 1.5

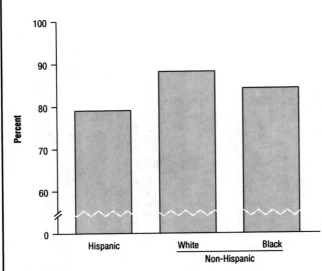

Age- and sex-adjusted percentage of persons of all ages with a usual place to go for medical care, by race/ethnicity, January–September 2013

Notes: Data are based on household interviews of a sample of the civilian noninstitutionalized population. The usual place to go for medical care does not include a hospital emergency room. The analyses excluded the 0.4% of persons with an unknown usual place to go for medical care. Estimates are age-sex adjusted using the projected 2000 U.S. population as the standard population and using five age groups: under 18, 18–24, 25–44, 45–64, and 65 and over.

SOURCE: B. W. Ward, J. S. Schiller, and G. Freeman, "Figure 2.3. Age-Sex-Adjusted Percentage of Persons of All Ages with a Usual Place to Go for Medical Care, by Race/Ethnicity: United States, January–September 2013," in *Early Release of Selected Estimates Based on Data from the January–September 2013 National Health Interview Survey*, National Center for Health Statistics, March 2014, http://www.cdc.gov/nchs/data/nhis/earlyrelease/earlyrelease201403.pdf (accessed April 4, 2014)

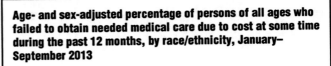
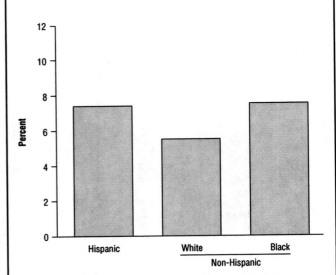

Age- and sex-adjusted percentage of persons of all ages who failed to obtain needed medical care due to cost at some time during the past 12 months, by race/ethnicity, January–September 2013

Notes: Data are based on household interviews of a sample of the civilian noninstitutionalized population. The analyses excluded the 0.1% of persons with unknown responses to the question on failure to obtain needed medical care due to cost. Estimates are age-sex adjusted using the projected 2000 U.S. population as the standard population and using three age groups: under 18, 18–64, and 65 and over.

SOURCE: B. W. Ward, J. S. Schiller, and G. Freeman, "Figure 3.3. Age-Sex-Adjusted Percentage of Persons of All Ages Who Failed to Obtain Needed Medical Care Due to Cost at Some Time during the Past 12 Months, by Race/Ethnicity: United States, January–September 2013," in *Early Release of Selected Estimates Based on Data from the January–September 2013 National Health Interview Survey*, National Center for Health Statistics, March 2014, http://www.cdc.gov/nchs/data/nhis/earlyrelease/earlyrelease201403.pdf (accessed April 4, 2014)

The type of health insurance a child had, if any, was related to whether or not they had a regular source of care. In 2012, 28% of children without health insurance did not have a usual place for health care, compared with just 1.8% of children with private health insurance. (See Table 1.1.)

Bloom, Jones, and Freeman also find that in 2012 a greater percentage of children with private health insurance (85%) received health care in a physician's office than children with Medicaid (62.4%), other health insurance (58.9%), or uninsured children (55.5%). (See Table 1.1.) These last three groups were notably more likely to receive routine care at a clinic than were children with private insurance.

Table 1.1 shows that children from poor and near-poor families were more likely to have no usual place for health care than children from families that were not poor. Bloom, Jones, and Freeman also report that these children were more likely to have unmet medical needs and to have delayed care because of costs than nonpoor

children. Health professionals are especially concerned about delayed or missed medical visits for children because well-child visits provide an opportunity for early detection of developmental problems, timely treatment of illnesses, and provision of the recommended schedule of immunizations.

According to Bloom, Jones, and Freeman, there was significant geographic variation in having a usual place for care. (See Table 1.1.) Children in the West were the most likely (5.1%) to not have a usual place for care in 2012, followed by those in the South (4.3%). By comparison, 3.2% of children in the Midwest, and just 1.5% of those in the Northeast, lacked a usual place for care.

HOW TO REDUCE DISPARITIES IN ACCESS TO CARE

Health care researchers believe many factors contribute to differences in access, including cultural perceptions and beliefs about health and illness, patient preferences, availability of services, and provider bias. They

FIGURE 1.6

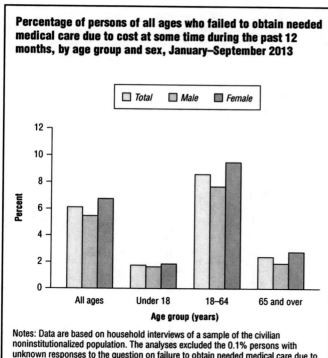

Percentage of persons of all ages who failed to obtain needed medical care due to cost at some time during the past 12 months, by age group and sex, January–September 2013

Notes: Data are based on household interviews of a sample of the civilian noninstitutionalized population. The analyses excluded the 0.1% persons with unknown responses to the question on failure to obtain needed medical care due to cost.

SOURCE: B. W. Ward, J. S. Schiller, and G. Freeman, "Figure 3.2. Percentage of Persons of All Ages Who Failed to Obtain Needed Medical Care Due to Cost at Some Time during the Past 12 Months, by Age Group and Sex: United States, January–September 2013," in *Early Release of Selected Estimates Based on Data from the January–September 2013 National Health Interview Survey*, National Center for Health Statistics, March 2014, http://www.cdc.gov/nchs/data/nhis/earlyrelease/earlyrelease201403.pdf (accessed April 4, 2014)

recommend special efforts to inform and educate minority health care consumers and to increase understanding and sensitivity among practitioners and other providers of care. Besides acquiring factual information, minority consumers must overcome the belief that they are at a disadvantage because of their race or ethnicity. Along with action to dispel barriers to access, educating practitioners, policy makers, and consumers can help reduce the perception of disadvantage.

For decades, health care researchers have documented sharp differences in the ability of ethnic and racial groups to access medical services. The federal government has repeatedly called for an end to these disparities. Although some observers believe universal health insurance coverage is an important first step in eliminating disparities, there is widespread concern that the challenge is more complicated and many calls for additional analysis and action.

In "Reducing Health Care Disparities: Where Are We Now?" (*Mathematica Policy Research*, March 2014), Marcia Gold estimates that full implementation of the ACA could reduce the differential in health insurance coverage between minorities and whites in part by expanding Medicaid coverage. The ACA aims to reduce disparities by emphasizing the concept of medical homes—patient-centered care that is comprehensive, coordinated, accessible, and focused on quality and safety—and addresses the social determinants of health such as income and discrimination. It also strives to improve equity by encouraging best practices—use of the best evidence to make decisions about patient care or the delivery of health services.

According to the White House press release "Fact Sheet: Affordable Care Act by the Numbers" (April 17, 2014, http://www.whitehouse.gov/the-press-office/2014/04/17/fact-sheet-affordable-care-act-numbers), as of April 2014, 8 million people had obtained health insurance in the health insurance marketplace established under the ACA. The ACA had also enabled 3 million young adults to gain coverage by staying on their parents' plans, and 3 million other people to enroll in Medicaid and CHIP. However, the White House estimated that 5.7 million people will remain uninsured in 2016 as a direct result of 24 states opting not to expand Medicaid.

AHRQ Report Documents Disparities in Access

In July 2003 the Agency for Healthcare Research and Quality (AHRQ) released its first *National Healthcare Disparities Report* (http://archive.ahrq.gov/qual/nhdr03/nhdr2003.pdf), a report requested by Congress that documented racial health disparities including access to care. Among other concerns, the report found that African Americans and low-income Americans have higher mortality rates for cancer than the general population because they are less likely to receive screening tests for certain forms of the disease and other preventive services. Although the report asserted that differential access may lead to disparities in quality, and observed that opportunities to provide preventive care are often missed, it conceded that knowledge about why disparities exist is limited.

The AHRQ report generated fiery debate in the health care community and among legislators and painted a rather bleak view of disparities. The report called for detailed data to support quality improvement initiatives and observed that "community-based participatory research has numerous examples of communities working to improve quality overall, while reducing healthcare disparities for vulnerable populations."

Highlights from the *National Healthcare Disparities Report 2012*

In *National Healthcare Disparities Report 2012* (May 2013, http://www.ahrq.gov/research/findings/nhqrdr/nhdr 12/nhdr12_prov.pdf), the AHRQ tracks the measures of access to care that the first report, *National Healthcare Disparities Report*, identified in 2003. These measures

TABLE 1.1

Age-adjusted percentages of selected measures of health care access for children under age 18, by selected characteristics, 2012

Selected characteristic	Has usual place of health care		All children under age 18 years with a usual place of health care	Type of place[b]					
	No	Yes		Clinic	Doctor's office	Emergency room	Hospital outpatient	Some other place	Doesn't go to one place most often
				Percent distribution[c]					
Total[d] (age-adjusted)	**3.8**	**96.2**	**100.0**	**23.9**	**74.2**	**0.4**	**1.0**	**0.4**	**0.1**
Total[f] (crude)	**3.8**	**96.2**	**100.0**	**23.9**	**74.2**	**0.4**	**1.0**	**0.4**	**0.1**
Sex									
Male	3.8	96.2	100.0	23.0	75.2	0.3	0.9	0.4	0.1*
Female	3.7	96.3	100.0	24.9	73.2	0.4	1.1	0.3	0.1*
Age[g]									
0–4 years	2.1	97.9	100.0	23.7	74.3	0.3*	1.5	0.1*	*
5–11 years	3.4	96.6	100.0	23.9	74.4	0.5	0.7	0.4	0.2*
12–17 years	5.6	94.4	100.0	24.2	73.9	0.2	1.0	0.5	0.2*
Race									
One race[i]	3.8	96.2	100.0	23.9	74.2	0.4	1.0	0.3	0.2
White	3.8	96.2	100.0	23.5	75.2	0.3	0.6	0.3	0.1*
Black or African American	3.2	96.8	100.0	24.6	71.4	0.7	2.6	*	*
American Indian or Alaska Native	3.0*	97.0	100.0	46.9	46.9	*	*	—	—
Asian	6.3	93.7	100.0	22.4	75.4	*	1.3*	—	0.5*
Native Hawaiian or other Pacific Islander	—	100.0	100.0	31.4*	65.6	*	—	*	—
Two or more races[g]	3.3	96.7	100.0	24.4	74.2	*	0.8*	*	—
Black or African American and white	4.1*	95.9	100.0	22.3	76.1	—	*	*	—
American Indian or Alaska Native and white	2.3*	97.7	100.0	28.1	69.9	—	*	*	—
Hispanic or Latino origin[h] and race									
Hispanic or Latino	5.9	94.1	100.0	38.4	59.2	0.6	1.3	0.3*	0.2*
Mexican or Mexican American	6.3	93.7	100.0	42.1	55.5	0.6*	1.1	0.3*	0.4*
Not Hispanic or Latino	3.2	96.8	100.0	19.5	78.9	0.3	0.9	0.4	0.1*
White, single race	2.9	97.1	100.0	17.2	81.8	0.2*	0.4	0.4	0.1*
Black or African American, single race	3.3	96.7	100.0	24.4	71.8	0.8	2.3	*	*
Family structure[i]									
Mother and father	3.4	96.6	100.0	21.8	76.7	0.2	0.9	0.4	0.1*
Mother, no father	3.8	96.2	100.0	27.8	70.0	0.6	1.1	0.3*	0.3*
Father, no mother	7.4	92.6	100.0	27.9	69.8	*	*	*	*
Neither mother nor father	4.9	95.1	100.0	34.4	59.2	*	4.2*	*	0.1
Parent's education[j]									
Less than high school diploma	6.0	94.0	100.0	47.8	49.5	0.7*	0.9	0.4	0.3*
High school diploma or GED[k]	5.7	94.3	100.0	29.0	68.6	0.6	1.3	0.4*	*
More than high school	2.8	97.2	100.0	17.7	80.9	0.2*	0.7	0.3	*
Family income[l]									
Less than $35,000	5.4	94.6	100.0	35.6	61.9	0.7	1.4	0.3*	0.2*
$35,000 or more	2.9	97.1	100.0	18.2	80.3	0.2*	0.7	0.4	0.1*
$35,000–$49,999	4.5	95.5	100.0	26.0	71.6	0.6*	1.2	*	0.2*
$50,000–$74,999	3.9	96.1	100.0	21.9	76.6	*	0.8	0.4*	*
$75,000–$99,999	2.4	97.6	100.0	15.2	83.3	*	0.7*	*	*
$100,000 or more	1.8	98.2	100.0	13.3	85.8	*	0.4*	0.3*	*
Poverty status[m]									
Poor	5.2	94.8	100.0	36.9	60.3	0.8	1.4	0.3*	0.2*
Near poor	4.8	95.2	100.0	30.5	67.2	0.5*	1.3	0.3*	0.3*

TABLE 1.1

Age-adjusted percentages of selected measures of health care access for children under age 18, by selected characteristics, 2012 [CONTINUED]

Selected characteristic	Has usual place of health care[a]		All children under age 18 years with a usual place of health care	Type of place[b]					
	No	Yes		Clinic	Doctor's office	Emergency room	Hospital outpatient	Some other place	Doesn't go to one place most often
				Percent distribution[c]					
Not poor	2.7	97.3	100.0	15.6	83.1	0.1*	0.6	0.4	0.1*
Health insurance coverage[d]									
Private	1.8	98.2	100.0	14.1	85.0	*	0.5	0.3	0.0*
Medicaid or other public	2.5	97.5	100.0	35.1	62.4	0.6	1.4	0.4*	0.1*
Other	2.6*	97.4	100.0	35.3	58.9	—	3.4*	1.9*	*
Uninsured	26.8	73.2	100.0	38.6	55.5	1.7*	1.8*	0.8*	1.6*
Place of residence[e]									
Large MSA	3.8	96.2	100.0	20.9	77.2	0.5	1.0	0.2*	0.1
Small MSA	3.8	96.2	100.0	24.5	73.6	0.2*	1.0	0.6	*
Not in MSA	3.7	96.3	100.0	33.1	65.0	0.2*	1.1*	0.3*	0.3*
Region									
Northeast	1.5	98.5	100.0	14.6	83.7	0.2*	1.3	*	*
Midwest	3.2	96.8	100.0	29.0	69.5	0.3*	0.9	0.3*	*
South	4.3	95.7	100.0	19.5	78.6	0.5	0.8	0.4	0.1*
West	5.1	94.9	100.0	32.6	65.1	0.4*	1.2	0.5*	0.3*
Current health status									
Excellent or very good	3.8	96.2	100.0	22.6	75.7	0.4	0.9	0.3	0.2
Good	3.3	96.7	100.0	31.3	66.2	0.4*	1.3*	0.6*	*
Fair or poor	4.4*	95.6	100.0	25.2	71.9	*	1.2*	*	*

* Estimates are considered unreliable.
—Quantity zero.
[a]Based on the question, "Is there a place that [child's name] usually goes when [he/she] is sick or you need advice about [his/her] health?"
[b]Based on the question, "What kind of place is it/What kind of place does [child's name] go to most often—clinic or health center, doctor's office or HMO (health maintenance organization), hospital emergency room, hospital outpatient department, or some other place?"
[c]Unknowns for the column variables are not included in the denominators when calculating percentages.
[d]Includes other races not shown separately and children with unknown family structure, parent's education, family income, poverty status, health insurance, or current health status. Estimates may not add to totals due to rounding.
[e]Estimates for age groups are not age-adjusted.
[f]Refers to children of only a single-race group, including those of Hispanic or Latino origin.
[g]Refers to children of more than one race group, including those of Hispanic or Latino origin. Only two combinations of multiple-race groups are shown due to small sample sizes for other combinations.
[h]Refers to children who are of Hispanic or Latino origin and may be of any race or combination of races. "Not Hispanic or Latino" refers to children who are not of Hispanic or Latino origin, regardless of race.
[i]Refers to parents living in the household. "Mother and father" can include biological, adoptive, step, in-law, or foster relationships. Legal guardians are classified in "Neither mother nor father."
[j]Refers to the education level of the parent with the higher level of education, regardless of that parent's age, provided that the parent lives in the household.
[k]GED is General Educational Development high school equivalency diploma.
[l]Includes children in families that reported a dollar amount or would not provide a dollar amount but provided an income interval.
[m]"Poor" children live in families defined as having income below the poverty threshold. "Near poor" children live in families with incomes of 100% to less than 200% of the poverty threshold. "Not poor" children live in families with incomes that are 200% of the poverty threshold or greater.
[n]Based on a hierarchy of mutually exclusive categories. Children with more than one type of health insurance were assigned to the first appropriate category in the hierarchy. "Uninsured" includes children who had no coverage, as well as those who had only Indian Health Service coverage or had only a private plan that paid for one type of service such as accidents or dental care.
[o]MSA is metropolitan statistical area. Large MSAs have a population size of 1 million or more; small MSAs have a population size of less than 1 million. "Not in MSA" consists of persons not living in a metropolitan statistical area.
Notes: Based on household interviews of a sample of the civilian noninstitutionalized population. This table is based on responses about the sample child, not all children in the family. Data came from the sample child file and were weighted using the sample child weight. Estimates of "All children under 18 years" in this table differ slightly from estimates of "All children under 18 years" in the other detailed tables that were based on the person file and were weighted using the person weight. Estimates are age-adjusted using the projected 2000 U.S. population as the standard population and using age groups 0–4 years, 5–11 years, and 12–17 years.

SOURCE: Adapted from Barbara Bloom, Lindsey I. Jones, and Gulnar Freeman, "Table 10. Age-Adjusted Percentages of Having a Usual Place of Health Care, and Age-Adjusted Percent Distributions of Type of Place for Children under 18 Years by Selected Characteristics: United States, 2012," in Summary Health Statistics for U.S. Children: National Health Interview Survey, 2012, National Center for Health Statistics, 2013, http://www.cdc.gov/nchs/data/series/sr_10/sr10_258.pdf (accessed April 4, 2014)

FIGURE 1.7

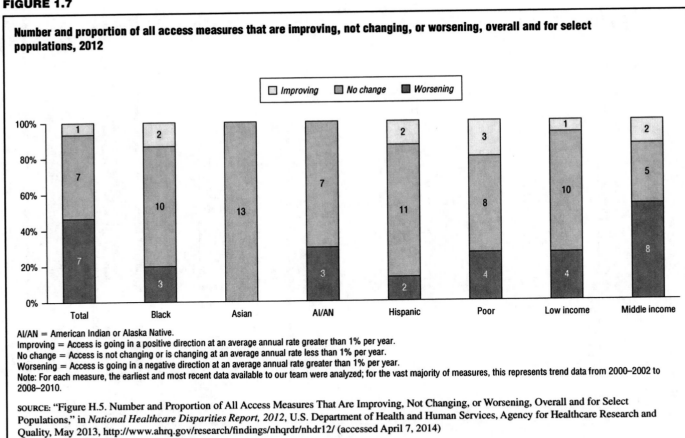

Number and proportion of all access measures that are improving, not changing, or worsening, overall and for select populations, 2012

AI/AN = American Indian or Alaska Native.
Improving = Access is going in a positive direction at an average annual rate greater than 1% per year.
No change = Access is not changing or is changing at an average annual rate less than 1% per year.
Worsening = Access is going in a negative direction at an average annual rate greater than 1% per year.
Note: For each measure, the earliest and most recent data available to our team were analyzed; for the vast majority of measures, this represents trend data from 2000–2002 to 2008–2010.

SOURCE: "Figure H.5. Number and Proportion of All Access Measures That Are Improving, Not Changing, or Worsening, Overall and for Select Populations," in *National Healthcare Disparities Report, 2012*, U.S. Department of Health and Human Services, Agency for Healthcare Research and Quality, May 2013, http://www.ahrq.gov/research/findings/nhqrdr/nhdr12/ (accessed April 7, 2014)

include factors that facilitated access, such as having a primary care provider, and factors that were barriers to access, such as having no health insurance.

The AHRQ reports that, although overall quality is improving, access to care is getting worse and disparities are not improving. For most racial, ethnic, and income groups, the number of access measures that were worsening or unchanged were greater than the number that were improving. Figure 1.7 shows the number and proportion of access measures that improved, were unchanged, or worsened.

Racial and ethnic minorities continued to encounter disproportionate barriers to care. For about one-third of all access measures analyzed, African Americans had worse access to care than whites. Hispanics had worse access to care than non-Hispanic whites across roughly two-thirds of the measures. Figure 1.8 reveals that disparities in access to care by race or ethnicity showed little change in 2012.

Socioeconomic status greatly affected access to care. The report found that poor people had worse access to care than high-income people across every measure in 2012. Low-income individuals had worse access than those with high incomes across 85.7% of measures, and middle-income people had worse access than high-income people

for 71.4% of measures. Figure 1.8 shows that these income-based disparities had grown somewhat worse since the previous report.

ACCESS TO MENTAL HEALTH CARE

Besides the range of barriers to access faced by all Americans trying to access the health care system, people seeking mental health care face unique challenges, not the least of which is that they are even less able than people in good mental health to successfully navigate the fragmented mental health service delivery system. Furthermore, because people with serious mental illness frequently suffer from unemployment and disability, they are likely to join the ranks of the impoverished, uninsured, and homeless, which only compounds access problems. Finally, the social stigmas (deeply held negative attitudes) that promote discrimination against people with mental illness are a powerful deterrent to seeking care.

Myths about mental illness persist, especially the mistaken beliefs that mental illness are a sign of moral weakness or that an affected individual can simply choose to "wish or will away" the symptoms of mental illness. People with mental illness cannot just "pull themselves together" and will themselves well. Without treatment, symptoms can worsen and persist for months or even years.

FIGURE 1.8

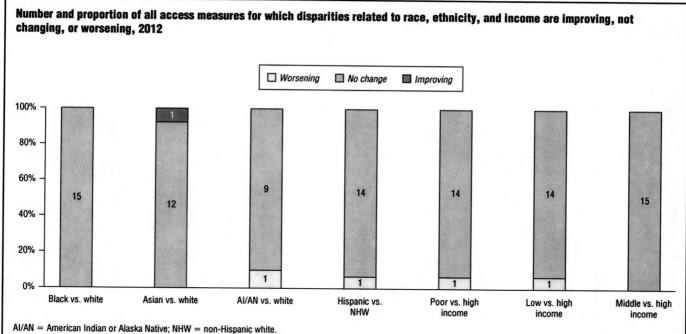

Number and proportion of all access measures for which disparities related to race, ethnicity, and income are improving, not changing, or worsening, 2012

AI/AN = American Indian or Alaska Native; NHW = non-Hispanic white.
Improving = Disparity is getting smaller at a rate greater than 1% per year.
No change = Disparity is not changing or is changing at a rate less than 1% per year.
Worsening = Disparity is getting larger at a rate greater than 1% per year.
Note: For each measure, the earliest and most recent data available to our team were analyzed; for the vast majority of measures, this represents data on change in disparities from 2000–2002 to 2008–2010.

SOURCE: "Figure H.7. Number and Proportion of All Access Measures for Which Disparities Related to Age, Race, Ethnicity, and Income are Improving, Not Changing, or Worsening," in *National Healthcare Disparities Report, 2012*, U.S. Department of Health and Human Services, Agency for Healthcare Research and Quality, May 2013, http://www.ahrq.gov/research/findings/nhqrdr/nhdr12/ (accessed April 7, 2014)

People with mental illness experience other types of social stigmas as well. They may face discrimination in the workplace, in school, and in finding housing. Thwarted in their efforts to maintain independence, people suffering from mental illness may become trapped in a cycle characterized by feelings of worthlessness and hopelessness and may be further isolated from the social and community supports and treatments most able to help them recover.

Disparities in Access to Mental Health Care

The principal barriers to access of mental health care are the cost of mental health services, the lack of sufficient insurance for these services, the fragmented organization of these services, mistrust of providers, and the social stigmas about mental illness. These obstacles may act as deterrents for all Americans, but for racial and ethnic minorities they are compounded by language barriers, ethnic and cultural compatibility of practitioners, and geographic availability of services.

The AHRQ finds in *National Healthcare Disparities Report 2012* that, when compared with whites, African Americans and Hispanics have less access to mental health care and are less likely to receive needed services. For example, according to the AHRQ, African Americans

and Hispanics suffering from depression were less likely than whites to receive timely treatment during 2008–10. (See Figure 1.9.)

HEALTH CARE REFORM PROMISES TO IMPROVE ACCESS

The 2010 enactment of the ACA was hailed as landmark legislation—the most sweeping social legislation since the enactment of Social Security in 1935 and Medicare and Medicaid in 1965. The act is intended to improve access to care by extending health care coverage to an estimated 27 million uninsured Americans by 2019 and by preventing health insurance companies from denying coverage to people with preexisting medical conditions or dropping them when they develop costly medical problems.

In the years after its passage, the ACA has remained controversial. Congressional Republicans, who had not supported the law's enactment, led numerous efforts to revise or repeal the ACA. Court challenges limited the ACA's effects in some ways, most notably by giving states the power to decide if they would expand Medicaid. And even the law's supporters were dismayed by highly visible problems with the ACA's rollout that caused difficulties for consumers.

FIGURE 1.9

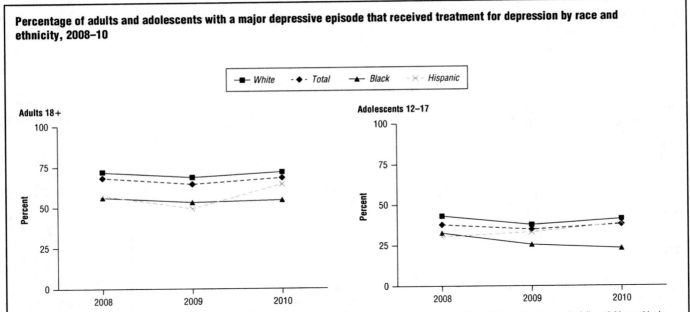

Percentage of adults and adolescents with a major depressive episode that received treatment for depression by race and ethnicity, 2008–10

Note: Major depressive episode is defined as a period of at least 2 weeks when a person experienced a depressed mood or loss of interest or pleasure in daily activities and had a majority of the symptoms of depression described in the fourth edition of the *Diagnostic and Statistical Manual of Mental Disorders*. Treatment for depression is defined as seeing or talking to a medical doctor or other professional or using prescription medication in the past year for depression. White and black are non-Hispanic; Hispanic includes all races.

SOURCE: "Figure 2.32. Adults (Left) and Adolescents (Right) with a Major Depressive Episode in the Past Year Who Received Treatment for Depression in the Past Year, by Age and Race/Ethnicity, 2008–2010," in *National Healthcare Disparities Report, 2012*, U.S. Department of Health and Human Services, Agency for Healthcare Research and Quality, May 2013, http://www.ahrq.gov/research/findings/nhqrdr/nhdr12/ (accessed April 7, 2014)

Concerns about the mandate that medium-sized (50 to 99 full-time workers) and large (100 plus full-time workers) businesses offer health insurance to their employees led to these provisions being delayed by the Obama administration. Implementation of these rules was first pushed back a year, from January 2014 to January 2015. Then, in February 2014, the Obama administration further delayed full implementation until January 2016. Opponents of the ACA pointed to these repeated delays and the difficult rollout of the HealthCare.gov marketplace as indications that that law was unworkable. As of late 2014 there was every indication that the ACA would continue to be a contentious issue for some time to come.

The ACA Delivers on Its Promise

Despite these problems and controversies, the ACA has improved access to care. "Fact Sheet: Affordable Care Act by the Numbers" states that an estimated 71 million Americans with private insurance gained coverage for at least one free preventive health care service—such as mammograms, birth control, or immunizations—in 2011 and 2012, and 37 million Medicare beneficiaries received at least one preventive service with no out of pocket cost. About 60 million Americans gained expanded mental health and substance use disorder benefits and/or federal parity protections. In addition, under the ACA, 105 million Americans no longer need to worry about losing their health benefits when they reach a lifetime limit.

IS ACCESS A RIGHT OR A PRIVILEGE?

The United States is the only developed country in the world that does not have a government-funded universal or national program of health insurance. As a result, Americans with greater incomes and assets are more likely than low-income families to have health insurance and have greater access to health care services. It is for this reason that many regard the ACA as groundbreaking. Supporters of this legislation assert that as previously uninsured people obtain insurance, access will be greatly improved.

However, the AHRQ and other health care researchers and policy makers observe that having health insurance does not necessarily ensure access to medical care. They contend that many other factors, including cost-containment measures put in place by private and public payers, have reduced access to care. They note that reduced access affects vulnerable populations—the poor, people with mental illness and other disabilities, and immigrants—more than others.

Various groups and organizations support the premise that health care is a fundamental human right, rather than a privilege. These organizations include Physicians for a National Health Program, the AARP, National Health Care for the Homeless, the Friends Committee on National Legislation (a Quaker public interest lobby), and the National Economic and Social Right Initiative

(NESRI). For example, in "Human Right to Health" (2014, http://www.nesri.org/programs/health), NESRI states that "the human right to health guarantees a system of health protection for all.... NESRI supports groups that seek to mobilize people to stand up for their right to health care and motivate policy makers to make health care a public good, with costs and benefits shared equitably. We have a right to get the health care we need, and a responsibility to ensure that everyone else can do the same."

Others disagree with the notion that access to health care is a fundamental right. For example, Richard M. Salsman argues in "Memo to the Supreme Court: Health Care Is Not a Right" (Forbes.com, April 3, 2012) that "health care is not a right. It's a valuable service provided by intelligent, hard-working professionals with years of painstaking education and training, people who, like other Americans, deserve equal protection under the law, people who, like other Americans, have a right to their own life, liberty, property and the pursuit of their own happiness." Salsman believes that because people pay for health care, as they do for other goods and services, it is a privilege. Furthermore, he opposes the ACA, contending that mandating health coverage and requiring hospitals to treat patients who cannot pay violate both personal rights and the U.S. Constitution.

Concurring with Salsman, many groups and organizations assert that health care is not a fundamental right. These include Americans for Free Choice in Medicine, the Atlas Society, the United States Conference of Catholic Bishops, and the Heritage Foundation.

CHAPTER 2
HEALTH CARE PRACTITIONERS

The art of medicine consists of amusing the patient while nature cures the disease.

—Voltaire

One of the first duties of the physician is to educate the masses not to take medicine.

—William Osler, *Sir William Osler: Aphorisms, from His Bedside Teachings and Writings* (1950)

PHYSICIANS

Physicians routinely perform medical examinations, provide preventive medicine services, diagnose illness, treat patients suffering from injury or disease, and offer counsel about how to achieve and maintain good health. There are two types of physicians trained in traditional Western medicine: the Doctor of Medicine (MD) is schooled in allopathic medicine and the Doctor of Osteopathy (DO) learns osteopathy. Allopathy is the philosophy and system of curing disease by producing conditions that are incompatible with disease, such as prescribing antibiotics to combat bacterial infection. The philosophy of osteopathy is different; it is based on recognition of the body's capacity for self-healing, and it emphasizes structural and manipulative therapies such as postural education, manual treatment of the musculoskeletal system (osteopathic physicians are trained in hands-on diagnosis and treatment), and preventive medicine. Osteopathy is also considered a holistic practice because it considers the whole person, rather than simply the diseased organ or system.

In modern medical practice, the philosophical differences may not be obvious to most health care consumers because MDs and DOs use many comparable methods of treatment, including prescribing medication and performing surgery. In fact, the American Osteopathic Association (2014, https://www.osteopathic.org/inside-aoa/about/Pages/default.aspx), the national medical professional society that represents more than 104,000 DOs and DO

students, admits that many people who seek care from osteopathic physicians may be entirely unaware of their physician's training. Like MDs, DOs complete four years of medical school and postgraduate residency training; may specialize in areas such as surgery, psychiatry, or obstetrics; and must pass state licensing examinations to practice.

Medical School, Postgraduate Training, and Qualifications

Modern medicine requires considerable skill and extensive training. The road to becoming a physician is long, difficult, and intensely competitive. Medical school applicants must earn excellent college grades, achieve high scores on entrance exams, and demonstrate emotional maturity and motivation to be admitted to medical school. Once admitted, they spend the first two years primarily in laboratories and classrooms learning basic medical sciences such as anatomy (detailed understanding of body structure), physiology (biological processes and vital functions), and biochemistry. They also learn how to take medical histories, perform complete physical examinations, and recognize symptoms of diseases. During their third and fourth years, medical students work under supervision at teaching hospitals and clinics. By completing clerkships—spending time in different specialties such as internal medicine, obstetrics and gynecology, pediatrics, psychiatry, and surgery—they acquire the necessary skills to diagnose and treat a wide variety of illnesses.

Following medical school, new physicians must complete a year of internship, also referred to as postgraduate year one, that emphasizes either general medical practice or one specific specialty and that provides clinical experience in various hospital services (e.g., inpatient care, outpatient clinics, emergency departments, and operating rooms). In the past, many physicians entered practice after this first year of postgraduate training. However, in the present era of specialization most physicians choose to continue in residency training, which lasts an additional three to six years, depending on the specialty. Those who choose a subspecialty such as cardiology, infectious diseases, oncology, or plastic surgery must spend additional years in residency and may then choose to complete fellowship training. Following residency, they are eligible to take an examination to earn board certification in their chosen specialty. Fellowship training involves a year or two of laboratory and clinical research work as well as opportunities to gain additional clinical and patient care expertise.

Medical School Applicants

The Association of American Medical Colleges (AAMC) states in "Applicants, First-Time Applicants, Acceptees, and Matriculants to U.S. Medical Schools by Sex, 2002–2013" (2014, https://www.aamc.org/download/321470/data/2013factstable7.pdf) that the number of students entering medical school for the 2013–14 academic year rose to 21,070, which was a 2.9% increase from the 2012 academic year. The students were selected from a pool of 48,010 applicants.

The High Costs and Long Hours of Medical Training

Medical school is very expensive. In "U.S. Medical Schools: Tuition and Student Fees—First Year Students 2013–2014 and 2012–2013 (2014, https://services.aamc.org/tsfreports/report_median.cfm?year_of_study=2014), the AAMC reports on the average costs of attending public medical schools (based on 84 schools reporting) and private medical schools (55 schools reporting) during the 2013–14 academic year. For public schools, the average was $31,804 for residents and $55,335 for nonresidents. At private schools, costs averaged $50,475 for residents and $52,092 for nonresidents.

Many medical students borrow money in order to pay for their education. The AAMC indicates in "Medical Student Education: Debt, Costs, and Loan Repayment Fact Card" (November 2013, https://www.aamc.org/download/152968/data/debtfactcard.pdf) that for the class of 2013, 87% of public medical school graduates had education debt, as did 84% of the graduates of private medical schools. (This education debt included debts incurred for education prior to medical school.) On average, indebted public medical school graduates had education debts of $162,736, and indebted private medical school graduates owed $181,058 in education debt.

Although a physician's earning power is considerable, and many students are able to repay their educational debt during their first years of practice, some observers believe the extent of medical students' indebtedness may unduly influence their career choices. They may train for higher-paying specialties and subspecialties rather than follow their natural interests, or opt not to practice in underserved geographic areas. The high cost of medical education is also believed to limit the number of minority applicants to medical school.

Historically, medical training has been difficult and involved long hours. This is particularly true for those in residency training. However, working long hours without adequate rest has been found to increase the occurrence of preventable medical errors and thereby adversely affect patient safety. Since July 1, 2011, the Accreditation Council for Graduate Medical Education (ACGME) restricts the duty hours of the more than 100,000 medical residents in the United States. The ACGME Common Program Requirements (2011, http://www.acgme.org/acgmeweb/Portals/0/PDFs/Common_Program_Requirements_07012011%5B2%5D.pdf) stipulate that:

- Residents' "duty hours must be limited to 80 hours per week, averaged over a four-week period"

- "Residents must be scheduled for a minimum of one day free of duty every week"

- First-year residents (interns) must not work more than 16 hours and "should have 10 hours, and must have eight hours, free of duty between scheduled duty periods"

- Second-year residents and above "may be scheduled to a maximum of 24 hours of continuous duty in the hospital"

- "Programs must encourage residents to use alertness management strategies in the context of patient care responsibilities. Strategic napping, especially after 16 hours of continuous duty and between the hours of 10:00 p.m. and 8:00 a.m., is strongly suggested."

In "Inpatient Safety Outcomes following the 2011 Residency Work-Hour Reform" (*Journal of Hospital Medicine*, vol. 366, no. 35, June 14, 2012), Lauren Block et al. report the results of a study to determine whether patient safety outcomes improved after the 2011 residency work-hour changes. Block et al. compared outcomes including length of stay, 30-day readmission, admission to intensive care, and inpatient deaths cared for by residents and hospitalists before and after the reform was instituted. They report, "after implementation of the 2011 work-hour reforms relative to prior years, we found no change in patient safety outcomes in patients treated by residents compared with patients treated by hospitalists."

Conventional and Newer Medical Specialties

Rapid advances in science and medicine and changing needs have resulted in a variety of new medical and surgical specialties, subspecialties, and concentrations.

For example, geriatrics, the medical subspecialty concerned with the prevention and treatment of diseases in older adults, has developed in response to growth in this population. The term *geriatrics* is derived from the Greek *geras* (old age) and *iatrikos* (physician). Geriatricians are physicians trained in primary care, such as internal medicine or family practice, who receive further training and gain certification as specialists in the medical care of older adults.

Another relatively new medical specialty has resulted in physician intensivists. Intensivists, as the name indicates, are trained to staff hospital intensive care units (ICUs, which are sometimes known as critical care units), where the most critically ill patients are cared for using a comprehensive array of state-of-the-art technology and equipment. This specialty arose in response to both the increasing complexity of care provided in ICUs and the demonstrated benefits of having highly trained physicians immediately available to care for critically ill patients. The Health Resources and Services Administration (HRSA) notes in *The Critical Care Workforce: A Study of the Supply and Demand for Critical Care Physicians* (July 2006, http://bhpr.hrsa.gov/healthworkforce/reports/studycriticalcarephys.pdf) that "demand for intensivists will continue to exceed available supply through the year 2020 if current supply and demand trends continue." Assuming optimal utilization, the HRSA predicts a shortfall of 1,500 intensivists in 2020. (See Figure 2.1.) Sajeesh Kumar, Shezana Merchant, and Rebecca Reynolds write in "Tele-ICU: Efficacy and Cost-Effectiveness of Remotely Managing Critical Care" (*Perspectives in Health Information Management*, vol. 10, Spring 2013) that in 2010 less than 15% of ICUs provided intensivist care because there is a limited number of board-certified intensivists in the United States. One promising solution is tele-ICU—exchanging health information from a hospital critical care unit via electronic communications—which enables intensivists to provide real-time services to multiple ICUs from an off-site command center.

Growing more than 8% per year, another newer specialty is hospitalists—physicians who are hospital based as opposed to office based and who provide a variety of services—such as caring for hospitalized patients who do not have personal physicians, explaining complex medical procedures to patients and families, and coordinating many aspects of inpatient care. The Society of Hospital Medicine estimated that there were more than 40,000 hospitalists in practice in 2014.

More traditional medical specialties include:

- Anesthesiologist—administers anesthesia (to induce partial or complete loss of sensation) and monitors patients in surgery

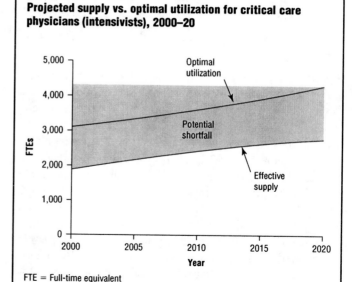

FIGURE 2.1

Projected supply vs. optimal utilization for critical care physicians (intensivists), 2000–20

FTE = Full-time equivalent

SOURCE: Elizabeth M. Duke, "Exhibit 15. Projected Supply vs. Optimal Utilization for Intensivists, 2000–2020," in *Report to Congress—The Critical Care Workforce: A Study of the Supply and Demand for Critical Care Physicians*, U.S. Department of Health and Human Services, Health Resources and Services Administration, May 2006, http://bhpr.hrsa.gov/healthworkforce/reports/studycriticalcarephys.pdf (accessed April 9, 2014)

- Cardiologist—diagnoses and treats diseases of the heart and blood vessels

- Dermatologist—diagnoses and treats diseases of the skin, hair, and nails

- Family practitioner—delivers primary care to people of all ages and, when necessary, refers patients to other physician specialists

- Gastroenterologist—specializes in digestive system disorders

- Internist—provides diagnosis and nonsurgical treatment of a broad array of illnesses affecting adults

- Neurologist—specializes in the nervous system and diagnosis and treatment of brain, spinal cord, and nerve disorders

- Obstetrician-gynecologist—provides health care for women and their reproductive systems, as well as care for mothers and babies before, during, and immediately following delivery

- Oncologist—provides diagnosis and treatment of cancer

- Otolaryngologist—skilled in the medical and surgical treatment of ear, nose, and throat disorders and related structures of the face, head, and neck

- Pathologist—uses skills in microscopic chemical analysis and diagnostics to detect disease in body tissues and fluids

- Psychiatrist—specializes in the prevention, diagnosis, and treatment of mental health and emotional disorders
- Pulmonologist—specializes in diseases of the lungs and respiratory system
- Urologist—provides diagnosis as well as medical and surgical treatment of the urinary tract in both men and women as well as male reproductive health services

The Number of Physicians in Practice Is Increasing

There were 809,492 actively practicing physicians in the United States in 2011 (the most recent data available to the federal government as of 2014), of which 309,672 (38.3%) were primary care physicians. (See Table 2.1.) Primary care physicians are the front line of the health care system—the first health professionals most people see for medical problems or routine care. Family practitioners, internists, pediatricians, obstetrician/gynecologists, and general practitioners are considered to be primary care physicians. Primary care physicians tend to see the same patients regularly and develop relationships with patients over time as they offer preventive services, scheduled visits, follow-up, and urgent medical care. When necessary, they refer patients for consultation with, and care from, physician specialists.

In 2011, 575,641 physicians of all types maintained office-based practices. (See Table 2.2.) There were an additional 79,182 physicians working full time at hospitals, aided by 112,959 residents and interns. Another 41,710 active doctors were engaged in teaching, research, or other activities rather than patient care. Of the 809,492 active doctors in 2011, 74.7% were graduates of U.S. or Canadian medical schools, while the remaining 25.3% received their medical education elsewhere.

Some states have more physicians engaged in patient care relative to their populations than do other states, making it easier for patients living in those areas to find a doctor. In 2011, the District of Columbia (68.3 physicians per 10,000 civilian population) and Massachusetts (41.1 per 10,000) had the highest ratios. (See Table 2.3.) Idaho (17.7 per 10,000) and Mississippi (17.9 per 10,000) had the lowest ratios.

TABLE 2.1

Doctors in primary care, by specialty, selected years 1949–2011

[Data are based on reporting by physicians]

Specialty	1949[a]	1960[a]	1970	1980	1990	1995	2000	2010	2011
					Number				
Total doctors of medicine[b]	201,277	260,484	334,028	467,679	615,421	720,325	813,770	985,375	1,004,635
Active doctors of medicine[c]	191,577	247,257	310,845	414,916	547,310	625,443	692,368	794,862	809,492
General primary care specialists	113,222	125,359	134,354	170,705	213,514	241,329	274,653	304,687	309,672
General practice/family medicine	95,980	88,023	57,948	60,049	70,480	75,976	86,312	94,746	95,274
Internal medicine	12,453	26,209	39,924	58,462	76,295	88,240	101,353	113,591	116,715
Obstetrics/gynecology	—	—	18,532	24,612	30,220	33,519	35,922	38,520	38,957
Pediatrics	4,789	11,127	17,950	27,582	36,519	43,594	51,066	57,830	58,726
Primary care subspecialists	—	—	3,161	16,642	30,911	39,659	52,294	76,122	79,751
Family medicine	—	—	—	—	—	236	483	1,445	1,593
Internal medicine	—	—	1,948	13,069	22,054	26,928	34,831	50,730	52,929
Obstetrics/gynecology	—	—	344	1,693	3,477	4,133	4,319	4,277	4,229
Pediatrics	—	—	869	1,880	5,380	8,362	12,661	19,670	21,000
					Percent of active doctors of medicine				
General primary care specialists	59.1	50.7	43.2	41.1	39.0	38.6	39.7	38.3	38.3
General practice/family medicine	50.1	35.6	18.6	14.5	12.9	12.1	12.5	11.9	11.8
Internal medicine	6.5	10.6	12.8	14.1	13.9	14.1	14.6	14.3	14.4
Obstetrics/gynecology	—	—	6.0	5.9	5.5	5.4	5.2	4.8	4.8
Pediatrics	2.5	4.5	5.8	6.6	6.7	7.0	7.4	7.3	7.3
Primary care subspecialists	—	—	1.0	4.0	5.6	6.3	7.6	9.6	9.9
Family medicine	—	—	0.0	0.0	0.0	0.0	0.1	0.2	0.2
Internal medicine	—	—	0.6	3.1	4.0	4.3	5.0	6.4	6.5
Obstetrics/gynecology	—	—	0.1	0.4	0.6	0.7	0.6	0.5	0.5
Pediatrics	—	—	0.3	0.5	1.0	1.3	1.8	2.5	2.6

—Data not available.

0.0 Percentage greater than zero but less than 0.05.

[a]Estimated by the Bureau of Health Professions, Health Resources and Services Administration. Active doctors of medicine (MDs) include those with address unknown and primary specialty not classified.

[b]Includes MDs engaged in federal and nonfederal patient care (office-based or hospital-based) and other professional activities.

[c]Starting with 1970 data, MDs who are inactive, have unknown address, or primary specialty not classified are excluded.

Notes: Data are as of December 31 except for 1990–1994 data, which are as of January 1, and 1949 data, which are as of midyear. Outlying areas include Puerto Rico, the U.S. Virgin Islands, and the Pacific Islands of Canton, Caroline, Guam, Mariana, Marshall, American Samoa, and Wake.

SOURCE: "Table 103. Doctors of Medicine in Primary Care, by Specialty: United States and Outlying U.S. Areas, Selected Years 1949–2011," in *Health, United States, 2013: With Special Feature on Prescription Drugs*, U.S. Department of Health and Human Services, Centers for Disease Control and Prevention, National Center for Health Statistics, May 2014, http://www.cdc.gov/nchs/data/hus/hus13.pdf (accessed May 14, 2014). Data from the American Medical Association (AMA).

TABLE 2.2

Medical doctors by activity and place of medical education, selected years 1975–2011

[Data are based on reporting by physicians]

Place of medical education and activity	1975	1985	1995	2000	2005	2009	2010	2011
				Number of doctors of medicine				
Total doctors of medicine	393,742	552,716	720,325	813,770	902,053	972,376	985,375	1,004,635
Active doctors of medicine[a]	340,280	497,140	625,443	692,368	762,438	792,805	794,862	809,492
Place of medical education								
U.S. medical graduates	—	392,007	481,137	527,931	571,798	591,835	595,908	604,737
International medical graduates[b]	—	105,133	144,306	164,437	190,640	200,970	198,954	204,755
Activity								
Patient care[c, d]	287,837	431,527	564,074	631,431	718,473	749,566	752,572	767,782
Office-based practice	213,334	329,041	427,275	490,398	563,225	560,381	565,024	575,641
General and family practice	46,347	53,862	59,932	67,534	74,999	76,514	77,098	77,723
Cardiovascular diseases	5,046	9,054	13,739	16,300	17,519	17,443	17,454	17,477
Dermatology	3,442	5,325	6,959	7,969	8,795	9,192	9,272	9,495
Gastroenterology	1,696	4,135	7,300	8,515	9,742	10,293	10,466	10,735
Internal medicine	28,188	52,712	72,612	88,699	107,028	109,305	110,612	114,110
Pediatrics	12,687	22,392	33,890	42,215	51,854	52,420	53,054	55,084
Pulmonary diseases	1,166	3,035	4,964	6,095	7,321	7,677	7,846	8,074
General surgery	19,710	24,708	24,086	24,475	26,079	24,536	24,327	24,408
Obstetrics and gynecology	15,613	23,525	29,111	31,726	34,659	34,092	34,083	34,420
Ophthalmology	8,795	12,212	14,596	15,598	16,580	15,731	15,723	15,882
Orthopedic surgery	8,148	13,033	17,136	17,367	19,115	19,205	19,325	19,428
Otolaryngology	4,297	5,751	7,139	7,581	8,206	8,025	7,964	8,024
Plastic surgery	1,706	3,299	4,612	5,308	6,011	6,110	6,180	6,248
Urological surgery	5,025	7,081	7,991	8,460	8,955	8,678	8,606	8,574
Anesthesiology	8,970	15,285	23,770	27,624	31,887	31,294	31,819	32,096
Diagnostic radiology	1,978	7,735	12,751	14,622	17,618	17,100	17,503	17,770
Emergency medicine	—	—	11,700	14,541	20,173	19,978	20,654	21,393
Neurology	1,862	4,691	7,623	8,559	10,400	10,433	10,547	10,972
Pathology, anatomical/clinical	4,195	6,877	9,031	10,267	11,747	10,554	10,688	10,880
Psychiatry	12,173	18,521	23,334	24,955	27,638	26,235	25,690	25,802
Radiology	6,970	7,355	5,994	6,674	7,049	6,837	7,032	7,114
Other specialty	15,320	28,453	29,005	35,314	39,850	38,729	39,081	39,932
Hospital-based practice	74,503	102,486	136,799	141,033	155,248	189,185	187,548	192,141
Residents and interns[e]	53,527	72,159	93,650	95,125	95,391	109,065	108,142	112,959
Full-time hospital staff	20,976	30,327	43,149	45,908	59,857	80,120	79,406	79,182
Other professional activity[f]	24,252	44,046	40,290	41,556	43,965	43,239	42,290	41,710
Inactive	21,449	38,646	72,326	75,168	99,823	121,704	125,928	134,168
Not classified	26,145	13,950	20,579	45,136	39,304	57,427	64,153	60,131
Unknown address	5,868	2,980	1,977	1,098	488	440	432	844

—Data not available.

[a]Doctors of medicine who are inactive, have unknown address, or primary specialty not classified are excluded.
[b]International medical graduates received their medical education in schools outside the United States and Canada.
[c]Specialty information is based on the physician's self-designated primary area of practice. Categories include generalists and specialists.
[d]Starting with 2003 data, estimates include federal and nonfederal doctors of medicine. Prior to 2003, estimates were for nonfederal doctors of medicine only.
[e]Starting with 1990, clinical fellows are included in this category. In prior years, clinical fellows were included in the other professional activity category.
[f]Includes medical teaching, administration, research, and other. Prior to 1990, this category also included clinical fellows.
Notes: Data for doctors of medicine are as of December 31, except for 1990–1994 data, which are as of January 1. Outlying areas include Puerto Rico, the U.S. Virgin Islands, and the Pacific Islands of Canton, Caroline, Guam, Mariana, Marshall, American Samoa, and Wake.

SOURCE: "Table 102. Doctors of Medicine, by Place of Medical Education and Activity: United States and Outlying U.S. Areas, Selected Years 1975–2011," in *Health, United States, 2013: With Special Feature on Prescription Drugs*, U.S. Department of Health and Human Services, Centers for Disease Control and Prevention, National Center for Health Statistics, May 2014, http://www.cdc.gov/nchs/data/hus/husl3.pdf (accessed May 14, 2014). Data from the American Medical Association (AMA).

Physician Working Conditions and Earnings

In its *Occupational Outlook Handbook* (January 8, 2014, http://www.bls.gov/ooh), the U.S. Bureau of Labor Statistics (BLS) reports that most physicians and surgeons work full time, and that many "work long, irregular, and overnight hours." Physicians in salaried positions, such as those employed by health maintenance organizations, usually have more regular hours and enjoy more flexible work schedules than those in private practice. Instead of working as solo practitioners, growing numbers of physicians work in clinics or are partners in group practices or other integrated health care systems. Medical group practices allow physicians to have more flexible schedules, to realize purchasing economies of scale, to pool their money to finance expensive medical equipment, and to be better able to adapt to changes in health care delivery, financing, and reimbursement.

Physicians' earnings are among the highest of any profession. (See Figure 2.2.) The BLS notes that the median annual compensation (the point at which half

TABLE 2.3

Active physicians and physicians in patient care, by state, selected years 1975–2011

[Data are based on reporting by physicians]

State	Active physicians[a, b]						Physicians in patient care[a, b, c]					
	1975	1985	1995	2000[d]	2010	2011	1975	1985	1995	2000[d]	2010	2011
	Number per 10,000 civilian population											
United States	15.3	20.7	24.2	25.8	27.2	27.5	13.5	18.0	21.3	22.7	24.0	26.1
Alabama	9.2	14.2	18.4	19.8	21.4	21.4	8.6	13.1	17.0	18.2	20.6	20.7
Alaska	8.4	13.0	15.7	18.5	24.3	24.3	7.8	12.1	14.2	16.3	23.3	23.3
Arizona	16.7	20.2	21.4	20.9	22.6	23.8	14.1	17.1	18.2	17.6	21.6	22.8
Arkansas	9.1	13.8	17.3	18.8	20.2	20.5	8.5	12.8	16.0	17.3	19.4	19.7
California	18.8	23.7	23.7	23.8	26.1	26.2	17.3	21.5	21.7	21.6	24.7	24.9
Colorado	17.3	20.7	23.7	24.0	26.9	27.4	15.0	17.7	20.6	20.9	25.5	26.0
Connecticut	19.8	27.6	32.8	33.7	36.0	36.5	17.7	24.3	29.5	30.3	33.6	34.1
Delaware	14.3	19.7	23.4	24.7	26.3	26.4	12.7	17.1	19.7	21.0	25.2	25.2
District of Columbia	39.6	55.3	63.6	62.5	76.9	76.4	34.6	45.6	53.6	54.5	68.8	68.3
Florida	15.2	20.2	22.9	24.1	26.0	25.8	13.4	17.8	20.3	21.2	25.0	24.8
Georgia	11.5	16.2	19.7	20.4	21.3	21.9	10.6	14.7	18.0	18.6	20.2	20.8
Hawaii	16.2	21.5	24.8	26.4	31.3	29.8	14.7	19.8	22.8	24.0	29.6	28.2
Idaho	9.5	12.1	13.9	15.8	18.4	18.1	8.9	11.4	13.1	14.4	17.9	17.7
Illinois	14.5	20.5	24.8	26.1	27.9	28.5	13.1	18.2	22.1	23.1	26.6	27.3
Indiana	10.6	14.7	18.4	20.0	22.2	22.2	9.6	13.2	16.6	18.0	21.3	21.3
Iowa	11.4	15.6	19.2	19.8	21.8	21.7	9.4	12.4	15.1	15.5	20.8	20.7
Kansas	12.8	17.3	20.8	21.8	24.0	24.3	11.2	15.1	18.0	18.8	23.1	23.4
Kentucky	10.9	15.1	19.2	20.6	23.1	23.2	10.1	13.9	18.0	19.1	22.2	22.3
Louisiana	11.4	17.3	21.7	23.8	25.4	26.0	10.5	16.1	20.3	22.4	24.5	25.1
Maine	12.8	18.7	22.3	26.8	31.8	31.7	10.7	15.6	18.2	21.7	30.2	30.2
Maryland	18.6	30.4	34.1	35.4	39.1	39.3	16.5	24.9	29.9	31.1	34.9	35.3
Massachusetts	20.8	30.2	37.5	38.6	43.4	44.5	18.3	25.4	33.2	34.4	40.0	41.1
Michigan	15.4	20.8	24.8	26.3	28.9	29.4	12.0	16.0	19.0	20.2	27.6	28.1
Minnesota	14.9	20.5	23.4	24.9	30.1	30.0	13.7	18.5	21.5	23.0	28.2	28.7
Mississippi	8.4	11.8	13.9	16.6	18.3	18.5	8.0	11.1	13.0	15.2	17.6	17.9
Missouri	15.0	20.5	23.9	24.7	26.3	27.1	11.6	16.3	19.7	20.2	25.1	25.9
Montana	10.6	14.0	18.4	20.4	22.5	22.1	10.1	13.2	17.1	18.8	21.8	21.4
Nebraska	12.1	15.7	19.8	21.7	24.5	24.7	10.9	14.4	18.3	20.1	23.4	23.6
Nevada	11.9	16.0	16.7	18.0	19.8	19.4	10.9	14.5	14.6	15.9	19.2	18.8
New Hampshire	14.3	18.1	21.5	23.8	29.5	30.1	13.1	16.7	19.8	21.7	28.2	28.7
New Jersey	16.2	23.4	29.3	31.1	31.8	32.0	14.0	19.8	24.9	26.2	30.1	30.4
New Mexico	12.2	17.0	20.2	20.9	23.8	23.8	10.1	14.7	18.0	18.5	22.5	22.5
New York	22.7	29.0	35.3	36.2	36.4	37.4	20.2	25.2	31.6	32.3	34.2	35.3
North Carolina	11.7	16.9	21.1	22.3	25.0	25.0	10.6	15.0	19.4	20.5	23.7	23.8
North Dakota	9.7	15.8	20.5	19.2	25.0	24.2	9.2	14.9	18.9	19.8	24.1	23.4
Ohio	14.1	19.9	23.8	25.4	28.5	29.1	12.2	16.8	20.0	21.3	27.3	27.9
Oklahoma	11.6	16.1	18.8	19.4	21.0	20.9	9.4	12.9	14.7	14.8	20.2	20.2
Oregon	15.6	19.7	21.6	22.9	28.3	29.0	13.8	17.6	19.5	20.5	26.9	27.6
Pennsylvania	16.6	23.6	30.1	31.6	32.6	33.0	13.9	19.2	24.6	25.4	30.7	31.1
Rhode Island	17.8	23.3	30.4	32.5	37.1	37.8	16.1	20.2	26.7	28.8	35.2	35.9
South Carolina	10.0	14.7	18.9	21.0	23.3	23.0	9.3	13.6	17.6	19.4	22.4	22.2
South Dakota	8.2	13.4	16.7	19.2	23.0	23.1	7.7	12.3	15.7	17.7	22.2	22.3
Tennessee	12.4	17.7	22.5	23.6	26.0	26.4	11.3	16.2	20.8	21.8	24.8	25.2
Texas	12.5	16.8	19.4	20.3	21.5	21.8	11.0	14.7	17.3	17.9	20.6	20.9
Utah	14.1	17.2	19.2	19.6	21.0	21.5	13.0	15.5	17.6	17.8	20.0	20.5
Vermont	18.2	23.8	26.9	32.0	35.7	35.7	15.5	20.3	24.2	28.8	33.4	33.4
Virginia	12.9	19.5	22.5	23.9	27.0	27.1	11.9	17.8	20.8	22.0	25.7	25.8
Washington	15.3	20.2	22.5	23.7	27.1	27.1	13.6	17.9	20.2	21.2	25.5	25.5
West Virginia	11.0	16.3	21.0	23.5	25.5	25.6	10.0	14.6	17.9	19.5	24.5	24.6
Wisconsin	12.5	17.7	21.5	23.1	26.8	26.8	11.4	15.9	19.6	20.9	25.6	25.7
Wyoming	9.5	12.9	15.3	17.3	19.7	19.3	8.9	12.0	13.9	15.7	19.1	18.7

[a]Includes active doctors of medicine (MDs) and active doctors of osteopathy (DOs).
[b]Starting with 2003 data, federal and nonfederal physicians are included. Data prior to 2003 included nonfederal physicians only.
[c]Prior to 2006, excludes DOs. Excludes physicians in medical teaching, administration, research, and other nonpatient care activities. Includes residents.
[d]Data for DOs are as of January 2001.
Notes: Data for MDs are as of December 31. Data for DOs are as of May 31, unless otherwise specified. Starting with *Health, United States, 2012*, data for DOs for 2009 and beyond are from the American Medical Association (AMA). Prior to 2009, data for DOs are from the American Osteopathic Association (AOA).

SOURCE: "Table 101. Active Physicians and Physicians in Patient Care, by State: United States, Selected Years 1975–2011," in *Health, United States, 2013: With Special Feature on Prescription Drugs*, U.S. Department of Health and Human Services, Centers for Disease Control and Prevention, National Center for Health Statistics, May 2014, http://www.cdc.gov/nchs/data/hus/hus13.pdf (accessed May 14, 2014). Data from the American Medical Association (AMA).

earn more and half earn less) for all physicians in 2012 was $187,200; however, many specialists earn more. In 2012 family practitioners had a median annual compensation of $207,117 and pediatricians had a median annual compensation of $216,069. By contrast, the median annual compensation for general surgeons was $367,885 and for anesthesiologists it was $431,977. (See Table 2.4.) Salaries vary widely and are based on a physician's specialty, the

FIGURE 2.2

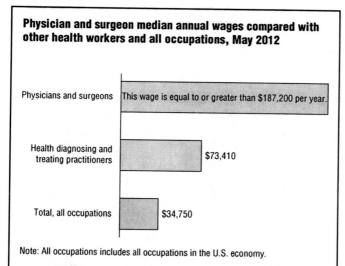

Physician and surgeon median annual wages compared with other health workers and all occupations, May 2012

SOURCE: "Physicians and Surgeons Median Annual Wages, May 2012," in *Occupational Outlook Handbook, 2014–15 Edition: Physicians and Surgeons*, U.S. Department of Labor, Bureau of Labor Statistics, January 8, 2014, http://www.bls.gov/ooh/healthcare/physicians-and-surgeons.htm#tab-5 (accessed April 11, 2014). Data from the Medical Group Management Association.

FIGURE 2.3

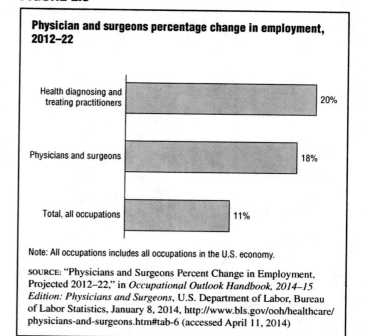

Physician and surgeons percentage change in employment, 2012–22

SOURCE: "Physicians and Surgeons Percent Change in Employment, Projected 2012–22," in *Occupational Outlook Handbook, 2014–15 Edition: Physicians and Surgeons*, U.S. Department of Labor, Bureau of Labor Statistics, January 8, 2014, http://www.bls.gov/ooh/healthcare/physicians-and-surgeons.htm#tab-6 (accessed April 11, 2014)

TABLE 2.4

Median annual compensation for selected medical specialties, 2012

Anesthesiology	$431,977
General surgery	367,885
Obstetrics/gynecology	301,737
Internal medicine	224,110
Psychiatry	220,252
Pediatrics/adolescent medicine	216,069
Family practice (without obstetrics)	207,117

SOURCE: "Median Annual Compensations for Selected Specialties in 2012," in *Occupational Outlook Handbook, 2014–15 Edition: Physicians and Surgeons*, U.S. Department of Labor, Bureau of Labor Statistics, January 8, 2014, http://www.bls.gov/ooh/healthcare/physicians-and-surgeons.htm#tab-5 (accessed April 11, 2014). Data from the Medical Group Management Association.

number of years in practice, the hours worked, and the geographic location.

The BLS expects that physician employment will increase 18% between 2012 and 2022, outpacing many other occupations. (See Figure 2.3.) This increase is attributable to an aging population and continued demand for physician services.

Physician Satisfaction

In *Factors Affecting Physician Professional Satisfaction and Their Implications for Patient Care, Health Systems, and Health Policy* (2013, http://www.rand.org/content/dam/rand/pubs/research_reports/RR400/RR439/RAND_RR439.pdf), Mark W. Friedberg et al. of the Rand Corporation report the results of a study into physician satisfaction sponsored by the American Medical Association. Friedberg et al. state that most of the physicians studied were "generally satisfied" with their medical practices. One of their main sources of satisfaction was the belief that they are providing quality care or that their practices facilitate delivery of such care. Physicians also cited income stability as contributing to their satisfaction and relatively few expressed dissatisfaction with their incomes.

Freidberg et al. indicate, however, that a substantial minority of physicians were not satisfied with their practices, and that even generally satisfied physicians reported a number of factors about their jobs that dissatisfied them: fear of declining income; having to deal with increased rules, regulations, and documentation requirements; and time pressures interfering with the ability to deliver the best possible care. Many of these sources of dissatisfaction are related to changes in the health care delivery system. For example, the shift from traditional fee-for-service practice to managed care has brought with it efforts to standardize medical practice, which reduces the ability of physicians to manage their time, schedules, and professional relationships. Other changes, including decreasing reimbursement and an ever-increasing emphasis on documentation to satisfy government and private payers, as well as administrative requirements that infringe on the time physicians would rather spend caring for patients, have also increased physician dissatisfaction.

Physician Visits

In 2010 Americans made more than 1 million physician-office visits. (See Table 2.5.) More than half (55.2%) of

TABLE 2.5

Visits to physician offices by age, selected years 1995–2011

[Data are based on reporting by a sample of office-based physicians, hospital outpatient departments, and hospital emergency departments]

Age, sex, and race	All places[a]				Physician offices			
	1995	2000	2010	2011	1995	2000	2010	2011
Age	Number of visits, in thousands							
Total	860,859	1,014,848	1,239,387	—	697,082	823,542	1,008,802	—
Under 18 years	194,644	212,165	246,228	—	150,351	163,459	191,500	—
18–44 years	285,184	315,774	342,797	—	219,065	243,011	261,941	—
45–64 years	188,320	255,894	352,001	—	159,531	216,783	296,385	—
45–54 years	104,891	142,233	171,039	—	88,266	119,474	140,819	—
55–64 years	83,429	113,661	180,962	—	71,264	97,309	155,566	—
65 years and over	192,712	231,014	298,362	—	168,135	200,289	258,976	—
65–74 years	102,605	116,505	151,075	—	90,544	102,447	132,201	—
75 years and over	90,106	114,510	147,287	—	77,591	97,842	126,775	—
	Number of visits per 100 persons							
Total, age-adjusted[b]	334	374	401	—	271	304	325	—
Total, crude	329	370	408	—	266	300	332	—
Under 18 years	275	293	331	—	213	226	257	—
18–44 years	264	291	310	—	203	224	237	—
45–64 years	364	422	441	—	309	358	371	—
45–54 years	339	385	388	—	286	323	320	—
55–64 years	401	481	505	—	343	412	434	—
65 years and over	612	706	767	—	534	612	666	—
65–74 years	560	656	713	—	494	577	624	—
75 years and over	683	766	831	—	588	654	715	—
Sex and age								
Male, age-adjusted[b]	290	325	350	—	232	261	283	—
Male, crude	277	314	350	—	220	251	283	—
Under 18 years	273	302	340	—	209	231	262	—
18–44 years	190	203	205	—	139	148	151	—
45–54 years	275	316	324	—	229	260	265	—
55–64 years	351	428	460	—	300	367	396	—
65–74 years	508	614	680	—	445	539	597	—
75 years and over	711	771	871	—	616	670	760	—
Female, age-adjusted[b]	377	420	452	—	309	345	367	—
Female, crude	378	424	464	—	310	348	379	—
Under 18 years	277	285	322	—	217	221	252	—
18–44 years	336	377	415	—	265	298	323	—
45–54 years	400	451	450	—	339	384	372	—
55–64 years	446	529	546	—	382	453	469	—
65–74 years	603	692	741	—	534	609	647	—
75 years and over	666	763	804	—	571	645	685	—
Race and age[c]								
White, age-adjusted[b]	339	380	408	—	282	315	336	—
White, crude	338	381	421	—	281	316	349	—
Under 18 years	295	306	341	—	237	243	270	—
18–44 years	267	301	319	—	211	239	249	—
45–54 years	334	386	389	—	286	330	326	—
55–64 years	397	480	505	—	345	416	440	—
65–74 years	557	641	727	—	496	568	642	—
75 years and over	689	764	838	—	598	658	723	—
Black or African American, age-adjusted[b]	309	353	439	—	204	239	316	—
Black or African American, crude	281	324	425	—	178	214	303	—
Under 18 years	193	264	351	—	100	167	241	—
18–44 years	260	257	339	—	158	149	222	—
45–54 years	387	383	466	—	281	269	339	—
55–64 years	414	495	617	—	294	373	481	—
65–74 years	553	656	715	—	429	512	565	—
75 years and over	534	745	845	—	395	568	682	—

—Data not available. Estimates for all places and physician offices will be published on the *Health, United States* website when the data are available.

[a]All places includes visits to physician offices and hospital outpatient and emergency departments.

[b]Estimates are age-adjusted to the year 2000 standard population using six age groups: under 18 years, 18–44 years, 45–54 years, 55–64 years, 65–74 years, and 75 years and over.

[c]Estimates by racial group should be used with caution because information on race was collected from medical records. In 2010, race data were missing and imputed for 23% of visits to physician offices, and in 2011, for 17% of visits to hospital outpatient departments, and 15% of visits to hospital emergency departments. Information on the race imputation process used in each data year is available in the public-use file documentation. Starting with 1999 data, the instruction for the race item on the Patient Record Form was changed so that more than one race could be recorded. In previous years only one race could be recorded. Estimates for race in this table are for visits where only one race was recorded. Because of the small number of responses with more than one racial group recorded, estimates for visits with multiple races recorded are unreliable and are not presented.

SOURCE: Adapted from "Table 89. Visits to Physician Offices, Hospital Outpatient Departments, and Hospital Emergency Departments, by Age, Sex, and Race: United States, Selected Years 1995–2011," in *Health, United States, 2013: With Special Feature on Prescription Drugs*, U.S. Department of Health and Human Services, Centers for Disease Control and Prevention, National Center for Health Statistics, May 2014, http://www.cdc.gov/nchs/data/hus/hus13.pdf (accessed May 14, 2014)

these visits were to primary care physicians. (See Table 2.6.) Younger Americans were particularly likely to see a primary care generalist when they visited a physician; 80.9% of visits by people age 17 and younger were to generalists, as were 62.7% of visits by those aged 18 to 44 years. Americans aged 45 years and older saw specialists for more than half of their physician visits in 2010.

REGISTERED NURSES

Registered nurses (RNs) are licensed by the state to care for the sick and to promote health. RNs supervise hospital care, administer medication and treatment as prescribed by physicians, monitor the progress of patients, and provide health education. Nurses work in a variety of settings, including hospitals, nursing homes, physicians' offices, clinics, and schools.

Education for Nurses

There are three types of education for RNs: associate's degree (two-year community college programs), baccalaureate degree (four-year programs), and postgraduate degree (master's and doctorate programs).

TABLE 2.6

Visits to physician offices, by selected characteristics, selected years 1980–2010

[Data are based on reporting by a sample of office-based physicians]

	All primary care generalists				Type of primary care generalist physician[a] — General and family practice				Internal medicine			
Age, sex, and race	1980	1990	2000	2010	1980	1990	2000	2010	1980	1990	2000	2010
Age						Percent distribution						
Total	66.2	63.6	58.9	55.2	33.5	29.9	24.1	21.1	12.1	13.8	15.3	13.9
Under 18 years	77.8	79.5	79.7	80.9	26.1	26.5	19.9	15.3	2.0	2.9	*	*
18–44 years	65.3	65.2	62.1	62.7	34.3	31.9	28.2	27.8	8.6	11.8	12.7	11.6
45–64 years	60.2	55.5	51.2	46.7	36.3	32.1	26.4	23.1	19.5	18.6	20.1	18.5
45–54 years	60.2	55.6	52.3	48.7	37.4	32.0	27.8	26.2	17.1	17.1	18.7	15.7
55–64 years	60.2	55.5	49.9	44.8	35.4	32.1	24.7	20.4	21.8	20.0	21.7	21.0
65 years and over	61.6	52.6	46.5	38.3	37.5	28.1	20.2	16.4	22.7	23.3	24.5	20.5
65–74 years	61.2	52.7	46.6	37.3	37.4	28.1	19.7	17.5	22.1	23.0	24.5	18.2
75 years and over	62.3	52.4	46.4	39.2	37.6	28.0	20.8	15.4	23.5	23.7	24.5	22.8
Sex and age												
Male												
Under 18 years	77.3	78.1	77.7	80.1	25.6	24.1	18.3	15.7	2.0	3.0	*	*
18–44 years	50.8	51.8	51.5	51.7	38.0	35.9	34.2	33.7	11.5	15.0	14.4	16.4
45–64 years	55.6	50.6	49.4	43.7	34.4	31.0	28.7	24.4	20.5	19.2	19.8	19.1
65 years and over	58.2	51.2	43.1	36.6	35.6	27.7	19.3	16.2	22.3	23.3	23.8	20.3
Female												
Under 18 years	78.5	81.1	82.0	81.7	26.6	29.1	21.7	14.9	2.0	2.8	*	*
18–44 years	72.1	71.3	67.2	67.9	32.5	30.0	25.3	25.0	7.3	10.3	11.9	9.4
45–64 years	63.4	58.8	52.5	48.9	37.7	32.8	24.9	22.2	18.9	18.2	20.2	18.1
65 years and over	63.9	53.5	48.9	39.6	38.7	28.3	20.9	16.7	22.9	23.3	25.0	20.5
Race and age[b]												
White												*
Under 18 years	77.6	79.2	78.5	79.6	26.4	27.1	21.2	15.6	2.0	2.3	*	11.1
18–44 years	64.8	64.4	61.4	61.2	34.5	31.9	29.2	27.9	8.6	10.6	11.0	17.5
45–64 years	59.6	54.2	49.3	45.2	36.0	31.5	27.3	22.8	19.2	17.6	17.1	19.7
65 years and over	61.4	51.9	45.1	37.6	36.6	27.5	20.3	16.6	23.3	23.1	23.0	
Black or African American												
Under 18 years	79.9	85.5	87.3	88.0	23.7	20.2	*	16.5*	2.2*	9.8	*	*
18–44 years	68.5	68.3	65.0	72.6	31.7	31.9	22.0	29.4	9.0	18.1	20.9	14.0*
45–64 years	66.1	61.6	61.7	57.0	38.6	31.2	23.3	26.7	22.6	26.9	35.9	24.5
65 years and over	64.6	58.6	52.8	45.2	49.0	28.9	18.5*	18.6*	14.2	28.7	33.4	25.4*

	Type of primary care generalist physician[a] — Obstetrics and gynecology				Pediatrics				Specialty care physicians			
Age, sex, and race	1980	1990	2000	2010	1980	1990	2000	2010	1980	1990	2000	2010
Age						Percent distribution						
Total	9.6	8.7	7.8	7.8	10.9	11.2	11.7	12.4	33.8	36.4	41.1	44.8
Under 18 years	1.3	1.2	1.1*	1.3*	48.5	48.9	57.3	63.4	22.2	20.5	20.3	19.1
18–44 years	21.7	20.8	20.4	22.3	0.7	0.7	0.9*	1.0	34.7	34.8	37.9	37.3
45–64 years	4.2	4.6	4.5	4.9	*	*	*	*	39.8	44.5	48.8	53.3
45–54 years	5.6	6.3	5.6	6.7	*	*	*	*	39.8	44.4	47.7	51.3
55–64 years	2.9	3.1	3.3	3.3	*	*	*	*	39.8	44.5	50.1	55.2
65 years and over	1.4	1.1	1.5	1.3	*	*	*	*	38.4	47.4	53.5	61.7
65–74 years	1.7	1.6	2.0	1.7	*	*	*	*	38.8	47.3	53.4	62.7
75 years and over	1.0	0.6*	1.0*	1.0*	*	*	*	*	37.7	47.6	53.6	60.8

TABLE 2.6

Visits to physician offices, by selected characteristics, selected years 1980–2010 [CONTINUED]

[Data are based on reporting by a sample of office-based physicians]

| | Type of primary care generalist physician[a] | | | | | | | | Specialty care physicians | | | |
| | Obstetrics and gynecology | | | | Pediatrics | | | | | | | |
Age, sex, and race	1980	1990	2000	2010	1980	1990	2000	2010	1980	1990	2000	2010
Sex and age					Percent distribution							
Male												
Under 18 years	—	—	—	—	49.4	50.7	58.0	63.7	22.7	21.9	22.3	19.9
18–44 years	—	—	—	—	1.0	0.7	1.7*	1.4*	49.2	48.2	48.5	48.3
45–64 years	—	—	—	—	*	*	*	*	44.4	49.4	50.6	56.3
65 years and over	—	—	—	—	*	*	*	*	41.8	48.8	56.6	63.4
Female												
Under 18 years	2.5	2.3	2.1	2.8*	47.4	46.9	56.5	63.1	21.5	18.9	18.0	18.3
18–44 years	31.7	30.4	29.6	32.5	0.6	0.7	*	0.9*	27.9	28.7	32.8	32.1
45–64 years	6.7	7.7	7.3	8.5	*	*	*	*	36.6	41.2	47.5	51.1
65 years and over	2.1	1.8	2.6	2.4	*	*	*	*	36.1	46.5	51.1	60.4
Race and age[b]												
White												
Under 18 years	1.1	1.0	1.2*	1.3*	48.2	48.8	54.7	61.7	22.4	20.8	21.5	20.4
18–44 years	21.0	21.1	20.4	21.1	0.7	0.7	0.8*	1.1*	35.2	35.6	38.6	38.8
45–64 years	4.1	4.8	4.7	4.7	*	*	*	*	40.4	45.8	50.7	54.8
65 years and over	1.4	1.2	1.5	1.3*	*	*	*	*	38.6	48.1	54.9	62.4
Black or African American												
Under 18 years	2.8	3.4*	*	*	51.2	52.1	75.0	70.2	20.1	14.5	12.7*	12.0*
18–44 years	27.1	17.9	20.7	28.4	*	*	*	*	31.5	31.7	35.0	27.4
45–64 years	4.8	3.5	2.4*	5.6*	*	*	*	*	33.9	38.4	38.3	43.0
65 years and over	*	*	*	1.2*	*	*	*	*	35.4	41.4	47.2	54.8

*Estimates are considered unreliable.

—Category not applicable.

[a]Type of physician is based on physician's self-designated primary area of practice. Primary care generalist physicians are defined as practitioners in the fields of general and family practice, general internal medicine, general obstetrics and gynecology, and general pediatrics and exclude primary care specialists. Primary care generalists in general and family practice exclude primary care specialties, such as sports medicine and geriatrics. Primary care internal medicine physicians exclude internal medicine specialists, such as allergists, cardiologists, and endocrinologists. Primary care obstetrics and gynecology physicians exclude obstetrics and gynecology specialties, such as gynecological oncology, maternal and fetal medicine, obstetrics and gynecology critical care medicine, and reproductive endocrinology. Primary care pediatricians exclude pediatric specialists, such as adolescent medicine specialists, neonatologists, pediatric allergists, and pediatric cardiologists.

[b]Estimates by racial group should be used with caution because information on race was collected from medical records. In 2010, race data were missing and imputed for 23% of visits. Information on the race imputation process used in each data year is available in the public-use file documentation. Starting with 1999 data, the instruction for the race item on the Patient Record Form was changed so that more than one race could be recorded. In previous years only one racial category could be checked. Estimates for racial groups presented in this table are for visits where only one race was recorded. Because of the small number of responses with more than one racial group checked, estimates for visits with multiple races checked are unreliable and are not presented.

Notes: This table presents data on visits to physician offices and excludes visits to other sites, such as hospital outpatient and emergency departments. In 1980, the survey excluded Alaska and Hawaii. Data for all other years include all 50 states and the District of Columbia. Visits with specialty of physician unknown are excluded.

SOURCE: "Table 90. Visits to Primary Care Generalist and Specialist Physicians, by Selected Characteristics and Type of Physician: United States, Selected Years 1980–2010," in *Health, United States, 2013: With Special Feature on Prescription Drugs*, U.S. Department of Health and Human Services, Centers for Disease Control and Prevention, National Center for Health Statistics, May 2014, http://www.cdc.gov/nchs/data/hus/hus13.pdf (accessed May 14, 2014)

The baccalaureate degree provides more knowledge of community health services, as well as the psychological and social aspects of caring for patients, than does the associate's degree. Those who complete the four-year baccalaureate degree and the other advanced degrees are generally better prepared to eventually attain administrative or management positions and may have greater opportunities for upward mobility in related disciplines such as research, teaching, and public health.

The *Occupational Outlook Handbook* indicates that in 2012 there were more than 2.7 million RN jobs in the United States. It predicts that employment of RNs will grow 19% between 2012 and 2022, faster than it will for all occupations. (See Figure 2.4.)

NEED FOR NURSES EXCEEDS SUPPLY. Although the number of RNs holding baccalaureate degrees increased sharply during the 1990s, there is still a shortage of nurses that is predicted to persist through 2020. Figure 2.4 shows employment projections for RNs between 2010 and 2020. Figure 2.5 shows that the gap between supply and demand for RNs is projected to widen through 2020. In "United States Registered Nurse Workforce Report Card and Shortage Forecast" (*American Journal of Medical Quality*, vol. 27, no. 3, May–June 2012), Stephen P. Juraschek et al. forecast a national RN deficit of 300,000 to 1 million RN jobs in 2020. The researchers assert that the aging U.S. population and growing demand for health services are responsible for the shortage, and opine that it "will reach epic proportions in years when RN services are in highest demand."

FIGURE 2.4

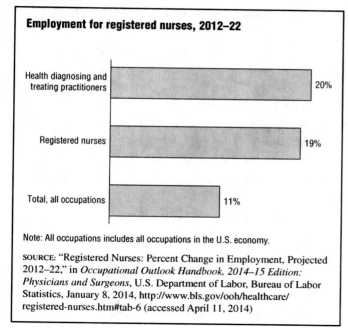

Employment for registered nurses, 2012–22

Note: All occupations includes all occupations in the U.S. economy.

SOURCE: "Registered Nurses: Percent Change in Employment, Projected 2012–22," in *Occupational Outlook Handbook, 2014–15 Edition: Physicians and Surgeons*, U.S. Department of Labor, Bureau of Labor Statistics, January 8, 2014, http://www.bls.gov/ooh/healthcare/registered-nurses.htm#tab-6 (accessed April 11, 2014)

FIGURE 2.5

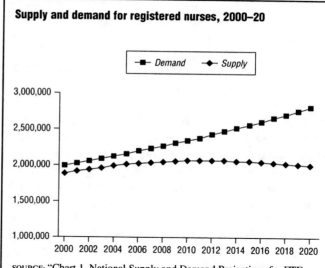

Supply and demand for registered nurses, 2000–20

SOURCE: "Chart 1. National Supply and Demand Projections for FTE Registered Nurses: 2000 to 2020," in *Projected Supply, Demand, and Shortages of Registered Nurses: 2000–2020*, U.S. Department of Health and Human Services, Health Resources and Services Administration, Bureau of Health Professions, National Center for Health Workforce Analysis, July 2002, http://www.ahcancal.org/research_data/staffing/Documents/Registered_Nurse_Supply_Demand.pdf (accessed April 11, 2014)

Industry observers believe other factors have contributed to the shortage, including expanding opportunities for women to pursue other careers, a sicker population of hospitalized patients requiring more labor-intensive care, and the public perception that nursing is a thankless, unglamorous job that requires grueling physical labor, long hours, and low pay. Observers also note that the public, particularly high school students who are considering careers in health care, are unaware of the many new opportunities in nursing, such as advanced practice nursing, which offers additional independence and increased earning potential, and the technology-driven field of applied informatics (computer management of information).

In "The Best Jobs of 2014" (USNews.com, January 23, 2014), Jada A. Graves explains that registered nurse ranked number six in terms of the career options with the brightest prospects, based on the high projected demand for these workers.

ADVANCED PRACTICE NURSES AND PHYSICIAN ASSISTANTS

Much of the preventive medical care and treatment usually delivered by physicians may also be provided by midlevel practitioners—health professionals with less formal education and training than physicians. Advanced practice nurses make up a group that includes certified nurse midwives, nurse practitioners (NPs; RNs with advanced academic and clinical experience), and clinical nurse specialists (RNs with advanced nursing degrees who specialize in areas such as mental health, gerontology, cardiac or cancer care, or community or neonatal health). Physician assistants (PAs) are midlevel practitioners who work under the auspices, supervision, or direction of physicians. They conduct physical examinations, order and interpret laboratory and radiological studies, and prescribe medication. They even perform procedures (e.g., biopsy, suturing, casting, and administering anesthesia) that were once performed exclusively by physicians.

The origins of each profession are key to understanding the differences between them. Nursing has the longer history, and nurses are recognized members of the health care team. For this reason, NPs were easily integrated into many practice settings.

PA is the newer of the two disciplines. PAs have been practicing in the United States since the early 1970s. The career originated as civilian employment for returning Vietnam War (1954–1975) veterans who had worked as medics. The veterans needed immediate employment and few had the educational prerequisites, time, or resources to pursue the training necessary to become physicians. At the same time, the United States was projecting a dire shortage of primary care physicians, especially in rural and inner-city practices. The use of NPs and PAs was seen as an ideal rapid response to the demand for additional medical services. They could be deployed quickly to serve remote communities or underserved populations for a fraction of the costs associated with physicians.

The numbers of NPs and PAs have increased dramatically since the beginning of the 1990s. The HRSA states in *The U.S. Health Workforce Chartbook* (November 2013, http://bhpr.hrsa.gov/healthworkforce/supplydemand/usworkforce/chartbook/chartbookbrief.pdf) that in 2008–2010 there were 110,042 NPs, 35,570 nurse anesthetists, 12,383 nurse midwives, and 99,651 PAs.

Training, Certification, and Practice

Advanced practice nurses usually have considerable clinical nursing experience before completing certificate or master's degree NP programs. Key components of NP programs are instruction in nursing theory and practice and a period of direct supervision by a physician or NP. The American Association of Nurse Practitioners explains in "State Practice Environment" (2014, http://www.aanp.org/legislation-regulation/state-practice-environment) that NPs are a scope of practice that varies from state to state. For example, some states require state certification as well as national certification and some states permit independent practice for NPs (not requiring any physician involvement).

The Commission on Accreditation of Allied Health Education Programs accredits PA training programs. In "Becoming a PA" (2014, http://www.aapa.org/your_pa_career/becoming_a_pa.aspx), the American Academy of Physician Assistants notes that most students have an undergraduate degree and health care experience before they enter a PA training program, which lasts about 27 months. Graduates sit for a national certifying examination and, once certified, must earn 100 hours of continuing medical education every two years and pass a recertification exam every six years. PAs must also obtain a state license.

PA practice is always delegated by the physician and conducted with physician supervision. The extent and nature of physician supervision varies from state to state. For example, Connecticut permits a physician to supervise up to six PAs, whereas California limits a supervising physician to two. Although PAs work interdependently with physicians, supervision is not necessarily direct and onsite; some PAs working in remote communities are supervised primarily by telephone.

Graves reports that NP was ranked number four in terms of best jobs in 2014, with a median salary of $89,960. According to the BLS the median salary of PAs in 2012 was $90,930.

Expanding Role of Midlevel Practitioners

The role of NPs has been gradually expanding over time, but the Patient Protection and Affordable Care Act (ACA) may accelerate the broadening the responsibilities of NPs, because it extends health insurance coverage to millions of previously uninsured Americans. This creates additional demand for services—especially time-consuming preventive care—that cannot be met by physicians alone.

In "Conquering the Doctor Shortage" (Cincinnati.com, February 8, 2014), Lisa Bernard-Kuhn explains that expanded roles for NPs and PAs could help to ease the projected physician shortage. However, Bernard-Kuhn asserts that "restrictive regulations—including those on the books in Ohio, Kentucky and Indiana—limit nurse practitioners from reaching more patients."

Several provisions of the ACA expand the role of nurses by encouraging training and increasing compensation. These include:

- $50 million to clinics managed by nurses that provide care to low-income patients

- $50 million annually between 2012 and 2015 for hospitals to train nurses with advanced degrees to care for Medicare patients

- 10% bonuses from Medicare between through 2016 to primary care providers, including NPs, who work in physician-shortage areas

- Increasing Medicare reimbursement for certified nurse midwives, giving them the same compensation as physicians

According to the American Association of Nurse Practitioners, as of October 2014, 19 states and the District of Columbia allowed NPs to work independently—without a supervising physician. During 2013 and 2014, lawmakers in several states introduced legislation to expand the scope of practice for NPs, including Florida, which has strict limits on NPs. In "Milestone New York Legislation Eases Practice Restrictions on NPs" (Nurse.com, May 5, 2014), Robin Farmer reports that, in April 2014, New York expanded the authority of NPs effective January 1, 2015. This is despite the fact that in New York and elsewhere, many physician groups have opposed allowing NPs to work independently, asserting that they lack the training to diagnose, treat, and prescribe medication without physician oversight.

DENTISTS

Dentists diagnose and treat problems of the teeth, gums, and mouth, take x-rays, apply protective plastic sealants to teeth, fill cavities, straighten teeth, and treat gum disease. The *Occupational Outlook Handbook* reports that dentists held about 146,800 jobs in 2012.

Fluoridation of community water supplies and improved dental hygiene have dramatically improved the dental health of Americans. Dental caries (cavities) among all age groups have declined significantly. As a result, many dental services are shifting focus from young people to adults. In the 21st century many adults are choosing to have orthodontic services, such as straightening their teeth. In addition, the growing older adult population generally requires more complex dental procedures, such as endodontic (root canal) services, bridges, and dentures.

Many dentists own solo dental practices, where only one dentist operates in each office. Others are partners in a practice with other general dentists or dental specialists. Most dentists manage a small staff, which may include dental hygienists and assistants. The BLS reports most dentists work full time and many work evenings and weekends to accommodate their patients.

Dental Specialists

In "Specialty Definitions" (2014, http://www.ada .org/495.aspx), the American Dental Association identifies nine recognized specialties. Orthodontists, who straighten teeth, make up the largest group of specialists. The next largest group, oral, and maxillofacial surgeons, operates on the mouth and jaw. Other specialties are: pediatric dentistry (dentistry for children), periodontics (treating the gums), prosthodontics (making dentures and artificial teeth), endodontics (root canals), public health dentistry (community dental health), and oral pathology (diseases of the mouth).

Training to Become a Dentist

Entry into dental schools requires two to four years of college-level pre-dental education—most dental students have earned excellent grades and have at least a bachelor's degree when they enter dental school. Dentists should have good visual memory, excellent judgment about space and shape, a high degree of manual dexterity, and scientific ability. Development and maintenance of a successful private practice requires business acumen, the ability to manage and organize people and materials, and strong interpersonal skills.

Dental schools require applicants to take the Dental Admission Test (DAT). During the admission process, schools consider scores earned on the DAT, applicants' grade-point averages, and information gleaned from recommendations and interviews. Dental school usually lasts four academic years. Students begin by studying the basic sciences, including anatomy, microbiology, biochemistry, and physiology. During the last two years students receive practical experience by treating patients, usually in dental clinics that are supervised by licensed dentists.

Visiting a Dentist

In 2012, 66.2% of Americans aged two years and older had visited a dentist at least once in the past year. (See Table 2.7.) Children aged 2 to 17 years (82.3%) were more likely to have visited a dentist than any other age group. Women (68.5%) were somewhat more likely to have seen a dentist than men (63.8%). The proportion of non-Hispanic whites (68.9%) who had visited a dentist was higher than the proportions of non-Hispanic African Americans (62%) and Hispanics (58.8%) who had done so. People who were poor or near poor were much less likely to have visited a dentist in the past year than those who were not poor. For example, 51.5% of people who were below the poverty level had visited a dentist in the past year, compared with 81.1% of people who with incomes above 400% of the poverty level.

Shortages of Dentists in Some Areas

Although the United States boasts the highest concentration of dentists of any country in the world, large swaths of the country have few dentists. Not unexpectedly, poor, rural regions are disproportionately affected. The Department of Health and Human Services reports in *Health, United States, 2013: With Special Feature on Prescription Drugs* that Arkansas had just 4.2 dentists per 10,000 people in the civilian population in 2011, compared with the District of Columbia, which boasted 10.8 dentists per 10,000 population. For the entire country, there were 6.2 dentists per 10,000 people in the civilian population.

ALLIED HEALTH CARE PROVIDERS

Many health care services are provided by an interdisciplinary team of health professionals. The complete health care team may include not just physicians and nurses, but a variety of allied health professionals. Table 2.8 describes some of these allied health professions. Specific health care teams are assembled to meet the varying needs of patients. For example, the team involved in stroke rehabilitation might include a physician, a nurse, a speech-language pathologist, a social worker, and physical and occupational therapists.

Table 2.9 shows the growth in numbers of health care practitioners, allied health professionals, and health care support occupations such as assistants, aides, and massage therapists as well as their mean hourly wages during the first decade of the 21st century. For example, pharmacists saw a 4.2% annual increase in hourly wages between 2001 and 2012, whereas psychiatric aides realized a 1.1% increase during the same period.

Physical and Occupational Therapists

Physical therapists (PTs) are licensed practitioners who work with patients to preserve and restore function, improve capabilities and mobility, and regain independence following an illness or injury. They also aim to prevent or limit disability and slow the progress of debilitating diseases. Treatment involves exercise to improve range of motion, balance, coordination, flexibility, strength, and endurance. PTs may also use electrical

TABLE 2.7

Dental visits in the past year by selected characteristics, 1997–2012

[Data are based on household interviews of a sample of the civilian noninstitutionalized population]

Characteristic	2 years and over			2–17 years			18–64 years			65 years and over[a]		
	1997	2010	2012	1997	2010	2012	1997	2010	2012	1997	2010	2012
	Percent of persons with a dental visit in the past year[b]											
Total[c]	**65.1**	**64.7**	**66.2**	**72.7**	**78.9**	**82.3**	**64.1**	**61.1**	**61.6**	**54.8**	**57.7**	**61.8**
Sex												
Male	62.9	61.7	63.8	72.3	78.3	82.7	60.4	56.8	57.7	55.4	56.2	60.5
Female	67.1	67.5	68.5	73.0	79.6	81.8	67.7	65.4	65.4	54.4	58.9	62.8
Race[d]												
White only	66.4	65.6	66.8	74.0	79.2	82.3	65.7	62.4	62.5	56.8	59.3	63.4
Black or African American only	58.9	58.8	62.1	68.8	79.0	83.1	57.0	53.1	56.4	35.4	40.6	45.1
American Indian or Alaska Native only	55.1	57.4	65.0	66.8	73.2	89.8	49.9	49.8	53.6	*	72.2	48.9*
Asian only	62.5	66.5	65.5	69.9	74.8	78.9	60.3	64.6	61.7	53.9	61.9	65.3
Native Hawaiian or other Pacific Islander only	—	*	*	—	*	*	—	*	*	—	*	*
2 or more races	—	65.2	68.9	—	77.9	80.5	—	54.7	60.1	—	48.1	47.3
Black or African American; White	—	72.5	71.8	—	78.4	77.2	—	62.1	61.7	—	*	67.8*
American Indian or Alaska Native; White	—	54.7	60.4	—	70.0	86.1	—	49.0	51.0	—	54.5*	44.8*
Hispanic origin and race												
Hispanic or Latino	54.0	56.5	58.8	61.0	74.8	80.4	50.8	48.5	49.2	47.8	42.1	47.1
Not Hispanic or Latino	66.4	66.2	67.7	74.7	80.1	82.9	65.7	63.4	64.1	55.2	59.0	63.0
White only	68.0	67.6	68.9	76.4	80.9	83.3	67.5	65.4	65.8	57.2	60.9	65.0
Black or African American only	58.8	58.7	62.0	68.8	79.2	82.9	56.9	53.1	56.5	35.3	40.5	45.2
Percent of poverty level[e]												
Below 100%	50.5	50.6	51.5	62.0	73.2	76.4	46.9	41.0	41.5	31.5	32.8	32.8
100%–199%	50.8	51.6	54.1	62.5	73.4	79.2	48.3	44.1	45.8	40.8	43.8	44.6
200%–399%	66.2	63.5	64.9	76.1	79.0	82.5	63.4	59.6	59.8	60.7	57.9	60.8
400% or more	78.9	79.3	81.1	85.7	88.0	89.8	77.7	77.5	78.8	74.7	77.2	82.4
Hispanic origin and race and percent of poverty level[d, e]												
Hispanic or Latino:												
Below 100%	45.7	50.8	52.5	55.9	74.3	77.9	39.2	34.7	37.3	33.6	32.4	36.5
100%–199%	47.2	50.8	55.2	53.8	71.1	80.3	43.5	40.2	43.1	47.9	39.5	41.0
200%–399%	61.2	59.1	59.9	70.5	76.5	81.6	57.5	54.1	52.8	57.0	46.0	47.9
400% or more	73.0	73.3	75.9	82.4	84.2	85.9	70.8	71.6	73.0	64.9	54.3	71.9
Not Hispanic or Latino:												
White only:												
Below 100%	51.7	49.3	49.2	64.4	69.1	73.8	50.6	44.4	43.2	32.0	36.4	32.6
100%–199%	52.4	52.7	52.7	66.1	75.3	76.7	50.4	47.2	46.7	42.2	45.4	45.9
200%–399%	67.5	64.7	66.0	77.1	79.6	82.5	65.0	61.4	61.5	61.9	59.8	62.9
400% or more	79.7	79.8	82.2	86.8	88.6	90.9	78.5	77.9	80.0	75.5	78.8	83.2
Black or African American only:												
Below 100%	52.8	52.0	53.9	66.1	78.0	78.1	46.2	39.7	42.7	27.7	20.9	25.6
100%–199%	48.7	50.0	57.5	61.2	75.9	84.8	46.3	41.5	49.0	26.9	33.6	39.0
200%–399%	63.3	61.2	62.6	75.0	81.2	85.1	60.7	57.2	57.8	41.5	45.3	48.7
400% or more	74.6	77.2	78.3	81.8	87.2	90.4	73.4	75.9	76.4	66.1	69.8	76.1

*Estimates are considered unreliable.

—Data not available.

[a]Based on the 1997–2012 National Health Interview Surveys, about 21%–30% of persons aged 65 and over were edentulous (having lost all their natural teeth). In 1997–2012, about 69%–73% of older dentate persons, compared with 17%–23% of older edentate persons, had a dental visit in the past year.

[b]Respondents were asked "About how long has it been since you last saw or talked to a dentist?"

[c]Includes all other races not shown separately and unknown disability status.

[d]The race groups, white, black, American Indian or Alaska Native, Asian, Native Hawaiian or other Pacific Islander, and 2 or more races, include persons of Hispanic and non-Hispanic origin. Persons of Hispanic origin may be of any race. Starting with 1999 data, race-specific estimates are tabulated according to the 1997 Revisions to the Standards for the Classification of Federal Data on Race and Ethnicity and are not strictly comparable with estimates for earlier years. The five single-race categories plus multiple-race categories shown in the table conform to the 1997 Standards. Starting with 1999 data, race-specific estimates are for persons who reported only one racial group; the category 2 or more races includes persons who reported more than one racial group. Prior to 1999, data were tabulated according to the 1977 Standards with four racial groups, and the Asian only category included Native Hawaiian or Other Pacific Islander. Estimates for single-race categories prior to 1999 included persons who reported one race or, if they reported more than one race, identified one race as best representing their race. Starting with 2003 data, race responses of other race and unspecified multiple race were treated as missing, and then race was imputed if these were the only race responses. Almost all persons with a race response of other race are of Hispanic origin.

[e]Percent of poverty level is based on family income and family size and composition using U.S. Census Bureau poverty thresholds. Missing family income data were imputed for 1997 and beyond.

SOURCE: Adapted from "Table 91. Dental Visits in the Past Year, by Selected Characteristics: United States, Selected Years 1997–2012," in *Health, United States, 2013: With Special Feature on Prescription Drugs*, U.S. Department of Health and Human Services, Centers for Disease Control and Prevention, National Center for Health Statistics, May 2014, http://www.cdc.gov/nchs/data/hus/hus13.pdf (accessed May 14, 2014)

TABLE 2.8

Allied health care providers

Dental hygienists provide services for maintaining oral health. Their primary duty is to clean teeth.

Emergency medical technicians (EMTs) provide immediate care to critically ill or injured people in emergency situations.

Home health aides provide nursing, household, and personal care services to patients who are homebound or disabled.

Licensed practical nurse (LPNs) are trained and licensed to provide basic nursing care under the supervision of registered nurses and doctors.

Medical records personnel analyze patient records and keep them up-to-date, complete, accurate, and confidential.

Medical technologists perform laboratory tests to help diagnose diseases and to aid in identifying their causes and extent.

Nurses' aides, orderlies, and attendants help nurses in hospitals, nursing homes, and other facilities.

Occupational therapists help disabled persons adapt to their disabilities. This may include helping a patient relearn basic living skills or modifying the environment.

Optometrists measure vision for corrective lenses and prescribe glasses.

Pharmacists are trained and licensed to make up and dispense drugs in accordance with a physician's prescription.

Physician assistants (PAs) work under a doctor's supervision. Their duties include performing routine physical exams, prescribing certain drugs, and providing medical counseling.

Physical therapists work with disabled patients to help restore function, strength and mobility. PTs use exercise, heat, cold, water, and electricity to relieve pain and restore function.

Podiatrists diagnose and treat diseases, injuries, and abnormalities of the feet. They may use drugs and surgery to treat foot problems.

Psychologists are trained in human behavior and provide counseling and testing services related to mental health.

Radiation technicians take and develop x-ray photographs for medical purposes.

Registered dietitians (RDs) are licensed to use dietary principles to maintain health and treat disease.

Respiratory therapists treat breathing problems under a doctor's supervision and help in respiratory rehabilitation.

Social workers help patients to handle social problems such as finances, housing, and social and family problems that arise out of illness or disability.

Speech pathologists diagnose and treat disorders of speech and communication.

SOURCE: "Allied Health Care Providers," U.S. Department of Commerce, Washington, DC

stimulation to promote healing, hot and cold packs to relieve pain and inflammation (swelling), and therapeutic massage.

According to the *Occupational Outlook Handbook*, PTs worked at 204,200 jobs in 2012. Employment of PTs was forecast to increase 36% from 2012 to 2022. (See Figure 2.6.) PTs work in hospitals and physicians' offices, outpatient rehabilitation clinics, nursing homes, and home health agencies. Although most work in rehabilitation, PTs may specialize in areas such as sports medicine, pediatrics, or neurology. PTs often work as members of a health care team and may supervise PT assistants or aides. The BLS notes that in 2012 the median annual wage for a PT was $79,860.

The BLS indicates that PTs are required to earn a master's or doctorate degree from an accredited physical therapy program. To practice physical therapy, PTs must obtain state licensure. Although the requirements vary by state, licensure generally requires graduation from an accredited physical therapy education program and passing a national examination. Many states also require continuing education as a condition of maintaining licensure.

Occupational therapists (OTs) focus on helping people relearn and improve their abilities to perform the "activities of daily living," meaning the tasks they perform during the course of their work and home life. Examples of activities of daily living that OTs help patients regain are dressing, bathing, and meal preparation. For people with long-term or permanent disabilities, OTs may assist them to find new ways to accomplish their responsibilities on the job, sometimes by using adaptive equipment or by asking employers to accommodate workers with special needs such as people in wheelchairs. OTs use computer programs and simulations to help patients restore fine motor skills and practice reasoning, decision making, and problem solving.

A master's degree or higher in occupational therapy is the minimum educational requirement. The American Occupational Therapy Association states in "Occupational Therapy's Role in Health Care Reform" (2014, http://www.aota.org/About-Occupational-Therapy/Professionals/HCR.aspx) that in addition to providing some of the essential benefits of the ACA such as rehabilitation, OTs also focus on prevention and helping people remain in the community as opposed to entering long-term care facilities. All of these services help to improve health outcomes and decrease costs.

The *Occupational Outlook Handbook* reports that in 2012 OTs filled 113,200 jobs and that their median annual wages were $75,400.

The demand for OTs is expected to exceed the available supply through 2020, growing 29% between 2012 and 2022. Besides hospital and rehabilitation center jobs, it is anticipated that PTs and OTs will increasingly be involved in school program efforts to meet the needs of disabled and special education students.

Pharmacists

Pharmacists are involved in many more aspects of patient care than simply compounding and dispensing medication from behind the drugstore counter. According to the American Pharmacists Association, pharmacists provide pharmaceutical care that both improves patient adherence to prescribed drug treatment and reduces the frequency of drug therapy mishaps, which can have serious and even life-threatening consequences.

Studies citing the value of pharmacists in patient care describe pharmacists improving the rates of immunization against disease (pharmacists can provide immunization in all 50 states, the District of Columbia, and Puerto Rico), assisting patients to better control chronic diseases such as asthma and diabetes, reducing the frequency and severity of drug interactions and adverse reactions, and helping patients effectively manage pain and symptoms of disease, especially at the end of life. Pharmacists also

TABLE 2.9

Health care workers and wages, selected years 2001–12

[Data are based on a semiannual mail survey of nonfarm establishments]

Occupation title	Employment[a]				AAPC[b] 2001–2012	Mean hourly wage[c]				AAPC[b] 2001–2012
	2001	2005	2009	2012		2001	2005	2009	2012	
Healthcare practitioners and technical occupations										
Audiologists	11,040	10,030	12,590	12,060	0.8	$23.89	$27.72	$32.14	$35.04	3.5
Cardiovascular technologists and technicians	40,990	43,560	48,070	50,530	1.9	17.55	19.99	23.91	25.51	3.5
Dental hygienists	149,880	161,140	173,900	190,290	2.2	27.30	29.15	32.63	33.99	2.0
Diagnostic medical sonographers	32,990	43,590	51,630	57,700	5.2	23.08	26.65	30.60	31.90	3.0
Dietetic technicians	28,940	23,780	24,510	24,660	−1.4	11.23	12.20	13.72	13.79	1.9
Dietitians and nutritionists	43,200	48,850	53,220	58,240	2.8	19.74	22.09	25.59	27.00	2.9
Emergency medical technicians and paramedics	170,690	196,880	217,920	232,860	2.9	12.24	13.68	15.88	16.53	2.8
Licensed practical and licensed vocational nurses	683,790	710,020	728,670	718,800	0.5	15.14	17.41	19.66	20.39	2.7
Magnetic resonance imaging technologists	—	—	—	29,560	—	—	—	—	31.45	—
Medical and clinical laboratory technicians	146,920	142,330	152,420	157,920	0.7	14.52	15.95	18.20	18.91	2.4
Medical and clinical laboratory technologists	145,400	155,250	166,860	160,700	0.9	20.70	23.37	26.74	28.19	2.8
Medical records and health information technicians	142,170	160,450	170,580	182,370	2.3	12.20	13.81	16.29	17.68	3.4
Nuclear medicine technologists	17,360	18,280	21,670	20,480	1.5	24.65	29.10	32.91	34.06	3.0
Nurse anesthetists	—	—	—	34,180	—	—	—	—	74.22	—
Nurse midwives	—	—	—	5,710	—	—	—	—	43.78	—
Nurse practitioners	—	—	—	105,780	—	—	—	—	43.97	—
Occupational therapists	77,080	87,430	97,840	105,540	2.9	25.10	28.41	33.98	36.73	3.5
Opticians, dispensing	63,120	70,090	60,840	64,930	0.3	13.49	14.80	16.73	16.83	2.0
Pharmacists	223,630	229,740	267,860	281,560	2.1	35.02	42.62	51.27	55.27	4.2
Pharmacy technicians	207,140	266,790	331,890	353,340	5.0	10.82	12.19	13.92	14.63	2.8
Physical therapists	126,450	151,280	174,490	191,460	3.8	28.43	31.42	36.64	38.99	2.9
Physician assistants	56,200	63,350	76,900	83,640	3.7	30.00	34.17	40.78	44.45	3.6
Psychiatric technicians	59,750	62,040	70,730	67,760	1.2	12.94	14.04	14.77	15.93	1.9
Radiation therapists	13,460	14,120	15,570	18,230	2.8	25.71	30.59	37.18	38.66	3.8
Radiologic technologists[c]	168,240	184,580	213,560	194,790	1.3	18.68	22.60	26.05	27.14	3.5
Recreational therapists	26,830	23,260	21,960	19,180	−3.0	14.92	16.90	19.84	21.29	3.3
Registered nurses[d]	2,217,990	2,368,070	2,583,770	2,633,980	1.6	23.19	27.35	31.99	32.66	3.2
Respiratory therapists	82,930	95,320	107,270	116,960	3.2	19.17	22.24	26.06	27.50	3.3
Respiratory therapy technicians	28,700	22,060	15,100	13,460	−6.7	16.93	18.57	21.96	22.84	2.8
Speech-language pathologists	83,110	94,660	111,640	121,690	3.5	24.20	27.89	32.86	34.97	3.4
Healthcare support occupations										
Dental assistants	267,840	270,720	294,020	300,160	1.0	13.29	14.41	16.35	16.86	2.2
Home health aides	560,190	663,280	955,220	839,930	3.8	8.90	9.34	10.39	10.49	1.5
Massage therapists	26,440	37,670	55,920	71,040	9.4	15.93	19.33	19.13	19.40	1.8
Medical assistants	345,930	382,720	495,970	553,140	4.4	11.71	12.58	14.16	14.69	2.1
Medical equipment preparers	33,540	41,790	47,070	50,230	3.7	11.29	12.42	14.32	15.51	2.9
Medical transcriptionists	94,090	90,380	82,810	74,810	−2.1	12.99	14.36	16.03	16.66	2.3
Nursing assistants[e]	1,307,600	1,391,430	1,438,010	1,420,020	0.8	9.54	10.67	12.01	12.32	2.4
Occupational therapy aides	7,560	6,220	8,040	7,950	0.5	11.70	13.20	13.89	14.36	1.9
Occupational therapy assistants	17,520	22,160	26,680	29,500	4.9	17.39	19.13	24.44	25.52	3.5
Pharmacy aides	58,130	46,610	52,230	42,600	−2.8	9.22	9.76	10.74	11.28	1.9
Physical therapist aides	35,250	41,930	44,160	48,700	3.0	10.45	11.01	12.01	12.22	1.4
Physical therapist assistants	47,810	58,670	63,750	69,810	3.5	17.18	18.98	23.36	25.15	3.5
Psychiatric aides	59,640	56,150	62,610	77,880	2.5	11.42	11.47	13.19	12.83	1.1

[a]Employment is the number of filled positions. This table includes both full-time and part-time wage and salary positions. Estimates do not include business establishments where persons are self-employed, owners and partners in unincorporated firms, household workers, or unpaid family workers. Estimates were rounded to the nearest 10.

[b]AAPC is average annual percent change.

[c]The mean hourly wage rate for an occupation is the total wages that all workers in the occupation earn in an hour, divided by the total number of employees in the occupation.

[d]2012 data are not comparable to earlier data. Starting with 2012 data, the registered nurses occupation category was split into four occupations as part of the 2010 SOC revision: Registered nurses (29–1141), plus three advanced nursing occupations: Nurse anesthetists (29–1151), Nurse midwives (29–1161), and Nurse practitioners (29–1171).
(SOC = Standard Occupational Classification.)

[e]2012 data are not comparable to earlier data. Starting with 2012 data, the nursing aides, orderlies, and attendants occupation category was split into two occupations as part of the 2010 SOC revision: Nursing assistants (31–1014) and Orderlies (31–1015).

Notes: This table excludes occupations such as dentists, physicians, and chiropractors, which have a large percentage of workers who are self-employed. Challenges in using Occupational Employment Statistics (OES) data as a time series include changes in the occupational, industrial, and geographical classification systems, changes in the way data are collected, changes in the survey reference period, and changes in mean wage estimation methodology, as well as permanent features of the methodology.

SOURCE: "Table 105. Healthcare Employment and Wages, by Selected Occupations: United States, Selected Years 2001–2012," in *Health, United States, 2013: With Special Feature on Prescription Drugs*, U.S. Department of Health and Human Services, Centers for Disease Control and Prevention, National Center for Health Statistics, May 2014, http://www.cdc.gov/nchs/data/hus/hus13.pdf (accessed May 14, 2014)

offer public health education programs about prescription medication safety, prevention of poisoning, appropriate use of nonprescription (over-the-counter) drugs, and medical self-care.

Pharmacists must obtain a doctoral degree, called a PharmD, from an accredited school of pharmacy. Training for the PharmD generally takes four years to complete, and some PharmD graduates obtain additional

FIGURE 2.6

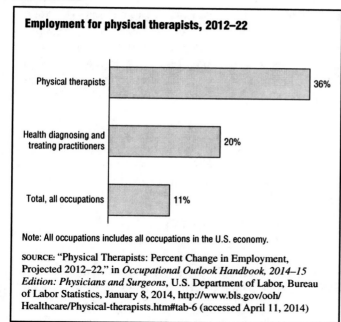

Employment for physical therapists, 2012–22

Physical therapists — 36%

Health diagnosing and treating practitioners — 20%

Total, all occupations — 11%

Note: All occupations includes all occupations in the U.S. economy.

SOURCE: "Physical Therapists: Percent Change in Employment, Projected 2012–22," in *Occupational Outlook Handbook, 2014–15 Edition: Physicians and Surgeons*, U.S. Department of Labor, Bureau of Labor Statistics, January 8, 2014, http://www.bls.gov/ooh/Healthcare/Physical-therapists.htm#tab-6 (accessed April 11, 2014)

training. All states require prospective pharmacists to pass two exams to obtain a license to practice pharmacy. Some states also require additional exams and all require a stipulated number of hours of experience in a practice setting as a prerequisite for licensure.

The *Occupational Outlook Handbook* reports that pharmacists worked at 286,400 jobs in 2012. Approximately 43% worked in community pharmacies—either independently owned or part of a drugstore chain, 23% worked in hospitals, 8% worked in grocery stores, 5% in department stores, and 5% in other mass merchandisers. The median annual wages of pharmacists in 2012 were $116,670.

MENTAL HEALTH PROFESSIONALS

The mental health sector includes a range of professionals—psychiatrists, psychologists, psychiatric nurses, clinical social workers, and counselors—whose training, orientation, philosophy, and practice styles differ, even within a single discipline. For example, different clinical psychologists may endorse and offer dramatically different forms of therapy—ranging from long-term psychoanalytic psychotherapy to short-term cognitive-behavioral therapy.

Psychiatrists

Psychiatrists are physicians who have completed residency training in the prevention, diagnosis, and treatment of mental illness, mental retardation, and substance abuse disorders. Because they are trained physicians, psychiatrists are especially well equipped to care for people who have coexisting medical diseases and mental health problems. As doctors, they can prescribe medication including psychoactive drugs. Psychiatrists may also obtain additional training that prepares them to treat certain populations, such as children and adolescents or older adults (this subspecialty is called geriatric psychiatry or geropsychiatry), or they may specialize in a specific treatment modality.

Psychologists

Psychologists are professionals trained in the study and treatment of people's cognitive, emotional, and social issues. They are distinct from psychiatrists in that they are not trained as physicians. Psychologists can engage in a wide variety of specialties and subspecialties, only some of which involve providing health care.

Research psychologists investigate the physical, cognitive, emotional, or social aspects of human behavior. They work at academic and private research centers and for business, nonprofit, and governmental organizations.

Clinical psychologists help mentally and emotionally disturbed clients better manage their symptoms and behaviors. Some work in rehabilitation, treating patients with spinal cord injuries, chronic pain or illness, stroke, arthritis, and neurologic conditions. Others help people cope during times of personal crisis, such as divorce or the death of a loved one. Psychologists are also called on to help communities recover from the trauma of natural or human-made disasters by working with, for example, people who have lost their homes to earthquakes, fires, or floods, or with students who have witnessed school violence.

Subspecialties open to clinical psychologists include health psychology, neuropsychology, and geropsychology. Health psychologists promote healthy lifestyles and behaviors and provide counseling such as smoking cessation, weight reduction, and stress management to assist people to reduce their health risks. Neuropsychologists often work in stroke rehabilitation and head injury programs, and geropsychologists work with older adults in institutional and community settings.

School psychologists identify, diagnose, and address students' learning and behavior problems. They work with teachers and school personnel to improve classroom management strategies and to design educational programs for students with disabilities or gifted and talented students. They also work with parents to help improve parenting skills.

Industrial-organizational psychologists aim to improve productivity and the quality of life in the workplace. They screen prospective employees and conduct training and development, counseling, and organizational development and analysis. Industrial-organizational psychologists examine aspects of work life. They work in organizational consultation, market research, systems design, or other applied psychology fields. For example, industrial-organizational psychologists may be involved in efforts to understand and influence consumer-purchasing behaviors.

Social psychologists consider interpersonal relationships and interactions with the social environment and social experience. Many social psychologists specialize in particular aspects of social psychology, such as group behavior, leadership, aggression, attitudinal change, or social perception.

EDUCATION, TRAINING, LICENSURE, AND EARNINGS. Most psychologists hold a doctorate degree in psychology, which requires between five and seven years of graduate study. Clinical psychologists usually earn a Doctor of Philosophy or a Doctor of Psychology degree and complete an internship that lasts at least one year. An educational specialist degree qualifies an individual to work as a school psychologist; however, most school psychologists complete a master's degree followed by a one-year internship. People with a master's degree in psychology might also work as industrial-organizational psychologists, or as psychological assistants under the supervision of doctoral-level psychologists, and conduct research or psychological evaluations. Vocational and guidance counselors usually need two years of graduate education in counseling and one year of counseling experience. A master's degree in psychology requires at least two years of full-time graduate study. People with undergraduate degrees in psychology assist psychologists and other professionals in community mental health centers, vocational rehabilitation offices, and correctional programs.

Psychologists in clinical practice must be certified or licensed in all states and the District of Columbia. According to the *Occupational Outlook Handbook*, the median annual wage for clinical, counseling, and school psychologists was $67,650 in 2012.

Psychiatric Nurses

Psychiatric nurses are required to have a degree in nursing, be licensed as RNs, and have additional experience in psychiatry. Advanced practice psychiatric nurses (RNs prepared at the master's level) may prescribe psychotropic medications and conduct individual, group, and family psychotherapy as well as perform crisis intervention and case management functions. Along with primary care physicians, they are often the first points of contact for people seeking mental health help.

The American Psychiatric Nurses Association is the professional society that represents psychiatric nurses. In "About Psychiatric-Mental Health Nurses" (2014, http://www.apna.org/i4a/pages/index.cfm?pageid=3292), the association explains that the pay scale for psychiatric nurses and psychiatric nurse practitioners "depends on many factors, such as level of education, years of experience, size of the agency or hospital, and geographic location." According to PayScale (2014, http://www.pay scale.com/research/US/Job=Registered_Psychiatric_Nurse_(RPN)/Hourly_Rate), a service that collects salary data, psychiatric nurses' salaries range from $43,535 to $83,706.

Social Workers

Social workers help people cope with challenges in their lives. They work in a variety of settings and specialties, only some of which are specifically related to health care.

Health care social workers help people to deal with illnesses and disabilities. For instance, they help people transition from care in a hospital back to living in their homes and communities, a process that may include making adjustments to lifestyle and housing. Mental health and substance abuse social workers specialize in helping people deal with mental illnesses and addictions, such as by directing them to 12-step programs.

Some social workers are specifically licensed to diagnose and treat mental, behavioral, and emotional disorders. They are known as clinical social workers or licensed clinical social workers. They offer psychotherapy or counseling and a range of diagnostic services in public agencies, clinics, and private practice.

According to the *Occupational Outlook Handbook*, social workers held 607,300 positions in the United States in 2012. Health care social workers' median wages were $49,830, and mental health and substance abuse social workers earned $39,980 on average.

EDUCATION, CERTIFICATION, AND LICENSURE. A bachelor's degree in social work is usually the minimum requirement for employment as a social worker, and an advanced degree has become the standard for many positions. A master's degree in social work is necessary for positions in health and mental health settings and is typically required for certification for clinical work. Licensed clinical social workers hold a master's degree in social work along with additional clinical training. Supervisory, administrative, and staff training positions usually require an advanced degree, and university teaching positions and research appointments normally require a doctorate in social work.

All the states and the District of Columbia have licensing, certification, or registration requirements that delineate the scope of social work practice and the use of professional titles; however, standards for licensing vary by state. The National Association of Social Workers (2014, https://www.socialworkers.org/nasw/default.asp) represents 132,000 professional social workers and "works to enhance the professional growth and development of its members, to create and maintain professional standards, and to advance sound social policies."

Counselors

Counselors assist people with personal, family, educational, mental health, and job-related challenges and problems. Their roles and responsibilities depend on the clients they serve and on the settings in which they work; only some types of counselors are involved in providing health care. The *Occupational Outlook Handbook* indicates that a master's degree is required to become a licensed counselor. The American Counseling Association (2014, http://www.counseling.org) is the world's largest association for professional counselors and represents nearly 55,000 professional counselors in various practice settings. The association has taken an active role in advocating for certification, licensure, and registry of counselors.

Rehabilitation counselors help people to gain independence and employment despite personal, social, and vocational challenges that stem from birth defects, illness, disease, accidents, or the stress of daily life. They help design and coordinate activities for people in rehabilitation treatment facilities and perform client evaluations. Rehabilitation counselors plan and implement rehabilitation programs that may include personal and vocational counseling, training, and job placement. The *Occupational Outlook Handbook* indicates that a master's degree is required to become a rehabilitation counselor. There were 117,500 jobs in this field in 2012, with an average pay of $33,880 annually.

Mental health counselors work in prevention programs to promote optimum mental health and provide a wide range of counseling services. They work closely with other mental health professionals, including psychiatrists, psychologists, clinical social workers, psychiatric nurses, and school counselors. Marriage and family therapists help people with problems with their family and relationships. The *Occupational Outlook Handbook* reports that there were 166,330 jobs for these types of counselors and therapists in 2012, with an average annual salary of $41,500. A master's degree is required and license to practice is typically required for these positions.

Substance abuse and behavioral disorder counselors help people overcome addictions to alcohol, drugs, gambling, and eating disorders. They counsel individuals, families, and groups in clinics, hospital-based outpatient treatment programs, community mental health centers, and inpatient chemical dependency treatment programs. In the *Occupational Outlook Handbook*, the BLS states that "educational requirements range from a high school diploma and certification to a master's degree," depending on the location, but that workers with more education are typically permitted to provide more services with less supervision. There were 89,600 jobs in this field in 2012, paying an average of $38,520 annually.

Pastoral counselors offer a type of psychotherapy that combines spiritual resources with psychological understanding for healing and growth. According to the "Mission Statement" of the American Association of Pastoral Counselors (AAPC; 2014, http://www.aapc.org/home/mission-statement.aspx), this therapeutic modality is more than simply the comfort, support, and encouragement a religious community can offer; instead, it aims to provide "healing, hope, and wholeness to individuals, families, and communities by expanding and equipping spiritually grounded and psychologically informed care, counseling, and psychotherapy." Typically, an AAPC-certified counselor has obtained a bachelor's degree from a college or university, a three-year professional degree from a seminary, and a specialized master's or doctorate degree in the mental health field.

The AAPC asserts that demand for spiritually based counseling is on the rise, in part because interest in spirituality is on the rise in the United States. The organization believes that despite increased interest in psychotherapy and increasing numbers of therapists, managed mental health care has reduced the availability of, and payment for, counseling services for many people. As a result, more people are turning to clergy for help with personal, marital, and family issues as well as with faith issues. For many Americans, free or low-cost counseling from pastoral counselors is the most accessible, available, affordable, and acceptable form of mental health care.

PRACTITIONERS OF COMPLEMENTARY AND ALTERNATIVE MEDICINE

The field of complementary and alternative medicine (CAM) is attracting a growing number of professionals. In "Complementary, Alternative, or Integrative Health: What's in a Name?" (July 2014, http://nccam.nih.gov/health/whatiscam) the federal government's National Center for Complementary and Alternative Medicine (NCCAM) explains that the terms *complementary medicine*, *alternative medicine*, and *integrative medicine* "are often used to mean the array of health care approaches with a history of use or origins outside of mainstream medicine, [but] they are actually hard to define and may mean different things to different people."

The NCCAM further defines alternative medicine as being a nonmainstream approach used in place of conventional medicine. By contrast, complementary medicine combines nonmainstream approaches with conventional medicine. As for integrative medicine, the NCCAM states that "this term is often used when conventional and complementary approaches are offered together by a health care provider, health care facility, or system."

CAM techniques and products are considered non-mainstream by the NCCAM because they are not a part of conventional medical training, and because they have generally not undergone the sort of scientific testing associated with mainstream medicine.

Examples of CAM include acupuncture, dietary supplements, mediation, spinal manipulation, and traditional Chinese medicine. While these and other CAM approaches are not considered conventional medicine in the United States, that does not mean they are uncommon. Research shows that there is considerable enthusiasm for, and use of, CAM approaches and practices. Figure 2.7 shows the results of a 2012 survey of U.S. adults conducted by the U.S. Centers for Disease Control. The survey found that a substantial percentage of Americans had used various CAM techniques in the previous 12 months.

The most commonly used CAM therapies were:

- Nonvitamin, nonmineral dietary supplements (17.9% of respondents)
- Chiropractic and osteopathic care (8.5%)
- Yoga (8.4%)
- Massage (6.8%)
- Meditation (4.1%)
- Special diets (3%)

Homeopathic Medicine

Homeopathic medicine (also called homeopathy) is a CAM approach based on the belief that "like cures like" and uses very diluted amounts of natural substances to encourage the body's own self-healing mechanisms. Homeopathy was developed by the German physician Samuel Hahnemann (1755–1843) during the 1790s. Hahnemann found that he could produce symptoms of particular diseases by injecting small doses of various herbal substances. This discovery inspired him to administer to sick people extremely diluted formulations of substances that would produce the same symptoms they suffered from in an effort to stimulate natural recovery and regeneration.

According to Lex Rutten et al., in "Plausibility and Evidence: The Case of Homeopathy" (*Medicine, Health Care and Philosophy*, vol. 16, no. 3, August 2013), studies evaluating homeopathy report varied results from "comparable to conventional medicine" to "no evidence of effects beyond placebo." (Patients sometimes report improvement even when their treatment is a placebo—something that has no physical effects—because people expect to feel better when they are being treated and this expectation colors their perceptions of their conditions.) Rutten et al. observe that there are many unanswered questions and unresolved issues about the efficacy of homeopathy but they "remain convinced that these will eventually be resolved by application of authentic scientific method...."

Furthermore, Peter Fisher of the Royal London Hospital for Integrated Medicine observes in "What Is

FIGURE 2.7

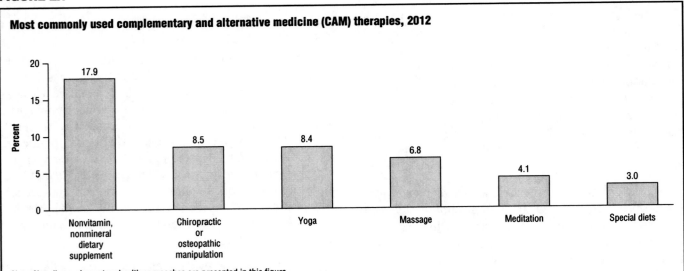

Most commonly used complementary and alternative medicine (CAM) therapies, 2012

Note: Not all complementary health approaches are presented in this figure.

SOURCE: Jennifer A. Peregoy et al., "Figure 1. Percentage of Adults Who Used Complementary Health Approaches in the Past 12 Months, by Type of Approach: United States, 2012," in "Regional Variation in Use of Complementary Health Approaches by U.S. Adults," *NCHS Data Brief*, no. 146, April 2014, http://www.cdc.gov/nchs/data/databriefs/db146.pdf (accessed April 18, 2014)

Homeopathy? An Introduction" (*Frontiers in Bioscience*, no. 4, January 1, 2012) that despite widespread condemnation, homeopathy continues to be employed by thousands of conventionally trained physicians. Fisher asserts that "there is a significant body of clinical research including randomised clinical trials and meta-analyses of such trials which suggest that homeopathy has actions which are not placebo effects."

Naturopathic Medicine

As its name suggests, naturopathic medicine (also called naturopathy) uses naturally occurring substances to prevent, diagnose, and treat disease. Although it is now considered to be an alternative medicine system, it is one of the oldest medicine systems and has its origins in Native American culture and even draws from Greek, Chinese, and East Indian ideas about health and illness.

The guiding principles of modern naturopathic medicine are "first, do no harm" and "nature has the power to heal." Naturopathy seeks to treat the whole person, because disease is seen as arising from many causes rather than from a single cause. Naturopathic physicians are taught that "prevention is as important as cure" and to view creating and maintaining health as equally important as curing disease. They are instructed to identify and treat the causes of diseases rather than to act only to relieve symptoms.

Naturopathic treatment methods include nutritional counseling; use of dietary supplements, herbs, and vitamins; hydrotherapy (water-based therapies, usually involving whirlpool or other baths); exercise; manipulation; massage; heat therapy; and electrical stimulation. Because naturopathy draws on Chinese and Indian medical techniques, naturopathic physicians often use Chinese herbs, acupuncture, and East Indian medicines to treat disease.

In "Integrating Naturopathy: Can We Move Forward?" (*Permanente Journal*, vol. 17, no. 4, Fall 2013), Charles R. Elder describe naturopathy as "a whole system medical practice guiding the selection and prescription of relatively complex, individualized treatment regimens." Elder explains that "Naturopathic medicine owns a history of promoting holistic, prevention-oriented care in North America and has established infrastructure for the accredited training and licensing of practitioners. Naturopathic physicians can offer the patient and health care team unique expertise in herbal medicine, diet and nutrition, stress reduction, disease prevention, and other areas to help optimize chronic disease management." Elder claims that naturopathy is potentially effective for many conditions including osteoarthritis, menopausal symptoms, irritable bowels, headache, chronic fatigue, and eczema.

Traditional Chinese Medicine

Traditional Chinese medicine (TCM) uses nutrition, acupuncture, massage, herbal medicine, and Qi Gong (exercises to improve the flow of vital energy through the body) to help people achieve balance and unity of their mind, body, and spirit. Practiced for more than 3,000 years by about a quarter of the world's population, TCM has been adopted by naturopathic physicians, chiropractors, and other CAM practitioners in the United States.

TCM views balancing *qi* (pronounced "chee"), the vital life force that flows over the surface of the body and through internal organs, as central to health, wellness, disease prevention, and treatment. This vital force or energy is thought to flow through the human body in meridians (channels). TCM practitioners believe that pain and disease develop when there is any sort of disturbance in the natural flow. TCM also seeks to balance the feminine and masculine qualities of yin and yang by using other techniques such as moxibustion, which is the stimulation of acupuncture points with heat, and cupping, in which the practitioner increases circulation by putting a heated jar on the skin of a body part. Herbal medicine is the most commonly prescribed treatment.

Acupuncture

Acupuncture is a Chinese practice that dates back more than 5,000 years. Chinese medicine describes acupuncture—the insertion of extremely thin, sterile needles to any of 360 specific points on the body—as a way to balance *qi*. When an acupuncturist determines that there is an imbalance in the flow of energy, needles are inserted at specific points along the meridians. Each point controls a different part of the body. Once the needles are in place, they are rotated gently or are briefly charged with a small electric current.

Traditional Western medicine explains the acknowledged effectiveness of acupuncture as the result of triggering the release of neurotransmitters and neuropeptides that influence brain chemistry and of pain-relieving substances called endorphins that occur naturally in the body. Besides providing lasting pain relief, acupuncture has demonstrated success in helping people with substance abuse problems, relieving nausea, heightening immunity by increasing total white blood cells and T-cell production, and assisting patients to recover from stroke and other neurological impairments. Imaging techniques confirm that acupuncture acts to alter brain chemistry and function.

Chiropractic Physicians

Chiropractic physicians treat patients whose health problems are associated mainly with the body's structural and neurological systems, especially the spine. These practitioners believe that interference with these systems can impair normal functions and lower resistance to disease. Chiropractic medicine asserts that misalignment or compression of, for example, the spinal nerves can alter many important body functions. According to the American Chiropractic Association, in "About Chiropractic" (2014, http://www.acatoday.org/level1_css.cfm?T1ID=42), *chiropractic* is "a health care profession that focuses on disorders of the musculoskeletal system and the nervous system, and the effects of these disorders on general health. Chiropractic care is used most often to treat neuromusculoskeletal complaints, including but not limited to back pain, neck pain, pain in the joints of the arms or legs, and headaches." Doctors of chiropractic medicine do not use or prescribe pharmaceutical drugs or perform surgery. Instead, they rely on adjustment and manipulation of the musculoskeletal system, particularly the spinal column.

Many chiropractors use nutritional therapy and prescribe dietary supplements; some employ a technique known as applied kinesiology to diagnose and treat disease. Applied kinesiology is based on the belief that every organ problem is associated with weakness of a specific muscle. Chiropractors who use this technique claim they can accurately identify organ system dysfunction without any laboratory or other diagnostic tests.

Besides manipulation, chiropractors use a variety of other therapies to support healing and relax muscles before they make manual adjustments. These treatments include:

- Heat and cold therapy to relieve pain, speed healing, and reduce swelling

- Hydrotherapy to relax muscles and stimulate blood circulation

- Immobilization such as casts, wraps, traction, and splints to protect injured areas

- Electrotherapy to deliver deep tissue massage and boost circulation

- Ultrasound to relieve muscle spasms and reduce swelling

All states and the District of Columbia license chiropractors that meet the educational and examination requirements established by the state. According to the *Occupational Outlook Handbook*, chiropractors worked at 44,400 jobs in 2012, and most were self-employed and in solo practice. In 2012 the median annual wage for chiropractors was $66,160. Visits to chiropractors are most often for treatment of lower back pain, neck pain, and headaches.

INCREASE IN HEALTH CARE EMPLOYMENT

The number of people working in health care services has increased steadily since the middle of the 20th century. Figure 2.8 shows the projected increases in employment in selected health care occupations between 2006 and 2016. The largest employment increases forecasted are for RNs; personal and home care aides; home health aides; nursing aides, orderlies, and attendants; medical assistants; and licensed practical and licensed vocational nurses.

Why Is Health Care Booming?

Three major factors appear to have influenced the escalation in health care employment: advances in technology, the increasing amounts of money spent on health care, and the aging of the U.S. population. In other sectors of the economy, technology often replaces humans in the labor force. However, health care technology has increased the demand for highly trained specialists to operate the sophisticated equipment. Because of technological advances, patients are likely to undergo more tests and diagnostic procedures, take more drugs, see more specialists, and be subjected to more aggressive treatments than ever before.

The second factor involves the amount of money the nation spends on keeping its citizens in good health. The Centers for Medicare and Medicaid Services forecasts in *National Health Expenditure Projections 2010–2020* (September 2011, https://www.cms.gov/Research-Statistics-Data-and-Systems/Statistics-Trends-and-Reports/National HealthExpendData/downloads/proj2010.pdf) that national health expenditures will rise from an average of $10,535 per person in 2015 to $13,709 per person in 2020. For each year that the amount of money spent on health care continues to grow, employment in the field grows as well. Some health care industry observers believe that government and private financing for the health care industry, unlike most other fields, is virtually unlimited.

The third factor contributing to the rise in the number of health care workers is the aging of the nation's population. There are greater numbers of older adults in the United States than ever before, and they are living longer. The U.S. Census Bureau states in the press release "Census Bureau Reports World's Older Population Projected to Triple by 2050" (June 23, 2009, http://www.census.gov/newsroom/releases/archives/international_population/cb09-97.html), the U.S. population aged 65 years and older will more than double by 2050, rising from 39 million in 2009 to 89 million in 2050.

The increase in the number of older people is expected to boost the demand for home health care services, assisted living, and nursing home care. Many nursing homes now offer special care for stroke patients, people with Alzheimer's disease (a progressive cognitive impairment), and people who need a respirator to breathe. To care for such patients, nursing homes need more PTs, nursing aides, and respiratory

FIGURE 2.8

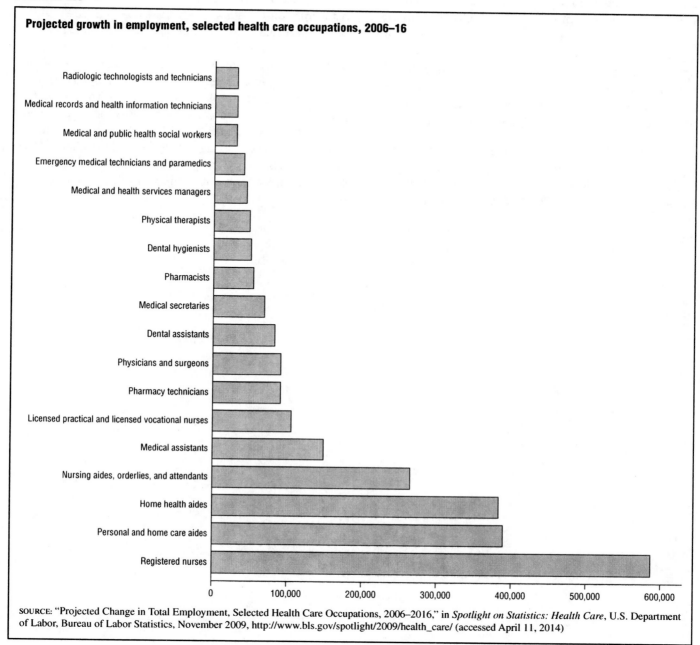

Projected growth in employment, selected health care occupations, 2006–16

SOURCE: "Projected Change in Total Employment, Selected Health Care Occupations, 2006–2016," in *Spotlight on Statistics: Health Care*, U.S. Department of Labor, Bureau of Labor Statistics, November 2009, http://www.bls.gov/spotlight/2009/health_care/ (accessed April 11, 2014)

therapists. Figure 2.8 shows the projected growth of these health care occupations.

Another factor that will likely further increase the demand for health care workers is the full implementation of the ACA, which is expected to occur in 2015. As millions of previously uninsured Americans obtain coverage and enter the health care system, additional health care resources (i.e., workers and facilities) will be required. The legislation also aims to improve the way in which physicians and other health care workers deliver care. For example, previously uninsured Americans who may have used hospital emergency departments to obtain needed medical care will be able to access preventive services in physicians' offices and clinics. This group may also seek care when the symptoms of sickness first appear, when diseases and disorders are more amenable to treatment, rather than waiting until the situation requires emergency treatment.

The ACA expanded training programs for health professionals and established the National Health Care Workforce Commission to meet the growing demand for health care professionals. In "Projecting the Supply and Demand for Primary Care Practitioners through 2020" (November 2013, http://bhpr.hrsa.gov/healthworkforce/supplydemand/usworkforce/primarycare/projectingprimarycare.pdf) the National Center for Health Workforce

Analysis attributes 81% of the increased demand for primary care services from 2010 and 2020 to population growth and the aging population. The balance of the projected increase in demand is associated with expanded coverage under the ACA. There will be a corresponding demand for services from clinical laboratory professionals, imaging technicians, pharmacists and other pharmacy personnel, and health educators.

In "The Effects of Expanding Primary Care Access for the Uninsured: Implications for the Health Care Workforce under Health Reform" (*Academic Medicine*, vol. 88, no. 12, December 2013), Alan W. Dow et al. note that increasing demand for health services will exacerbate strain on the already overloaded health care system. They assert that access to care in areas that already suffer from primary care physician shortages will be further compromised. Dow et al. opine that implementation of the ACA "offers researchers and leaders an opportunity to understand the needs of communities, to implement targeted strategies of care, and to define which approaches best align the existing health care workforce and systems of care with the needs of the newly insured population. The results of these new strategies, approaches, and initiatives could reshape health care, improving quality, cost, and equity across the system."

CHAPTER 3
HEALTH CARE INSTITUTIONS

A hospital is no place to be sick.
—Samuel Goldwyn

HOSPITALS

The first hospitals in the United States were established over 200 years ago. No records of hospitals in the early colonies exist, but almshouses, which sheltered the poor, also cared for those who were ill. The first almshouse opened in 1662 in the Massachusetts Bay Colony. In 1756 the Pennsylvania Hospital in Philadelphia became the first U.S. institution devoted entirely to care of the sick.

Until the late 1800s, U.S. hospitals had a bad reputation. The upper classes viewed hospitals as places for the poor who could not afford home care, and the poor saw hospitalization as a humiliating consequence of personal economic failure. People from all walks of life thought hospitals were places to go to die. These attitudes changed as the quality of care available in hospitals improved.

TYPES OF HOSPITALS

The American Hospital Association (AHA) notes in "Fast Facts on U.S. Hospitals" (January 2, 2014, http://www.aha.org/research/rc/stat-studies/fast-facts.shtml) that in 2012 there were 5,723 registered hospitals in the United States. These included both short-stay and long-term facilities. Short-stay facilities include community, teaching, and public hospitals. Sometimes short-stay hospitals are referred to as acute care facilities because the services provided within them focus on pressing problems or medical conditions, such as a heart attack, rather than on long-term chronic conditions, such as the need for rehabilitation following a head injury. Long-term hospitals are usually rehabilitation and psychiatric hospitals or facilities for the treatment of tuberculosis or other pulmonary (respiratory) diseases.

Hospitals are also distinguished by their ownership, scope of services, and whether they are teaching hospitals with academic affiliations. Hospitals may be operated as proprietary (for-profit) businesses—owned either by corporations or individuals, such as the physicians on staff—or they may be voluntary—owned by nonprofit corporations or religious organizations or operated by federal, state, or city governments. Voluntary, nonprofit hospitals are usually governed by a board of trustees, who are selected from among community business and civic leaders and who serve without pay to oversee hospital operations.

Most community hospitals offer emergency services as well as a range of inpatient and outpatient medical and surgical services. There are more than 1,000 tertiary hospitals in the United States, which are hospitals that provide highly specialized services such as neonatal intensive care units (for care of sick newborns), trauma services, or cardiovascular surgery programs. A majority of tertiary hospitals serve as teaching hospitals.

Teaching hospitals are those community and tertiary hospitals affiliated with medical schools, nursing schools, or allied health professions training programs. Teaching hospitals are the primary sites for training new physicians, where interns and residents work under the supervision of experienced physicians. Nonteaching hospitals may also maintain affiliations with medical schools and some serve as sites for nursing and allied health professions students as well as for physicians-in-training.

Table 3.1 shows that the total number of U.S. hospitals declined from 7,156 in 1975 to 5,724 in 2011. Occupancy rates also declined during this period. Although the number of community nonprofit and state and local hospitals declined during this period, the number of for-profit hospitals grew, from 775 in 1975 to 1,025 in 2011.

TABLE 3.1

Hospitals, beds, and occupancy rates, by type of ownership and size of hospital, selected years 1975–2011

[Data are based on reporting by a census of hospitals]

Type of ownership and size of hospital	1975	1980	1990	1995	2000	2005	2010	2011
Hospitals					Number			
All hospitals	7,156	6,965	6,649	6,291	5,810	5,756	5,754	5,724
Federal	382	359	337	299	245	226	213	208
Nonfederal[a]	6,774	6,606	6,312	5,992	5,565	5,530	5,541	5,516
Community[b]	5,875	5,830	5,384	5,194	4,915	4,936	4,985	4,973
Nonprofit	3,339	3,322	3,191	3,092	3,003	2,958	2,904	2,903
For profit	775	730	749	752	749	868	1,013	1,025
State-local government	1,761	1,778	1,444	1,350	1,163	1,110	1,068	1,045
6–24 beds	299	259	226	278	288	370	424	445
25–49 beds	1,155	1,029	935	922	910	1,032	1,167	1,177
50–99 beds	1,481	1,462	1,263	1,139	1,055	1,001	970	955
100–199 beds	1,363	1,370	1,306	1,324	1,236	1,129	1,029	1,005
200–299 beds	678	715	739	718	656	619	585	582
300–399 beds	378	412	408	354	341	368	352	353
400–499 beds	230	266	222	195	182	173	185	184
500 beds or more	291	317	285	264	247	244	273	272
Beds								
All hospitals	1,465,828	1,364,516	1,213,327	1,080,601	983,628	946,997	941,995	924,333
Federal	131,946	117,328	98,255	77,079	53,067	45,837	44,940	38,065
Nonfederal[a]	1,333,882	1,247,188	1,115,072	1,003,522	930,561	901,160	897,055	886,268
Community[b]	941,844	988,387	927,360	872,736	823,560	802,311	804,943	797,403
Nonprofit	658,195	692,459	656,755	609,729	582,988	561,106	555,768	547,804
For profit	73,495	87,033	101,377	105,737	109,883	113,510	124,652	128,371
State-local government	210,154	208,895	169,228	157,270	130,689	127,695	124,523	121,228
6–24 beds	5,615	4,932	4,427	5,085	5,156	6,316	7,261	7,616
25–49 beds	41,783	37,478	35,420	34,352	33,333	33,726	37,446	37,680
50–99 beds	106,776	105,278	90,394	82,024	75,865	71,737	69,470	67,844
100–199 beds	192,438	192,892	183,867	187,381	175,778	161,593	148,090	143,843
200–299 beds	164,405	172,390	179,670	175,240	159,807	151,290	142,616	141,308
300–399 beds	127,728	139,434	138,938	121,136	117,220	126,899	121,749	122,269
400–499 beds	101,278	117,724	98,833	86,459	80,763	76,894	82,071	81,699
500 beds or more	201,821	218,259	195,811	181,059	175,638	173,856	196,240	195,144
Occupancy rate[c]					Percent			
All hospitals	76.7	77.7	69.5	65.7	66.1	69.3	66.6	66.5
Federal	80.7	80.1	72.9	72.6	68.2	66.0	65.3	69.1
Nonfederal[a]	76.3	77.4	69.2	65.1	65.9	69.5	66.6	66.4
Community[b]	75.0	75.6	66.8	62.8	63.9	67.3	64.5	64.3
Nonprofit	77.5	78.2	69.3	64.5	65.5	69.1	66.2	66.0
For profit	65.9	65.2	52.8	51.8	55.9	59.6	57.1	57.0
State-local government	70.4	71.1	65.3	63.7	63.2	66.7	64.4	64.5
6–24 beds	48.0	46.8	32.3	36.9	31.7	33.5	32.3	31.9
25–49 beds	56.7	52.8	41.3	42.6	41.3	47.1	44.8	44.3
50–99 beds	64.7	64.2	53.8	54.1	54.8	59.0	55.1	55.6
100–199 beds	71.2	71.4	61.5	58.8	60.0	63.2	60.4	59.7
200–299 beds	77.1	77.4	67.1	63.1	65.0	67.7	64.0	63.7
300–399 beds	79.7	79.7	70.0	64.8	65.7	70.1	67.4	66.7
400–499 beds	81.1	81.2	73.5	68.1	69.1	71.2	68.5	68.4
500 beds or more	80.9	82.1	77.3	71.4	72.2	75.9	73.0	73.2

[a]The category of nonfederal hospitals comprises psychiatric hospitals, tuberculosis and other respiratory diseases hospitals, and long-term and short-term general and other special hospitals.
[b]Community hospitals are nonfederal short-term general and special hospitals whose facilities and services are available to the public.
[c]Estimated percentage of staffed beds that are occupied. Occupancy rate is calculated as the average daily census (from the American Hospital Association) divided by the number of hospital beds.

SOURCE: "Table 107. Hospitals, Beds, and Occupancy Rates, by Type of Ownership and Size of Hospital: United States, Selected Years 1975–2011," in *Health, United States, 2013: With Special Feature on Prescription Drugs*, U.S. Department of Health and Human Services, Centers for Disease Control and Prevention, National Center for Health Statistics, May 2014, http://www.cdc.gov/nchs/data/hus/husl3.pdf (accessed May 14, 2014). Data from American Hospital Association (AHA) Annual Survey of Hospitals.

Community Hospitals

The most common type of hospital in the United States is the community, or general, hospital. Community hospitals, where most people receive care, are typically small, with 50 to 500 beds. The AHA reports in "Fast Facts on U.S. Hospitals" that in 2012 there were 4,999 community hospitals, with 800,566 staffed beds, in the United States. These hospitals normally provide quality care for routine medical and surgical problems. Since the 1980s many smaller hospitals have closed down because they are no longer profitable. The larger ones, usually located in cities and adjacent suburbs, are often equipped with a full complement of medical and surgical personnel and state-of-the-art equipment.

Some community hospitals are nonprofit corporations that are supported by local funding. These include hospitals supported by religious, cooperative, or osteopathic organizations. During the 1990s increasing numbers of nonprofit community hospitals converted their ownership status, becoming proprietary hospitals that are owned and operated on a for-profit basis by corporations. These hospitals joined investor-owned corporations because they needed additional financial resources to maintain their existence in an increasingly competitive industry. Investor-owned corporations acquire nonprofit hospitals to build market share, expand their provider networks, and penetrate new health care markets. According to the AHA, there were 2,894 nonprofit community hospitals and 1,068 investor-owned, for-profit community hospitals in 2012.

Teaching Hospitals

Teaching hospitals, which provide clinical training for medical students and other health care professionals, are affiliated with a medical school and have several hundred beds. Many of the physicians on staff at the hospital also hold teaching positions at the university that is affiliated with the hospital. These physicians may serve as classroom instructors as well as teaching physicians-in-training at the bedsides of the patients. Patients in teaching hospitals understand that they may be examined by medical students and residents as well as by their primary attending physician.

One advantage of obtaining care at a university-affiliated teaching hospital is the opportunity to receive treatment from highly qualified physicians with access to the most advanced technology and equipment. A disadvantage is the inconvenience and invasion of privacy that may result from multiple examinations performed by residents and students. When compared with smaller community hospitals, some teaching hospitals have reputations for being impersonal; however, patients with complex, unusual, or difficult diagnoses usually benefit from the presence of acknowledged medical experts and more comprehensive resources that are available at these facilities.

Public Hospitals

Public hospitals are owned and operated by federal, state, or city governments. Many have a continuing tradition of caring for the poor. They are usually located in the inner cities and are often in precarious financial situations because many of their patients are unable to pay for services. These hospitals depend heavily on Medicaid payments that are supplied by federal and state agencies or on grants from local governments.

Medicaid is a program run by both the federal and state governments for the provision of health care insurance to people younger than 65 years of age who cannot afford to pay for private health insurance. The federal government matches the states' contribution to provide a certain minimal level of available coverage, and the states may offer additional services at their own expense. In "Fast Facts on U.S. Hospitals," the AHA indicates that there were 1,037 state and local government community hospitals and 211 federal government hospitals in 2012.

TREATING SOCIETY'S MOST VULNERABLE MEMBERS. Increasingly, public hospitals must bear the burden of the weaknesses in the nation's health care system. Many of the major problems in U.S. society are readily apparent in the emergency departments and corridors of public hospitals: poverty, drug and alcohol abuse, crime victimization, domestic violence, untreated or inadequately treated chronic conditions such as high blood pressure and diabetes, and infectious diseases such as acquired immunodeficiency syndrome (AIDS) and tuberculosis.

LOSING MONEY. The typical public hospital provides millions of dollars in health care and fails to recoup these costs from reimbursement by private insurance, Medicaid, and Medicare (a federal health insurance program for people aged 65 years and older and people with disabilities). Jack Zwanziger, Nasreen Khan, and Anil Bamezai note in "The Relationship between Safety Net Activities and Hospital Financial Performance" (*BMC Health Services Research*, vol. 10, no. 1, January 14, 2010) that at the close of the 20th century all U.S. hospitals were forced to take steps to reduce health care costs and faced reduced Medicare and Medicaid reimbursement. These changes, however, disproportionately affected the nation's public hospitals, which provide "safety net" services and serve vulnerable populations such as poor and uninsured patients. (According to the Institute of Medicine, in *America's Health Care Safety Net: Intact but Endangered* [January 2000, http://www.iom.edu], safety net services are offered by providers "that deliver a significant level of health care to uninsured, Medicaid, and other vulnerable patients." The institute also explains that "these providers have two distinguishing characteristics: [1] either by legal mandate or explicitly adopted mission, they offer care to patients regardless of their ability to pay for those services; and [2] a substantial share of their patient mix are uninsured, Medicaid, and other vulnerable patients.") In response to these fiscal pressures, some hospitals closed and others decreased the range of services provided. Others responded by streamlining services and pursuing paying patients.

According to Steven Ross Johnson in "Outlook 2014: Public Hospitals" (ModernHealthCare.com, January 4, 2014), under the Patient Protection and Affordable

Care Act (ACA) the financial outlook for public hospitals in states that expanded Medicaid enrollment should improve, despite the fact that Medicare and Medicaid payments for uncompensated care will be reduced, because hospitals will see an increased number of patients with health coverage. In states that have not expanded Medicaid coverage, public hospitals may suffer cutbacks in per-patient payments from Medicare and Medicaid without an increase in the number of covered patients in their service areas.

PROVIDING NEEDED SERVICES. America's Essential Hospitals (formerly the National Association of Public Hospitals and Health Systems) is an association of hospitals and health systems dedicated to serving vulnerable patients. In 2014 the organization represented nearly 250 hospitals and health care systems that provided care to patients and served as community resources.

Many of the members of America's Essential Hospitals are disproportionate share hospitals (DSHs), meaning that an especially large percentage of their patients cannot pay their medical bills. In "Key Facts about Our Members" (2014, http://essentialhospitals.org/newsroom/key-facts), America's Essential Hospitals reports that although its members represented a scant 2% of all acute care hospitals in the United States, they provided 20% of all uncompensated care.

Medicaid reimburses DSHs for some of the costs of providing care to indigent patients. The ACA, however, reduces funding for this compensation program, under the assumption that it will be less important as more people are enrolled in medical insurance. When President Barack Obama (1961–) announced a fiscal year 2015 budget plan in February 2014, it included a proposed cut to DSH reimbursements of $3.2 billion. Bruce Siegel, the president and chief executive officer of America's Essential Hospitals, expressed the organization's opposition to cuts in funding for essential hospitals in the press release, "Statement on President's Fiscal Year 2015 Budget Proposal" (March 5, 2014, http://essentialhospitals .org/general/statement-on-presidents-fiscal-year-2015-budget-proposal). Siegel stated that "we caution strongly against further reductions in federal support for essential hospitals and call on policy makers to revisit Affordable Care Act cuts in light of greatly reduced Medicaid expansion and other coverage shortfalls."

The ACA requires all insurance plans offered on the insurance marketplace it created to include some "essential community providers." These are health care providers that care for persons who are low income or medically underserved and include critical access hospitals, federally qualified health centers and Ryan White HIV/AIDS providers (which provide HIV-related care for those who do not have sufficient coverage or resources).

Under the ACA, safety net providers have opportunities to coordinate care and serve as medical homes—sources of patient-centered, comprehensive, and coordinated care. The ACA approved the creation of the Center for Medicare and Medicaid Innovation, which is testing innovative payment and delivery system models, such as medical homes. The law also offers states the option to receive federal matching funds to implement or expand health home programs for Medicaid beneficiaries with chronic conditions, which are akin to medical homes. Furthermore, the law funds initiatives to pilot and assess novel delivery system and payment models, especially those that incentivize providers to coordinate and integrate care for vulnerable populations. For example, the Medicare Shared Savings Program creates incentives for providers to work together in accountable care organizations to improve health care quality and efficiency.

HOSPITAL EMERGENCY DEPARTMENTS: MORE THAN THEY CAN HANDLE

For many Americans, the hospital emergency department (ED) has replaced the physician's office as the place to seek health care services. With no insurance and little money, many people go to the only place that will take them without question. Insurance companies and health care planners estimate that more than half of all ED visits are for nonemergency treatment.

During 2012, 17.8% of all children under the age of 18 years visited a hospital emergency room at least once. (See Table 3.2.) The poorest children were the most likely to have visited an ED. Almost one-quarter (24.9%) of children whose families lived below the poverty level visited an ED in 2012, as did 19.7% of children whose families were between 100% and 199% of the poverty level. By comparison, only 12.9% of children whose families were at or above 400% of the poverty level visited an ED that year. In 2012, 24.8% of children on Medicaid (at the time the government surveyed them) had visited EDs at least once, as opposed to 13% of children who were privately insured and 15.6% of uninsured children.

In the 18 years and older age group, 19.5% of the population visited an ED at least once during 2012. (See Table 3.3.) As with children, poorer adults were the most likely to have visited an ED, with 29.6% of people living below 100% of the poverty level and 23.9% of those living between 100% and 199% of the poverty level making at least one visit that year. By contrast only 14.1% of those with incomes at or above 400% of the poverty level had visited an ED. Among adults aged 18 to 64 years, 39.7% of people who were insured under Medicaid (at the time the government surveyed them) had visited the ED at least once in 2012, as opposed to 15% of those who were privately insured and 18.8% of those who were uninsured.

TABLE 3.2

Emergency department visits within the past 12 months among children under age 18, by selected characteristics, 1997, 2010, and 2012

[Data are based on household interviews of a sample of the civilian noninstitutionalized population]

Characteristic	Under 18 years			Under 6 years			6–17 years		
	1997	2010	2012	1997	2010	2012	1997	2010	2012
	Percent of children with one or more emergency department visits								
All children[a]	19.9	22.1	17.8	24.3	27.8	24.4	17.7	19.1	14.6
Sex									
Male	21.5	23.3	18.4	25.2	29.3	25.4	19.6	20.1	15.0
Female	18.3	20.9	17.2	23.3	26.3	23.4	15.7	18.2	14.1
Race[b]									
White only	19.4	21.2	16.8	22.6	26.6	23.2	17.8	18.4	13.7
Black or African American only	24.0	27.6	24.1	33.1	34.0	32.8	19.4	24.2	19.7
American Indian or Alaska Native only	24.1*	20.9	22.4*	24.3*	35.4*	*	24.0*	*	22.7*
Asian only	12.6	15.0	8.8	20.8	18.4	11.6*	8.6	13.3	7.4
Native Hawaiian or other Pacific Islander only	—	*	*	—	*	*	—	*	*
2 or more races	—	27.2	22.1	—	34.9	30.6	—	21.6	17.6
Hispanic origin and race[b]									
Hispanic or Latino	21.1	23.6	16.8	25.7	30.2	25.2	18.1	19.4	12.1
Not Hispanic or Latino	19.7	21.7	18.1	24.0	27.0	24.1	17.6	19.0	15.3
White only	19.2	20.4	16.9	22.2	25.1	22.6	17.7	18.2	14.3
Black or African American only	23.6	27.2	24.1	32.7	34.4	32.3	19.2	23.3	20.2
Percent of poverty level[c]									
Below 100%	25.1	30.6	24.9	29.5	35.4	32.7	22.2	27.6	20.1
100%–199%	22.0	25.7	19.7	28.0	31.6	26.0	19.0	22.3	16.6
200%–399%	18.0	18.4	15.0	21.4	22.7	20.4	16.4	16.4	12.5
400% or more	16.3	15.9	12.9	19.1	21.7	18.1	15.1	13.3	10.7
Hispanic origin and race and percent of poverty level[b, c]									
Hispanic or Latino:									
Percent of poverty level:									
Below 100%	21.9	27.0	19.4	25.0	32.0	27.9	19.6	23.4	14.1
100%–199%	20.8	23.3	16.6	28.8	31.6	26.4	15.6	18.0	11.4
200%–399%	21.4	19.5	13.7	24.6	25.2	18.1	19.6	16.1	11.2
400% or more	17.7	21.4	15.3	20.2*	28.6	25.7	16.4	18.0	9.9*
Not Hispanic or Latino:									
White only:									
Percent of poverty level:									
Below 100%	25.5	33.7	28.7	27.2	37.4	38.0	24.4	31.6	22.9
100%–199%	22.3	26.3	19.5	25.8	29.2	23.1	20.7	24.7	17.8
200%–399%	17.8	17.6	15.4	20.9	21.2	19.9	16.3	15.9	13.3
400% or more	16.5	15.5	12.5	19.0	21.0	17.2	15.4	13.2	10.6
Black or African American only:									
Percent of poverty level:									
Below 100%	29.3	32.4	28.9	39.5	41.6	33.4	23.0	26.6	26.1
100%–199%	22.5	27.5	26.8	31.7	34.5	37.8	18.5	23.7	22.2
200%–399%	18.5	22.3	17.6	23.9	24.6	28.1	16.3	21.4	13.5
400% or more	16.1	18.9	13.9	18.8*	24.1*	20.7*	15.2	16.1	11.2*
Health insurance status at the time of interview[d]									
Insured	19.8	22.3	18.0	24.4	28.1	24.7	17.5	19.2	14.6
Private	17.5	17.1	13.0	20.9	21.8	17.0	15.9	14.9	11.2
Medicaid	28.2	30.0	24.8	33.0	35.5	32.7	24.1	26.4	19.7
Uninsured	20.2	19.4	15.6	23.0	24.0	18.0	18.9	17.6	14.9
Health insurance status prior to interview[d]									
Insured continuously all 12 months	19.6	22.2	17.8	24.1	28.1	24.5	17.3	19.1	14.5
Uninsured for any period up to 12 months	24.0	23.7	20.3	27.1	28.0	26.8	21.9	21.3	17.0
Uninsured more than 12 months	18.4	17.6	12.9	19.3	21.3*	*	18.1	16.7	12.9

Majority of ED Patients Have Health Insurance

Because people without health insurance or a usual source of care often resort to using hospital EDs, industry observers sometimes assume that the crowding and long waits in EDs are at least in part caused by uninsured patients seeking care for routine problems such as colds, allergies, or back pain. In "Frequent Users of Emergency Departments: The Myths, the Data, and the Policy Implications" (*Annals of Emergency Medicine*, vol. 56, no. 1, July 2010), Eduardo LaCalle and Elaine Rabin of the

TABLE 3.2

Emergency department visits within the past 12 months among children under age 18, by selected characteristics, 1997, 2010, and 2012 [CONTINUED]

[Data are based on household interviews of a sample of the civilian noninstitutionalized population]

*Estimates are considered unreliable.
—Data not available.
[a]Includes all other races not shown separately and unknown health insurance status.
[b]The race groups, white, black, American Indian or Alaska Native, Asian, Native Hawaiian or other Pacific Islander, and 2 or more races, include persons of Hispanic and non-Hispanic origin. Persons of Hispanic origin may be of any race. Starting with 1999 data, race-specific estimates are tabulated according to the 1997 Revisions to the Standards for the Classification of Federal Data on Race and Ethnicity and are not strictly comparable with estimates for earlier years. The five single-race categories plus multiple-race categories shown in the table conform to the 1997 Standards. Starting with 1999 data, race-specific estimates are for persons who reported only one racial group; the category 2 or more races includes persons who reported more than one racial group. Prior to 1999, data were tabulated according to the 1977 Standards with four racial groups, and the Asian only category included Native Hawaiian or other Pacific Islander. Estimates for single-race categories prior to 1999 included persons who reported one race or, if they reported more than one race, identified one race as best representing their race. Starting with 2003 data, race responses of other race and unspecified multiple race were treated as missing, and then race was imputed if these were the only race responses. Almost all persons with a race response of other race were of Hispanic origin.
[c]Percent of poverty level is based on family income and family size and composition using U.S. Census Bureau poverty thresholds. Missing family income data were imputed for 1997 and beyond.
[d]Health insurance categories are mutually exclusive. Persons who reported both Medicaid and private coverage are classified as having private coverage. Starting with 1997 data, state-sponsored health plan coverage is included as Medicaid coverage. Starting with 1999 data, coverage by the Childrens Health Insurance Program (CHIP) is included with Medicaid coverage. In addition to private and Medicaid, the insured category also includes military, other government, and Medicare coverage. Persons not covered by private insurance, Medicaid, CHIP, state-sponsored or other government-sponsored health plans (starting in 1997), Medicare, or military plans are considered to have no health insurance coverage. Persons with only Indian Health Service coverage are considered to have no health insurance coverage.

SOURCE: Adapted from "Table 86. Emergency Department Visits within the Past 12 Months among Children under Age 18, by Selected Characteristics: United States, 1997–2012," in *Health, United States, 2013: With Special Feature on Prescription Drugs*, U.S. Department of Health and Human Services, Centers for Disease Control and Prevention, National Center for Health Statistics, May 2014, http://www.cdc.gov/nchs/data/hus/hus13.pdf (accessed May 14, 2014)

Mount Sinai School of Medicine refute this hypothesis. They characterize frequent users of emergency medical care (adults who make four or more ED visits in one year) as people with insurance who also make frequent use of other health care services, such as clinics and physicians' offices. The researchers conclude that "frequent ED users are a heterogeneous group along many dimensions and defy popular assumptions ... and many frequent users present with true medical needs, which may explain why existing attempts to address the phenomena have had mixed success at best."

Some industry observers opine that under the ACA, states that extend and expand Medicaid to cover persons previously uninsured will increase access to primary care and reduce ED use. However, in "Medicaid Increases Emergency-Department Use: Evidence from Oregon's Health Insurance Experiment" (*Science*, vol. 343, no. 6168, January 4, 2014), Sarah Taubman et al. report that Medicaid expansion increased ED use in Oregon. The researchers analyzed data from that state, which in 2008 began a limited expansion of Medicaid that drew names from a waiting list by lottery to provide coverage. Taubman et al. speculate that Medicaid did not decrease ED use because it did not improve access to and use of primary care.

Hospitals Cater to Special Populations

The oldest Americans are the most likely age group to visit an ED. Table 3.3 shows that in 2012, 25.3% of those aged 75 years and older did so at least once, and 9.2% did so two or more times. This has led some hospitals to create special areas in the EDs for them, or even dedicating EDs to meet their needs. For example, Anemona Hartocollis reports in "For the Elderly, Emergency Rooms of Their Own" (NYTimes.com, April 9, 2012) that Mount Sinai Hospital in New York City is among a growing number of hospitals with an ED dedicated to serving older adults. Also known as a "geri-ed," it looks more like a clinic than an ED and has features such as nonskid floors, wall rails, reclining chairs, and thicker mattresses to improve the comfort of patients aged 65 years and older. Volunteers interact with patients in a calm environment that is designed to allay anxiety and enhance patient satisfaction. Patients use iPads to initiate two-way conversations with nurses and can order lunch, pain medication, or music using the touchscreen.

In "Emergency Rooms Are No Place for the Elderly" (NYTimes.com, March 13, 2014), Pauline W. Chen reports that by 2014, about 50 medical centers had made changes to their emergency departments to better serve older adults, such as hiring specially trained providers and installing nonslip flooring to prevent falls. These EDs also arrange transportation for patients, help to fill prescriptions, and supply patients with medical equipment such as canes and walkers when they are discharged.

HOSPITALIZATION

In *Health, United States, 2013: With Special Feature on Prescription Drugs* (May 2014, http://www.cdc.gov/nchs/data/hus/hus13.pdf), the National Center for Health Statistics (NCHS) reports that in 2009–10, there were 35.6 million discharges from nonfederal short-stay hospitals. That is, hospitals treated and discharged patients that many times. The hospital discharge rate was 1,125.1

TABLE 3.3

Emergency department visits within the past 12 months among adults, by selected characteristics, selected years 1997–2012

[Data are based on household interviews of a sample of the civilian noninstitutionalized population]

Characteristic	One or more emergency department visits				Two or more emergency department visits			
	1997	2000	2010	2012	1997	2000	2010	2012
	Percent of adults with emergency department visits							
18 years and over, age-adjusted[a, b]	19.6	20.2	21.4	19.5	6.7	6.9	7.8	7.2
18 years and over, crude[a]	19.6	20.1	21.3	19.4	6.7	6.8	7.7	7.1
Age								
18–44 years	20.7	20.5	22.0	19.4	6.8	7.0	8.4	7.4
18–24 years	26.3	25.7	25.4	22.3	9.1	8.8	9.6	9.0
25–44 years	19.0	18.8	20.7	18.4	6.2	6.4	8.0	6.8
45–64 years	16.2	17.6	19.2	18.0	5.6	5.6	6.7	6.4
45–54 years	15.7	17.9	18.6	18.0	5.5	5.8	6.6	6.7
55–64 years	16.9	17.0	19.8	18.0	5.7	5.3	6.8	6.0
65 years and over	22.0	23.7	23.7	22.2	8.1	8.6	7.7	7.8
65–74 years	20.3	21.6	20.7	19.9	7.1	7.4	6.4	6.7
75 years and over	24.3	26.2	27.4	25.3	9.3	10.0	9.4	9.2
Sex[b]								
Male	19.1	18.7	18.5	17.0	5.9	5.7	6.0	5.7
Female	20.2	21.6	24.3	22.0	7.5	7.9	9.6	8.7
Race[b, c]								
White only	19.0	19.4	20.7	18.8	6.2	6.4	7.2	6.7
Black or African American only	25.9	26.5	28.6	26.4	11.1	10.8	12.6	11.6
American Indian or Alaska Native only	24.8	30.3	22.6	22.1	13.1	12.6*	11.8*	10.2*
Asian only	11.6	13.6	13.3	10.9	2.9*	3.8*	3.3	3.0
Native Hawaiian or other Pacific Islander only	—	*	*	*	—	*	*	*
2 or more races	—	32.5	29.7	31.2	—	11.3	11.1	12.7
American Indian or Alaska Native; White	—	33.9	31.1	37.7	—	9.4*	15.2*	12.8
Hispanic origin and race[b, c]								
Hispanic or Latino	19.2	18.3	19.8	18.2	7.4	7.0	6.9	7.2
Mexican	17.8	17.4	18.1	14.8	6.4	7.1	6.1	5.4
Not Hispanic or Latino	19.7	20.6	21.9	20.0	6.7	6.9	8.1	7.3
White only	19.1	19.8	21.1	19.3	6.2	6.4	7.4	6.9
Black or African American only	25.9	26.5	29.0	26.4	11.0	10.8	12.7	11.6
Percent of poverty level[b, d]								
Below 100%	28.1	29.0	30.6	29.6	12.8	13.3	14.9	14.8
100%–199%	23.8	23.9	25.6	23.9	9.3	9.6	10.5	10.3
200%–399%	18.3	19.8	20.4	18.6	5.9	6.3	6.8	5.9
400% or more	15.9	16.8	17.0	14.1	3.9	4.5	4.7	3.8
Hispanic origin and race and percent of poverty level[b, c, d]								
Hispanic or Latino:								
Below 100%	22.1	22.4	23.6	22.0	9.8	9.7	11.5	11.2
100%–199%	19.2	18.1	19.9	16.9	8.1	6.7	6.3	7.5
200%–399%	18.5	17.3	18.1	18.0	6.0	7.4	5.2	5.5
400% or more	14.6	16.4	18.8	17.3	3.8*	4.3*	5.5*	4.0*
Not Hispanic or Latino:								
White only:								
Below 100%	29.5	30.1	33.3	32.2	13.0	13.9	15.5	15.7
100%–199%	24.3	25.5	26.8	26.3	9.1	10.4	11.2	11.9
200%–399%	18.1	20.1	20.3	18.7	5.8	6.3	6.5	5.8
400% or more	15.8	16.3	16.9	14.0	3.8	4.1	4.9	3.8
Black or African American only:								
Below 100%	34.6	35.4	36.9	38.2	17.5	17.4	20.2	20.4
100%–199%	29.2	28.5	33.5	29.9	12.8	12.2	15.9	13.5
200%–399%	20.8	23.2	25.7	22.4	8.1	8.0	10.2	9.0
400% or more	18.2	22.6	18.8	16.3	5.9	8.8	4.0*	4.4*

per 10,000 population, down from 1,132.8 in 2000. The rate for females was 1,283.5 per 10,000 population, and for males it was 975.3 per 10,000 population. Male patients had longer average lengths of stay (ALOS) than female patients: 5.3 days compared with 4.5 days. ALOS and discharge rates varied by region; ALOS ranged from 4.3 days in the Midwest to 5.4 days in the Northeast.

Furthermore, the discharge rate per 10,000 population ranged from 932.7 in the West to 1,299.6 in the Northeast.

Organ Transplants

Organ transplants are a viable means of saving lives. According to the United Network for Organ Sharing's (UNOS) "Organ Procurement and Transplantation

TABLE 3.3

Emergency department visits within the past 12 months among adults, by selected characteristics, selected years 1997–2012 [CONTINUED]

[Data are based on household interviews of a sample of the civilian noninstitutionalized population]

Characteristic	One or more emergency department visits				Two or more emergency department visits			
	1997	2000	2010	2012	1997	2000	2010	2012
Health insurance status at the time of interview[e, f]	Percent of adults with emergency department visits							
18–64 years:								
Insured	18.8	19.5	20.8	19.1	6.1	6.4	7.5	6.9
Private	16.9	17.6	17.4	15.0	4.7	5.1	5.2	4.1
Medicaid	37.6	42.2	40.2	39.7	19.7	21.0	21.1	22.8
Uninsured	20.0	19.3	21.3	18.8	7.5	6.9	8.9	7.8
Health insurance status prior to interview[e, f]								
18–64 years:								
Insured continuously all 12 months	18.3	19.0	20.2	18.3	5.8	6.1	7.1	6.5
Uninsured for any period up to 12 months	25.5	28.2	26.0	27.4	9.4	10.3	12.5	12.6
Uninsured more than 12 months	18.9	17.3	20.6	16.9	7.1	6.4	8.1	6.9

*Estimates are considered unreliable. Data preceded by an asterisk have a relative standard error (RSE) of 20%–30%. Data not shown have an RSE greater than 30%.

—Data not available.

[a]Includes all other races not shown separately, unknown health insurance status, and unknown disability status.

[b]Estimates are for persons aged 18 and over and are age-adjusted to the year 2000 standard population using five age groups: 18–44 years, 45–54 years, 55–64 years, 65–74 years, and 75 years and over.

[c]The race groups, white, black, American Indian or Alaska Native, Asian, Native Hawaiian or other Pacific Islander, and 2 or more races, include persons of Hispanic and non-Hispanic origin. Persons of Hispanic origin may be of any race. Starting with 1999 data, race-specific estimates are tabulated according to the 1997 Revisions to the Standards for the Classification of Federal Data on Race and Ethnicity and are not strictly comparable with estimates for earlier years. The five single-race categories plus multiple-race categories shown in the table conform to the 1997 Standards. Starting with 1999 data, race-specific estimates are for persons who reported only one racial group; the category 2 or more races includes persons who reported more than one racial group. Prior to 1999, data were tabulated according to the 1977 Standards with four racial groups, and the Asian only category included Native Hawaiian or Other Pacific Islander. Estimates for single-race categories prior to 1999 included persons who reported one race or, if they reported more than one race, identified one race as best representing their race. Starting with 2003 data, race responses of other race and unspecified multiple race were treated as missing, and then race was imputed if these were the only race responses. Almost all persons with a race response of other race were of Hispanic origin.

[d]Percent of poverty level is based on family income and family size and composition using U.S. Census Bureau poverty thresholds. Missing family income data were imputed for 1997 and beyond.

[e]Estimates for persons ages 18–64 are age-adjusted to the year 2000 standard population using three age groups: 18–44 years, 45–54 years, and 55–64 years.

[f]Health insurance categories are mutually exclusive. Persons who reported both Medicaid and private coverage are classified as having private coverage. Starting with 1997 data, state-sponsored health plan coverage is included as Medicaid coverage. Starting with 1999 data, coverage by the Childrens Health Insurance Program (CHIP) is included with Medicaid coverage. In addition to private and Medicaid, the insured category also includes military, other government, and Medicare coverage. Persons not covered by private insurance, Medicaid, CHIP, state-sponsored or other government-sponsored health plans (starting in 1997), Medicare, or military plans are considered to have no health insurance coverage. Persons with only Indian Health Service coverage are considered to have no health insurance coverage.

SOURCE: Adapted from "Table 87. Emergency Department Visits within the Past 12 Months among Adults Aged 18 Years and Over, by Selected Characteristics: United States, Selected Years 1997–2012," in *Health, United States, 2013: With Special Feature on Prescription Drugs*, U.S. Department of Health and Human Services, Centers for Disease Control and Prevention, National Center for Health Statistics, May 2014, http://www.cdc.gov/nchs/data/hus/hus13.pdf (accessed May 14, 2014)

Network" (OPTN; April 11, 2014, http://optn.transplant .hrsa.gov), 28,954 transplants were performed in 2013. The UNOS compiles data on organ transplants, distributes organ donor cards, and maintains a registry of patients waiting for organ transplants. It reports that as of October 17, 2014, 123,931 Americans were waiting for a transplant. Because demand for organs continues to outpace supply, many patients die while waiting for an organ transplant.

In February 2004 the UNOS/OPTN revised and strengthened its policies to guard against potential medical errors in transplant candidate and donor matching. The policy revisions were developed in response to a systematic review of a medical error in February 2003, when a teenager named Jésica Sántillan (1985–2003) died after receiving a heart-lung transplant from a blood-type incompatible donor at Duke University Medical Center. News of this tragic error immediately prompted transplant centers throughout the United States to perform internal audits of their protocols and procedures to ensure appropriate donor-recipient matching.

The key policy revisions included stipulations that:

- The blood type of each transplant candidate and donor must be independently verified by two staff members at the institution involved at the time blood type is entered into the national database.

- Each transplant program and organ procurement organization must establish a protocol to ensure blood-type data for transplant candidates and donors are accurately entered into the national database and communicated to transplant teams. The UNOS will verify the existence and effective use of these protocols during routine audits of organ procurement organizations and transplant programs.

- Organs must only be offered to candidates specifically identified on the computer-generated list of medically suitable transplant candidates for a given organ offer. If the organ offer is not accepted for any candidate on a given match run, an organ procurement organization may give transplant programs the opportunity to update transplant candidate data and rerun a match to see if any additional candidates are identified.

The UNOS resolved to continuously review national policies and procedures for organ placement and to recommend policy and procedure enhancements to maximize the efficiency of organ placement and the safety of transplant candidates and recipients. As of 2014, there were no further reported occurrences of unintentional blood-type incompatible transplants.

The risks associated with organ transplant were, however, publicized again in 2005 and 2006, when two transplant recipients from the same organ donor contracted West Nile virus, a potentially serious illness that is transmitted by mosquitoes. Both developed encephalitis (a brain infection), fell into comas, and died. These cases catalyzed transplant physicians and public health officials to intensify organ safety protocols and procedures.

Following a review of more than 200 reports of unexpected disease transmission through organ transplantation, Debbie L. Seem et al. published "PHS Guideline for Reducing Transmission of Human Immunodeficiency Virus (HIV), Hepatitis B Virus (HBV), and Hepatitis C Virus (HCV) through Solid Organ Transplantation" (September 21, 2011, http://www.regulations.gov/#!docket Detail;dct=FR%252BPR%252BN%252BO%252BSR;rpp= 10;po=0;D=CDC-2011-0011) to reduce the risk and occurrence of unintended disease in organ recipients. The guidelines recommend enhancing donor screening practices and improving organ testing procedures to enable patients and physicians to make more informed risk-benefit decisions about organs that are available for transplant.

UNOS continually updates its policies. *OPTN Policies* (October 1, 2014, http://optn.transplant.hrsa.gov/ContentDocuments/OPTN_Policies.pdf) details procedures for every aspect of transplantation from blood type verification and organ recovery to waiting periods and data collection.

SURGICAL CENTERS AND URGENT CARE CENTERS

Ambulatory surgery centers (also called surgicenters) are equipped to perform routine surgical procedures that do not require an overnight hospital stay. A surgical center requires less sophisticated and expensive equipment than a hospital operating room. Minor surgery, such as biopsies, abortions, hernia repair, and many cosmetic surgery procedures, are performed at outpatient surgical centers. Most procedures are done under local anesthesia, and patients go home the same day.

Most ambulatory surgery centers are freestanding, but some are located on hospital campuses or are next to physicians' offices or clinics. Facilities are licensed by their state and must be equipped with at least one operating room, an area for preparing patients for procedures, a patient recovery area, and x-ray and clinical laboratory services. Also, surgical centers must have a registered nurse on the premises when patients are in the facility.

Urgent care centers (also called urgicenters) are usually operated by private, for-profit organizations and provide up to 24-hour care on a walk-in basis. These centers fill several special needs in a community. They provide convenient, timely, and easily accessible care in an emergency when the nearest hospital may be miles away. The centers are often open during the hours when most physicians' offices are closed, and they are economical to operate because they do not provide hospital beds. They usually treat problems such as cuts that require sutures, sprains and bruises from accidents, and various infections. Many provide inexpensive immunizations, and some offer routine health care for people who do not have a regular source of medical care. Urgent care may be more expensive than a visit to the family physician, but an urgent care center visit is usually less expensive than treatment from a traditional hospital ED.

Clinics in Stores and Malls

Retail-based clinics in grocery stores, drug stores, or "big box" stores offer more than simply convenient locations. Many welcome walk-in patients and offer urgent care as well as extended hours, flat fees for physician visits, low-cost immunizations, and comfortable surroundings. They also emphasize unscheduled care much more than do most primary care practices. Furthermore, some clinics telephone all patients within 48 hours of being seen for care, a measure that serves to improve both quality of care and patient satisfaction.

The American Academy of Pediatrics (AAP), observes that there were more than 6,000 retail-based clinics in 2012. Although studies suggest that the care the clinics provide is comparable and costs less than care in other settings such as hospital EDs, the AAP asserts that the clinics do not provide infants, children and adolescents with the "high-quality, regular preventive health care" they need.

Specifically, in a policy statement issued in March 2014, "AAP Principles Concerning Retail-Based Clinics" (*Pediatrics*, vol. 133, no. 3), the AAP cited concerns including: fragmentation of care; lack of access to complete, central health records; use of diagnostic tests without proper follow-up; and potential public health problems when patients with infectious diseases such as measles, mumps, or strep throat are seen in a retail environment rather than isolated to prevent the spread of infection. The AAP also notes that visits with pediatricians in conventional offices offer opportunities to identify and discuss problems, catch up on immunizations, and strengthen relationships with children and their families.

LONG-TERM-CARE FACILITIES

Families are the primary caretakers for older, dependent, and disabled individuals in U.S. society. However, the number of people aged 65 years and older living in long-term-care facilities such as nursing homes is rising because the population in this age group is increasing rapidly. Although many older people now live longer, healthier lives, the increase in overall length of life has expanded the need for long-term-care facilities.

Growth of the home health care industry during the early 1990s only slightly slowed the increase in the numbers of Americans entering nursing homes. Assisted-living and continuing-care retirement communities offer other alternatives to nursing home care. When it is possible, many older adults prefer to remain in the community and receive health care in their home.

Types of Nursing Homes

Nursing homes fall into three broad categories: residential care facilities, intermediate care facilities, and skilled nursing facilities. Each provides a different range and intensity of services:

- A residential care facility normally provides meals and housekeeping for its residents, plus some basic medical monitoring, such as administering medications. This type of home is for people who are fairly independent and do not need constant medical attention but need help with tasks such as laundry and cleaning. Many residential care facilities also provide social activities and recreational programs for their residents.

- An intermediate care facility offers room and board and nursing care as necessary for people who can no longer live independently. As in the residential care facility, exercise and social programs are provided, and some intermediate care facilities also offer physical therapy and rehabilitation programs.

- A skilled nursing facility provides around-the-clock nursing care, plus on-call physician coverage. A skilled nursing facility is for patients who need intensive nursing care and services such as occupational therapy, physical therapy, respiratory therapy, and rehabilitation.

Nursing Home Beds, Residents, and Occupancy Rates

The NCHS reports that in 2012 there were 15,673 certified nursing homes in the United States, which housed more than 1.7 million beds and had an average occupancy rate of 81.2%. (See Table 3.4.)

The National Nursing Home Survey (NNHS) was a continuing series of national sample surveys of nursing homes, their residents, and their staff. The surveys were conducted in 1973–74, 1977, 1985, 1995, 1997, 1999, and 2004. Although each survey focused on different aspects of care, they all provided some common basic information about nursing homes, their residents, and their staff from two perspectives: the provider of services and the recipient. Data about the facilities included characteristics such as size, ownership, Medicare/Medicaid certification, occupancy rate, number of days of care provided, and expenses. The surveys gathered demographic data, health status, and services received by nursing home residents. The last NNHS was conducted in 2004 and its results were published in *2004 National Nursing Home Survey* (December 2006, http://www.cdc.gov/nchs/data/nnhsd/nursinghomefacilities2006.pdf).

The NNHS found that most residents of nursing homes are the "oldest old" (people aged 85 years and older). Of nursing home residents aged 65 years and older in 2004, the so-called oldest old accounted for 674,500 (52%) of all nursing home residents.

In December 2008 the Centers for Medicare and Medicaid Services (CMS) began the Five-Star Quality Rating System for the nation's certified nursing homes. The CMS offers the online "Nursing Home Compare" (http://www.medicare.gov/NHCompare/Include/Data Section/Questions/ProximitySearch.asp), which contains detailed information, updated around the third Thursday of every month, about every Medicare- and Medicaid-certified nursing home in the country.

Diversification of Nursing Homes

To remain competitive with home health care and the increasing array of alternative living arrangements for the elderly, many nursing homes offer alternative services and programs. These services include adult day care and visiting nurse services for people who still live at home. Other programs include respite plans that allow caregivers who need to travel for business or vacation to leave an elderly relative in a nursing home temporarily.

One of the most popular nontraditional services is subacute care, which is comprehensive inpatient treatment for people recovering from acute illnesses such as pneumonia, injuries (e.g., a broken hip), and chronic diseases such as arthritis that do not require intensive, hospital-level treatment. This level of care also enables nursing homes to expand their markets by offering services to younger patients.

TABLE 3.4

Nursing home beds, residents, and occupancy rates, selected years 1995–2012

[Data are based on a census of certified nursing facilities]

State	Residents				Occupancy rate*			
	1995	2000	2011	2012	1995	2000	2011	2012
	Number							
United States	1,479,550	1,480,076	1,389,241	1,383,488	84.5	82.4	81.6	81.2
Alabama	21,691	23,089	22,855	22,673	92.9	91.4	85.6	85.0
Alaska	634	595	607	591	77.9	72.5	91.7	87.0
Arizona	12,382	13,253	11,472	11,426	76.6	75.9	69.9	68.8
Arkansas	20,823	19,317	18,071	17,982	69.5	75.1	73.5	73.2
California	109,805	106,460	102,377	102,587	78.3	80.8	84.7	84.2
Colorado	17,055	17,045	16,099	16,136	85.7	84.2	80.0	79.2
Connecticut	29,948	29,657	25,748	24,948	91.2	91.4	88.6	89.5
Delaware	3,819	3,900	4,195	4,268	80.6	79.5	84.1	86.7
District of Columbia	2,576	2,858	2,610	2,604	80.3	92.9	94.2	94.1
Florida	61,845	69,050	72,068	72,286	85.1	82.8	87.3	87.1
Georgia	35,933	36,559	34,272	34,122	94.3	91.8	86.0	85.6
Hawaii	2,413	3,558	3,800	3,738	96.0	88.8	88.1	88.6
Idaho	4,697	4,640	4,315	4,074	81.7	75.1	70.4	68.7
Illinois	83,696	83,604	74,580	73,849	81.1	75.5	74.3	74.0
Indiana	44,328	42,328	38,994	39,310	74.5	74.6	66.3	66.3
Iowa	27,506	29,204	25,121	25,077	68.8	78.9	77.2	71.5
Kansas	25,140	22,230	18,877	18,596	83.8	82.1	73.5	73.1
Kentucky	20,696	22,730	23,242	23,051	89.1	89.7	89.6	88.7
Louisiana	32,493	30,735	25,586	25,906	86.0	77.9	71.1	72.7
Maine	8,587	7,298	6,391	6,395	92.9	88.5	89.7	90.6
Maryland	24,716	25,629	24,683	24,543	87.0	81.4	85.8	85.0
Massachusetts	49,765	49,805	42,801	42,204	91.3	88.9	87.2	86.7
Michigan	43,271	42,615	39,545	39,307	87.5	84.1	84.3	84.2
Minnesota	41,163	38,813	28,529	27,789	93.8	92.1	90.2	89.9
Mississippi	15,247	15,815	16,447	16,304	94.9	92.7	88.3	88.0
Missouri	39,891	38,586	37,519	37,998	75.7	70.4	68.1	68.9
Montana	6,415	5,973	4,799	4,657	89.0	77.9	69.3	68.7
Nebraska	16,166	14,989	12,522	12,235	89.0	83.8	77.6	76.6
Nevada	3,645	3,657	4,717	4,625	91.2	65.9	78.8	77.2
New Hampshire	6,877	7,158	6,906	6,938	92.8	91.3	89.6	91.7
New Jersey	40,397	45,837	45,486	45,499	91.9	87.8	88.0	87.3
New Mexico	6,051	6,503	5,645	5,669	86.8	89.2	83.1	82.2
New York	103,409	112,957	108,077	107,481	96.0	93.7	91.6	91.6
North Carolina	35,511	36,658	37,486	37,313	92.7	88.6	84.4	84.7
North Dakota	6,868	6,343	5,733	5,694	96.4	91.2	90.0	90.7
Ohio	79,026	81,946	78,673	78,075	73.9	78.0	85.0	84.7
Oklahoma	26,377	23,833	19,491	19,315	77.8	70.3	67.0	66.9
Oregon	11,673	9,990	7,498	7,334	84.1	74.0	61.3	60.0
Pennsylvania	84,843	83,880	80,253	80,055	91.6	88.2	90.2	90.4
Rhode Island	8,823	9,041	8,053	7,978	91.8	88.0	91.6	91.9
South Carolina	14,568	15,739	17,240	16,900	87.3	86.9	87.9	86.1
South Dakota	7,926	7,059	6,471	6,371	95.5	90.0	93.9	91.7
Tennessee	33,929	34,714	31,437	31,189	91.5	89.9	84.4	83.2
Texas	89,354	85,275	92,133	93,710	72.6	68.2	69.1	69.8
Utah	5,832	5,703·	5,448	5,423	82.1	74.5	65.0	63.9
Vermont	1,792	3,349	2,833	2,761	96.2	89.5	87.2	86.3
Virginia	28,119	27,091	28,308	28,260	93.5	88.5	87.5	87.5
Washington	24,954	21,158	17,578	17,272	87.7	81.7	80.6	79.4
West Virginia	10,216	10,334	9,448	9,535	93.7	90.5	87.6	87.9
Wisconsin	43,998	38,911	29,801	29,000	90.2	83.9	83.1	82.5
Wyoming	2,661	2,605	2,401	2,435	87.7	83.5	80.9	81.6

*Percentage of beds occupied (number of nursing home residents per 100 nursing home beds).
Notes: Annual numbers of nursing homes, beds, and residents are based on the Online Survey Certification and Reporting Database reporting cycle. Data for additional years are available.

SOURCE: "Table 110. Nursing Homes, Beds, Residents, and Occupancy Rates, by State: United States, Selected Years 1995–2012," in *Health, United States, 2013: With Special Feature on Prescription Drugs*, U.S. Department of Health and Human Services, Centers for Disease Control and Prevention, National Center for Health Statistics, May 2014, http://www.cdc.gov/nchs/data/hus/hus13.pdf (accessed May 14, 2014). Data from Cowles Research Group.

Innovation Improves Quality of Nursing Home Care

Industry observers and the media frequently raise concerns about the care provided in nursing homes and publicize instances of elder abuse and other quality of care issues. Several organizations have actively sought to develop models of health service delivery that improve the clinical care and quality of life for nursing home residents. In *Evaluation of the Wellspring Model for Improving Nursing Home Quality* (August 2002, http://www.cmwf.org/usr_doc/stone_wellspringevaluation.pdf), a benchmark report that examines one such model in eastern Wisconsin, Robyn Stone et al. evaluate the Wellspring model of nursing home quality improvement.

Wellspring is a group of nonprofit nursing homes that are governed by a group called the Wellspring Alliance. Founded in 1994, the alliance aims to improve the clinical care delivered to its nursing home residents and the work environment for its employees. Based on the Wellspring philosophy that education and collaboration are paramount to success, the program began by equipping nursing home personnel with the skills needed to perform their jobs and by organizing employees in teams working toward shared goals. The Wellspring model of service delivery uses a multidisciplinary clinical team approach (nurse practitioners, social service professionals, food service personnel, nursing assistants, and facility and housekeeping personnel) to solve problems and develop approaches to better meet residents' needs. Each of these teams represents an important innovation because it allows health professionals and other workers to interact as peers and share resources, information, and decision making in a cooperative, supportive environment.

Stone et al. observe that there was more cooperation, responsibility, and accountability within the teams and the institutions than what was noted at other comparable facilities. Besides finding a strong organizational culture that seemed committed to quality patient care, the researchers document measurable improvements in specific areas including:

- Wellspring facilities had lower rates of staff turnover than comparable Wisconsin facilities during the same period, probably because Wellspring workers felt valued by management and experienced greater job satisfaction than other nursing home personnel

- The Wellspring model did not require additional resources to institute, and Wellspring facilities operated at lower costs than comparable facilities

- Wellspring facilities' performance, as measured by a federal survey, improved

- Wellspring personnel appeared more attentive to residents' needs and problems and sought to anticipate and promptly resolve problems

- An organizational commitment to training and shared decision making, along with improved quality of interactions and relationships among staff and between staff and residents, significantly contributed to enhanced quality of life for residents

In "Person-Centered Care for Nursing Home Residents: The Culture-Change Movement" (*Health Affairs*, vol. 29, no. 2, February 2010), Mary Jane Koren of the Commonwealth Fund enumerates the principles of the culture-change movement championed by organizations such as Wellspring. These include:

- Resident direction—supporting residents to make their own choices and decisions about personal issues such as food choices, clothing, and activities

- Homelike environment—using strategies such as replacing larger institutional units with smaller groups of residents and eliminating public address systems

- Relationship cultivation—improving continuity of care by having the same staff provide care to a resident

- Staff empowerment—by providing necessary training and granting them authority, staff are better able to respond to residents' needs

- Collaborative decision making—direct caregivers, working in teams, should have the authority to make decisions about residents' care

- Quality improvement—culture change should be understood as continuous performance improvement

Koren observes that about one-third of nursing homes have adopted some culture-change practices and an additional one-third are planning to make some changes. She encourages policy changes to support the wider adoption of comprehensive culture change.

"Green House Model" (2014, http://thegreenhouse project.org) describes "a model for long-term care designed to look and feel like a real home." Facilities following this model are designed for 10 to 12 residents, who have private rooms and share common spaces. The Green House Project claims its model has been proven to be "to be effective, feasible and sustainable." In "9 Green House Homes Receive Best Nursing Home Honor" (March 7, 2014, http://blog.thegreenhouseproject .org/8-green-house-homes-receive-best-nursing-home- honor), Tara Gugelman-McMahon reports that a *U.S. News & World Report* evaluation of more than 16,000 facilities looked at their state health inspections, the amount of time nurses spend with residents, and the quality of medical care provided. The publication gave less than 25 percent of facilities a five star rating, but nine Green House homes earned the five star rating.

In "Who Are the Innovators? Nursing Homes Implementing Culture Change" (*Gerontologist*, vol. 54, Suppl. 1, February 2014), David C. Grabowski et al. observe that a key aim of the ACA is to "transform both institutional and community-based long-term care into a more person-centered system." Grabowski et al. looked at the resident, facility, and state characteristics of nursing homes identified by experts as having implemented culture change between 2004 and 2011. The 291 facilities identified by experts as having implemented culture change were more often nonprofit-owned, larger, and had fewer Medicaid and Medicare residents. Nursing homes that had instituted culture change also had better quality ratings, fewer health-related survey deficiencies, and higher levels of licensed practical nurse and nurse aide staffing.

MENTAL HEALTH FACILITIES

In earlier centuries mental illness was often considered to be a sign of possession by the devil or, at best, a moral weakness. A change in these attitudes began during the late 18th century, when mental illness was perceived to be a treatable condition. It was then that the concept of asylums was developed, not only to lock the mentally ill away but also to provide them with "relief" from the conditions they found troubling.

In the 21st century mental health care is provided in a variety of treatment settings by different types of organizations. The following mental health organizations offer diagnostic and therapeutic mental health services:

- A psychiatric hospital (public or private) provides 24-hour inpatient care to people with mental illnesses in a hospital setting. It may also offer 24-hour residential care and less than 24-hour care, but these are not requirements. Psychiatric hospitals are operated under state, county, private for-profit, and private nonprofit auspices.

- General hospitals with separate psychiatric services, units, or designated beds are under governmental or nongovernmental auspices and maintain assigned staff for 24-hour inpatient care, 24-hour residential care, and less than 24-hour care (outpatient care or partial hospitalization) to provide mental health diagnosis, evaluation, and treatment.

- Veterans Administration (VA) hospitals are operated by the U.S. Department of Veterans Affairs and include VA general hospital psychiatric services and VA psychiatric outpatient clinics that exclusively serve people entitled to VA benefits.

- Outpatient mental health clinics that provide only ambulatory mental health services. Generally, a psychiatrist has overall medical responsibility for clients and establishes the philosophy and orientation of the mental health program.

- Community mental health centers were funded under the Federal Community Mental Health Centers Act of 1963 and subsequent amendments to the act. During the early 1980s, when the federal government reverted to funding mental health services through block grants to the states rather than by funding them directly, the federal government stopped tracking these mental health organizations individually, and statistical reports include them in the category "all other mental health organizations." This category also includes freestanding psychiatric outpatient clinics, freestanding partial care organizations, and multiservice mental health organizations such as residential treatment centers. These so-called community mental health centers have sliding scale fees and accept Medicaid, Medicare, private health insurance, and private fee-for-service (paid for each visit, procedure, or treatment that is delivered) payment. Mental health care is also available from nonprofit mental health or counseling services offered by health and social service agencies, such as Catholic Social Services, family and children's service agencies, Jewish Family Services, and Lutheran Social Services, that are staffed by qualified mental health professionals to provide counseling services.

- Residential treatment centers for emotionally disturbed children serve children and youth primarily under the age of 18 years, provide 24-hour residential services, and offer a clinical program that is directed by a psychiatrist, psychologist, social worker, or psychiatric nurse who holds a master's or doctorate degree.

Where Are the Mentally Ill?

The chronically mentally ill reside in mental hospitals, in intermediate care facilities, or in community settings, such as with families, in boarding homes and shelters, in single-room-occupancy hotels (usually inexpensive hotels or boardinghouses), in prison, or even on the streets as part of the homeless population. The institutionalized mentally ill are those people with psychiatric diagnoses who have lived in mental hospitals for more than one year or those with diagnosed mental illness who are living in nursing homes.

Declining mental health expenditures have resulted in fewer available services for specific populations of the mentally ill, particularly those who could benefit from inpatient or residential care. Even for people without conditions requiring institutional care there are barriers to access. The U.S. surgeon general's landmark report *Mental Health: A Report of the Surgeon General, 1999* (1999, http://profiles.nlm.nih.gov/ps/retrieve/Resource Metadata/NNBBHS) describes the U.S. mental health service system as largely uncoordinated and fragmented, in part because it involves so many different sectors—health and social welfare agencies, public and private hospitals, housing, criminal justice, and education—and because it is funded through many different sources. Finally, inequalities in insurance coverage for mental health, coupled with the stigma associated with mental illness and treatment, have also limited access to services.

The NCHS reveals in *Health, United States, 2011* that the number of mental health organizations for 24-hour inpatient treatment steadily declined from 3,942 in 1990 to 3,130 in 2008. (See Table 3.5.) Except for

Department of Veterans Affairs medical centers and residential treatment centers for children, all other service sites and types of organizations diminished in capacity. The number of beds per 100,000 civilian population fell from 128.5 in 1990 to just 78.6 in 2008. There was a similar decline in the number of intermediate care facilities specializing in psychiatric care—the number of beds declined from 689 in 1995 to 508 in 2010. This decline was not necessarily a result of better treatment for the mentally ill but a consequence of reduced funding for inpatient facilities. Many of the patients who were once housed in mental institutions (including some who had been lifelong residents in these facilities) were forced to fend for themselves on the streets or in prison.

Besides mental health units or beds in acute care medical/surgical hospitals and physicians' offices, mental health care and treatment is offered in the offices of other mental health clinicians such as psychologists, clinical social workers, and marriage and family therapists, as well as in other settings. Private psychiatric hospitals provide outpatient mental health evaluation and therapy in day programs as well as inpatient care. Like acute care hospitals, these facilities are accredited by the Joint Commission and may offer outpatient services by way of referral to a local network of qualified mental health providers.

National Goals for Mental Health Service Delivery

The federal government's Healthy People initiative sets 10-year national objectives for improving the health of Americans. In "Mental Health and Mental Disorders" (October 22, 2014, http://www.healthypeople.gov/2020/topics-objectives/topic/mental-health-and-mental-disorders), the initiative describes the 12 mental health objectives that the government hopes to achieve by 2020:

1. Reduce the suicide rate

2. Reduce suicide attempts by adolescents

3. Reduce the proportion of adolescents who engage in disordered eating behaviors in an attempt to control their weight

TABLE 3.5

Mental health organizations and beds for 24-hour hospital and residential treatment, by type of organization, selected years 1986–2008

Type of organization	1986	1990	1994	2000	2002	2004	2008[a]
	Number of mental health organizations						
All organizations	3,512	3,942	3,853	3,211	3,044	2,891	3,130
State psychiatric hospitals	285	278	270	229	227	237	241
Private psychiatric hospitals	314	464	432	271	255	264	256
Nonfederal general hospitals with psychiatric services	1,351	1,577	1,539	1,325	1,231	1,230	1,292
Department of Veterans Affairs medical centers[b]	139	131	136	134	132	—	130
Residential treatment centers for children with emotional disturbance	437	501	472	476	510	458	538
All other organizations[c]	986	991	1,004	776	689	702	673
	Number of beds						
All organizations	267,613	325,529	293,139	214,186	211,040	212,231	239,014
State psychiatric hospitals	119,033	102,307	84,063	61,833	57,314	57,034	37,450
Private psychiatric hospitals	30,201	45,952	42,742	26,402	24,996	28,422	25,406
Nonfederal general hospitals with psychiatric services	45,808	53,576	53,455	40,410	40,520	41,403	54,390
Department of Veterans Affairs medical centers[b]	26,874	24,779	21,346	8,989	9,581	—	11,991
Residential treatment centers for children with emotional disturbance	24,547	35,170	32,691	33,508	39,407	33,835	50,063
All other organizations[c]	21,150	63,745	58,842	43,044	39,222	51,536	59,715
	Beds per 100,000 civilian population[d]						
All organizations	111.7	128.5	110.9	74.8	72.2	71.2	78.6
State psychiatric hospitals	49.7	40.4	31.8	21.6	19.6	19.1	12.3
Private psychiatric hospitals	12.6	18.1	16.2	9.2	8.6	9.5	8.4
Nonfederal general hospitals with psychiatric services	19.1	21.2	20.2	14.1	13.9	13.9	17.9
Department of Veterans Affairs medical centers[b]	11.2	9.8	8.1	3.1	3.3	—	3.9
Residential treatment centers for children with emotional disturbance	10.3	13.9	12.4	11.7	13.5	11.4	16.5
All other organizations[c]	8.8	25.2	22.2	15.0	13.4	17.3	19.6

Notes: Data for additional years are available.
—Data not available.
[a]Data for 2008 are not strictly comparable with data for earlier years due to the survey redesign, including a new name, National Survey of Mental Health Treatment Facilities.
[b]Department of Veterans Affairs medical centers (VA general hospital psychiatric services and VA psychiatric outpatient clinics) were not included in the 2004 survey.
[c]Includes residential treatment facilities for adults, freestanding psychiatric outpatient clinics, partial care organizations, and multiservice mental health organizations.
[d]Civilian population estimates for 2000 and beyond are based on the 2000 census as of July 1; population estimates for 1992–1998 are 1990 postcensal estimates.

SOURCE: "Table 117. Mental Health Organizations and Beds for 24-Hour Hospital and Residential Treatment, by Type of Organization: United States, Selected Years 1986–2008," in Health, United States, 2011: With Special Feature on Socioeconomic Status and Health, U.S. Department of Health and Human Services, Centers for Disease Control and Prevention, National Center for Health Statistics, May 2012, http://www.cdc.gov/nchs/data/hus/hus11.pdf (accessed May 14, 2014)

4. Reduce the proportion of persons who experience major depressive episodes [a serious depression with symptoms such as despondency, feelings of worthlessness, and even suicidal thoughts]

5. Increase the proportion of primary care facilities that provide mental health treatment onsite or by paid referral

6. Increase the proportion of children with mental health problems who receive treatment

7. Increase the proportion of juvenile residential facilities that screen admissions for mental health problems

8. Increase the proportion of persons with serious mental illness who are employed

9. Increase the proportion of adults with mental disorders who receive treatment

10. Increase the proportion of persons with co-occurring substance abuse and mental disorders who receive treatment for both disorders

11. Increase depression screening by primary care providers

12. Increase the proportion of homeless adults with mental health problems who receive mental health services

HOME HEALTH CARE

The concept of home health care began as postacute care after hospitalization, an alternative to longer, costlier lengths of stay in regular hospitals. Home health care services have grown tremendously since the 1980s, when prospective payment (payments made before, rather than after, care is received) for Medicare patients sharply reduced hospital lengths of stay. During the mid-1980s Medicare began reimbursing hospitals using a rate scale based on diagnosis-related groups—hospitals received a fixed amount for providing services to Medicare patients based on their diagnoses. This form of payment gave hospitals powerful financial incentives to use fewer resources because they could keep the difference between the prospective payment and the amount they actually spent to provide care. Hospitals experienced losses when patients had longer lengths of stay and used more services than were covered by the standardized diagnosis-related group prospective payment.

According to the article "Home Health Care" (*Family Economics and Nutrition Review*, Spring 1996), home health care grew faster during the early 1990s than any other segment of health services. Its growth may be attributable to the fact that in many cases caring for patients at home is preferable to, and more cost effective than, care provided in a hospital, nursing home, or some other residential facility. Oftentimes, older adults are more comfortable and much happier living in their own home or with family members. Disabled people may also be able to function better at home with limited assistance than in a residential setting with full-time monitoring.

Home health care agencies provide a wide variety of services. Services range from helping with activities of daily living—such as bathing, doing light housekeeping, and making meals—to skilled nursing care, such as the nursing care needed by AIDS or cancer patients. The number of Medicare-certified home health agencies has varied in response to reimbursement, growing from 2,924 in 1980 to 8,437 in 1996, then declining to 7,857 in 2000. (See Table 3.6.) In 2011 the number of Medicare-certified

TABLE 3.6

Medicare-certified providers and suppliers, selected years 1975–2011

[Data are compiled from various Centers for Medicare & Medicaid Services data systems]

Providers or suppliers	1975	1980	1985	1990	1996	2000	2005	2009	2010	2011
					Number of providers or suppliers					
Skilled nursing facilities	—	5,052	6,451	8,937	—	14,841	15,006	15,071	15,084	15,132
Home health agencies	2,242	2,924	5,679	5,661	8,437	7,857	8,090	10,184	10,914	11,930
Clinical Laboratory Improvement Amendments facilities	—	—	—	4,828	159,907	171,018	196,296	218,139	224,679	229,611
End-stage renal disease facilities	—	999	1,393	1,987	2,876	3,787	4,755	5,476	5,631	5,766
Outpatient physical therapy	117	419	854	1,144	2,302	2,867	2,962	2,640	2,536	2,351
Portable x-ray	132	216	308	435	555	666	553	546	561	577
Rural health clinics	—	391	428	517	2,775	3,453	3,661	3,752	3,845	3,940
Comprehensive outpatient rehabilitation facilities	—	—	72	184	307	522	634	406	354	298
Ambulatory surgical centers	—	—	336	1,165	2,112	2,894	4,445	5,260	5,316	5,335
Hospices	—	—	164	772	1,927	2,326	2,872	3,405	3,509	3,630
Critical access hospitals	...	...	...	...	...	—	—	1,311	1,325	1,331

—Data not available.
...Category not applicable.
Notes: Data for 1975–1990 are as of July 1. Data for 1996–2011 are as of December 31.

SOURCE: "Table 111. Medicare-Certified Providers and Suppliers: United States, Selected Years 1975–2011," in *Health, United States, 2013: With Special Feature on Prescription Drugs*, U.S. Department of Health and Human Services, Centers for Disease Control and Prevention, National Center for Health Statistics, May 2014, http://www.cdc.gov/nchs/data/hus/hus13.pdf (accessed May 14, 2014)

home health agencies rose to 11,930, the highest level since at least 1975.

In 1972 Medicare extended home health care coverage to people under 65 years of age only if they were disabled or suffered from end-stage renal disease. Before 2000 Medicare coverage for home health care was limited to patients immediately following discharge from the hospital. By 2000 Medicare covered beneficiaries' home health care services with no requirement for previous hospitalization. There were also no limits to the number of professional visits or to the length of coverage. As long as the patient's condition warranted it, the following services were provided:

- Part-time or intermittent skilled nursing and home health aide services

- Speech-language pathology services

- Physical and occupational therapy

- Medical social services

- Medical supplies

- Durable medical equipment (with a 20% co-payment)

Over time, the population receiving home health care services has changed. Since 2000 much of home health care is associated with rehabilitation from critical illnesses, and fewer users are long-term patients with chronic conditions. This changing pattern of utilization reflects a shift from longer-term care for chronic conditions to short-term, postacute care. Compared with postacute care users, the long-term patients are older, more functionally disabled, more likely to be incontinent, and more expensive to serve.

Medicare Limits Home Health Care Services

The Balanced Budget Act of 1997 cut approximately $16.2 billion from the federal government's home health care expenditures over a period of five years. The act sought to return home health care to its original concept of short-term care plus skilled nursing and therapy services. As a result of this shift away from personal care and "custodial care" services and toward short-term, skilled nursing services, some Medicare beneficiaries who received home health care lost coverage for certain personal care services, such as assistance with bathing, dressing, and eating.

The Balanced Budget Act sharply curtailed the growth in home health care spending, which affected health care providers. Nonetheless, the aging population and the financial imperative to prevent or minimize institutionalization (hospitalization or placement in a long-term-care facility) combined to generate increasing expenditures for home health care services. Medicare expenditures for home health care rose from $4 billion in 2000 to $6.8 billion in 2012, which represented 1.2%

of Medicare expenditures. (See Table 3.7.) In contrast, payments to skilled nursing facilities accounted for 4.9% ($28 billion) of expenditures in 2012, and inpatient hospital expenditures were 24.3% ($139.7 billion) of the total.

Sharply reduced Medicare spending for home health care under the ACA reduced planned funding for home care 14% between 2014 and 2018, and may slow the growth of home health care jobs and services. In "The ACA's Cuts to Medicare Threaten Home Health Care Jobs, Patients" (NewsObserver.com, February 5, 2014), home health clinician Connie Dolin opines that the cuts "will directly affect nearly 5,000 small-business providers that today serve nearly 1.5 million seniors and are responsible for nearly 500,000 jobs from coast to coast." Dolin asks federal lawmakers to reconsider the cuts.

HOSPICE CARE

In medieval times hospices were refuges for the sick, the needy, and travelers. The modern hospice movement developed in response to the need to provide humane care to terminally ill patients, while at the same time offering support to their families. British physician Cicely Saunders (1918–2005) pioneered the hospice concept in Britain during the late 1960s and helped introduce it in the United States during the 1970s. The care provided by hospice workers is called palliative care, and it aims to relieve patients' pain and the accompanying symptoms of terminal illness without seeking to cure the illness.

Hospice is a philosophy, an approach to care for the dying, and it is not necessarily a physical facility. Hospice may refer to a place—a freestanding facility or a designated floor in a hospital or nursing home—or to a program such as hospice home care, where a team of health professionals helps the dying patient and family at home. Hospice teams may involve physicians, nurses, social workers, pastoral counselors, and trained volunteers. The goal of hospice care is to provide support and care for people at the end of life, enabling them to remain as comfortable as possible.

Hospice workers consider the patient and family as the "unit of care" and focus their efforts on attending to emotional, psychological, and spiritual needs as well as to physical comfort and well-being. The programs provide respite care, which offers relief at any time for families who may be overwhelmed and exhausted by the demands of caregiving and may be neglecting their own needs for rest and relaxation. Finally, hospice programs work to prepare relatives and friends for the loss of their loved ones. Hospice offers bereavement support groups and counseling to help deal with grief and may even help with funeral arrangements.

TABLE 3.7

Medicare enrollees and expenditures by type of service, selected years 1970–2012

[Data are compiled from various sources by the Centers for Medicare & Medicaid Services]

Medicare program and type of service	1970	1980	1990	1995	2000	2005	2008	2009	2010	2011	2012[a]
Enrollees					Number, in millions						
Total Medicare[b]	**20.4**	**28.4**	**34.3**	**37.6**	**39.7**	**42.6**	**45.5**	**46.6**	**47.7**	**48.9**	**50.7**
Hospital insurance	20.1	28.0	33.7	37.2	39.3	42.2	45.1	46.3	47.4	48.5	50.3
Supplementary medical insurance (SMI)[c]	19.5	27.3	32.6	35.6	37.3	—	—	—	—	—	—
Part B	19.5	27.3	32.6	35.6	37.3	39.8	42.0	42.9	43.9	44.9	46.4
Part D[d]	—	—	—	—	—	1.8	32.6	33.6	34.8	35.7	37.4
Expenditures					Amount, in billions						
Total Medicare	**$7.5**	**$36.8**	**$111.0**	**$184.2**	**$221.8**	**$336.4**	**$468.2**	**$509.0**	**$522.9**	**$549.1**	**$574.2**
Total hospital insurance (HI)	**5.3**	**25.6**	**67.0**	**117.6**	**131.1**	**182.9**	**235.6**	**242.5**	**247.9**	**256.7**	**266.8**
HI payments to managed care organizations[e]	—	0.0	2.7	6.7	21.4	24.9	50.6	59.4	60.7	64.6	70.2
HI payments for fee-for-service utilization	5.1	25.0	63.4	109.5	105.1	156.6	172.8	179.5	183.3	187.0	189.5
Inpatient hospital	4.8	24.1	56.9	82.3	87.1	123.3	130.3	133.9	136.0	134.0	139.7
Skilled nursing facility	0.2	0.4	2.5	9.1	11.1	19.3	24.5	26.3	27.0	32.0	28.0
Home health agency	0.1	0.5	3.7	16.2	4.0	6.0	6.7	7.1	7.2	7.0	6.8
Hospice	—	—	0.3	1.9	2.9	8.0	11.4	12.3	13.1	14.0	15.0
Other programs[f]	—	—	—	—	—	—	—	—	—	0.9	2.5
Home health agency transfer[g]	—	—	—	—	1.7	—	—	—	—	—	—
Medicare Advantage premiums[h]	—	—	—	—	—	—	0.1	0.1	0.2	0.2	0.2
Accounting error (CY 2005–2008)[i]	—	—	—	—	—	−1.9	8.5	—	—	—	—
Administrative expenses[j]	0.2	0.5	0.9	1.4	2.9	3.3	3.6	3.5	3.8	4.0	4.3
Total supplementary medical insurance (SMI)[c]	**2.2**	**11.2**	**44.0**	**66.6**	**90.7**	**153.5**	**232.6**	**266.5**	**274.9**	**292.5**	**307.4**
Total Part B	**2.2**	**11.2**	**44.0**	**66.6**	**90.7**	**152.4**	**183.3**	**205.7**	**212.9**	**225.3**	**240.5**
Part B payments to managed care organizations[e]	0.0	0.2	2.8	6.6	18.4	22.0	48.1	53.4	55.2	59.1	66.0
Part B payments for fee-for-service utilization[k]	1.9	10.4	39.6	58.4	72.2	125.0	140.5	149.0	154.3	162.3	170.3
Physician/supplier[l]	1.8	8.2	29.6	—	—	—	—	—	—	—	—
Outpatient hospital[m]	0.1	1.9	8.5	—	—	—	—	—	—	—	—
Independent laboratory[n]	0.0	0.1	1.5	—	—	—	—	—	—	—	—
Physician fee schedule	—	—	—	31.7	37.0	57.7	60.6	61.8	63.9	67.5	69.6
Durable medical equipment	—	—	—	3.7	4.7	8.0	8.6	8.2	8.3	8.2	8.4
Laboratory[o]	—	—	—	4.3	4.4	6.9	7.9	8.7	8.9	8.9	9.7
Other[p]	—	—	—	9.9	13.6	26.7	29.6	32.4	33.2	34.5	36.3
Hospital[q]	—	—	—	8.7	8.1	18.7	23.6	26.2	27.9	30.9	34.4
Home health agency	0.0	0.2	0.1	0.2	4.5	7.1	10.3	11.8	12.1	12.4	11.8
Home health agency transfer[g]	—	—	—	—	−1.7	—	—	—	—	—	—
Medicare Advantage premiums[h]	—	—	—	—	—	—	0.1	0.1	0.2	0.2	0.2
Accounting error (CY 2005–2008)[i]	—	—	—	—	—	1.9	−8.5	—	—	—	—
Administrative expenses[j]	0.2	0.6	1.5	1.6	1.8	2.8	3.1	3.2	3.2	3.7	4.0
Part D start-up costs[r]	—	—	—	—	—	0.7	0.0	—	—	—	—
Total Part D[d]	**—**	**—**	**—**	**—**	**—**	**1.1**	**49.3**	**60.8**	**62.1**	**67.1**	**66.9**
					Percent distribution of expenditures						
Total hospital insurance (HI)	**100.0**	**100.0**	**100.0**	**100.0**	**100.0**	**100.0**	**100.0**	**100.0**	**100.0**	**100.0**	**100.0**
HI payments to managed care organizations[e]	—	0.0	4.0	5.7	16.3	13.6	21.5	24.5	24.5	25.2	26.3
HI payments for fee-for-service utilization	97.0	97.9	94.6	93.1	80.2	85.6	73.4	74.0	73.9	72.8	71.0
Inpatient hospital	91.4	94.3	85.0	70.0	66.4	67.4	55.3	55.2	54.9	52.2	52.4
Skilled nursing facility	4.7	1.5	3.7	7.8	8.5	10.6	10.4	10.8	10.9	12.5	10.5
Home health agency	1.0	2.1	5.5	13.8	3.1	3.3	2.8	2.9	2.9	2.7	2.5
Hospice	—	—	0.5	1.6	2.2	4.4	4.8	5.1	5.3	5.4	5.6
Other programs[f]	—	—	—	—	—	—	—	—	—	0.3	0.9
Home health agency transfer[g]	—	—	—	—	1.3	—	—	—	—	—	—
Medicare Advantage premiums[h]	—	—	—	—	—	—	0.0	0.1	0.1	0.1	0.1
Accounting error (CY 2005–2008)[i]	—	—	—	—	—	−1.0	3.6	—	—	—	—
Administrative expenses[j]	3.0	2.1	1.4	1.2	2.2	1.8	1.5	1.4	1.5	1.6	1.6

The hospice concept is different from most other health care services because it focuses on care rather than on cure. Hospice workers try to minimize the two greatest fears associated with dying: fear of isolation and fear of pain. Potent, effective medications are offered to patients in pain, with the goal of controlling pain without impairing alertness so that patients may be as comfortable as possible.

Hospice care also emphasizes living life to its fullest. Patients are encouraged to stay active for as long as possible, to do things they enjoy, and to learn something new each day. Quality of life, rather than length of life, is the focus. In addition, whenever it is possible, family and friends are urged to be the primary caregivers in the home. Care at home helps both patients and family members enrich their lives and face death together.

—Category not applicable or data not available. CY = Calendar year. 0.0 = Quantity more than zero but less than 0.05.

[a]Preliminary estimates.

[b]Average number enrolled in the hospital insurance (HI) and/or supplementary medical insurance (SMI) programs for the period.

[c]Starting with 2004 data, the SMI trust fund consists of two separate accounts: Part B (which pays for a portion of the costs of physicians' services, outpatient hospital services, and other related medical and health services for voluntarily enrolled individuals) and Part D (Medicare Prescription Drug Account, which pays private plans to provide prescription drug coverage).

[d]The Medicare Modernization Act, enacted December 8, 2003, established within SMI two Part D accounts related to prescription drug benefits: the Medicare Prescription Drug Account and the Transitional Assistance Account. The Medicare Prescription Drug Account is used in conjunction with the broad, voluntary prescription drug benefits that began in 2006. The Transitional Assistance Account was used to provide transitional assistance benefits, beginning in 2004 and extending through 2005, for certain low-income beneficiaries prior to the start of the new prescription drug benefit. The amounts shown for Total Part D expenditures—and thus for total SMI expenditures and total Medicare expenditures—for 2006 and later years include estimated amounts for premiums paid directly from Part D beneficiaries to Part D prescription drug plans.

[e]Medicare-approved managed care organizations.

[f]Includes Community-Based Care Transitions Program ($0.1 billion in each of 2011 and 2012), Electronic Health Records Incentive Program ($0.7 billion in 2011 and $2.7 billion in 2012), and Accountable Care Organizations (–$0.3 billion in 2012).

[g]For 1998 to 2003 data, reflects annual home health HI to SMI transfer amounts.

[h]When a beneficiary chooses a Medicare Advantage plan whose monthly premium exceeds the benchmark amount, the additional premiums (that is, amounts beyond those paid by Medicare to the plan) are the responsibility of the beneficiary. Beneficiaries subject to such premiums may choose to either reimburse the plans directly or have the additional premiums deducted from their Social Security checks. The amounts shown here are only those additional premiums deducted from Social Security checks. These amounts are transferred to the HI trust and SMI trust funds and then transferred from the trust funds to the plans.

[i]Represents misallocation of benefit payments between the HI trust fund and the Part B account of the SMI trust fund from May 2005 to September 2007, and the transfer made in June 2008 to correct the misallocation.

[j]Includes expenditures for research, experiments and demonstration projects, peer review activity (performed by Peer Review Organizations from 1983 to 2001 and by Quality Review Organizations from 2002 to present), and to combat and prevent fraud and abuse.

[k]Type-of-service reporting categories for fee-for-service reimbursement differ before and after 1991.

[l]Includes payment for physicians, practitioners, durable medical equipment, and all suppliers other than independent laboratory through 1990. Starting with 1991 data, physician services subject to the physician fee schedule are shown. Payments for laboratory services paid under the laboratory fee schedule and performed in a physician office are included under Laboratory beginning in 1991. Payments for durable medical equipment are shown separately beginning in 1991. The remaining services from the Physician/-supplier category are included in other.

[m]Includes payments for hospital outpatient department services, skilled nursing facility outpatient services, Part B services received as an inpatient in a hospital or skilled nursing facility setting, and other types of outpatient facilities. Starting with 1991 data, payments for hospital outpatient department services, except for laboratory services, are listed under Hospital. Hospital outpatient laboratory services are included in the Laboratory line.

[n]Starting with 1991 data, those independent laboratory services that were paid under the laboratory fee schedule (most of the independent laboratory category) are included in the Laboratory line; the remaining services are included in the Physician fee schedule and Other lines.

[o]Payments for laboratory services paid under the laboratory fee schedule performed in a physician office, independent laboratory, or in a hospital outpatient department.

[p]Includes payments for physician-administered drugs; freestanding ambulatory surgical center facility services; ambulance services; supplies; freestanding end-stage renal disease (ESRD) dialysis facility services; rural health clinics; outpatient rehabilitation facilities; psychiatric hospitals; and federally qualified health centers.

[q]Includes the hospital facility costs for Medicare Part B services that are predominantly in the outpatient department, with the exception of hospital outpatient laboratory services, which are included on the Laboratory line. Physician reimbursement is included on the Physician fee schedule line.

[r]Part D start-up costs were funded through the SMI Part B account in 2004–2008.

Notes: Estimates are subject to change as more recent data become available. Totals may not equal the sum of the components because of rounding. Estimates are for Medicare-covered services furnished to Medicare enrollees residing in the United States, Puerto Rico, Virgin Islands, Guam, other outlying areas, foreign countries, and unknown residence. Estimates in this table have been revised and differ from previous editions of Health, United States.

SOURCE: Adapted from "Table 127. Medicare Enrollees and Expenditures and Percent Distribution, by Medicare Program and Type of Service: United States and Other Areas, Selected Years 1970–2012," in *Health, United States, 2013: With Special Feature on Prescription Drugs*, U.S. Department of Health and Human Services, Centers for Disease Control and Prevention, National Center for Health Statistics, May 2014, http://www.cdc.gov/nchs/data/hus/hus13.pdf (accessed May 14, 2014)

Ira Byock, the former president of the American Academy of Hospice and Palliative Medicine, explains the concept of hospice care in *Dying Well: The Prospect for Growth at the End of Life* (1997): "Hospice care differs noticeably from the modern medical approach to dying. Typically, as a hospice patient nears death, the medical details become almost automatic and attention focuses on the personal nature of this final transition— what the patient and family are going through emotionally and spiritually. In the more established system, even as people die, medical procedures remain the first priority. With hospice, they move to the background as the personal comes to the fore."

According to the National Hospice and Palliative Care Organization (NHPCO), in *NHPCO's Facts and Figures: Hospice Care in America 2013 Edition* (2013, http://www.nhpco.org/sites/default/files/public/Statistics _Research/2013_Facts_Figures.pdf), the use of hospice care is increasing in the United States. The NHPCO estimates that between 1.5 million and 1.6 million patients received hospice care in 2012. That same year Medicare expenditures for hospice care totaled $15 billion and accounted for 2.6% of Medicare expenditures. (See Table 3.7.)

MANAGED CARE ORGANIZATIONS

Managed health care is the sector of the health insurance industry in which health care providers are not independent businesses run by, for example, private medical practitioners, but are instead administrative firms that manage the allocation of health care benefits. In contrast to conventional indemnity insurers that do not govern the provision of medical care services and simply pay for them, managed care firms have a significant voice in how services are administered to enable them to exert better control over health care costs. (Indemnity insurance is traditional fee-for-service coverage in which providers are paid according to the service performed.)

The beneficiaries of employer-funded health plans (people who receive health benefits from their employers), as well as Medicare and Medicaid recipients, often find themselves in this type of health care program. The term *managed care organization* covers several types of health care delivery systems, such as health maintenance organizations (HMOs), preferred provider organizations (PPOs), and utilization review groups that oversee diagnoses, recommend treatments, and manage costs for their beneficiaries.

Health Maintenance Organizations

HMOs began to grow during the 1970s as alternatives to traditional health insurance, which was becoming increasingly expensive. The HMO Act of 1973 was a federal law requiring employers with more than 24 employees to offer an alternative to conventional indemnity insurance in the form of a federally qualified HMO. The intent of the act was to stimulate HMO development, and the federal government has continued to promote them since then, maintaining that groups of physicians following certain rules of practice can slow rising medical costs and improve health care quality.

HMOs are health insurance programs organized to provide complete coverage for subscribers' (also known as enrollees or members) health needs for negotiated, prepaid prices. The subscribers (and/or their employers) pay a fixed amount each month; in turn, the HMO group provides, at no extra charge or at a minimal charge, preventive care, such as routine checkups, screening, and immunizations, and care for any illness or accident. The monthly fee also covers inpatient hospitalization and referral services. HMO members benefit from reduced out-of-pocket costs (they do not pay deductibles), they do not have to file claims or fill out insurance forms, and they generally pay only nominal co-payments for each office visit. Members are usually locked into the plan for a specified period—typically one year. If the necessary service is available within the HMO, patients must normally use an HMO doctor. There are several types of HMOs:

- Staff model—the "purest" form of managed care. All primary care physicians are employees of the HMO and practice in a centralized location such as an outpatient clinic that may also house a laboratory, pharmacy, and facilities for other diagnostic testing. The staff model offers the HMO the greatest opportunity to manage both cost and quality of health care services.

- Group model—in which the HMO contracts with a group of primary care and multispecialty health providers. The group is paid a fixed amount per patient to provide specific services. The administration of the medical group determines how the HMO payments will be distributed among the physicians and other health care providers. Group model HMOs are usually located in hospitals or in clinic settings and have on-site pharmacies. Participating physicians usually do not have any fee-for-service patients.

- Network model—in which the HMO contracts with two or more groups of health providers that agree to provide health care at negotiated prices to all members enrolled in the HMO.

- Independent practice association (IPA) model—in which the HMO contracts with individual physicians or medical groups that then provide medical care to HMO members at their own offices. The individual physicians agree to follow the practices and procedures of the HMO when caring for the HMO members; however, they generally also maintain their own private practices and see fee-for-service patients as well as HMO members. IPA physicians are paid by capitation (literally, per head) for the HMO patients and by conventional methods for their fee-for-service patients. Physician members of the IPA guarantee that the care for each HMO member for which they are responsible will be delivered within a fixed budget. They guarantee this by allowing the HMO to withhold an amount of their payments (usually about 20% per year). If at year's end the physician's cost for providing care falls within the preset amount, then the physician receives all the monies withheld. If the physician's costs of care exceed the agreed-on amount, the HMO may retain any portion of the monies it has withheld. This arrangement places physicians and other providers such as hospitals, laboratories, and imaging centers at risk for keeping down treatment costs, and this at-risk formula is the key to HMO cost-containment efforts.

Some HMOs offer an open-ended or point-of-service (POS) option that allows members to choose their own physicians and hospitals, either within or outside the HMO. However, a member who chooses an outside provider will generally have to pay a larger portion of the expenses. Physicians not contracting with the HMO but who see HMO patients are paid according to the services performed. POS members are given an incentive to seek care from contracted network physicians and other health care providers through comprehensive coverage offerings.

The Kaiser Family Foundation is a nonprofit organization that studies health care issues. It indicates in "Health Insurance & Managed Care" (2014, http://kff .org/state-category/health-insurance-managed-care/hmos) that as of July 2012, 73.6 million HMO members were served by 545 HMOs operating in the United States. In *Health, United States, 2007: With Chartbook on Trends in the Health of Americans* (2007, http://www.cdc.gov/nchs/data/hus/hus07.pdf), the NCHS notes that HMO enrollment grew during the 1990s and reached about 30% of the U.S. population in 2000. However, the Kaiser Family Foundation states that by July 2012 HMO enrollment had declined to just 23.3% of the U.S population.

HMO enrollment varies by geographic region. According to the Kaiser Family Foundation, 64.1% of the population of Puerto Rico was enrolled in an HMO in July 2012, as was 58.1% of the population in Hawaii and 43.5% in California. In contrast, 0.1% of the population of Alaska, 1% of Wyoming's population, and 2.9% of people in North Dakota were covered by HMOs.

HMOs Have Fans and Critics

HMOs have been the subject of considerable debate among physicians, payers, policy makers, and health care consumers. Many physicians feel HMOs interfere in the physician-patient relationship and effectively prevent them from practicing medicine the way they have traditionally practiced. These physicians claim they know their patients' conditions and are, therefore, in the best position to recommend treatment. The physicians resent being advised and overruled by insurance administrators. (Physicians can recommend the treatment they believe is best, but if the insurance company will not cover the costs, patients may be unwilling to undergo the recommended treatment.)

The HMO industry counters that its evidence-based determinations (judgments about the appropriateness of care that reflect scientific research) are based on the experiences of many thousands of physicians and, therefore, it knows which treatments are most likely to be successful. The industry maintains that, in the past, physician-chosen treatments were not scrutinized or even assessed for effectiveness, and as a result most physicians did not really know whether the treatment they prescribed was optimal for the specific medical condition.

Furthermore, the HMO industry cites the slower increase in health care expenses as another indicator of its management success. Industry spokespeople note that any major change in how the HMO industry is run would lead to increasing costs. They claim that HMOs and other managed care programs are bringing a more rational approach to the health care industry while maintaining health care quality and controlling costs.

Still, many physicians resent that, with a few exceptions, HMOs are not financially liable for their decisions. When a physician chooses to forgo a certain procedure and negative consequences result, the physician may be held legally accountable. When an HMO informs a physician

that it will not cover a recommended procedure and the HMO's decision is found to be wrong, it cannot be held directly liable. Many physicians assert that because HMOs make such choices, they are practicing medicine and should, therefore, be held accountable. The HMOs counter that these are administrative decisions and deny that they are practicing medicine.

The legal climate seemed to be changing for HMOs during the mid-1990s. Both the Third Circuit Federal Court of Appeals in *Dukes v. U.S. Healthcare* (57 F.3d 350 [1995]) and the 10th Circuit Federal Court of Appeals in *PacifiCare of Oklahoma, Inc. v. Burrage* (59 F.3rd 151 [1995]) agreed that HMOs were liable for malpractice and negligence claims against the HMO and HMO physicians. In *Frappier Estate v. Wishnov* (678 So.2d 884 [1996]), the Florida District Court of Appeals, Fourth District, agreed with the earlier findings. It appeared that these court decisions would be backed by a new federal law when both houses of Congress passed legislation (the Patients' Bill of Rights) that would give patients more recourse to contest the decisions of HMOs. However, disagreements about the specific rights to be provided under the law ultimately led to its defeat.

In June 2004 the U.S. Supreme Court struck down a law in California and in several other states that allowed patients to sue their health plans for denying them health care services. Although patients can still sue in federal court for reimbursement of denied benefits, they no longer may sue for damages in federal or state courts.

PPOs

In response to HMOs and other efforts by insurance groups to cut costs, physicians began forming or joining PPOs during the 1990s. PPOs are managed care organizations that offer integrated delivery systems (networks of providers) available through a wide array of health plans and are readily accountable to purchasers for access, cost, quality, and services of their networks. They use provider selection standards, utilization management, and quality assessment programs to complement negotiated fee reductions (discounted rates from participating physicians, hospitals, and other health care providers) as effective strategies for long-term cost control. Under a PPO benefit plan, covered people retain the freedom of choice of providers but are offered financial incentives such as lower out-of-pocket costs to use the preferred provider network. PPO members may use other physicians and hospitals, but they usually have to pay a higher proportion of the costs. PPOs are marketed directly to employers and to third-party administrators who then market PPOs to their employer clients.

Exclusive provider organizations (EPOs) are a more restrictive variation of PPOs in which members must seek care from providers on the EPO panel. If a member visits an outside provider who is not on the EPO panel, then the EPO will offer either limited or no coverage for the office or hospital visit.

According to the Kaiser Family Foundation, in "Employer Health Benefits: 2013 Summary of Findings" (August 2013, http://kff.org/report-section/2013-summary-of-findings), 57% of U.S. workers with insurance through their jobs were enrolled in PPO plans in 2012. By contrast, only 14% of these workers were enrolled in HMO plans and 9% in POS plans.

Accountable Care Organizations

Accountable care organizations (ACOs) are groups of health care providers that offer coordinated care and chronic disease management in an effort to improve the quality of care Medicare patients receive. Under the ACA, the CMS has established the Medicare Shared Savings Program for ACOs. ACOs that choose to join the program commit to containing or reducing costs while also achieving health care quality goals set by the CMS. (There were 33 quality measures in place in October 2014.) ACOs that meet these standards share in the savings they achieve, receiving payments equal to as much as 60% of the money they saved the Medicare program. However, if an ACO fails to generate savings, and instead charges more for its services than the standards call for, it is required to pay back some of these funds to the Medicare program.

In September 2014 the Department of Health and Human Services issued a press release, "New Affordable Care Act Tools and Payment Models Deliver $372 Million in Savings, Improve Care" (http://www.hhs.gov/news/press/2014pres/09/20140916a.html), discussing the impact of the Medicare Shared Savings Program and the Pioneer ACO Model (a smaller program in which participating ACOs share savings, and risks, at a higher level). The release states that 23 Pioneer ACOs and 220 Shared Savings Program ACOs had collectively saved Medicare $372 million, and that "the ACOs outperformed published benchmarks for quality and patient experience last year and improved significantly on almost all measures of quality and patient experience this year."

Health Care Reform Affects Managed Care Plans

The ACA has a significant impact on the benefits provided by managed care plans (and other forms of health insurance). It requires insurers to change certain underwriting practices and benefit structures. The plans must cover children with preexisting conditions, cannot cancel coverage when enrollees require costly treatment, cannot cap lifetime benefits, and must allow children to remain on their parents' insurance until they turn 27 years old.

In "National Health Expenditure Projections, 2012–2022: Slow Growth until Coverage Expands and Economy Improves" (*Health Affairs*, vol. 32, no. 10, October 2013), Gigi A. Cuckler et al. of the CMS explain that because the ACA extends Medicaid eligibility to more low-income people, and some states are trying to reduce Medicaid costs by shifting recipients into managed care plans, Medicaid managed care plans have experienced increased enrollment. By contrast, the act reduces reimbursement to Medicare managed care plans, and some plans have lost enrollees as a result of decreasing benefits in response to the diminished reimbursement.

In the article "New Evidence on the Affordable Care Act: Coverage Impacts of Early Medicaid Expansions" (*Health Affairs*, vol. 31, no.1, January 2014), Benjamin D. Sommers, Genevieve M. Kenney, and Arnold M. Epstein analyzed data from three states—California, Connecticut, Minnesota—and the District of Columbia that extended Medicaid eligibility to some low-income childless adults who previously had not been eligible. Some of the these adults had been ineligible because their income was too high or their assets too great; others had been eligible but did not enroll until the Medicaid expansion under the ACA, which offered more generous coverage.

Sommers, Kenney, and Epstein report that initially a disproportionate number of new enrollees were likely to be in poor health. They predict that there will likely be some loss of enrollment in private plans as newly eligible people migrate from private to Medicaid plans. Their research also suggests that Medicaid enrollment may continue to rise well beyond the first year of the expansion.

In "April 18: UnitedHealth Braces for Affordable Care Act Changes" (StarTribune.com, August 15, 2013), Jackie Crosby reports that UnitedHealth, America's largest managed care company in terms of revenue and enrollment, experienced "better-than-expected growth" in membership, which offset the cost of providing ACA-mandated services. Industry observers scrutinized the plan's financial performance for clues about how other managed care plans will fare as the full implementation of the ACA occurs.

CHAPTER 4
RESEARCHING, MEASURING, AND MONITORING THE QUALITY OF HEALTH CARE

Many agencies, institutions, and organizations are dedicated to researching, quantifying (measuring), monitoring, and improving health in the United States. Some are federally funded public entities such as the many institutes and agencies governed by the U.S. Department of Health and Human Services (HHS). Others are professional societies and organizations that develop standards of care, represent the views and interests of health care providers, and ensure the quality of health care facilities, such as the American Medical Association and the Joint Commission. Still other voluntary health organizations, such as the American Heart Association, the American Cancer Society, and the March of Dimes, promote research and education about prevention and treatment of specific diseases.

AFFORDABLE CARE ACT INITIATIVES AND MEASURES TO IMPROVE QUALITY

The Patient Protection and Affordable Care Act (ACA) of 2010 authorized a wide range of quality initiatives, including measures that "pay-for-performance"— offering financial incentives for health care providers to achieve optimal outcomes for patients. These incentives may include bonuses for meeting or exceeding agreed upon quality standards and penalties for failing to meet specified objectives. Examples of ACA quality measures include:

- Development of quality data collection and reporting tools such as a quality rating system and a quality improvement strategy, as well as an enrollee satisfaction survey system to assess health plans offered by health insurance marketplaces and exchanges

- Requiring health plans to report their quality improvement activities—benefits or coverage and provider reimbursement that improve health outcomes, prevent hospital readmissions, improve patient safety, and reduce medical errors

- Use of core measures to assess the quality of health care received by Medicaid enrollees.

- Instituting quality reporting requirements for inpatient rehabilitation facilities

- Research on health delivery system improvement and best practices to improve the quality, safety, and efficiency of health care delivery

Effectively implementing these measures requires cooperation and collaboration between federal government agencies and state and local agencies, as well as health care providers and voluntary health organizations.

U.S. DEPARTMENT OF HEALTH AND HUMAN SERVICES

The HHS is the nation's lead agency for ensuring the health of Americans by planning, operating, and funding delivery of essential human services, especially for society's most vulnerable populations. According to the HHS, in "About HHS" (2014, http://www.hhs.gov/about), it includes by 11 divisions, 10 regional offices, and the Office of the Secretary. It is the largest grant-making agency in the federal government, funding several thousand grants each year as well as the HHS Medicare program, the nation's largest health insurer, which processes over 1 billion claims per year. For fiscal year (FY) 2015, the HHS had a budget of $1.02 trillion, which was an increase of $57.7 billion from FY 2014. (See Table 4.1.)

HHS Milestones

The HHS notes in "Historical Highlights" (2014, http://www.hhs.gov/about/hhshist.html) that it began with the 1798 opening of the first Marine Hospital in Boston, Massachusetts, to care for sick and injured merchant seamen. Under President Abraham Lincoln (1809–1865) the agency that would become the U.S. Food and

TABLE 4.1

U.S. Department of Health and Human Services budget, fiscal years 2013–15

[Dollars in millions]

Category	2013	2014	2015
Budget Authority	873,535	962,554	1,020,284
Total outlays	**886,472**	**958,077**	**1,010,479**
Fulltime equivalents (FTE)	74,992	77,457	79,540

SOURCE: "FY 2015 President's Budget for HHS," in *HHS FY2015 Budget in Brief*, U.S. Department of Health and Human Services, 2014, http://www.hhs.gov/budget/fy2015-hhs-budget-in-brief/hhs-fy2015budget-in-brief-overview.html (accessed April 21, 2014)

Drug Administration was established in 1862. The National Institutes of Health (NIH) dates back to 1887 and eventually became part of the Public Health Service. The 1935 enactment of the Social Security Act spurred the development of the Federal Security Agency in 1939 to direct programs in health, human services, insurance, and education. In 1946 the Communicable Disease Center, which would become the Centers for Disease Control and Prevention (CDC), was established, and 19 years later, in 1965, Medicare (a federal health insurance program for people aged 65 years and older and people with disabilities) and Medicaid (a state and federal health insurance program for low-income people) were enacted to improve access to health care for older, disabled, and low-income Americans. That same year the Head Start program was developed to provide education, health, and social services to preschool-aged children.

In 1970 the National Health Service Corps was established to help meet the health care needs of underserved areas and populations. The following year the National Cancer Act became law, which established cancer research as a national research priority. In 1984 the human immunodeficiency virus (HIV), the virus that causes acquired immunodeficiency syndrome (AIDS), was identified by the Public Health Service and French research scientists. The National Organ Transplant Act became law in 1984, and in 1990 the Human Genome Project was initiated.

In 1994 NIH-funded research isolated the genes responsible for inherited breast cancer, colon cancer, and the most frequently occurring type of kidney cancer. In 1998 efforts were launched to eliminate racial and ethnic disparities (differences) in health, and in 2000 the human genome sequencing was published. In 2001 the Health Care Financing Administration was replaced by the Centers for Medicaid and Medicare Services, and the HHS responded to the first reported cases of bioterrorism (anthrax attacks) and developed new strategies to detect and prevent threats of bioterrorism. In 2003 the Medicare Prescription Drug Improvement and Modernization Act expanded Medicare and included prescription drug benefits. In 2010 landmark health care reform legislation—the Patient Protection and Affordable Care Act and the Health Care and Education Reconciliation Act (which are now commonly known as the ACA)—was enacted.

According to the HHS, in *2015 HHS Budget Press Conference* (March 4, 2014, http://www.hhs.gov/secretary/about/speeches/sp20140304.html), significant initiatives funded in the FY 2015 budget include implementing the ACA, which entails continuing to expand access to health insurance coverage. The budget includes $4.6 billion for community health centers in the United States to enable access to care for 31 million people at 9,500 existing sites and 150 new center sites. The budget includes $15 million to expand prevention efforts in primary care practices, nursing homes, and other health care settings. It also allocates $45 million for global health security activities, as well as $30 million to prevent the spread of antibiotic-resistant pathogens.

HHS Agencies and Institutes Provide Comprehensive Health and Social Services

Besides the CDC and the NIH, the HHS explains in *U.S. Department of Health and Human Services Budget in Brief, Fiscal Year 2015* (2014, http://www.hhs.gov/budget/fy2015/fy-2015-budget-in-brief.pdf) that the following agencies and programs research, plan, direct, oversee, administer, and provide health care services:

- Administration for Community Living (ACL) consists of the Administration on Aging, the Office on Disability, and the Administration on Developmental Disabilities and provides services aimed at helping older Americans and persons with disabilities retain their independence. The ACL develops policies that support and direct programs that provide transportation, in-home services, and other community living services. For FY 2015 the ACL planned for a budget of $2.1 billion and 178 employees.

- Administration for Children and Families (ACF) provides services for families and children in need, administers Head Start, and works with state foster care and adoption programs. The ACF was allotted a budget of $51.3 billion and 1,402 employees for FY 2015.

- Agency for Healthcare Research and Quality (AHRQ) researches access to health care, quality of care, and efforts to control health care costs. It also looks at the safety of health care services and the ways to prevent medical errors. Figure 4.1 shows how the AHRQ researches health system problems by performing a continuous process of needs assessment, gaining knowledge, interpreting and communicating information, and evaluating the effects of this process on the health problem. Figure 4.2 shows the process that

FIGURE 4.1

Cycle of health care research

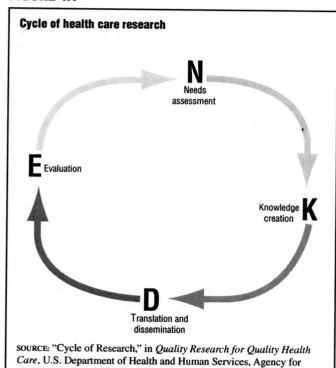

SOURCE: "Cycle of Research," in *Quality Research for Quality Health Care*, U.S. Department of Health and Human Services, Agency for Healthcare Research and Quality, March 2001, http://archive.ahrq.gov/about/qr4qhc/chart4.htm (accessed April 21, 2014)

FIGURE 4.2

Health care research pipeline

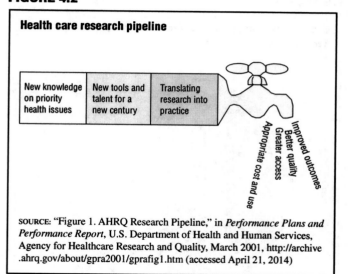

SOURCE: "Figure 1. AHRQ Research Pipeline," in *Performance Plans and Performance Report*, U.S. Department of Health and Human Services, Agency for Healthcare Research and Quality, March 2001, http://archive.ahrq.gov/about/gpra2001/gprafig1.htm (accessed April 21, 2014)

transforms new information about health care issues into actions to improve access, costs, outcomes (how patients fare as a result of the care they receive), and quality. For FY 2015 the AHRQ planned for a budget of $440 million and 326 employees. The AHRQ budgeted $73 million for patient safety research and activities and $23 million for research about how to use health information technology to improve health care quality.

• Agency for Toxic Substances and Disease Registry seeks to prevent exposure to hazardous waste. The agency's FY 2015 budget of $75 million represented no change from FY 2014.

• Centers for Medicare and Medicaid Services (CMS) administers programs that provide health insurance for about 100 million Americans (older adults, those in financial need, and uninsured children); manages the Health Insurance Marketplace (also known as exchanges, the ACA created the marketplace, which enables consumers to compare health plans based on price, benefits, and other features); and regulates all laboratory testing, except testing performed for research purposes, in the United States. For FY 2015 the CMS planned for a budget of $897.3 billion. Figure 4.3 shows the allocation of the CMS budget—58.4% was devoted to Medicare, 37.4% to Medicaid, 1.2% to the Children's Health Insurance Plan, and 1.1% to administration.

• Children's Health Insurance Program Reauthorization Act (which is implemented by the AHRQ) identified an initial core set of 24 health care quality measures for voluntary use by Medicaid and the Children's Health Insurance Program and continues to improve, expand, and strengthen these measures. Measures added in 2011 and 2012 included human papillomavirus vaccination in female adolescents and medication management for children with asthma.

• U.S. Food and Drug Administration (FDA) acts to ensure the safety and efficacy (the ability of an intervention to produce the intended diagnostic or therapeutic effect in optimal circumstances) of dietary supplements, pharmaceutical drugs, and medical devices and monitors food safety and purity. The FDA planned for a budget of $4.7 billion in FY 2015 and 16,905 employees. The FDA budget included an increase of $358 million more than the FY 2014 budget to ensure the safety and security of the food supply and to provide other safety and prevention measures.

• Health Resources and Services Administration provides services for medically underserved populations such as migrant workers, the homeless, and public housing residents. This agency oversees the nation's organ transplant program, directs efforts to improve maternal and child health, and delivers services through the Ryan White CARE Act to people with AIDS. In FY 2015 it planned to have 1,983 employees and a budget of $10.8 billion.

• Indian Health Service (IHS) serves 566 tribes through a network of more than 632 hospitals, clinics and health stations. In FY 2015 the IHS planned to employ 15,760 workers and have a budget of $6 billion.

FIGURE 4.3

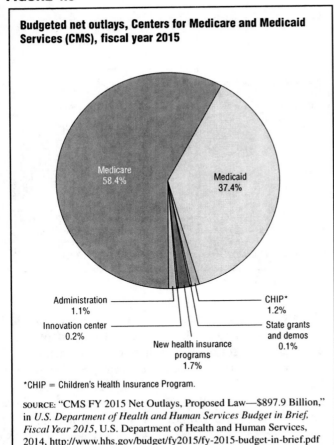

Budgeted net outlays, Centers for Medicare and Medicaid Services (CMS), fiscal year 2015

Medicare 58.4%

Medicaid 37.4%

Administration 1.1%

Innovation center 0.2%

New health insurance programs 1.7%

CHIP* 1.2%

State grants and demos 0.1%

*CHIP = Children's Health Insurance Program.

SOURCE: "CMS FY 2015 Net Outlays, Proposed Law—$897.9 Billion," in *U.S. Department of Health and Human Services Budget in Brief, Fiscal Year 2015*, U.S. Department of Health and Human Services, 2014, http://www.hhs.gov/budget/fy2015/fy-2015-budget-in-brief.pdf (accessed April 21, 2014)

- General Departmental Management provides the HHS's leadership and oversees the 11 staff divisions and offices of the HHS. It also advises the president about health, welfare, human service, and income security issues. In FY 2015 it was allotted 1,590 employees and a budget of $535 million.

- Substance Abuse and Mental Health Services Administration (SAMHSA) seeks to improve access to, and availability of, substance abuse prevention and treatment programs as well as other mental health services. SAMHSA was budgeted $3.6 billion in FY 2015 and had 655 employees.

The HHS agencies work with state, local, and tribal governments as well as with public and private organizations to coordinate and deliver a wide range of services including:

- Conducting preventive health services such as surveillance to detect outbreaks of disease and immunization programs through efforts directed by the CDC and the NIH

- Ensuring food, drug, and cosmetic safety through efforts of the FDA

- Improving maternal and child health and preschool education in programs such as Head Start, which serves more than 1 million children per year, according to the National Head Start Association (2014, http://www.nhsa.org/about_nhsa)

- Preventing child abuse, domestic violence, and substance abuse, as well as funding substance abuse treatment through programs directed by the ACF

- Ensuring the delivery of health care services to about 2.2 million Native Americans and Alaskan Natives through the IHS, a network of hospitals, health centers, and other programs and facilities (2014, http://www.ihs.gov/newsroom/factsheets/ihsyear2014profile)

- Administering Medicare and Medicaid via the CMS

- Providing financial assistance and support services for low-income and older Americans, such as home-delivered meals (Meals on Wheels) coordinated by the Administration on Aging

SUBSTANTIAL BUDGET HELPS THE HHS TO ACHIEVE ITS OBJECTIVES. Table 4.2 displays how the FY 2015 HHS budget was allocated and provides comparisons between 2013, 2014, and 2015 outlays. The FY 2015 budget is a net increase of $147 billion over the FY 2013 budget and aims to provide funds to help improve access to and quality of health care, prevent disease, and support scientific research. In *U.S. Department of Health and Human Services Budget in Brief, Fiscal Year 2015*, the HHS explains that it provides funds "to improve health care and expand coverage, create opportunity, give children the chance to succeed, protect vulnerable populations, promote science and innovation, protect the nation's public health and national security, and focus on responsible stewardship of taxpayer dollars."

U.S. PUBLIC HEALTH SERVICE COMMISSIONED CORPS. The U.S. Public Health Service Commissioned Corps (November 22, 2011, http://www.usphs.gov/aboutus/history.aspx) was originally the uniformed service component of the early Marine Hospital Service, which adopted a military model for a group of career health professionals who traveled from one marine hospital to another as their services were needed. By examining newly arrived immigrants and directing state quarantine (the period and place where people suspected of having contagious diseases are detained and isolated) functions, it also assisted the Marine Hospital Service to prevent infectious diseases from entering the country. A law enacted in 1889 established this group as the Commissioned Corps, and in 1912 the Marine Hospital Service was renamed the Public Health Service (PHS) to reflect its broader scope of activities.

TABLE 4.2

Health and Human Services budget, by operating division, 2013–15

Mandatory and discretionary dollars in millions	2013	2014	2015
Food and Drug Administration[a]			
Budget authority	2,073	2,642	2,586
Outlays	1,537	2,668	2,877
Health Resources and Services Administration			
Budget authority	8,370	9,142	10,404
Outlays	8,645	9,121	9,514
Indian Health Service			
Budget authority	4,287	4,590	4,792
Outlays	4,274	4,607	4,883
Centers for Disease Control and Prevention			
Budget authority	6,273	7,170	6,674
Outlays	6,617	6,783	6,624
National Institutes of Health			
Budget authority	29,291	30,142	30,353
Outlays	30,976	31,124	29,705
Substance Abuse and Mental Health Services Administratior			
Budget authority	3,226	3,497	3,356
Outlays	3,225	3,701	3,409
Agency for Healthcare Research and Quality			
Budget authority	6	7	—
Program level	430	464	440
Outlays	319	343	113
Centers for Medicare & Medicaid Services[b]			
Budget authority	769,182	850,810	906,799
Outlays	777,258	844,379	897,235
Administration for Children and Families			
Budget authority	49,592	51,158	51,316
Outlays	50,430	50,072	51,490
Administration for Community Living			
Budget authority	1,407	1,647	2,058
Outlays	1,440	1,563	1,903
Office of the National Coordinator			
Budget authority	15	16	—
Outlays	551	414	53
Office of Medicare Hearings and Appeals			
Budget authority	69	82	100
Outlays	73	91	100
Office for Civil Rights			
Budget authority	39	39	41
Outlays	40	39	41
General Departmental Management			
Budget authority	470	481	416
Outlays	582	855	590
Health Insurance Reform Implementation Fund[c]			
Budget authority	—	—	—
Outlays	221	163	100
Public Health and Social Services Emergency Fund			
Budget authority	588	1,243	1,423
Outlays	1,769	1,784	1,905
Office of Inspector General			
Budget authority	52	71	75
Outlays	41	66	81
Program Support Center (retirement pay, medical benefits, misc. trust funds)			
Budget authority	636	658	678
Outlays	515	1,145	643
Offsetting Collections			
Budget authority	−2,041	−841	−787
Outlays	−2,041	−841	−787
Total, health and human services			
Budget authority	873,535	962,554	1,020,284
Outlays	886,472	958,077	1,010,479
Full-time equivalents	74,992	77,457	79,540

[a]In fiscal year 2013, the difference is due to the timing and availability of user fee collections, and in fiscal year 2014, the inclusion of sequestered user fees made available in fiscal year 2014.
[b]Budget authority includes Non-Centers for Medicare and Medicaid Services Budget authority for hospital insurance and Supplementary Medical Insurance for the Social Security Administration and MedPAC.
[c]Includes outlays for all agencies receiving resources from the fund.

SOURCE: "HHS Budget by Operating Division," in *U.S. Department of Health and Human Services Budget in Brief, Fiscal Year 2015*, U.S. Department of Health and Human Services, 2014, http://www.hhs.gov/budget/fy2015/fy-2015-budget-in-brief.pdf (accessed April 21, 2014)

Throughout the 20th century the corps grew to include a wide range of health professionals. Besides physicians, the corps employed nurses, dentists, research scientists, planners, pharmacists, sanitarians, engineers, and other public health professionals. These PHS-commissioned officers played important roles in disease prevention and detection, acted to ensure food and drug safety, conducted research, provided medical care to underserved groups such as Native Americans and Alaskan Natives, and assisted in disaster relief programs. As one of the seven uniformed services in the United States (the other six are the U.S. Navy, the U.S. Army, the U.S. Marine Corps, the U.S. Air Force, the U.S. Coast Guard, and the National Oceanic and Atmospheric Administration Commissioned Corps), the PHS Commissioned Corps continues to perform all these functions and identifies environmental threats to health and safety, promotes healthy lifestyles for Americans, and is involved with international agencies to help address global health problems.

The Office of the Surgeon General notes in "Mission of the U.S. Public Health Service Commissioned Corps" (http://www.surgeongeneral.gov/about/corps/index.html) that as of 2014 the PHS Commissioned Corps numbered more than 6,800 health professionals. These people report to the U.S. surgeon general, who holds the rank of vice admiral in the PHS. Corps officers work in PHS agencies and in other agencies including the U.S. Bureau of Prisons, the U.S. Coast Guard, the U.S. Environmental Protection Agency, and the Commission on Mental Health of the District of Columbia. The surgeon general is a physician who is appointed by the U.S. president to serve in a medical leadership position for a four-year term of office. The surgeon general reports to the assistant secretary of health, and the Office of the Surgeon General (2014, http://www.surgeongeneral.gov/aboutoffice.html) is part of the Office of Public Health and Science. Eighteen surgeons general, plus nine acting surgeons general, have served since the 1870s. In July 2013 Rear Admiral Boris D. Lushniak (1959–, http://www.surgeongeneral.gov/about/biographies/biosg.html) began to serve as the acting surgeon general.

CENTERS FOR DISEASE CONTROL AND PREVENTION

The CDC is the primary HHS agency responsible for ensuring the health and safety of the nation's citizens in the United States and abroad. The CDC's responsibilities include researching and monitoring health, detecting and investigating health problems, researching and instituting prevention programs, developing health policies, ensuring environmental health and safety, and offering education and training.

In "CDC Fact Sheet" (April 24, 2014, http://www.cdc.gov/about/resources/facts.htm), the CDC indicates that it employs over 15,000 people in nearly 170 disciplines and in more than 50 countries. Besides research scientists, physicians, nurses, and other health practitioners, the CDC employs epidemiologists, who study disease in populations as opposed to individuals. Epidemiologists measure disease occurrences, such as incidence and prevalence of disease, and work with clinical researchers to answer questions about causation (how particular diseases arise and the factors that contribute to their development), whether new treatments are effective, and how to prevent specific diseases.

In "CDC Organization" (April 14, 2014, http://www.cdc.gov/about/organization/cio.htm) the CDC list the national centers and various institutes and offices that it is home to. Among the best known are the National Center for Health Statistics, which collects vital statistics, and the National Institute for Occupational Safety and Health, which seeks to prevent workplace injuries and accidents through research and prevention. Thomas R. Frieden (1960–) was named the director of the CDC in June 2009. Figure 4.4 shows the organization and leadership of the CDC in 2014.

CDC Actions to Protect the Health of the Nation

The CDC is part of the first response to natural disasters, outbreaks of disease, other public health emergencies, and urgent public health problems. For example, the agency produces *Public Health Grand Rounds* (http://www.publichealthgrandrounds.unc.edu), a monthly webcast intended to stimulate discussion of significant public

FIGURE 4.4

Centers for Disease Control and Prevention organization and leadership, 2014

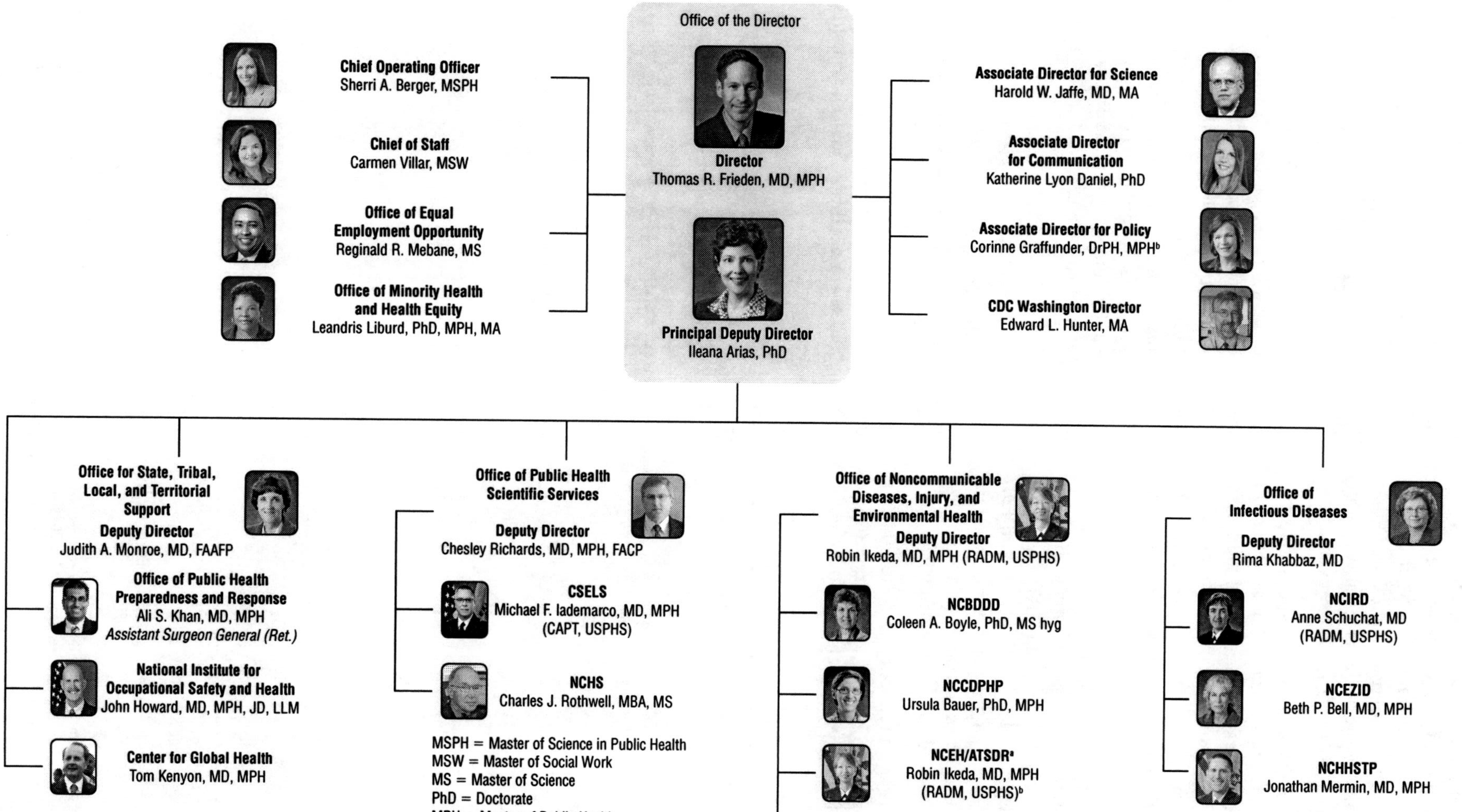

Office of the Director

Director
Thomas R. Frieden, MD, MPH

Principal Deputy Director
Ileana Arias, PhD

Associate Director for Science
Harold W. Jaffe, MD, MA

Associate Director for Communication
Katherine Lyon Daniel, PhD

Associate Director for Policy
Corinne Graffunder, DrPH, MPH[b]

CDC Washington Director
Edward L. Hunter, MA

Chief Operating Officer
Sherri A. Berger, MSPH

Chief of Staff
Carmen Villar, MSW

Office of Equal Employment Opportunity
Reginald R. Mebane, MS

Office of Minority Health and Health Equity
Leandris Liburd, PhD, MPH, MA

Office for State, Tribal, Local, and Territorial Support
Deputy Director
Judith A. Monroe, MD, FAAFP

Office of Public Health Preparedness and Response
Ali S. Khan, MD, MPH
Assistant Surgeon General (Ret.)

National Institute for Occupational Safety and Health
John Howard, MD, MPH, JD, LLM

Center for Global Health
Tom Kenyon, MD, MPH

Office of Public Health Scientific Services
Deputy Director
Chesley Richards, MD, MPH, FACP

CSELS
Michael F. Iademarco, MD, MPH (CAPT, USPHS)

NCHS
Charles J. Rothwell, MBA, MS

Office of Noncommunicable Diseases, Injury, and Environmental Health
Deputy Director
Robin Ikeda, MD, MPH (RADM, USPHS)

NCBDDD
Coleen A. Boyle, PhD, MS hyg

NCCDPHP
Ursula Bauer, PhD, MPH

NCEH/ATSDR[a]
Robin Ikeda, MD, MPH (RADM, USPHS)[b]

NCIPC
Daniel Sosin, MD, MPH, FACP[b]

Office of Infectious Diseases
Deputy Director
Rima Khabbaz, MD

NCIRD
Anne Schuchat, MD (RADM, USPHS)

NCEZID
Beth P. Bell, MD, MPH

NCHHSTP
Jonathan Mermin, MD, MPH

CAPT = Captain
DrPH = Doctor of Public Health
FAAFP = Fellow of the American Academy of Emergency Physicians
FACP = Fellow of the American College of Physicians
JD = Juris Doctor
LLM = Master of Laws

MSPH = Master of Science in Public Health
MSW = Master of Social Work
MS = Master of Science
PhD = Doctorate
MPH = Master of Public Health
MA = Master of Arts
MD = Medical Doctor
RADM = Rear Admiral
USPHS = United States Public Health Service
MS hyg = Master of Science, hygiene

[a]ATSDR is an OPDIV within DHHS but is managed by a common director's office.
[b]Acting.

SOURCE: "Organizational Chart," in *CDC Organization* Centers for Disease Control and Prevention, 2014, http://www.cdc.gov/about/pdf/organization/cdc-org-chart-3.20.14.pdf (accessed April 21, 2014)

health issues. Each session describes a specific health challenge and considers leading-edge scientific evidence and the possible impact of different interventions. In 2014 the series focused on a variety of topics, including hepatitis C, autism, multidrug-resistant tuberculosis, preventing heart attacks and strokes, and HIV prevention.

The CDC also monitors and plans responses to the emerging threat of seasonal influenza and other influenza viruses. In 2009 the CDC tracked and reported the H1N1 flu outbreak. Figure 4.5 compares influenza cases in selected seasons including the 2009–10 pandemic flu and reveals that the 2013–14 season was mild compared with other recent years.

Among the many recent CDC initiatives to address threats to public health are intensified efforts to improve antibiotic use and prevent infection and the spread of antibiotic-resistant infections. The CDC works with federal, state and local agencies and organizations to obtain data about antibiotic-resistant infections and to develop diagnostic tests to track the development of resistance.

The CDC also focuses on reducing prescription drug abuse and overdose. Efforts aim to reduce misuse and the number of deaths from painkiller overdoses while simultaneously ensuring that patients with pain receive safe, effective pain relief.

The CDC partners with national, state, local, public, and private agencies and organizations to deliver services. Examples of these collaborative efforts include the global battle against HIV/AIDS via the Leadership and Investment in Fighting an Epidemic initiative and the CDC Coordinating Center for Health Information and Service, which was created to improve public health through increased efficiencies and to foster stronger collaboration between the CDC and international health foundations, health care practitioners, community and philanthropic organizations, schools and universities, nonprofit and voluntary organizations, and state and local public health departments.

NATIONAL INSTITUTES OF HEALTH

The NIH (January 16, 2013, http://www.nih.gov/about/history.htm) began as a one-room laboratory in 1887 and eventually became the world's premier medical research center. The NIH conducts research in its own facilities and supports research in universities, medical schools, and hospitals throughout and outside the United

FIGURE 4.5

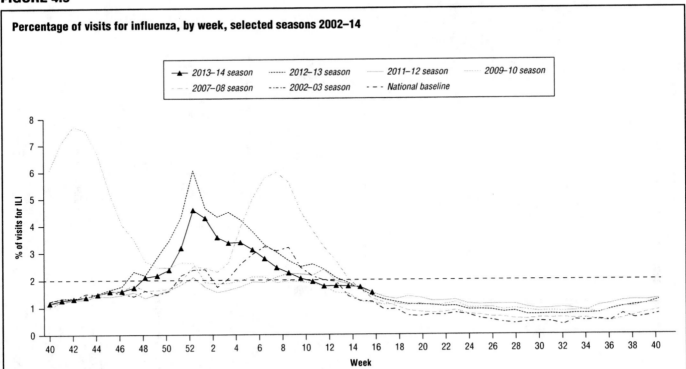

Percentage of visits for influenza, by week, selected seasons 2002–14

Notes: On a regional level, the percentage of outpatient visits for ILI ranged from 0.6% to 3.6% during week 15. Two of 10 regions reported a proportion of outpatient visits for ILI at or above their region-specific baseline level.
ILI = Influenza-like Illness.

SOURCE: "Percentage of Visits for Influenza-like Illness (ILI) Reported by the U.S. Outpatient Influenza-like Illness Surveillance Network (ILINet), Weekly National Summary, 2013–14 and Selected Previous Seasons," in *2013–14 Influenza Season Week 15 ending April 12, 2014*, Centers for Disease Control and Prevention, National Center for Immunization and Respiratory Diseases (NCIRD), April 12, 2014, http://www.cdc.gov/flu/weekly/pdf/External_F1415.pdf (accessed April 21, 2014)

States. The NIH trains research scientists and other investigators and serves to communicate medical and health information to professional and consumer audiences.

The NIH (August 20, 2013, http://www.nih.gov/about/organization.htm) consists of 27 centers and institutes and is housed in more than 75 buildings on a 300-acre (121-ha) campus in Bethesda, Maryland. Among the better-known centers and institutes are the National Cancer Institute, the National Human Genome Research Institute, the National Institute of Mental Health, and the National Center for Complementary and Alternative Medicine.

In "Facts at a Glance" (June 9, 2014, http://clinical center.nih.gov/about/welcome/fact.shtml), the NIH explains that patients arrive at the NIH Warren Grant Magnuson Clinical Center in Bethesda to participate in clinical research trials. About 5,800 patients per year are treated as inpatients, and an additional 102,000 receive outpatient treatment. The National Library of Medicine—which maintains MEDLINE, a comprehensive medical bibliographic database with more than 21 million references to articles published in around 5,600 biomedical journals from the United States and over 80 foreign countries—is in the NIH Lister Hill Center. According to the NIH, in "The NIH Almanac: Chronology of Events" (August 19, 2014, http://www.nih.gov/about/almanac/historical/chronology_of_events.htm), in 2010 the National Library of Medicine released ReUnite, an iPhone application to improve post-disaster family reunification. Within one week of its release, ReUnite was downloaded by more than 1,000 people. By 2014 the NIH offered 20 apps, ranging from Health Hotlines, a directory of nearly 9,000 biomedical organizations and resources with toll-free telephone numbers, to the Wireless System for Emergency Responders, which assists emergency responders in hazardous materials incidents.

The NIH budget for FY 2015 was $30.4 billion. Table 4.3 shows NIH funding allocation by institute. In "About the National Institutes of Health" (2014, http://science.education.nih.gov/supplements/nih1/Genetic/about/about-nih.htm), the NIH states that it works to achieve its ambitious research objectives "to acquire new knowledge to help prevent, detect, diagnose, and treat disease and disability, from the rarest genetic disorder to the common cold" by investing in promising biomedical research. The NIH makes grants and contracts to support research and training in every state in the country, at more than 2,000 institutions. The NIH allocated more than half (53.4%) of its FY 2015 budget to research project grants, 11.3% to intramural research (work conducted at NIH facilities), 10% to research and development contracts, and 9% to research centers. (See Figure 4.6.)

Establishing Research Priorities

By law, all 27 institutes and centers of the NIH must be funded, and each institute and center must allocate its funding to specific areas and aspects of research within its domain. About half of each institute's or center's budget is dedicated to supporting the best research proposals presented, in terms of their potential to contribute to advances that will combat the diseases the institute or center is charged with researching. Some of the other criteria that are used to determine research priorities include:

- Public health need—the NIH responds to health problems and diseases based on their incidence (the rate of development of a disease in a group during a given period) and severity and on the costs associated with them. Examples of other measures used to weigh and assess need are the mortality rate (the number of deaths caused by disease), the morbidity rate (the degree of disability caused by disease), the economic and social consequences of the disease, and whether rapid action is required to control the spread of the disease.

- Rigorous peer review—proposals are scrutinized by accomplished researchers to determine the potential return on investment of resources.

- Flexibility and expansiveness—the NIH experience demonstrates that important findings for commonly occurring diseases may come from research on rarer ones. The NIH attempts to fund the broadest possible array of research opportunities to stimulate creative solutions to pressing problems.

- Commitment to human resources and technology—the NIH invests in people and equipment in the pursuit of scientific advancement.

Because not even the most gifted scientists can accurately predict the next critical discovery or stride in biomedical research, the NIH must analyze each research opportunity in terms of competition for the same resources, public interest, scientific merit, and the potential to build on current knowledge.

NIH Achievements

The HHS notes in *U.S. Department of Health and Human Services Budget in Brief, Fiscal Year 2015* that in FY 2015 the NIH had 18,234 employees. The NIH recruits and attracts the most capable research scientists in the world. In fact, the NIH indicates in "The NIH Almanac: Nobel Laureates" (October 21, 2014, http://www.nih.gov/about/almanac/nobel/index.htm) that as of October 2014, 145 scientists who conducted NIH research or were supported by NIH grants had received Nobel Prizes. Several Nobel Prize winners made their prize-winning discoveries in NIH laboratories.

Equally important, NIH research has contributed to great improvements in the health of the nation. The following are some of the NIH's (August 19, 2014,

TABLE 4.3

National Institutes of Health total funding, fiscal years 2013–15

[Dollars in millions]

Institutes	2013	2014	2015	2015 +/– 2014
National Cancer Institute	4,783	4,923	4,931	+8
National Heart, Lung and Blood Institute	2,900	2,983	2,988	+5
National Institute of Dental and Craniofacial Research	387	397	397	+0
National Inst. of Diabetes & Digestive & Kidney Diseases	1,835	1,881	1,893	+12
National Institute of Neurological Disorders and Stroke	1,532	1,586	1,608	+23
National Institute of Allergy and Infectious Diseases	4,230	4,393	4,423	+31
National Institute of General Medical Sciences	2,291	2,362	2,369	+7
Eunice K. Shriver Natl. Inst. of Child Health & Human Dev	1,245	1,281	1,283	+3
National Eye Institute	656	674	675	+1
National Institute of Environmental Health Sciences:				
Labor/HHS appropriation	646	665	665	+7
Interior appropriation	75	77	77	—
National Institute on Aging	1,039	1,169	1,171	+1
Natl. Inst. of Arthritis & Musculoskeletal & Skin Diseases	505	519	520	+1
Natl. Inst. on Deafness and Communication Disorders	392	403	404	+0
National Institute of Mental Health	1,394	1,417	1,440	+23
National Institute on Drug Abuse	992	1,016	1,023	+8
National Institute on Alcohol Abuse and Alcoholism	433	445	446	+1
National Institute of Nursing Research	136	140	140	+0
National Human Genome Research Institute	483	497	498	+1
Natl. Institute of Biomedical Imaging and Bioengineering	319	326	329	+2
Natl. Institute on Minority Health and Health Disparities	260	268	268	—
Natl. Center for Complementary and Alternative Medicine	121	124	125	+0
National Center for Advancing Translational Sciences	542	632	657	+25
Fogarty International Center	66	67	68	+0
National Library of Medicine	360	375	381	+6
Office of the Director	1,411	1,400	1,452	+52
Buildings and facilities	118	129	129	—
Total, program level	**29,151**	**30,151**	**30,362**	**+211**
Less funds allocated from other sources				
PHS evaluation funds (NLM)	−8	−8	−8	—
Type 1 diabetes research (NIDDK)*	−142	−139	−150	−11
Total, discretionary budget authority	**29,001**	**30,003**	**30,203**	**+200**
Labor/HHS appropriation	28,926	29,926	30,126	+200
Interior appropriation	75	77	77	—
Full-time equivalents	18,234	18,234	18,234	—

*These mandatory funds were pre-appropriated in P.L. 111-309, the Medicare and Medicaid Extenders Act of 2010, and P.L. 112-240, the American Taxpayer Relief Act of 2012, and are proposed for reauthorization in fiscal year 2015.

Notes: PHS = Public Health Service. NLM = National Library of Medicine. NIDDK = National Institute of Diabetes and Digestive and Kidney Diseases.

SOURCE: "National Institutes of Health," in *U.S. Department of Health and Human Services Budget in Brief, Fiscal Year 2015*, U.S. Department of Health and Human Services, 2014, http://www.hhs.gov/budget/fy2015/fy-2015-budget-in-brief.pdf (accessed April 22, 2014)

http://www.nih.gov/about/almanac/historical/chronology_of_events.htm) recent achievements (from 2011 to 2014):

- A large NIH-funded clinical trial found that early treatment of HIV-positive patients significantly lowers their risk of transmitting HIV.

- NIH research found that a "primer" vaccine followed by an avian flu vaccine dramatically increased flu-fighting antibodies compared with the flu vaccine alone.

- Using computers and genomic data (information about the full set of chromosomes and all the inheritable traits), researchers identified new applications for existing FDA-approved drugs.

- NIH established the National Center for Advancing Translational Sciences, which aims to develop new methods and technologies to reduce, remove, or bypass bottlenecks in delivering new drugs, diagnostics, and medical devices to patients.

- The Human Connectome Project, which is mapping connections between the brain's neurons, showed that nerve fibers in the brain are not a jumble of overlapping wires. Instead, they form a structured 3-D grid—nerve pathways run parallel to one another and cross at right angles.

- NIH-funded research enabled paralyzed patients to reach and grasp objects using a robotic arm controlled by their thoughts.

- NIH-supported research found that programs that help to prevent or delay the onset of type

FIGURE 4.6

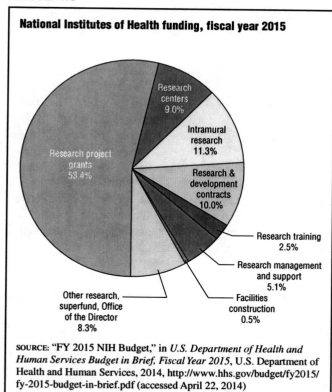

National Institutes of Health funding, fiscal year 2015

SOURCE: "FY 2015 NIH Budget," in *U.S. Department of Health and Human Services Budget in Brief, Fiscal Year 2015*, U.S. Department of Health and Human Services, 2014, http://www.hhs.gov/budget/fy2015/fy-2015-budget-in-brief.pdf (accessed April 22, 2014)

2 diabetes are cost-effective because these programs reduce overall medical care costs and improve quality of life.

- NIH launched a partnership with 10 biopharmaceutical companies and several nonprofits to transform the model for identifying promising targets for new diagnostics and drug development.

In "A Conversation with Francis Collins" (AARP .org, March 2014), an interview conducted by Gabrielle DeGroot Redford with Francis Collins (1950–), the director of the NIH, explains that one of the NIH's biggest projects is the Brain Research through Advancing Innovative Neurotechnologies (BRAIN) initiative. Over the next decade, the BRAIN project aims to determine exactly how the brain works—how it processes information and how it creates memories and retrieves them.

ACCREDITATION

Accreditation of health care providers (facilities and organizations) offers consumers, payers, and other stakeholders the assurance that accredited facilities and organizations have been certified as meeting or exceeding predetermined standards. Accreditation refers to both the process during which the quality of care delivered is measured and the resulting official endorsement that quality standards have been met. Besides promoting accreditation to health care consumers and other purchasers of care

such as employer groups, accreditation assists health care facilities and organizations to recruit and retain qualified staff, increase organizational efficiencies to reduce costs, identify ways to improve service delivery, and reduce liability insurance premiums.

The Joint Commission

The Joint Commission (2014, http://www.jointcommission.org/about_us/fact_sheets.aspx) surveys and accredits more than 20,500 health care organizations and programs throughout the United States. The Joint Commission is a nonprofit organization and is headquartered in Oakbrook Terrace, Illinois, with a satellite office in Washington, D.C. The Joint Commission notes in "Facts about the Joint Commission" (July 16, 2014, http://www.jointcommission.org/about_us/who_we_are.aspx) that it has more than 1,000 surveyors—physicians, nurses, pharmacists, hospital and health care organization administrators, laboratory medical technologists, and other health professionals—who are qualified and trained to evaluate specific aspects of health care quality.

Working closely with medical and other professional societies, purchasers of health care services, and management experts as well as with other accrediting organizations, the Joint Commission develops the standards that health care organizations are expected to meet. Besides developing benchmarks and standards of organizational quality, the Joint Commission is credited with promoting improvement in infection control, safety, and patients' rights.

THE JOINT COMMISSION GROWS TO BECOME THE PREEMINENT ACCREDITING BODY. In *The Joint Commission History* (February 2013, http://www.jointcommission.org/assets/1/6/Joint_Commission_History.pdf), the Joint Commission explains that early efforts to standardize and evaluate care delivered in hospitals began in 1913 by the American College of Surgeons. Thirty-eight years later, in 1951, the Joint Commission on Accreditation of Hospitals (JCAH) was established. In 1966 the JCAH began offering accreditation to long-term-care facilities, and in 1972 the Social Security Act was amended to require the HHS secretary to validate JCAH findings and include them in the HHS annual report to Congress. In subsequent years the JCAH's mandate was expanded to include a variety of other health care facilities, and in 1987 it was renamed the Joint Commission on Accreditation of Healthcare Organizations. Today it is known simply as The Joint Commission.

In 1992 the Joint Commission instituted a requirement that accredited hospitals prohibit smoking in the hospital, and in 1993 it began performing random, surprise surveys (unannounced site visits) of 5% of accredited organizations. The Joint Commission also moved to emphasize performance improvement standards by revising its policies on medical errors.

In 1999 the Joint Commission required hospitals to begin collecting and reporting data about the care they provide for five specific diagnoses: acute myocardial infarction (heart attack), congestive heart failure, pneumonia, pregnancy and related medical conditions, and surgical procedures and complications. The Joint Commission calls these diagnoses "core measure data" and uses these data to compare facilities and assess the quality of service delivered. In 2002 the Joint Commission moved to make its recommendations more easily understood by consumers so they can make informed choices about health care providers.

In 2006 the Joint Commission shifted to an unannounced survey program—meaning that organizations receive no advanced notice of their survey date. Before this policy change, the leaders of the nation's more than 4,500 Medicare-participating hospitals had ample notice and time to prepare for Joint Commission visits and inspections. The policy change was intended to shift hospitals' orientation from preparing for the next Joint Commission survey to preparing for the next patient. The policy also required hospitals to conduct an annual periodic performance review using their own internal evaluators to assess their own level of standards compliance and to communicate the results of their audit to the Joint Commission.

This policy change, presumably implemented to improve hospital vigilance about safety, care, and quality, coincided with another, seemingly contradictory Joint Commission policy change, which allowed hospitals to accumulate a higher number of deficiencies (patient care lapses and other violations) before sanctions are imposed on them. The Joint Commission defends this practice by explaining that it would rather identify more problems and have hospitals resolve them than deny hospitals accreditation.

In "Statement from the Joint Commission Regarding Enactment of Health Care Reform Bill" (*Joint Commission Perspectives*, vol. 30, no. 5, May 2010), a statement about the ACA, the Joint Commission asserts that "the United States has the most technologically sophisticated care in the world, and a cadre of dedicated and skilled health professionals beyond rival. At the same time, there are persistent issues in health care delivery that keep the health care system from attaining the highest achievable levels of quality and safety for every patient in every setting." The Joint Commission explains that it is working with health care facilities, providers, the CMS, safety advocates, Congress, and other stakeholders to effectively address urgent health and safety issues.

Joint Commission efforts appear to be effective. Stephen P. Schmaltz et al. demonstrate in "Hospital Performance Trends on National Quality Measures and the Association with Joint Commission Accreditation" (*Journal of Hospital Medicine*, vol. 6, no. 8, October 2011) that hospitals accredited by the Joint Commission outperform nonaccredited hospitals on nationally standardized quality measures.

Nonetheless, in "High-Reliability Health Care: Getting There from Here" (*Milbank Quarterly*, vol. 91, no. 3, September 2013), Mark R. Chassin and Jerod M. Loeb observe that despite efforts to improve safety and quality, patients still suffer preventable harm in hospitals. Chassin and Loeb assert, "No hospitals or health systems have achieved consistent excellence throughout their institutions. High-reliability science is the study of organizations in industries like commercial aviation and nuclear power that operate under hazardous conditions while maintaining safety levels that are far better than those of health care." Chassin and Loeb propose a framework to assist hospitals to improve quality by focusing on leadership, a culture of safety, and robust process improvement—philosophy and tools aimed at improving the outcomes of a process and preparing organizations to accept, implement, and sustain these improved processes.

Improving America's Hospitals: The Joint Commission's Annual Report on Quality and Safety 2013 (2014, http://www.jointcommission.org/assets/1/6/TJC_Annual_Report_2013.pdf), named and ranked 1,099 hospitals (33% of all Joint Commission–accredited hospitals reportingaccountability measure performance data for 2012) distinguished as top performers in the use of evidence-based care processes (approaches and methods based on the results of research), which are closely linked to positive patient outcomes (how patients fare as a result of treatment). The number of hospitals recognized as top performers increased 77% from the previous year and, of the top performers, 424 achieved the distinction for the past two years and 182 for the last three consecutive years.

National Committee for Quality Assurance

The National Committee for Quality Assurance (NCQA) is another well-respected accrediting organization that focuses its attention on the managed care industry. The NCQA began surveying and accrediting managed care organizations (MCOs) in 1991. The NCQA notes in the press release "4 out of 5 Exchange Health Plans Hold NCQA Accreditation" (September 30, 2013, http://www.ncqa.org/Newsroom/NewsArchive/2013News Archive/NewsReleaseSeptember302013.aspx) that by late 2013 the majority—nearly 85%—of the health plans offered by the health insurance exchange marketplaces that opened in October 2013 were accredited by the NCQA. Moreover, almost 60 plans that had not previously been accredited chose NCQA accreditation in anticipation of participating in the exchange marketplace. Accreditation by an approved, national group is a requirement for participation in exchange marketplaces.

NCQA surveys use more a set of more than 60 standards, each focusing on a specific aspect of health plan operations, for all types of health plans, such as MCOs, health maintenance organizations (HMOs), and preferred provider organizations (PPOs). The standards address access and service, the qualifications of providers, the organization's commitment to prevention programs and health maintenance, the quality of care delivered to members when they are ill or injured, and the organization's approach to helping members manage chronic diseases such as diabetes, heart disease, and asthma. To ensure fair comparisons between managed health care plans and to track their progress and improvement over time, the NCQA considers many standards, including:

- Management of asthma and effective use of medication

- Controlling hypertension (high blood pressure)

- Effective and appropriate use of antidepressant medications

- Childhood and adult weight and body mass index assessment

- Rates of breast cancer screening

- The frequency and consistency with which beta blockers (drug treatment) are used following heart attack

- Rates of immunization among children and teens

The NCQA combines the Healthcare Effectiveness Data and Information Set (HEDIS) with national and regional benchmarks of quality in a national database called the Quality Compass. This national database enables employers and health care consumers to compare health plans to one another and make choices about coverage based on quality and value rather than simply on price and participating providers (physicians, hospitals, and other providers that offer services to the managed care plan members).

The NCQA issues health plan report cards that rate HMOs and MCOs, and health care consumers and other stakeholders can access them at the NCQA website. After the NCQA review, the plans may be granted the NCQA's full accreditation for three years, indicating a level of excellence that exceeds NCQA standards. Those that need some improvement are granted one-year accreditation with recommendations about areas that need improvement, and MCOs that meet some but not all NCQA standards may be denied accreditation or granted provisional accreditation.

In *The State of Health Care Quality Report 2013* (October 2013, http://www.ncqa.org/Portals/0/News room/SOHC/2013/SOHC-web_version_report.pdf), the NCQA acknowledges that "annual studies like *The State of Health Care Quality* confirm that care is better in many ways than it was 10 years ago—or even 5 years ago. For all the complexity and political partisanship that roils health care today, it is encouraging to see how far we have come." The NCQA describes two key trends that are of concern—overuse of antibiotics, which leads to antibiotic resistance, continues to be a problem, and the proportion of people suffering from substance abuse that receive timely, recommended treatment has declined dramatically. The NCQA also documents, however, trends that indicate significant progress—there have been substantial gains in measures to assess and combat childhood obesity, such as counseling children and their families about nutrition and physical activity. Children enrolled in Medicaid HMOs are receiving recommended immunizations for influenza and rotavirus. Additionally, with the implementation of the ACA, Medicaid enrollment is growing; satisfaction with care received from Medicaid HMOs is also growing.

Accreditation Association for Ambulatory Health Care

Another accrediting organization, the Accreditation Association for Ambulatory Health Care (AAAHC), was formed in 1979 and focuses exclusively on ambulatory (outpatient) facilities and programs. Outpatient clinics, group practices, student health services, occupational medicine clinics, ambulatory surgery centers, and medical homes (primary care practices that aim to serve as centralized overseers of all the health care needs of individuals) are among the organizations that are evaluated by the AAAHC.

In 2009 the AAAHC established standards for reviewing medical homes. The term *medical home* is a relatively new descriptor of the long-standing practice of having a primary care practitioner (for adults usually an internist or family practitioner and for children a pediatrician) provide and coordinate needed care.

The medical home model of primary care is patient-centered, comprehensive, team-based, coordinated, and accessible, and emphasizes quality and safety. It is a philosophy of health care delivery that urges providers and care teams to meet patients where they are, from the most simple to the most complex chronic conditions. It endeavors to treat patients with respect, dignity, and compassion and to foster strong and trusting relationships with providers and staff. It is a model for quality primary care excellence that is delivered in the manner that best suits a patient's needs. The AAAHC offers certification and accreditation for medical homes based on the following standards:

- Patient rights and responsibilities

- Organizational governance and administration

- The patient/care team relationship

- Comprehensiveness, continuity, and accessibility of care

- Clinical records and health information

- Quality of care

The AAAHC accreditation process involves a self-assessment by the organization seeking accreditation, peer-review, continuing education, and a survey that is conducted by AAAHC surveyors who are all practicing professionals. The AAAHC grants accreditation for periods ranging from six months to three years. By 2014 the AAAHC (http://www.aaahc.org/en/about) was accrediting over 5,000 organizations.

In 2002 the AAAHC and the Joint Commission signed a collaborative accreditation agreement that permits ambulatory health care organizations to use their AAAHC accreditation to satisfy the Joint Commission's requirements. That same year the CMS granted the AAAHC authority to review health plans that provide coverage for Medicare beneficiaries. HMOs, PPOs, and ambulatory surgery centers are now considered to be Medicare-certified on their receipt of accreditation from the AAAHC.

National Quality Forum

In 2006 two other national quality organizations, the National Quality Forum and the National Committee on Quality Health Care, merged to become a new organization, also named the National Quality Forum (NQF; http://www.qualityforum.org). The NQF is a private, nonprofit membership organization created to develop and implement a national strategy for health care quality measurement and reporting. Its mission is to improve health and health care quality in the United States through measurement. In 2014 the NQF had more than 400 organizational members.

In the press release "CEO Chris Cassel, MD Announces NQF 15th Anniversary" (2014, http://www.qualityforum.org/15-Anniversary_Marks_Successes.aspx), the NQF states that reduction in hospital-acquired infections and hospital readmissions and improvements in maternity and nursing care are among the outcomes demonstrating how health care quality has improved since the NQF was founded. In 2014 the NQF initiated a program aimed at exploring the concept of affordable care from the consumer's perspective. In *Measuring Affordability from the Patient's Perspective* (September 16, 2014, http://www.qualityforum.org/Publications/2014/09/Measuring_Afford ability_from_the_Patient_s_Perspective.aspx), the NQF considers the current consumer experience and the impact of health care costs on consumers. The program aims to "explore what healthcare affordability means from the consumer and patient perspective and

to understand what information patients and consumers need to find affordable care."

PROFESSIONAL SOCIETIES

There are professional and membership organizations and societies for all health professionals, such as physicians, nurses, psychologists, and hospital administrators, as well as for institutional health care providers, such as hospitals, managed care plans, and medical groups. These professional organizations represent the interests and concerns of their members, advocate on their behalf, and frequently compile data and publish information about working conditions, licensing, accreditation, compensation, and scientific advancements of interest to members.

American Medical Association

The American Medical Association (AMA) is a powerful voice for U.S. physicians' interests. The AMA concerns itself with a wide range of health-related issues including medical ethics, medical education, physician and patient advocacy, and development of national health policy. The AMA publishes the highly regarded *JAMA: The Journal of the American Medical Association*, as well as nine journals known as the JAMA Network. From 1958 to 2013, it also published the *American Medical News*.

Founded in 1847, the AMA has worked to upgrade medical education by expanding medical school curricula and establishing standards for licensing and accreditation of practitioners and postgraduate training programs. Recent activities of the AMA include campaigning to avert a Medicare pay cut for physicians, combating childhood obesity, and supporting the 2010 health care reform legislation. In the press release "AMA: Physicians Generate $1.6 Trillion in Economic Activity, Support 10 Million Jobs" (April 16, 2014, http://www.ama-assn.org/ama/pub/news/news/2014/2014-04-16-physicians-economic-impact-study.page), the AMA explains that in addition to their vital role as healers, physicians have a significant impact on national, state, and local economies—they create jobs and commerce and generate taxes that support public services. The AMA reports that "Each physician supported an average of $2.2 million in economic output and contributed to a total of $1.6 trillion in economic output nationwide." Each physician supported about 14 jobs for a total of 10 million jobs and supported $90,449 in local and state tax revenues, resulting in a total of $65.2 billion in local and state tax revenues nationwide. The study concluded that the economic impact of physicians exceeded many other industries including higher education, home health care, legal services, and nursing.

American Nurses Association

The American Nurses Association (ANA; 2014, http://www.nursingworld.org/FunctionalMenuCategories/AboutANA) is a professional organization that represents 3.1 million registered nurses and promotes high standards of nursing practice and education as well as the rights and responsibilities of nurses in the workplace. On behalf of its members, the ANA works to protect patients' rights, lobbies to advocate for health care issues that affect nurses and the public, champions workplace safety, and provides career and continuing education opportunities. The ANA publishes the *American Journal of Nursing* and actively seeks to improve the public image of nurses among health professionals and the community at large.

American Hospital Association

The American Hospital Association (AHA; 2014, http://www.aha.org/about/index.shtml) represents nearly 5,000 hospitals, health care systems, networks, and other health care providers and 43,000 individual members. Originally established as a membership organization for hospital superintendents in 1898, the AHA eventually expanded its mission to address all facets of hospital care and quality. Besides national advocacy activities and participation in the development of health policy, the AHA oversees research and pilot programs to improve health service delivery. It also gathers and disseminates hospital and other related health care data, publishes information of interest for its members, and sponsors educational opportunities for health care managers and administrators.

VOLUNTARY HEALTH ORGANIZATIONS

American Heart Association

The American Heart Association's mission is to decrease disability and death from cardiovascular disease and stroke. The association's national headquarters is in Dallas, Texas, and seven regional affiliate offices serve the balance of the United States. The American Heart Association explains in "History of the American Heart Association" (March 7, 2011, http://www.heart.org/HEARTORG/General/History-of-the-American-Heart-Association_UCM_308120_Article.jsp) that it was started by a group of physicians and social workers in New York City in 1915. The early efforts of this group, called the Association for the Prevention and Relief of Heart Disease, were to educate physicians and the general public about heart disease. The first fund-raising efforts were launched in 1948 during a radio broadcast, and since then the association has raised millions of dollars to fund research, education, and treatment programs.

Besides research, fund-raising, and generating public awareness about reducing the risk of developing heart disease, the American Heart Association has published many best-selling cookbooks that feature heart-healthy recipes and meal planning ideas. The association is also considered to be one of the world's most trusted authorities about heart health among physicians and scientists. It publishes five print journals, *Circulation*, *Circulation Research*, *Stroke*, *Hypertension*, and *Atherosclerosis, Thrombosis, and Vascular Biology*, also available online, and seven online-only journals.

The American Heart Association supports many initiatives to prevent heart disease and educate the community at large. In the press release "American Heart Association Launches Its First Online Pediatric First Aid & CPR Course" (April 16, 2014, http://newsroom.heart.org/news/american-heart-association-launches-its-first-online-pediatric-first-aid-cpr-course), for example, the association announces a new web-based, self-directed education program for parents and child care providers that teaches first aid and pediatric cardiopulmonary resuscitation (CPR; an emergency lifesaving procedure that is performed when breathing or heartbeat has stopped).

The American Heart Association also educates consumers about the importance of controlling high blood pressure. For example, in the press release "Heart Health as Young Adult Linked to Mental Function in Mid-life" (March 31, 2014, http://newsroom.heart.org/news/heart-health-as-young-adult-linked-to-mental-function-in-mid-life), the association describes research finding that heart health at ages 18 to 30 may determine whether adults remain mentally sharp in middle age. Young adults with high blood pressure, blood sugar, and cholesterol levels were not as sharp in their 40s and 50s as their heart healthy peers. Another study, described in the press release "Consistent Blood Pressure Control May Cut Rate of Second Stroke in Half" (March 27, 2014, http://newsroom.heart.org/news/consistent-blood-pressure-control-may-cut-rate-of-second-stroke-in-half), finds that stroke survivors who consistently control their blood pressure reduce the prospect of a second stroke by more than half.

American Cancer Society

The American Cancer Society (ACS; 2014, http://www.cancer.org/AboutUs/WhoWeAre/index) is headquartered in Atlanta, Georgia, and has more than 350 local offices across the country. The ACS's mission (November 11, 2008, http://www.cancer.org/AboutUs/WhoWeAre/acsmissionstatements) is "eliminating cancer as a major health problem by preventing cancer, saving lives, and diminishing suffering from cancer, through research, education, advocacy, and service."

The ACS is the biggest source of private, nonprofit funding for cancer research—second only to the federal government. In "Facts about ACS" (2014, http://www.cancer.org/AboutUs/WhoWeAre/acs-fact-sheet), the ACS states that it has invested over $4 billion in cancer research at leading centers throughout the United States and has funded 47 Nobel Prize winners early in their careers. It also supports epidemiological research to provide cancer surveillance information about occurrence rates, risk factors, mortality, and availability of treatment services. The ACS publishes an array of patient information brochures and three clinical journals for health professionals: *Cancer, Cancer Cytopathology,* and *CA: A Cancer Journal for Clinicians.* The ACS also maintains a 24-hour consumer telephone line that is staffed by trained cancer information specialists and a website with information for professionals, patients and families, and the media.

Besides education, prevention, and patient services, the ACS advocates for cancer survivors, their families, and every potential cancer patient. The ACS seeks to obtain support and passage of laws, policies, and regulations that benefit people who are affected by cancer. The ACS is especially concerned with developing strategies to better serve the poor and people with little formal education, who historically have been disproportionately affected by cancer.

March of Dimes

The March of Dimes was founded in 1938 by President Franklin D. Roosevelt (1882–1945) to help protect American children from polio. Besides supporting the research that produced the polio vaccine, the nonprofit organization has advocated for birth defects research and the fortification of food supplies with folic acid to prevent neural tube defects. It has also supported increasing access to quality prenatal care and the growth of neonatal intensive care units to help improve the chances of survival for babies born prematurely or with serious medical conditions.

The March of Dimes continues to partner with volunteers, scientific researchers, educators, and community outreach workers to help prevent birth defects. It funds genetic research; investigates the causes and treatment of premature birth; educates pregnant women; and provides health care services for women and children, such as immunizations, checkups, and treatment for childhood illnesses.

In the press release "March of Dimes Awards $250,000 Prize to Scientist Who Discovered Genetic Mutations Responsible for Autism Spectrum Disorders" (May 5, 2014, http://www.marchofdimes.com/news/march-of-dimes-awards-250000-prize-to-scientist-who-discovered-genetic-mutations-responsible-for-autism-spectrum-disorders.aspx), the March of Dimes announces that it awarded the 2014 March of Dimes Prize in Developmental Biology to Huda Y. Zoghbi, a physician, professor, and medical researcher who identified genetic mutations that cause Rett syndrome, one of the most common causes of intellectual disability in girls, and other neurological disorders.

CHAPTER 5
THE INCREASING COST OF HEALTH CARE

HOW MUCH DOES HEALTH CARE COST?

American society places a high value on human life and generally wants—and expects—quality medical care. However, quality care comes with an increasingly high cost. In 1970 the United States spent 7.2% of its gross domestic product (GDP; the total market value of final goods and services produced within an economy in a given year) on health care. By 2011 health care expenditures reached 17.9% of the GDP. Table 5.1 shows the growth in health care expenditures, the growth in the GDP, and the annual percent change for select years between 1960 and 2011. Table 5.2 shows that the average annual percent change in health expenditures has decreased over time from a high of 13.1% between 1970 and 1980 to a low of 3.9% from 2010 to 2011.

For many years the consumer price index (CPI; a measure of the average change in prices paid by consumers) increased at a greater rate for medical care than for any other commodity. In 1990 the average annual increase in the overall CPI was 4.7%, whereas the average annual increase in the medical care index stood at 8.1%. (See Table 5.3.) In 2000 the average annual growth in the medical care index fell to 3.4%, but in 2005 it rose again to 4.4%, outpacing overall inflation, which was 2.5%. In 2012 the increase in the medical care index was 3.7%, still higher than overall inflation of 2.1%. The medical care index has consistently outpaced the CPI in each decade. Of all the components of health care delivery, the sharpest price increases in 2012 were in health insurance (12.1%) and hospital services (5.1%).

The Centers for Medicare and Medicaid Services (CMS) projects that by 2022 the national health expenditure will exceed $5 trillion, reaching 19.9% of the GDP, from 18.4% in 2015. (See Table 5.4.) (Because the numbers in Table 5.4 are projections, they may differ from the actual numbers presented in some other tables and figures that appear in this chapter.) In *National Health*

Expenditures Projections 2012–2022 (2013, http://www.cms.gov/Research-Statistics-Data-and-Systems/Statistics-Trends-and-Reports/NationalHealthExpendData/downloads/proj2012.pdf), the CMS indicates that health spending is anticipated to increase at an average annual rate of 5.8% from 2012 to 2022.

Generally, projections are most accurate for the near future and less accurate for the distant future. For example, predictions for 2030 should be viewed more warily than predictions for 2016 because it is unlikely that the conditions on which the projections are based will remain the same. As a result, the CMS cautions that its projections should not be viewed as predictions for the future. Rather, they are intended to help policy makers evaluate the costs or savings of proposed legislative or regulatory changes.

Total Health Care Spending

The CMS, along with the Centers for Disease Control and Prevention and the U.S. Government Accountability Office, maintain most of the nation's statistics on health care costs. The CMS reports that the United States will spend $3.3 trillion for health care in 2015, up from $2.7 trillion in 2011. (See Table 5.4.)

Implementation of the Patient Protection and Affordable Care Act (ACA) coverage expansions and the aging of the population contribute to the 6.2% average annual projected growth in health spending from 2015 to 2022. The ACA is anticipated to reduce the number of uninsured Americans by 30 million by 2022. It is forecast to increase average annual health spending 0.1 percentage-point and increase health spending by an estimated $621 billion from 2012 to 2022. Table 5.5 shows the projected impact of the ACA on health spending through 2022.

More than $1.3 trillion of the 2014 health care expenditures came from private funds (out-of-pocket payments

TABLE 5.1

Gross domestic product (GDP), national health expenditures, per capita amounts, and average annual percentage change, selected years 1960–2011

[Data are compiled from various sources by the Centers for Medicare & Medicaid Services]

Gross domestic product and national health expenditures	1960	1970	1980	1990	2000	2005	2010	2011
				Amount, in billions				
Gross domestic product (GDP)	$526	$1,038	$2,788	$5,801	$9,952	$12,623	$14,499	$15,076
				Deflator (2005 = 100.0)				
Price deflator for GDP[a]	18.6	24.3	47.8	72.3	88.7	100.0	111.0	113.4
				Amount, in billions				
National health expenditures	$27.4	$74.9	$255.8	$724.3	$1,377.2	$2,030.5	$2,600.0	$2,700.7
Health consumption expenditures	24.8	67.1	235.7	675.6	1,289.6	1,904.0	2,450.8	2,547.2
Personal health care	23.4	63.1	217.2	616.8	1,165.4	1,697.1	2,190.0	2,279.3
Administration and net cost of private health insurance	1.1	2.6	12.0	38.8	81.2	150.9	181.5	188.9
Public health	0.4	1.4	6.4	20.0	43.0	56.0	79.3	79.0
Investment[b]	2.6	7.8	20.1	48.7	87.5	126.5	149.1	153.5
				Deflator (2005 = 100.0)				
Chain-weighted national health expenditure deflator[a]	—	—	—	—	—	100.0	114.6	117.3
				Per capita amount, in dollars				
National health expenditures	$147	$356	$1,110	$2,854	$4,878	$6,875	$8,417	$8,680
Health consumption expenditures	133	319	1,023	2,662	4,568	6,447	7,934	8,187
Personal health care	125	300	943	2,430	4,128	5,746	7,090	7,326
Administration and net cost of private health insurance	6	12	52	153	288	511	588	607
Public health	2	6	28	79	152	190	257	254
Investment[b]	14	37	87	192	310	428	483	493
				Percent				
National health expenditures as percent of GDP	5.2	7.2	9.2	12.5	13.8	16.1	17.9	17.9
				Percent distribution				
National health expenditures	100.0	100.0	100.0	100.0	100.0	100.0	100.0	100.0
Health consumption expenditures	90.6	89.6	92.1	93.3	93.6	93.8	94.3	94.3
Personal health care	85.4	84.3	84.9	85.2	84.6	83.6	84.2	84.4
Administration and net cost of private health insurance	3.9	3.5	4.7	5.4	5.9	7.4	7.0	7.0
Public health	1.4	1.8	2.5	2.8	3.1	2.8	3.1	2.9
Investment[b]	9.4	10.4	7.9	6.7	6.4	6.2	5.7	5.7
				Average annual percent change from previous year shown				
GDP	...	7.0	10.4	7.6	5.5	4.9	2.8	4.0
National health expenditures	...	10.6	13.1	11.0	6.6	8.1	5.1	3.9
Health consumption expenditures	...	10.5	13.4	11.1	6.7	8.1	5.2	3.9
Personal health care	...	10.4	13.2	11.0	6.6	7.8	5.2	4.1
Administration and net cost of private health insurance	...	9.4	16.4	12.4	7.7	13.2	3.8	4.1
Public health	...	13.8	16.9	12.0	8.0	5.4	7.2	−0.5
Investment[b]	...	11.7	10.0	9.2	6.0	7.6	3.3	2.9
National health expenditures, per capita	...	9.3	12.0	9.9	5.5	7.1	4.1	3.1
Health consumption expenditures	...	9.1	12.4	10.0	5.5	7.1	4.2	3.2
Personal health care	...	9.1	12.1	9.9	5.4	6.8	4.3	3.3
Administration and net cost of private health insurance	...	8.1	15.4	11.3	6.5	12.2	2.8	3.3
Public health	...	12.5	15.8	10.9	6.8	4.4	6.3	−1.2
Investment[b]	...	10.4	8.9	8.2	4.9	6.7	2.4	2.2

and private health insurance), and the balance was paid with public money. (See Table 5.6.) The 2014 per capita cost for health care (the average per individual if spending was divided equally among all people in the country) was $9,697.

Of the $3.1 trillion that was spent on health care in 2014, nearly $2.6 trillion was spent on personal health services (expenses incurred by individuals as opposed to institutions). (See Table 5.5.) Some of the services included hospital care, physician and dental services,

nursing and home health care, prescription drugs, and durable medical equipment.

Table 5.5 shows the trends and annual percent changes in personal health care expenditures by category. In 2014 the nation spent $973 billion on hospital care, by far the largest amount of personal health care spending, followed by $840.7 billion on professional services. This expense was followed by $630.7 billion on physician and clinical services, $376 billion on retail outlet sales of medical products, $275.9 billion

TABLE 5.1

Gross domestic product (GDP), national health expenditures, per capita amounts, and average annual percentage change, selected years 1960–2011 [CONTINUED]

[Data are compiled from various sources by the Centers for Medicare & Medicaid Services]

—Data not available.
. . .Category not applicable.
ªYear 2005 = 100.
ᵇInvestment consists of research and structures and equipment.
Notes: Dollar amounts shown are in current dollars. Deflating health care spending separates the effects of price growth from growth attributable to all other factors. The dollar value of these estimates of real health care expenditures is determined by the index(es) chosen to remove price growth from spending. One approach to deflating health spending is to remove the effects of economy-wide inflation alone using the GDP deflator. An alternative approach to removing the effects of price growth from health spending for the National Health Expenditure Accounts is to deflate health care expenditures by a measure of medical specific price inflation. For personal health care (PHC) spending, this would involve directly deflating expenditures by price indexes associated with the services and goods provided; for non-PHC spending this would involve deflating by composite indexes matching the components of spending for each category. The data reflect preliminary annual estimates of the resident population of the United States as of July 1, 2011, excluding the armed forces overseas. Percents are calculated using unrounded data. Estimates may not add to totals because of rounding. Starting with *Health, United States*, 2010, estimates are based on a revised methodology that incorporates available source data and various methodological and definitional changes. These revisions are due to a comprehensive change in the classification structure of how estimates are defined and presented. Data have been revised and differ from previous editions of *Health, United States*.

SOURCE: "Table 112. Gross Domestic Product, National Health Expenditures, per Capita Amounts, Percent Distribution, and Average Annual Percent Change: United States, Selected Years 1960–2011, in *Health, United States, 2013: With Special Feature on Prescription Drugs*, U.S. Department of Health and Human Services, Centers for Disease Control and Prevention, National Center for Health Statistics, May 2014, http://www.cdc.gov/nchs/data/hus/hus13.pdf (accessed May 16, 2014)

on prescription drugs, and $164 billion on nursing home and continuing care.

WHO PAYS THE BILL?

In general, the government is the fastest-growing payer of health care expenses. In 2014 the public share (Medicare, Medicaid, other health insurance programs, and other third-party payers) of the nation's total health care bill was 56%, and it is projected to rise to 58.2% by 2022. (See Table 5.6.) In 2014 private health insurance, the major nongovernmental payer of health care costs, paid 33.5% of all health expenditures. The share of health care spending from private, out-of-pocket (paid by the patient) funds declined from 12.6% in 2006 to 10.5% in 2014.

Personal Health Care Bill

Much of the increase in government spending has occurred in the area of personal health care. In 2006 government sources (Medicare, Medicaid, other health insurance programs, and other third-party payers) paid 49.5% of personal health care expenditures; by 2014 they covered 52.9% of the $2.6 trillion spent on personal health care services. (See Table 5.7.) Some of the federal increase was attributed to Medicaid spending, which grew from 15.7% of all personal health care expenditures in 2006 to an estimated 17.2% in 2014.

WHY HAVE HEALTH CARE COSTS AND SPENDING INCREASED?

The increase in the cost of medical care is challenging to analyze because the methods and quality of health care change constantly and as a result are often not comparable. A hospital stay in 1970 did not include the same services offered in 2014. Furthermore, the care

received in a physician's office in 2014 is not comparable to that received a generation ago. One contributing factor to the rising cost of health care is the increase in bio-medical technology, much of which is now available for use outside of a hospital.

Other factors also contribute to the increase in health care costs. These include population growth, high salaries for physicians and some other health care workers, and the expense of malpractice insurance. Escalating malpractice insurance costs and professional liability premiums have prompted some physicians and other health care practitioners to refrain from performing high-risk procedures that increase their vulnerability or have caused them to relocate to states where malpractice premiums are lower. Furthermore, to protect themselves from malpractice suits, many health care practitioners routinely order diagnostic tests and prescribe treatments that may not be medically necessary and do not serve to improve their patients' health. This practice is known as defensive medicine, and although its precise contribution to rising health care costs is difficult to gauge, industry observers agree that it is a significant factor.

In *Cracking the Code on Health Care Costs* (January 2014, http://web1.millercenter.org/commissions/health care/HealthcareCommission-Report.pdf), John Thomasian et al. attribute high health care costs to nine key factors:

- U.S. physicians, hospitals, facilities and drug costs are the highest in the world.

- Americans make use of more expensive technologies and procedures. For example, magnetic resonance imaging (MRI) is used in the United States twice as often as it is in most other countries.

TABLE 5.2

National health expenditures, average annual percentage change and percentage distribution by type of expenditure, 1960–2011

[Data are compiled from various sources by the Centers for Medicare & Medicaid Services]

Type of national health expenditure	1960	1970	1980	1990	2000	2005	2010	2011
				Amount, in billions				
National health expenditures	$27.4	$74.9	$255.8	$724.3	$1,377.2	$2,030.5	$2,600.0	$2,700.7
Health consumption expenditures	24.8	67.1	235.7	675.6	1,289.6	1,904.0	2,450.8	2,547.2
Personal health care	23.4	63.1	217.2	616.8	1,165.4	1,697.1	2,190.0	2,279.3
Hospital care	9.0	27.2	100.5	250.4	415.5	609.4	815.9	850.6
Professional services	8.0	19.8	64.6	208.1	390.2	556.9	694.2	723.1
Physician and clinical services	5.6	14.3	47.7	158.9	290.9	417.2	519.1	541.4
Other professional services	0.4	0.7	3.5	17.4	37.0	52.7	69.8	73.2
Dental services	2.0	4.7	13.4	31.7	62.3	87.0	105.3	108.4
Other health, residential, and personal care	0.5	1.3	8.5	24.3	64.5	96.5	128.0	133.1
Home health care[a]	0.1	0.2	2.4	12.6	32.4	48.7	71.2	74.3
Nursing care facilities and continuing care retirement communities[a]	0.8	4.0	15.3	44.9	85.1	112.5	143.0	149.3
Retail outlet sales of medical products	5.0	10.6	25.9	76.5	177.6	273.2	337.8	348.9
Prescription drugs	2.7	5.5	12.0	40.3	120.9	204.7	255.7	263.0
Durable medical equipment	0.7	1.7	4.1	13.8	25.2	31.2	36.9	38.9
Other nondurable medical products	1.6	3.3	9.8	22.4	31.6	37.2	45.2	47.0
Government administration[b]	0.1	0.7	2.8	7.2	17.1	28.3	31.1	32.5
Net cost of health insurance[c]	1.0	1.9	9.3	31.6	64.1	122.6	150.4	156.4
Government public health activities[d]	0.4	1.4	6.4	20.0	43.0	56.0	79.3	79.0
Investment	2.6	7.8	20.1	48.7	87.5	126.5	149.1	153.5
Research[e]	0.7	2.0	5.4	12.7	25.5	40.3	49.0	49.8
Structures and equipment	1.9	5.8	14.7	36.0	62.1	86.2	100.1	103.7
			Average annual percent change from previous year shown					
National health expenditures	—	10.6	13.1	11.0	6.6	8.1	5.1	3.9
Health consumption expenditures	—	10.5	13.4	11.1	6.7	8.1	5.2	3.9
Personal health care	—	10.4	13.2	11.0	6.6	7.8	5.2	4.1
Hospital care	—	11.7	14.0	9.6	5.2	8.0	6.0	4.3
Professional services	—	9.5	12.6	12.4	6.5	7.4	4.5	4.2
Physician and clinical services	—	9.8	12.8	12.8	6.2	7.5	4.5	4.3
Other professional services	—	6.4	17.0	17.5	7.8	7.3	5.8	4.9
Dental services	—	9.0	11.0	9.0	7.0	6.9	3.9	3.0
Other health, residential, and personal care	—	11.4	20.4	11.1	10.3	8.4	5.8	4.0
Home health care[a]	—	14.5	26.9	18.1	9.9	8.5	7.9	4.5
Nursing care facilities and continuing care retirement communities[a]	—	17.4	14.2	11.4	6.6	5.7	4.9	4.4
Retail outlet sales of medical products	—	7.7	9.4	11.4	8.8	9.0	4.3	3.3
Prescription drugs	—	7.5	8.2	12.8	11.6	11.1	4.5	2.9
Durable medical equipment	—	9.0	8.8	13.0	6.2	4.4	3.4	5.3
Other nondurable medical products	—	7.4	11.4	8.6	3.5	3.4	4.0	4.0
Government administration[b]	—	29.9	14.1	10.0	9.1	10.6	1.9	4.7
Net cost of health insurance[c]	—	6.4	17.3	13.1	7.3	13.8	4.2	4.0
Government public health activities[d]	—	13.8	16.9	12.0	8.0	5.4	7.2	−0.5
Investment	—	11.7	10.0	9.2	6.0	7.6	3.3	2.9
Research[e]	—	10.9	10.8	8.9	7.2	9.6	4.0	1.7
Structures and equipment	—	12.0	9.7	9.4	5.6	6.8	3.0	3.6
				Percent distribution				
National health expenditures	100.0	100.0	100.0	100.0	100.0	100.0	100.0	100.0
Health consumption expenditures	90.6	89.6	92.1	93.3	93.6	93.8	94.3	94.3
Personal health care	85.4	84.3	84.9	85.2	84.6	83.6	84.2	84.4
Hospital care	32.8	36.3	39.3	34.6	30.2	30.0	31.4	31.5
Professional services	29.3	26.4	25.3	28.7	28.3	27.4	26.7	26.8
Physician and clinical services	20.6	19.1	18.7	21.9	21.1	20.5	20.0	20.0
Other professional services	1.4	1.0	1.4	2.4	2.7	2.6	2.7	2.7
Dental services	7.3	6.3	5.2	4.4	4.5	4.3	4.0	4.0
Other health, residential, and personal care	1.6	1.8	3.3	3.4	4.7	4.8	4.9	4.9
Home health care[a]	0.2	0.3	0.9	1.7	2.4	2.4	2.7	2.8
Nursing care facilities and continuing care retirement communities[a]	3.0	5.4	6.0	6.2	6.2	5.5	5.5	5.5
Retail outlet sales of medical products	18.4	14.1	10.1	10.6	12.9	13.5	13.0	12.9
Prescription drugs	9.8	7.3	4.7	5.6	8.8	10.1	9.8	9.7
Durable medical equipment	2.7	2.3	1.6	1.9	1.8	1.5	1.4	1.4
Other nondurable medical products	5.9	4.4	3.8	3.1	2.3	1.8	1.7	1.7
Government administration[b]	0.2	1.0	1.1	1.0	1.2	1.4	1.2	1.2
Net cost of health insurance[c]	3.7	2.5	3.6	4.4	4.7	6.0	5.8	5.8
Government public health activities[d]	1.4	1.8	2.5	2.8	3.1	2.8	3.1	2.9
Investment	9.4	10.4	7.9	6.7	6.4	6.2	5.7	5.7
Research[e]	2.5	2.6	2.1	1.8	1.8	2.0	1.9	1.8
Structures and equipment	6.8	7.8	5.7	5.0	4.5	4.2	3.9	3.8

TABLE 5.2

National health expenditures, average annual percentage change and percentage distribution by type of expenditure, 1960–2011 [CONTINUED]

[Data are compiled from various sources by the Centers for Medicare & Medicaid Services]

—Category not applicable.

aIncludes expenditures for care in freestanding facilities only. Additional services of this type are provided in hospital-based facilities and are considered hospital care.

bIncludes all administrative costs (federal and state and local employees' salaries; contracted employees, including fiscal intermediaries; rent and building costs; computer systems and programs; other materials and supplies; and other miscellaneous expenses) associated with insuring individuals enrolled in the following health insurance programs: Medicare, Medicaid, Children's Health Insurance Program, Department of Defense, Department of Veterans Affairs, Indian Health Service, workers' compensation, maternal and child health, vocational rehabilitation, Substance Abuse and Mental Health Services Administration, and other federal programs.

cNet cost of health insurance is calculated as the difference between calendar year incurred premiums earned and benefits incurred for private health insurance. This includes administrative costs, and in some cases additions to reserves, rate credits and dividends, premium taxes, and net underwriting gains or losses. Also included in this category is the difference between premiums earned and benefits incurred for the private health insurance companies that insure the enrollees of the following programs: Medicare, Medicaid, Children's Health Insurance Program, and workers' compensation (health portion only).

dIncludes personal care services delivered by government public health agencies.

eResearch and development expenditures of drug companies and other manufacturers and providers of medical equipment and supplies are excluded. These are included in the expenditure class in which the product falls because such expenditures are covered by the payment received for that product.

Notes: Percents and average annual percent change are calculated using unrounded data. Starting with *Health, United States, 2010,* estimates are based on a revised methodology that incorporates available source data and various methodological and definitional changes. These revisions are due to a comprehensive change in the classification structure of how estimates are defined and presented. Data have been revised and differ from previous editions of *Health, United States.*

SOURCE: "Table 114. National Health Expenditures, Average Annual Percent Change, and Percent Distribution, by Type of Expenditure: United States, Selected Years 1960–2011," in *Health, United States, 2013: With Special Feature on Prescription Drugs,* U.S. Department of Health and Human Services, Centers for Disease Control and Prevention, National Center for Health Statistics, May 2014, http://www.cdc.gov/nchs/data/hus/hus13.pdf (accessed May 16, 2014)

- Fragmented and uncoordinated care results in duplicative and unnecessary treatment and errors.

- Americans mistakenly believe that expensive care is quality care, and they often do not weigh the cost of care when making health care purchases or decisions.

- Fee-for-service payment, which reimburses hospitals and physicians for every service they provide, often incentivizes providers to maximize the volume and cost of services.

- Fragmented and unnecessarily complicated insurance and billing processes cost the U.S. health care system billions of dollars each year.

- Unhealthy lifestyles and behaviors cause or contribute to many chronic illnesses (such as heart disease, cancer, and diabetes) that are costly to treat.

- Americans' end-of-life care life is expensive, and unnecessary procedures and repeated hospitalizations do not benefit patients or the health care system.

- Mergers and acquisitions among hospitals, health systems, and physician groups are often prompted by the desire to increase market share, and while there may be some economies of scale, consolidation can also act to increase prices.

Other factors for the increase in health care costs include advanced biomedical procedures that require high-technology expertise and equipment, redundant (excessive and unnecessary) technology in hospitals, consumer demand for less restrictive insurance plans (ones that offer more choices, benefits, and coverage, but usually mean higher premiums), and consumer demand for the latest and most comprehensive testing and treatment. The growing number of older adults who use a disproportionate amount of health care services also accelerates health care spending.

As reported in *National Health Expenditures Projections 2012–2022,* the CMS expects government spending on health care to grow 6.2% per year from 2015 through 2022 in response to overall economic growth, continuing implementation of the ACA and the aging population. During the same period, Medicare spending is expected to grow 7.4%. Beginning in 2016 (following the 12.2% increase in Medicaid spending in 2014 attributable to the ACA expanded coverage), Medicaid spending is expected to grow by 6.6% per year.

Private health insurance spending is projected to grow 5.8% per year and out-of-pocket spending is projected to peak at growth of 5.6% in 2020. Largely because of the ACA, the out-of-pocket share of health spending is projected to fall from 11.4% of total spending in 2012 to 9.1% by 2022.

CONTROLLING HEALTH CARE SPENDING

In an effort to control health expenditures, the nation's health care system underwent some dramatic changes. Beginning in the late 1980s employers began looking for new ways to contain health benefit costs for their employees. Many enrolled their employees in managed care programs as alternatives to traditional, fee-for-service insurance. Managed care programs offered lower premiums by keeping a tighter control on costs and utilization and by emphasizing the importance of preventive care. Insurers negotiated discounts with providers

TABLE 5.3

Consumer price index and average annual percentage change for all items, selected items, and medical care costs, selected years 1960–2012

[Data are based on reporting by samples of providers and other retail outlets]

Items and medical care components	1960	1970	1980	1990	1995	2000	2005	2011	2012
	Consumer Price Index (CPI)								
All items	29.6	38.8	82.4	130.7	152.4	172.2	195.3	224.9	229.6
All items less medical care	30.2	39.2	82.8	128.8	148.6	167.3	188.7	216.3	220.6
Services	24.1	35.0	77.9	139.2	168.7	195.3	230.1	265.8	271.4
Food	30.0	39.2	86.8	132.4	148.4	167.8	190.7	227.8	233.8
Apparel	45.7	59.2	90.9	124.1	132.0	129.6	119.5	122.1	126.3
Housing	—	36.4	81.1	128.5	148.5	169.6	195.7	219.1	222.7
Energy	22.4	25.5	86.0	102.1	105.2	124.6	177.1	243.9	246.1
Medical care	22.3	34.0	74.9	162.8	220.5	260.8	323.2	400.3	414.9
Components of medical care									
Medical care services	19.5	32.3	74.8	162.7	224.2	266.0	336.7	423.8	440.3
Professional services	—	37.0	77.9	156.1	201.0	237.7	281.7	335.7	342.0
Physician services	21.9	34.5	76.5	160.8	208.8	244.7	287.5	340.3	347.3
Dental services	27.0	39.2	78.9	155.8	206.8	258.5	324.0	408.0	417.5
Eyeglasses and eye care[a]	—	—	—	117.3	137.0	149.7	163.2	178.3	179.9
Services by other medical professionals[a]	—	—	—	120.2	143.9	161.9	186.8	217.4	219.6
Hospital and related services	—	—	69.2	178.0	257.8	317.3	439.9	641.5	672.1
Hospital services[b]	—	—	—	—	—	115.9	161.6	241.2	253.6
Inpatient hospital services[b,c]	—	—	—	—	—	113.8	156.6	236.6	248.8
Outpatient hospital services[a,c]	—	—	—	138.7	204.6	263.8	373.0	546.9	574.0
Hospital rooms	9.3	23.6	68.0	175.4	251.2	—	—	—	—
Other inpatient services[a]	—	—	—	142.7	206.8	—	—	—	—
Nursing homes and adult day care[b]	—	—	—	—	—	117.0	145.0	182.2	188.8
Health insurance[d]	—	—	—	—	—	—	—	105.5	118.3
Medical care commodities	46.9	46.5	75.4	163.4	204.5	238.1	276.0	324.1	333.6
Medicinal drugs[e]	—	—	—	—	—	—	—	105.5	108.6
Prescription drugs[f]	54.0	47.4	72.5	181.7	235.0	285.4	349.0	425.0	440.1
Nonprescription drugs[e]	—	—	—	—	—	—	—	98.6	99.3
Medical equipment and supplies[e]	—	—	—	—	—	—	—	99.3	100.6
Nonprescription drugs and medical supplies[a,g]	—	—	—	120.6	140.5	149.5	151.7	—	—
Internal and respiratory over-the-counter drugs[h]	—	42.3	74.9	145.9	167.0	176.9	179.7	—	—
Nonprescription medical equipment and supplies[i]	—	—	79.2	138.0	166.3	178.1	180.6	—	—
	Average annual percent change from previous year shown								
All items	...	2.7	7.8	4.7	3.1	2.5	2.5	3.2	2.1
All items less medical care	...	2.6	7.8	4.5	2.9	2.4	2.4	3.2	2.0
Services	...	3.8	8.3	6.0	3.9	3.0	3.3	1.7	2.1
Food	...	2.7	8.3	4.3	2.3	2.5	2.6	3.7	2.6
Apparel	...	2.6	4.4	3.2	1.2	-0.4	-1.6	2.2	3.4
Housing	...	—	8.3	4.7	2.9	2.7	2.9	1.3	1.6
Energy	...	1.3	12.9	1.7	0.6	3.4	7.3	15.4	0.9
Medical care	...	4.3	8.2	8.1	6.3	3.4	4.4	3.0	3.7
Components of medical care									
Medical care services	...	5.2	8.8	8.1	6.6	3.5	4.8	3.1	3.9
Professional services	...	—	7.7	7.2	5.2	3.4	3.5	2.3	1.9
Physician services	...	4.6	8.3	7.7	5.4	3.2	3.3	2.7	2.1
Dental services	...	3.8	7.2	7.0	5.8	4.6	4.6	2.3	2.3
Eyeglasses and eye care[a]	...	—	—	—	3.2	1.8	1.7	0.9	0.9
Services by other medical professionals[a]	...	—	—	—	3.7	2.4	2.9	1.4	1.0
Hospital and related services	...	—	—	9.9	7.7	4.2	6.8	5.6	4.8
Hospital services[b]	...	—	—	—	—	—	6.9	6.2	5.1
Inpatient hospital services[b,c]	...	—	—	—	—	—	6.6	6.8	5.2
Outpatient hospital services[a,c]	...	—	—	—	8.1	5.2	7.2	5.1	5.0
Hospital rooms	...	9.8	11.2	9.9	7.4	—	—	—	—
Other inpatient services[a]	...	—	—	—	7.7	—	—	—	—
Nursing homes and adult day care[b]	...	—	—	—	—	—	4.4	2.9	3.6
Health insurance[d]	...	—	—	—	—	—	—	-1.1	12.1
Medical care commodities	...	-0.1	5.0	8.0	4.6	3.1	3.0	3.0	2.9
Medicinal drugs[e]	...	—	—	—	—	—	—	3.1	3.0
Prescription drugs[f]	...	-1.3	4.3	9.6	5.3	4.0	4.1	4.2	3.6
Nonprescription drugs[e]	...	—	—	—	—	—	—	-1.3	0.7
Medical equipment and supplies[e]	...	—	—	—	—	—	—	0.3	1.2
Nonprescription drugs and medical supplies[a,g]	...	—	—	—	3.1	1.2	0.3	—	—
Internal and respiratory over-the-counter drugs[h]	...	—	5.9	6.9	2.7	1.2	0.3	—	—
Nonprescription medical equipment and supplies[i]	...	—	—	5.7	3.8	1.4	0.3	—	—

(physicians, hospitals, clinical laboratories, and others) in exchange for guaranteed access to employer-insured groups. In 2014 private insurance paid for 33.5% of the nation's health costs. (See Table 5.6.) Public sources covered 56% of the nation's costs, and 10.5% of the costs came directly from consumers' pockets.

TABLE 5.3

Consumer price index and average annual percentage change for all items, selected items, and medical care costs, selected years 1960–2012 [CONTINUED]

[Data are based on reporting by samples of providers and other retail outlets]

—Data not available.
. . .Category not applicable.
[a]December 1986 = 100.
[b]December 1996 = 100.
[c]Special index based on a substantially smaller sample.
[d]December 2005 = 100.
[e]December 2009 = 100.
[f]Prior to 2006, this category included medical supplies.
[g]Starting with 2010 updates, this index series will no longer be published.
[h]Starting with 2010 updates, replaced by the series, nonprescription drugs.
[i]Starting with 2010 updates, replaced by the series, Medical equipment and supplies.
Notes: CPI for all urban consumers (CPI-U) U.S. city average, detailed expenditure categories. 1982–1984 = 100, except where noted. Data are not seasonally adjusted. Data for additional years are available.

SOURCE: "Table 113. Consumer Price Index and Average Annual Percent Change for All Items, Selected Items, and Medical Care Components: United States, Selected Years 1960–2012," in *Health, United States, 2013: With Special Feature on Prescription Drugs*, U.S. Department of Health and Human Services, Centers for Disease Control and Prevention, National Center for Health Statistics, May 2014, http://www.cdc.gov/nchs/data/hus/hus13.pdf (accessed May 16, 2014)

In "Small Ideas for Saving Big Health Care Dollars" (Rand Corporation, 2014, http://www.rand.org/content/dam/rand/pubs/research_reports/RR300/RR390/RAND_RR390.pdf), Jodi L. Liu et al. review a variety of additional small changes with the potential to reduce health care expenditures. Examples include substituting lower-cost treatments for more expensive ones, such as increasing the use of lower-cost antibiotics to treat middle ear infections since they are as effective as costlier antibiotics, increasing use of generic as opposed to brand-name drugs, and shifting some care from costlier sites such as emergency departments to retail clinics. Other recommended changes were intended to improve patient safety and prevent health care–associated infections and pressure ulcers (bedsores).

Liu et al. observe that these small changes could result in substantial cost savings. For example, if half of all people using brand-name drugs switched to $4 generics, the annual savings would be $5.9 billion. Preventing three common health care–associated infections could save nearly $200 million per year.

How Will the ACA Influence Health Care Spending?

Many aspects of the ACA spark fiery debate, but few are as divisive as the question of whether over time, its implementation will reduce health care costs. Proponents of the legislation claim that it will lower the federal budget deficit over time, whereas critics assert that it will inflate the deficit and national debt. As many key aspects of the ACA take effect, industry observers will assess how new provisions such as permitting the purchase of health insurance across state lines and malpractice reform affect U.S. expenditures for health care.

In "Deficit-Reducing Health Care Reform" (2014, http://www.whitehouse.gov/economy/reform/deficit-reduc

ing-health-care-reform), the White House explains that the ACA "reduces the deficit, saving over $200 billion over 10 years and more than $1 trillion in the second decade." In part, these savings accrue in response to rewarding providers that deliver high quality care, increasing the availability of generic drugs, and sharply reducing waste, fraud, and abuse. The reduction of waste, fraud, and abuse is projected to generate savings of $1.8 billion through 2015.

Vishal Persaud names in "How the Affordable Care Act Will Cut Health Spending" (NBCBayArea.com, March 31, 2014) specific provisions of the ACA that have the potential to control health care costs, including coverage for preventive services and reduced Medicare reimbursements to hospitals that release an excess number of patients who are readmitted within a month for heart attacks and pneumonia. Soon after this provision was finalized, overall 30-day hospital readmission rates for Medicare patients declined sharply from their average 2007–11 rates. (See Figure 5.1.)

In "Affordable Care Act's Role in Slowing Health Costs Debated" (NBCBayArea.com, March 31, 2014), Persaud observes that from 2009 through 2012 health care spending slowed to its lowest rates since government tracking began in 1960, but it is unclear whether the slower growth is entirely attributable to the effects of the ACA. Less spending during the economic recession also contributed to the lower rate.

The ACA will generate revenue because fewer people will be covered by employer-sponsored health coverage. As a result, taxable wages in proportion to nontaxable health coverage benefits will increase generating higher tax revenues totaling $152 billion.

TABLE 5.4

National health expenditures and annual percentage change, 2006–22

Item	2006	2007	2008	2009	2010	2011	2012	2013	Projected 2014	2015	2016	2017	2018	2019	2020	2021	2022
Amount in billions																	
National health expenditures	$2,163	$2,298	$2,407	$2,501	$2,600	$2,701	$2,807	$2,915	$3,093	$3,273	$3,458	$3,660	$3,889	$4,142	$4,416	$4,702	$5,009
Private health insurance—national health expenditures	742	779	809	835	864	896	931	962	1,036	1,100	1,156	1,215	1,287	1,374	1,459	1,549	1,636
Private health insurance—personal health care	640	674	707	738	757	786	814	836	899	953	1,005	1,058	1,126	1,201	1,277	1,356	1,434
Gross domestic product[a]	13,377	14,029	14,292	13,974	14,499	15,076	15,679	16,196	16,925	17,805	18,820	19,893	20,967	22,011	23,048	24,108	25,217
Level																	
Gross domestic product implicit price deflator, chain weighted 2005 base year	1.03	1.06	1.09	1.10	1.11	1.13	1.15	1.17	1.19	1.22	1.24	1.27	1.30	1.33	1.36	1.40	1.43
Consumer Price Index (CPI-U)—1982–1984 base	2.02	2.07	2.15	2.15	2.18	2.25	2.29	2.34	2.39	2.44	2.49	2.55	2.62	2.69	2.77	2.84	2.92
Millions																	
U.S. population[b]	298.2	301.0	303.8	306.4	308.9	311.1	313.6	316.3	319.0	321.8	324.7	327.5	330.4	333.2	336.0	338.8	341.6
Population age 65 years and older	37.0	37.7	38.7	39.6	40.4	41.3	42.6	44.1	45.4	46.8	48.3	49.8	51.3	53.0	54.7	56.5	58.3
Population age less than 65 years	261.2	263.3	265.1	266.8	268.5	269.8	271.0	272.2	273.5	275.0	276.4	277.8	279.0	280.2	281.3	282.3	283.3
Average annual percent change from previous year shown																	
National health expenditures	—	6.2%	4.7%	3.9%	3.9%	3.9%	3.9%	3.8%	6.1%	5.8%	5.6%	5.8%	6.2%	6.5%	6.6%	6.5%	6.5%
Private health insurance—national health expenditures	—	5.0	3.9	3.2	3.4	3.8	3.8	3.4	7.7	6.2	5.1	5.0	6.0	6.7	6.2	6.2	5.6
Private health insurance—personal health care		5.3	4.9	4.3	2.7	3.8	3.5	2.7	7.6	5.9	5.5	5.3	6.4	6.7	6.3	6.2	5.8
Gross domestic product	—	4.9	1.9	−2.2	3.8	4.0	4.0	3.3	4.5	5.2	5.7	5.7	5.4	5.0	4.7	4.6	4.6
Gross domestic product implicit price deflator, chain weighted 2005 base year	—	2.9	2.2	0.9	1.3	2.1	1.8	1.5	1.8	2.0	2.1	2.3	2.4	2.4	2.4	2.4	2.4
Consumer Price Index (CPI-U)—1982–1984 base	—	2.8	3.8	−0.4	1.6	3.2	2.0	1.9	2.0	2.1	2.2	2.4	2.6	2.8	2.8	2.8	2.8
U.S. population[a]	—	0.9	0.9	0.9	0.8	0.7	0.8	0.8	0.9	0.9	0.9	0.9	0.9	0.9	0.8	0.8	0.8
Population age 65 years and older	—	1.9	2.6	2.2	2.1	2.3	3.2	3.3	3.1	3.1	3.1	3.1	3.2	3.2	3.2	3.2	3.2
Population age less than 65 years	—	0.8	0.7	0.7	0.6	0.5	0.4	0.4	0.5	0.5	0.5	0.5	0.5	0.4	0.4	0.4	0.3
Per capita amount																	
National health expenditures	$7,255	$7,636	$7,922	$8,163	$8,417	$8,680	$8,948	$9,216	$9,697	$10,172	$10,651	$11,175	$11,771	$12,431	$13,142	$13,878	$14,664
Private health insurance—national health expenditures	2,487	2,588	2,665	2,725	2,796	2,881	2,967	3,043	3,248	3,418	3,561	3,708	3,896	4,123	4,343	4,572	4,791
Private health insurance—personal health care	2,147	2,240	2,329	2,408	2,452	2,526	2,595	2,642	2,820	2,961	3,095	3,230	3,408	3,604	3,799	4,001	4,199
Gross domestic product	44,862	46,608	47,044	45,605	46,939	48,452	49,989	51,213	53,061	55,329	57,965	60,733	63,461	66,055	68,588	71,153	73,825
Percent change in per capita from previous year shown																	
National health expenditures	—	5.2%	3.7%	3.0%	3.1%	3.1%	3.1%	3.0%	5.2%	4.9%	4.7%	4.9%	5.3%	5.6%	5.7%	5.6%	5.7%
Private health insurance—national health expenditures	—	4.0	3.0	2.3	2.6	3.0	3.0	2.5	6.7	5.2	4.2	4.1	5.1	5.8	5.3	5.3	4.8
Private health insurance—personal health care	—	4.3	4.0	3.4	1.9	3.0	2.7	1.8	6.7	5.0	4.5	4.4	5.5	5.8	5.4	5.3	5.0
Gross domestic product	—	3.9	0.9	−3.1	2.9	3.2	3.2	2.4	3.6	4.3	4.8	4.8	4.5	4.1	3.8	3.7	3.8
Percent																	
National health expenditures as a percent of gross domestic product	16.2%	16.4%	16.8%	17.9%	17.9%	17.9%	17.9%	18.0%	18.3%	18.4%	18.4%	18.4%	18.5%	18.8%	19.2%	19.5%	19.9%

[a] These projections incorporate estimates of GDP as of June 2013 and do not reflect the comprehensive revisions to GDP that were released in July 2013.

[b] July 1 Census resident based population estimates.

Note: Projections include effects of the Affordable Care Act and an alternative to the sustainable growth rate. Numbers and percents may not add to totals because of rounding.

SOURCE: "Table 1. National Health Expenditures and Selected Economic Indicators, Levels and Annual Percent Change: Calendar Years 2006–2022," in *National Health Expenditures Projections 2012–2022*, U.S. Department of Health and Human Services, Centers for Medicare and Medicaid Services, 2013, http://www.cms.gov/Research-Statistics-Data-and-Systems/Statistics-Trends-and-Reports/NationalHealthExpendData/downloads/proj2012.pdf (accessed May 16, 2014)

TABLE 5.5

Impact of the Affordable Care Act (ACA) on national health expenditures, by type of expenditure, 2006–22

Type of expenditure (billions $)

Type of expenditure	2006	2007	2008	2009	2010	2011	2012	2013	Projected 2014	2015	2016	2017	2018	2019	2020	2021	2022
National health expenditures	$2,163.3	$2,298.3	$2,406.6	$2,501.2	$2,600.0	$2,700.7	$2,806.6	$2,914.7	$3,093.2	$3,273.4	$3,458.3	$3,660.4	$3,889.1	$4,142.4	$4,416.2	$4,702.0	$5,008.8
Health consumption expenditures	2,032.4	2,154.6	2,252.8	2,355.1	2,450.8	2,547.2	2,648.4	2,753.1	2,923.1	3,094.4	3,269.2	3,459.4	3,674.6	3,913.7	4,172.9	4,443.9	4,735.6
Personal health care	1,804.4	1,914.1	2,010.4	2,111.6	2,190.0	2,279.3	2,365.8	2,452.3	2,594.0	2,743.2	2,902.3	3,075.2	3,271.8	3,484.7	3,717.8	3,960.2	4,224.3
Hospital care	651.9	692.5	729.2	777.9	815.9	850.6	892.4	929.0	973.0	1,027.5	1,091.6	1,158.1	1,232.3	1,310.7	1,397.4	1,485.2	1,581.3
Professional services	585.2	618.6	652.8	672.5	694.2	723.1	755.4	785.0	840.7	887.2	932.9	983.7	1,045.4	1,114.9	1,189.9	1,267.8	1,351.5
Physician and clinical services	438.8	461.8	486.4	503.2	519.1	541.4	566.5	588.0	630.7	664.9	698.0	736.5	782.8	834.6	890.7	948.9	1,012.0
Other professional services	55.0	59.5	64.0	66.8	69.8	73.2	76.8	79.5	87.5	93.0	99.2	105.6	112.9	120.7	129.3	138.3	148.2
Dental services	91.4	97.3	102.4	102.5	105.3	108.4	112.2	116.6	122.4	129.3	135.7	141.6	149.8	159.6	170.0	180.6	191.3
Other health, residential, and personal care	101.7	107.7	113.6	122.5	128.0	133.1	138.1	144.5	153.5	163.5	174.7	186.9	200.1	213.8	228.5	244.1	260.8
Home health care	52.6	57.8	62.3	67.3	71.2	74.3	77.9	81.8	86.8	92.9	99.5	106.9	115.5	124.5	134.3	144.9	157.2
Nursing care facilities and continuing care Retirement communities	117.3	126.4	132.6	138.5	143.0	149.3	151.2	156.8	164.0	172.2	182.0	193.2	205.4	218.1	231.9	246.8	264.2
Retail outlet sales of medical products	295.8	311.2	320.0	332.9	337.8	348.9	350.8	355.2	376.0	399.9	421.6	446.5	473.0	502.6	535.8	571.3	609.4
Prescription drugs	224.1	235.9	242.6	254.6	255.7	263.0	260.8	262.3	275.9	294.9	311.6	330.7	350.6	372.7	397.9	425.5	455.0
Other medical products	71.6	75.3	77.4	78.4	82.1	85.9	90.0	93.0	100.1	105.0	110.1	115.8	122.4	129.9	137.8	145.8	154.4
Durable medical equipment	32.9	34.3	34.9	34.9	36.9	38.9	40.9	42.2	43.8	46.1	47.8	50.1	52.8	55.9	59.3	62.8	66.7
Other non-durable medical products	38.7	41.0	42.5	43.5	45.2	47.0	49.1	50.7	56.3	58.9	62.3	65.7	69.7	74.0	78.5	83.0	87.8
Government administration	28.7	29.4	30.3	30.8	31.1	32.5	34.6	37.1	41.9	44.4	47.0	50.3	54.0	57.6	61.3	65.5	70.4
Net cost of private health insurance	136.9	142.4	139.5	137.1	150.4	156.4	166.3	180.0	199.4	215.3	224.3	233.8	243.6	261.1	277.8	296.2	313.2
Government public health activities	62.3	68.7	72.6	75.6	79.3	79.0	81.6	83.7	87.8	91.5	95.6	100.1	105.2	110.4	115.9	121.9	127.7
Investment	130.9	143.7	153.8	146.1	149.1	153.5	158.3	161.5	170.0	179.0	189.0	201.0	214.5	228.6	243.3	258.2	273.2
Research*	41.4	41.9	43.4	45.3	49.0	49.8	48.6	47.4	49.3	51.8	54.7	57.9	61.3	64.8	68.4	72.2	76.4
Structures & equipment	89.6	101.7	110.4	100.8	100.1	103.7	109.7	114.1	120.8	127.2	134.3	143.1	153.1	163.9	174.9	186.0	196.8

Annual percent change by type of expenditure (%)

Type of expenditure	2006	2007	2008	2009	2010	2011	2012	2013	Projected 2014	2015	2016	2017	2018	2019	2020	2021	2022
National health expenditures	—	6.2%	4.7%	3.9%	3.9%	3.9%	3.9%	3.8%	6.1%	5.8%	5.6%	5.8%	6.2%	6.5%	6.6%	6.5%	6.5%
Health consumption expenditures	—	6.0	4.6	4.5	4.1	3.9	4.0	4.0	6.2	5.9	5.6	5.8	6.2	6.5	6.6	6.5	6.6
Personal health care	—	6.1	5.0	5.0	3.7	4.1	3.8	3.7	5.8	5.8	5.8	6.0	6.4	6.5	6.7	6.5	6.7
Hospital care	—	6.2	5.3	6.7	4.9	4.3	4.9	4.1	4.7	5.6	6.2	6.1	6.4	6.4	6.7	6.3	6.5
Professional services	—	5.7	5.5	3.0	3.2	4.2	4.5	3.9	7.1	5.5	5.1	5.4	6.3	6.6	6.7	6.5	6.6
Physician and clinical services	—	5.2	5.3	3.5	3.1	4.3	4.6	3.9	7.1	5.4	5.0	5.5	6.3	6.6	6.7	6.5	6.6
Other professional services	—	8.2	7.6	4.4	4.6	4.9	4.8	3.6	10.1	6.3	6.6	6.4	6.9	6.9	7.1	7.0	7.2
Dental services	—	6.4	5.2	0.1	2.7	3.0	3.5	3.9	5.0	5.6	4.9	4.3	5.8	6.6	6.5	6.3	5.9
Other health, residential, and personal care	—	5.9	5.5	7.8	4.5	4.0	3.7	4.6	6.2	6.5	6.9	7.0	7.1	6.9	6.9	6.8	6.8
Home health care	—	9.9	7.8	8.0	5.8	4.5	4.8	5.0	6.1	7.0	7.1	7.4	8.1	7.8	7.9	7.9	8.5
Nursing care facilities and continuing care retirement communities	—	7.8	4.9	4.5	3.2	4.4	1.3	3.7	4.6	5.0	5.7	6.2	6.3	6.2	6.3	6.4	7.0
Retail outlet sales of medical products	—	5.2	2.8	4.1	1.5	3.3	0.5	1.3	5.8	6.4	5.4	5.9	5.9	6.3	6.6	6.6	6.7
Prescription drugs	—	5.2	2.8	5.0	0.4	2.9	-0.8	0.6	5.2	6.9	5.6	6.2	6.0	6.3	6.8	6.9	6.9
Other medical products	—	5.2	2.8	1.2	4.8	4.6	4.8	3.3	7.7	4.9	4.8	5.2	5.8	6.1	6.1	5.8	5.9
Durable medical equipment	—	4.4	1.7	-0.1	5.8	5.3	5.3	3.2	3.7	5.3	3.5	4.8	5.3	6.0	6.1	5.9	6.1
Other non-durable medical products	—	5.9	3.7	2.3	4.0	4.0	4.3	3.4	11.0	4.6	5.8	5.5	6.1	6.2	6.1	5.7	5.7
Government administration	—	2.4	2.9	1.8	0.7	4.7	6.3	7.3	13.0	6.0	5.9	7.0	7.3	6.7	6.5	6.8	7.4
Net cost of private health insurance	—	4.0	-2.0	-1.7	9.8	4.0	6.4	8.2	10.8	8.0	4.2	4.2	4.2	7.2	6.4	6.6	5.7
Government public health activities	—	10.3	5.8	4.1	4.9	-0.5	3.4	2.6	4.9	4.2	4.5	4.7	5.1	4.9	5.1	5.1	4.7
Investment	—	9.7	7.1	-5.0	2.1	2.9	3.1	2.1	5.3	5.3	5.6	6.4	6.7	6.6	6.4	6.1	5.8
Research*	—	1.3	3.5	4.3	8.2	1.7	-2.5	-2.3	3.8	5.1	5.6	6.0	5.8	5.6	5.6	5.6	5.8
Structures & Equipment	—	13.6	8.6	-8.7	-0.7	3.6	5.8	4.0	5.9	5.3	5.6	6.5	7.0	7.0	6.7	6.3	5.8

TABLE 5.5

Impact of the Affordable Care Act (ACA) on national health expenditures, by type of expenditure, 2006–22 [CONTINUED]

*Research and development expenditures of drug companies and other manufacturers and providers of medical equipment and supplies are excluded from research expenditures. These research expenditures are implicitly included in the expenditure class in which the product falls, in that they are covered by the payment for that product.

Notes: Numbers may not add to totals because of rounding. Projections include effect of the Affordable Care Act and an alternative to the sustainable growth rate.

SOURCE: "Table 2. National Health Expenditure Amounts with the Impacts of the Affordable Care Act, and Annual Percent Change by Type of Expenditure: Calendar Years 2006–2022," in *National Health Expenditures Projections 2012–2022*, U.S. Department of Health and Human Services, Centers for Medicare and Medicaid Services, 2013, http://www.cms.gov/Research-Statistics-Data-and-Systems/Statistics-Trends-and-Reports/NationalHealthExpendData/downloads/proj2012.pdf (accessed May 16, 2014)

TABLE 5.6

National health expenditures, by source of funds, 2006–22

Year	Total	Out-of-pocket payments	Health insurance[a] Total	Private health insurance	Medicare	Medicaid	Other health insurance programs[b]	Other third party payers[c]
Historical estimates				Amount in billions				
2006	$2,163.3	$271.6	$1,522.1	$741.6	$403.7	$306.9	$69.9	$369.5
2007	2,298.3	286.1	1,613.9	778.9	433.6	326.2	75.3	398.3
2008	2,406.6	293.0	1,705.2	809.5	468.2	344.9	82.6	408.5
2009	2,501.2	293.3	1,801.1	835.0	500.4	375.4	90.2	406.8
2010	2,600.0	299.4	1,879.4	863.7	522.0	397.7	96.0	421.1
2011	2,700.7	307.7	1,960.1	896.3	554.3	407.7	101.8	433.0
Projected								
2012	2,806.6	320.2	2,035.2	930.6	579.9	416.8	107.9	451.2
2013	2,914.7	329.0	2,117.4	962.2	604.2	436.6	114.5	468.3
2014	3,093.2	324.1	2,281.9	1,035.9	635.1	490.0	120.9	487.2
2015	3,273.4	333.7	2,429.0	1,099.9	669.3	530.7	129.1	510.7
2016	3,458.3	342.3	2,579.6	1,156.2	714.8	570.9	137.7	536.3
2017	3,660.4	356.3	2,733.9	1,214.6	767.1	608.1	144.1	570.3
2018	3,889.1	371.2	2,909.2	1,287.4	827.6	647.1	147.2	608.7
2019	4,142.4	390.0	3,106.6	1,374.0	885.6	691.1	155.9	645.8
2020	4,416.2	411.7	3,321.1	1,459.5	954.6	738.8	168.2	683.4
2021	4,702.0	434.5	3,545.3	1,549.2	1,029.0	787.6	179.4	722.3
2022	5,008.8	458.1	3,789.9	1,636.5	1,122.9	839.2	191.3	760.8
Historical estimates				Per capita amount				
2006	$7,255	$911	d	d	d	d	d	d
2007	7,636	950	d	d	d	d	d	d
2008	7,922	964	d	d	d	d	d	d
2009	8,163	957	d	d	d	d	d	d
2010	8,417	969	d	d	d	d	d	d
2011	8,680	989	d	d	d	d	d	d
Projected								
2012	8,948	1,021	d	d	d	d	d	d
2013	9,216	1,040	d	d	d	d	d	d
2014	9,697	1,016	d	d	d	d	d	d
2015	10,172	1,037	d	d	d	d	d	d
2016	10,651	1,054	d	d	d	d	d	d
2017	11,175	1,088	d	d	d	d	d	d
2018	11,771	1,124	d	d	d	d	d	d
2019	12,431	1,170	d	d	d	d	d	d
2020	13,142	1,225	d	d	d	d	d	d
2021	13,878	1,282	d	d	d	d	d	d
2022	14,664	1,341	d	d	d	d	d	d
Historical estimates				Percent distribution				
2006	100.0	12.6	70.4	34.3	18.7	14.2	3.2	17.1
2007	100.0	12.4	70.2	33.9	18.9	14.2	3.3	17.3
2008	100.0	12.2	70.9	33.6	19.5	14.3	3.4	17.0
2009	100.0	11.7	72.0	33.4	20.0	15.0	3.6	16.3
2010	100.0	11.5	72.3	33.2	20.1	15.3	3.7	16.2
2011	100.0	11.4	72.6	33.2	20.5	15.1	3.8	16.0
Projected								
2012	100.0	11.4	72.5	33.2	20.7	14.8	3.8	16.1
2013	100.0	11.3	72.6	33.0	20.7	15.0	3.9	16.1
2014	100.0	10.5	73.8	33.5	20.5	15.8	3.9	15.8
2015	100.0	10.2	74.2	33.6	20.4	16.2	3.9	15.6
2016	100.0	9.9	74.6	33.4	20.7	16.5	4.0	15.5
2017	100.0	9.7	74.7	33.2	21.0	16.6	3.9	15.6
2018	100.0	9.5	74.8	33.1	21.3	16.6	3.8	15.7
2019	100.0	9.4	75.0	33.2	21.4	16.7	3.8	15.6
2020	100.0	9.3	75.2	33.0	21.6	16.7	3.8	15.5
2021	100.0	9.2	75.4	32.9	21.9	16.8	3.8	15.4
2022	100.0	9.1	75.7	32.7	22.4	16.8	3.8	15.2
Historical estimates				Annual percent change from previous year shown				
2006	—	—	—	—	—	—	—	—
2007	6.2	5.3	6.0	5.0	7.4	6.3	7.7	7.8
2008	4.7	2.4	5.7	3.9	8.0	5.8	9.7	2.5
2009	3.9	0.1	5.6	3.2	6.9	8.8	9.3	−0.4
2010	3.9	2.1	4.4	3.4	4.3	5.9	6.4	3.5
2011	3.9	2.8	4.3	3.8	6.2	2.5	6.0	2.8

TABLE 5.6

National health expenditures, by source of funds, 2006–22 [CONTINUED]

			Health insurance[a]					
Year	Total	Out-of-pocket payments	Total	Private health insurance	Medicare	Medicaid	Other health insurance programs[b]	Other third party payers[c]
Projected			Annual percent change from previous year shown					
2012	3.9	4.1	3.8	3.8	4.6	2.2	6.0	4.2
2013	3.8	2.7	4.0	3.4	4.2	4.8	6.1	3.8
2014	6.1	−1.5	7.8	7.7	5.1	12.2	5.6	4.0
2015	5.8	3.0	6.4	6.2	5.4	8.3	6.8	4.8
2016	5.6	2.6	6.2	5.1	6.8	7.6	6.7	5.0
2017	5.8	4.1	6.0	5.0	7.3	6.5	4.7	6.3
2018	6.2	4.2	6.4	6.0	7.9	6.4	2.1	6.7
2019	6.5	5.1	6.8	6.7	7.0	6.8	5.9	6.1
2020	6.6	5.6	6.9	6.2	7.8	6.9	7.9	5.8
2021	6.5	5.5	6.7	6.2	7.8	6.6	6.7	5.7
2022	6.5	5.4	6.9	5.6	9.1	6.6	6.6	5.3

[a]Includes private health insurance (employer sponsored insurance and other private insurance, which includes marketplace plans), Medicare, Medicaid, Children's Health Insurance Program (Titles XIX and XXI), Department of Defense, and Department of Veterans' Affairs.
[b]Children's Health Insurance Program (Titles XIX and XXI), Department of Defense, and Department of Veterans' Affairs.
[c]Includes worksite health care, other private revenues, Indian Health Service, workers' compensation, general assistance, maternal and child health, vocational rehabilitation, other federal programs, Substance Abuse and Mental Health Services Administration, other state and local programs, and school health.
[d]Calculation of per capita estimates is not applicable.
Notes: Projections include effects of the Affordable Care Act and an alternative to the sustainable growth rate.
Per capita amounts based on July 1 Census resident based population estimates. Numbers and percents may not add to totals because of rounding.

SOURCE: "Table 3. National Health Expenditures; Aggregate and per Capita Amounts, Percent Distribution and Annual Percent Change by Source of Funds: Calendar Years 2006–2022," in *National Health Expenditures Projections 2012–2022*, U.S. Department of Health and Human Services, Centers for Medicare and Medicaid Services, 2013, http://www.cms.gov/Research-Statistics-Data-and-Systems/Statistics-Trends-and-Reports/NationalHealthExpendData/downloads/proj2012.pdf (accessed May 16, 2014)

Revenues also will be generated by a 0.9% increase in payroll taxes for individuals and couples with an income between $200,000 and $250,000. High-income taxpayers will also be required to pay a 3.8% tax on unearned income over the earning limits. In "Obamacare's 'Cadillac Tax' Could Help Reduce the Cost of Health Care" (Forbes.com, February 26, 2014), William H. Frist reports that a 40% excise tax (often referred to as a Cadillac tax because it applies to high-cost plans) starting in 2018 on richer, more costly health coverage is projected to raise $80 billion between 2018 and 2023. The ACA also raises the threshold for deducting out-of-pocket unreimbursed medical expenses from 7.5% of a taxpayer's adjusted gross income to 10%. Table 5.8 shows how the cost of coverage provisions are projected to effect the federal deficit from 2014 to 2023.

Prescription Drug Prices Continue to Rise

One of the fastest-growing components of health care is the market for prescription drugs. In 2014 Americans spent an estimated $275.9 billion on prescription medication. (See Table 5.9.) Private insurers paid $119.7 billion of the drug costs in 2014, an increase from $114.2 billion they paid for prescription drugs in 2013. (See Table 5.9.) The health needs and chronic conditions of the aging population have fueled growth in this sector of health services.

In *National Trends in Prescription Drug Expenditures and Projections for 2014* (*American Journal of Health-System Pharmacy*, vol. 71, no. 6, March 2014), Glen T. Schumock et al. note that like other health care expenditures, growth in prescription drug spending has slowed in recent years, and in 2012 spending decreased 0.8% from 2011. However, Schumock et al. anticipate that this trend will reverse itself because of ACA expanded insurance coverage, use of new and more expensive drugs, and increased per-capita drug use by older adults covered by Medicare.

The Medicare drug benefit, which was implemented in 2006 to provide prescription drug savings for older Americans and people with disabilities, increased government spending for prescription drugs. The program allows Medicare beneficiaries to choose from dozens of plans that are offered by health insurers and health plans called pharmacy benefit managers. The ACA reduced Medicare Part D enrollees' out-of-pocket drug costs when they reach the coverage gap, known as the so-called donut hole. Most Medicare Part D basic drug benefit plans require enrollees to pay all of their prescription drug costs after their drug spending exceeds the predesignated dollar amount that is their initial coverage limit until they satisfy the dollar amount that qualifies them for catastrophic coverage.

Under the ACA, in 2011 non-low-income Medicare Part D enrollees received a 50% discount on brand-name prescription drugs and a 7% discount on generic prescription drugs while they were in the coverage gap. In 2015

TABLE 5.7

Personal health expenditures, by source of funds, 2006–22

Year	Total	Out-of-pocket payments	Health insurance[a] Total	Private health insurance	Medicare	Medicaid	Other health insurance programs[b]	Other third party payers[c]
Historical estimates				Amount in billions				
2006	$1,804.4	$271.6	$1,372.2	$640.3	$382.3	$283.4	$66.2	$160.6
2007	1,914.1	286.1	1,456.5	674.1	409.5	301.7	71.1	171.6
2008	2,010.4	293.0	1,546.5	707.4	443.2	318.2	77.7	170.9
2009	2,111.6	293.3	1,641.2	737.7	471.9	346.8	84.8	177.0
2010	2,190.0	299.4	1,705.3	757.5	491.2	366.2	90.4	185.3
2011	2,279.3	307.7	1,779.1	786.1	521.6	374.5	97.0	192.5
Projected								
2012	2,365.8	320.2	1,843.0	813.9	543.8	382.1	103.3	202.6
2013	2,452.3	329.0	1,910.9	835.7	566.5	399.1	109.6	212.5
2014	2,594.0	324.1	2,053.3	899.5	592.8	445.1	115.9	216.6
2015	2,743.2	333.7	2,182.0	952.8	624.8	480.7	123.6	227.6
2016	2,902.3	342.3	2,320.9	1,005.0	668.2	516.0	131.8	239.0
2017	3,075.2	356.3	2,463.3	1,058.0	718.0	549.1	138.1	255.7
2018	3,271.8	371.2	2,626.5	1,125.8	775.2	583.9	141.7	274.0
2019	3,484.7	390.0	2,803.7	1,201.1	829.2	623.3	150.1	291.0
2020	3,717.8	411.7	2,998.4	1,276.7	893.6	666.5	161.7	307.7
2021	3,960.2	434.5	3,200.8	1,355.7	962.4	710.4	172.3	324.9
2022	4,224.3	458.1	3,424.4	1,434.4	1,049.5	756.9	183.5	341.8
Historical estimates				Per capita amount				
2006	$6,051	$911	d	d	d	d	d	d
2007	6,360	950	d	d	d	d	d	d
2008	6,618	964	d	d	d	d	d	d
2009	6,891	957	d	d	d	d	d	d
2010	7,090	969	d	d	d	d	d	d
2011	7,326	989	d	d	d	d	d	d
Projected								
2012	7,543	1,021	d	d	d	d	d	d
2013	7,754	1,040	d	d	d	d	d	d
2014	8,132	1,016	d	d	d	d	d	d
2015	8,525	1,037	d	d	d	d	d	d
2016	8,939	1,054	d	d	d	d	d	d
2017	9,389	1,088	d	d	d	d	d	d
2018	9,903	1,124	d	d	d	d	d	d
2019	10,458	1,170	d	d	d	d	d	d
2020	11,064	1,225	d	d	d	d	d	d
2021	11,688	1,282	d	d	d	d	d	d
2022	12,367	1,341	d	d	d	d	d	d
Historical estimates				Percent distribution				
2006	100.0	15.1	76.0	35.5	21.2	15.7	3.7	8.9
2007	100.0	14.9	76.1	35.2	21.4	15.8	3.7	9.0
2008	100.0	14.6	76.9	35.2	22.0	15.8	3.9	8.5
2009	100.0	13.9	77.7	34.9	22.3	16.4	4.0	8.4
2010	100.0	13.7	77.9	34.6	22.4	16.7	4.1	8.5
2011	100.0	13.5	78.1	34.5	22.9	16.4	4.3	8.4
Projected								
2012	100.0	13.5	77.9	34.4	23.0	16.2	4.4	8.6
2013	100.0	13.4	77.9	34.1	23.1	16.3	4.5	8.7
2014	100.0	12.5	79.2	34.7	22.9	17.2	4.5	8.3
2015	100.0	12.2	79.5	34.7	22.8	17.5	4.5	8.3
2016	100.0	11.8	80.0	34.6	23.0	17.8	4.5	8.2
2017	100.0	11.6	80.1	34.4	23.3	17.9	4.5	8.3
2018	100.0	11.3	80.3	34.4	23.7	17.8	4.3	8.4
2019	100.0	11.2	80.5	34.5	23.8	17.9	4.3	8.3
2020	100.0	11.1	80.6	34.3	24.0	17.9	4.3	8.3
2021	100.0	11.0	80.8	34.2	24.3	17.9	4.4	8.2
2022	100.0	10.8	81.1	34.0	24.8	17.9	4.3	8.1
Historical estimates				Annual percent change from previous year shown				
2006	—	—	—	—	—	—	—	—
2007	6.1	5.3	6.1	5.3	7.1	6.5	7.4	6.8
2008	5.0	2.4	6.2	4.9	8.2	5.5	9.2	−0.4
2009	5.0	0.1	6.1	4.3	6.5	9.0	9.2	3.6
2010	3.7	2.1	3.9	2.7	4.1	5.6	6.6	4.6
2011	4.1	2.8	4.3	3.8	6.2	2.3	7.3	3.9

TABLE 5.7

Personal health expenditures, by source of funds, 2006–22 [CONTINUED]

Year	Total	Out-of-pocket payments	Health insurance[a]					Other third party payers[c]
			Total	Private health insurance	Medicare	Medicaid	Other health insurance programs[b]	
Projected			Annual percent change from previous year shown					
2012	3.8	4.1	3.6	3.5	4.3	2.0	6.5	5.2
2013	3.7	2.7	3.7	2.7	4.2	4.4	6.2	4.9
2014	5.8	−1.5	7.5	7.6	4.7	11.5	5.7	1.9
2015	5.8	3.0	6.3	5.9	5.4	8.0	6.6	5.1
2016	5.8	2.6	6.4	5.5	6.9	7.3	6.6	5.0
2017	6.0	4.1	6.1	5.3	7.5	6.4	4.8	6.9
2018	6.4	4.2	6.6	6.4	8.0	6.3	2.6	7.2
2019	6.5	5.1	6.7	6.7	7.0	6.8	5.9	6.2
2020	6.7	5.6	6.9	6.3	7.8	6.9	7.7	5.8
2021	6.5	5.5	6.7	6.2	7.7	6.6	6.6	5.6
2022	6.7	5.4	7.0	5.8	9.1	6.5	6.5	5.2

[a]Includes private health insurance (employer sponsored insurance and other private insurance, which includes marketplace plans), Medicare, Medicaid, Children's Health Insurance Program (Titles XIX and XXI), Department of Defense, and Department of Veterans' Affairs.
[b]Children's Health Insurance Program (Titles XIX and XXI), Department of Defense, and Department of Veterans' Affairs.
[c]Includes worksite health care, other private revenues, Indian Health Service, workers' compensation, general assistance, maternal and child health, vocational rehabilitation, other federal programs, Substance Abuse and Mental Health Services Administration, other state and local programs, and school health.
[d]Calculation of per capita estimates is not applicable.
Notes: Projections include effects of the Affordable Care Act and an alternative to the sustainable growth rate.
Per capita amounts based on July 1 Census resident based population estimates. Numbers and percents may not add to totals because of rounding.

SOURCE: "Table 6. Personal Health Care Expenditures; Aggregate and per Capita Amounts, Percent Distribution and Annual Percent Change by Source of Funds: Calendar Years 2006–2022," in *National Health Expenditures Projections 2012–2022*, U.S. Department of Health and Human Services, Centers for Medicare and Medicaid Services, 2013, http://www.cms.gov/Research-Statistics-Data-and-Systems/Statistics-Trends-and-Reports/NationalHealthExpendData/downloads/proj2012.pdf (accessed May 16, 2014)

the coverage gap began after an individual had $2,960 in total drug costs and continued until out-of-pocket drug costs totaled $4,700. These discounts will continue growing until 2020, when the ACA's provisions are fully implemented, and the beneficiary coinsurance rate will drop to 25%. The ACA also reduces the out-of-pocket spending required for enrollees' eligibility for catastrophic coverage, which further reduces out-of-pocket costs for people with high prescription drug expenses.

HEALTH CARE FOR OLDER ADULTS, PEOPLE WITH DISABILITIES, AND THE POOR

Despite passage of the groundbreaking ACA, which expands health care coverage, the United States remains one of the few industrialized nations that does not have a government-funded national health care program that provides coverage for all of its citizens. Government-funded health care exists, and it forms a major part of the health care system, but it is available only to specific segments of the U.S. population. In other developed countries government-funded national medical care programs cover almost all their citizens' health-related costs, from maternity care to long-term care.

In the United States the major government health care entitlement programs are Medicare and Medicaid. They provide financial assistance for people aged 65 years and older, the poor, and people with disabilities. Before the existence of these programs, many older

Americans could not afford adequate medical care. For older adults who are beneficiaries, the Medicare program provides reimbursement for hospital and physician care, whereas Medicaid pays for the cost of nursing home care.

Medicare

The Medicare program, which was enacted under Title XVIII (Health Insurance for the Aged) of the Social Security Act, was approved in 1965. The program consists of four parts:

- Part A provides hospital insurance. Coverage includes physicians' fees, nursing services, meals, semiprivate rooms, special-care units, operating room costs, laboratory tests, and some drugs and supplies. Part A also covers rehabilitation services, limited posthospital care in a skilled nursing facility, home health care, and hospice care for the terminally ill.

- Part B (Supplemental Medical Insurance [SMI]) is elective medical insurance; that is, enrollees must pay premiums to obtain coverage. SMI covers outpatient physicians' services, diagnostic tests, outpatient hospital services, outpatient physical therapy, speech pathology services, home health services, and medical equipment and supplies.

- Part C is the Medicare+Choice program, which was established by the Balanced Budget Act of 1997 to expand beneficiaries' options and allow them to participate in private-sector health plans.

FIGURE 5.1

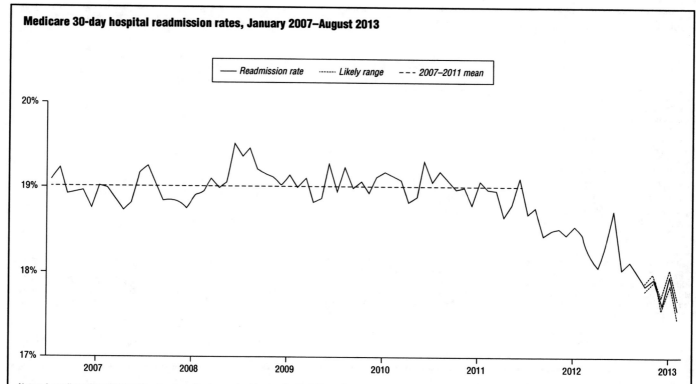

Medicare 30-day hospital readmission rates, January 2007–August 2013

— Readmission rate ⋯⋯ Likely range - - - 2007–2011 mean

Notes: A small number of claims for recent months have not yet been submitted. The estimates reported for recent months reflect the output of a CMS statistical model that accounts for this incomplete reporting. The dotted blue lines depict the range in which the final estimates are likely to fall once complete data are available, based on the output of the statistical model.
CMS = Centers for Medicare & Medicaid Services.

SOURCE: "Figure 4. Monthly Medicare 30-Day, All-Condition Hospital Readmission Rate, January 2007–August 2013," in *Trends in Health Care Cost Growth and the Role of the Affordable Care Act*, Office of the President of the United States, November 2013, http://www.whitehouse.gov/sites/default/files/docs/healthcostreport_final_noembargo_v2.pdf (accessed May 16, 2014)

- Part D is also elective and provides voluntary, subsidized access to prescription drug insurance coverage, for a premium, to individuals who are entitled to Part A or who are enrolled in Part B. Part D also has provisions (premium and cost-sharing subsidies) for low-income enrollees. Part D coverage began in 2006 and includes most prescription drugs approved by the U.S. Food and Drug Administration (FDA).

In general, Medicare reimburses physicians on a fee-for-service basis (payment for each visit, procedure, or treatment that is delivered), as opposed to per capita or per member per month. In response to the increasing administrative burden of paperwork, reduced compensation, and delays in reimbursements, some physicians opt out of Medicare participation. They do not provide services under the Medicare program and choose not to accept Medicare patients into their practice. Others still provide services to Medicare beneficiaries but do not "accept assignment," meaning that patients must pay out of pocket for services and then seek reimbursement from Medicare.

Because of these problems, the Tax Equity and Fiscal Responsibility Act of 1982 authorized a risk managed

care option for Medicare, based on agreed-on prepayments. Beginning in 1985 the Health Care Financing Administration (now known as the CMS) could contract to pay health care providers, such as health maintenance organizations (HMOs) or health care prepayment plans, to serve Medicare and Medicaid patients. These groups are paid a predetermined cost per patient for their services.

Medicare-Risk HMOs Control Costs, but Some Senior Health Plans Do Not Survive

During the 1980s and 1990s the federal government, employers that provided health coverage for retiring employees, and many states sought to control costs by encouraging Medicare and Medicaid beneficiaries to enroll in HMOs. The federal government paid the health plans that operated them fixed fees—a predetermined dollar amount per member per month (PMPM). For these fixed fees, Medicare recipients received a comprehensive, preset array of benefits. PMPM payment provided financial incentives for Medicare-risk HMO physicians to control costs, unlike physicians who were reimbursed on a fee-for-service basis.

TABLE 5.8

Effects of the insurance coverage provisions of the Affordable Care Act (ACA) on the federal deficit, 2014–23

	Effects on the cumulative federal deficit, 2014 to 2023[a] (billions of dollars)		
	May 2013 baseline	February 2014 baseline	Difference
Exchange subsidies and related spending[b]	1,075	1,058	−16
Medicaid and CHIP outlays	710	708	−2
Small-employer tax credits[c]	14	14	*
Gross cost of coverage provisions	1,798	1,780	−18
Penalty payments by uninsured people	−45	−45	*
Penalty payments by employers[c]	−140	−130	10
Excise tax on high-premium insurance plans[c]	−80	−80	0
Other effects on revenues and outlays[d]	−171	−171	−1
Net cost of coverage provisions	**1,363**	**1,354**	**−9**
Memorandum:			
Net collections and payments for risk adjustment, reinsurance, and risk corridors[i]	0	−8	−8

Note: CHIP = Children's Health Insurance Program.
*Between −$500 million and $500 million.
[a]Positive numbers indicate an increase in the deficit; negative numbers indicate a decrease in the deficit. They also exclude effects on the deficit of other provisions of the Affordable Care Act that are not related to insurance coverage. They also exclude federal administrative costs subject to appropriation.
[b]Includes spending for exchange grants to states and net collections and payments for risk adjustment, reinsurance, and risk corridors. Congressional Budget Office's (CBO) May 2013 baseline also included an estimated $1 billion in spending for high-risk pools, premium review activities, and loans to consumer-operated and -oriented plans over the 2014–2023 period.
[c]These effects on the deficit include the associated effects of changes in taxable compensation on revenues.
[d]Consists mainly of the effects of changes in taxable compensation on revenues.

SOURCE: Adapted from Jessica Banthin and Sarah Masi, "Comparison of CBO's Current and Previous Estimates of the Effects of the Insurance Coverage Provisions of the Affordable Care Act," in *Updated Estimates of the Insurance Coverage Provisions of the Affordable Care Act*, Congressional Budget Office, March 4, 2014, http://www.cbo.gov/publication/45159 (accessed May 19, 2014)

Although Medicare recipients were generally pleased with these HMOs (even when enrolling meant they had to change physicians and thereby end long-standing relationships with their family doctors), many of the health plans did not fare well financially. The health plans suffered for a variety of reasons: some had underestimated the service utilization rates of older adults, and some were unable to provide the stipulated range of services as cost effectively as they had believed possible. Other plans found that the PMPM payment was not sufficient to enable them to cover all the clinical services and their administrative overhead.

By the mid-1990s some Medicare-risk plans faced a challenge that proved daunting. Their enrollees had aged and required even more health care services than they had previously. For example, a senior member who had joined as a healthy 65-year-old could now be a frail 75-year-old with multiple chronic health conditions requiring many costly health services. Although the PMPM had increased over the years, for some plans it was insufficient to cover their costs. Some Medicare-risk plans, especially those operated by smaller health plans, were forced to end their programs abruptly, leaving thousands of older adults scrambling to join other health plans.

The Balanced Budget Act of 1997 produced another plan for Medicare recipients called Medicare+Choice. This plan offers Medicare beneficiaries a wider range of managed care plan options than just HMOs. Older adults may join preferred provider organizations (PPOs) and provider-sponsored organizations that generally offer greater freedom of choice of providers (physicians and hospitals) than what is available through HMO membership. These plans (as well as those formerly called Medicare-risk plans) are known as Medicare Advantage (MA) plans. MA plans include HMOs, PPOs, private fee-for-service plans, and medical savings account plans (which deposit money from Medicare into an account that can be used to pay medical expenses).

Medicare Faces Challenges

For the seventh consecutive year, the Social Security Act requires that the Trustees issue a "Medicare funding warning" because projected non-dedicated sources of revenues—primarily general revenues—are expected to continue to account for more than 45 percent of Medicare's outlays in 2013, a threshold breached for the first time in fiscal year 2010.

—Social Security and Medicare Boards of Trustees, *Status of the Social Security and Medicare Programs* (2013)

The Medicare program's continuing financial viability is in jeopardy. In 1995, for the first time since 1972, the Medicare trust fund lost money, a sign that the financial condition of Medicare was worse than previously assumed. The CMS did not expect a deficit until 1997; however, income to the trust fund, primarily from payroll taxes, was less than expected and spending was higher. The deficit is significant because losses are anticipated to grow from year to year.

TABLE 5.9

Prescription drug expenditures, by source of funds, 2006–22

Year	Total	Out-of-pocket payments	Health insurance[a]					Other third party payers[c]
			Total	Private health insurance	Medicare	Medicaid	Other health insurance programs[b]	
Historical estimates				Amount in billions				
2006	$224.1	$51.1	$168.9	$102.2	$39.6	$18.9	$8.2	$4.1
2007	235.9	51.8	180.2	107.7	46.0	18.1	8.4	3.8
2008	242.6	49.8	189.1	111.2	50.7	18.9	8.3	3.7
2009	254.6	49.6	201.4	118.3	54.6	19.8	8.7	3.6
2010	255.7	46.2	206.0	118.7	58.9	19.6	8.8	3.4
2011	263.0	45.0	214.3	122.2	63.7	19.0	9.4	3.7
Projected								
2012	260.8	42.9	214.3	118.8	66.8	18.7	10.0	3.5
2013	262.3	41.1	217.4	114.2	75.0	17.5	10.6	3.7
2014	275.9	38.0	233.7	119.7	80.6	22.2	11.2	4.2
2015	294.9	38.6	251.8	127.1	86.8	25.7	12.1	4.5
2016	311.6	38.1	268.6	134.4	93.5	27.6	13.0	4.9
2017	330.7	39.2	286.0	143.1	100.2	29.3	13.5	5.5
2018	350.6	39.7	304.9	153.1	107.7	30.6	13.5	6.1
2019	372.7	41.1	325.0	163.3	115.3	32.0	14.2	6.6
2020	397.9	42.9	347.9	173.8	125.1	33.4	15.5	7.1
2021	425.5	45.1	372.8	186.0	135.2	35.0	16.6	7.6
2022	455.0	47.3	399.5	198.8	146.4	36.5	17.8	8.1
Historical estimates				Per capita amount				
2006	$752	$171	d	d	d	d	d	d
2007	784	172	d	d	d	d	d	d
2008	798	164	d	d	d	d	d	d
2009	831	162	d	d	d	d	d	d
2010	828	150	d	d	d	d	d	d
2011	845	145	d	d	d	d	d	d
Projected								
2012	831	137	d	d	d	d	d	d
2013	829	130	d	d	d	d	d	d
2014	865	119	d	d	d	d	d	d
2015	916	120	d	d	d	d	d	d
2016	960	117	d	d	d	d	d	d
2017	1,010	120	d	d	d	d	d	d
2018	1,061	120	d	d	d	d	d	d
2019	1,119	123	d	d	d	d	d	d
2020	1,184	128	d	d	d	d	d	d
2021	1,256	133	d	d	d	d	d	d
2022	1,332	139	d	d	d	d	d	d
Historical estimates				Percent distribution				
2006	100.0	22.8	75.4	45.6	17.7	8.4	3.7	1.8
2007	100.0	22.0	76.4	45.7	19.5	7.7	3.6	1.6
2008	100.0	20.5	78.0	45.8	20.9	7.8	3.4	1.5
2009	100.0	19.5	79.1	46.5	21.4	7.8	3.4	1.4
2010	100.0	18.1	80.6	46.4	23.0	7.7	3.4	1.3
2011	100.0	17.1	81.5	46.5	24.2	7.2	3.6	1.4
Projected								
2012	100.0	16.5	82.2	45.6	25.6	7.2	3.8	1.4
2013	100.0	15.7	82.9	43.6	28.6	6.7	4.1	1.4
2014	100.0	13.8	84.7	43.4	29.2	8.0	4.1	1.5
2015	100.0	13.1	85.4	43.1	29.4	8.7	4.1	1.5
2016	100.0	12.2	86.2	43.1	30.0	8.9	4.2	1.6
2017	100.0	11.9	86.5	43.3	30.3	8.9	4.1	1.7
2018	100.0	11.3	87.0	43.7	30.7	8.7	3.8	1.7
2019	100.0	11.0	87.2	43.8	30.9	8.6	3.8	1.8
2020	100.0	10.8	87.4	43.7	31.4	8.4	3.9	1.8
2021	100.0	10.6	87.6	43.7	31.8	8.2	3.9	1.8
2022	100.0	10.4	87.8	43.7	32.2	8.0	3.9	1.8
Historical estimates				Annual percent change from previous year shown				
2006	—	—	—	—	—	—	—	—
2007	5.2	1.4	6.7	5.5	15.9	−4.2	2.7	−7.1
2008	2.8	−3.9	4.9	3.2	10.2	4.4	−1.2	−3.9
2009	5.0	−0.4	6.5	6.4	7.7	4.8	5.0	−2.2
2010	0.4	−6.8	2.3	0.4	8.0	−1.4	1.0	−4.2
2011	2.9	−2.6	4.0	2.9	8.1	−3.0	6.7	7.7

TABLE 5.9

Prescription drug expenditures, by source of funds, 2006–22 [CONTINUED]

Year	Total	Out-of-pocket payments	Health insurance[a]				Other health insurance programs[b]	Other third party payers[c]
			Total	Private health insurance	Medicare	Medicaid		
Projected			Annual percent change from previous year shown					
2012	−0.8	−4.7	0.0	−2.8	4.9	−1.2	6.2	−4.1
2013	0.6	−4.1	1.4	−3.8	12.3	−6.7	6.7	5.2
2014	5.2	−7.7	7.5	4.7	7.4	27.1	5.5	12.1
2015	6.9	1.6	7.7	6.2	7.7	15.9	8.1	8.0
2016	5.6	−1.3	6.7	5.7	7.7	7.4	7.2	8.0
2017	6.2	3.0	6.5	6.4	7.1	6.0	3.9	11.9
2018	6.0	1.1	6.6	7.0	7.6	4.4	−0.3	11.2
2019	6.3	3.7	6.6	6.7	7.1	4.7	5.7	9.1
2020	6.8	4.4	7.1	6.4	8.5	4.4	9.0	6.4
2021	6.9	4.9	7.2	7.0	8.1	4.5	6.9	7.6
2022	6.9	5.1	7.2	6.9	8.3	4.4	7.2	7.1

[a]Includes private health insurance (employer sponsored insurance and other private insurance, which includes marketplace plans), Medicare, Medicaid, Children's Health Insurance Program (Titles XIX and XXI), Department of Defense, and Department of Veterans' Affairs.
[b]Children's Health Insurance Program (Titles XIX and XXI), Department of Defense, and Department of Veterans' Affairs.
[c]Includes worksite health care, other private revenues, Indian Health Service, workers' compensation, general assistance, maternal and child health, vocational rehabilitation, other federal programs, Substance Abuse and Mental Health Services Administration, other state and local programs, and school health.
[d]Calculation of per capita estimates is not applicable.
Notes: Projections include effects of the Affordable Care Act and an alternative to the sustainable growth rate.
Per capita amounts based on July 1 Census resident based population estimates. Numbers and percents may not add to totals because of rounding.

SOURCE: "Table 11. Prescription Drug Expenditures; Aggregate and per Capita Amounts, Percent Distribution and Annual Percent Change by Source of Funds: Calendar Years 2006–2022," in *National Health Expenditures Projections 2012–2022*, U.S. Department of Health and Human Services, Centers for Medicare and Medicaid Services, 2013, http://www.cms.gov/Research-Statistics-Data-and-Systems/Statistics-Trends-and-Reports/NationalHealthExpendData/downloads/proj2012.pdf (accessed May 19, 2014)

A NATIONAL BIPARTISAN COMMISSION CONSIDERS THE FUTURE OF MEDICARE. The National Bipartisan Commission on the Future of Medicare was created by Congress in the Balanced Budget Act of 1997. The commission was charged with examining the Medicare program and drafting recommendations to avert a future financial crisis and reinforce the program in anticipation of the retirement of the baby boomers (the large generation of people born between 1946 and 1964 who would begin reaching retirement age in 2011).

The commission observed that much like Social Security, Medicare would suffer because there would be fewer workers per retiree to fund it. Furthermore, it predicted that beneficiaries' out-of-pocket costs would rise and forecast soaring Medicare enrollment.

When the commission disbanded in March 1999, it was unable to forward an official recommendation to Congress because its plan fell one vote short of the required majority needed to authorize an official recommendation. The plan would have changed Medicare into a premium system, where instead of Medicare directly covering beneficiaries, the beneficiaries would be given a fixed amount of money to purchase private health insurance. The plan would have also raised the age of eligibility from 65 to 67 (as had already been done with Social Security in 1983) and provided prescription drug coverage for low-income beneficiaries, much like the Medicare Prescription Drug, Improvement, and Modernization Act of 2003.

In February 2010 President Barack Obama (1961–) established the National Commission on Fiscal Responsibility and Reform to suggest strategies to reduce the federal budget deficit. Among the commission's tasks was to recommend ways to slow the growth in entitlement program spending. The 18-member commission issued its final report in January 2011, which contained a variety of controversial recommendations that were designed to balance the budget by 2015 such as a $200 billion reduction in discretionary spending achieved by reducing defense spending, decreasing the federal workforce by 10%, increasing the payroll tax, and raising the retirement age to 69.

The report was criticized by Republicans and Democrats alike. Republicans were displeased with the increased taxes, and Democrats decried the recommendations that might reduce retiree benefits. President Obama indicated his support for the commission's work but chose not to endorse its recommendations.

MEDICARE PRESCRIPTION DRUG, IMPROVEMENT, AND MODERNIZATION ACT AIMS TO REFORM MEDICARE. The Medicare Prescription Drug, Improvement, and Modernization Act of 2003 was a measure intended to introduce private-sector enterprise into a Medicare model in urgent need of reform.

Beginning 2004, Medicare beneficiaries saved 10% to 25% off the cost of most medicines by using a Medicare-approved drug discount card. In 2006, by joining a Medicare-approved plan, beneficiaries were able to reduce their prescription drug costs by at least 50%, in exchange for a monthly premium of about $35. Older adults with low incomes received additional assistance to help pay for their prescription drugs.

The act expanded coverage of preventive medical services, with new beneficiaries receiving a free physical examination along with laboratory tests to screen for heart disease and diabetes. The act also provides employers with subsidies and tax breaks to help offset the costs associated with maintaining retiree health benefits.

IMPACT OF THE ACA ON MEDICARE. In "Six Economic Benefits of the Affordable Care Act" (White House Council of Economic Advisers, February 6, 2014, http://www.whitehouse.gov/blog/2014/02/06/six-economic-benefits-affordable-care-act), Jason Furman observes that the Medicare provisions in the ACA aim to reduce costs by eliminating excessive payments to providers and private insurers and using innovative payment models to incentivize more efficient, quality care.

The CMS explains in "The Affordable Care Act & Medicare" (2014, http://www.medicare.gov/about-us/affordable-care-act/affordable-care-act.html) that the ACA ensures the future of Medicare. The viability of the Medicare Trust fund will be extended to at least 2029, which is 12 years longer than originally forecast, by savings resulting from reductions in Medicare costs as well as in waste, fraud, and abuse.

According to the CMS in "Medicare Premiums: Rules for Higher Income Beneficiaries" (2014, http://www.socialsecurity.gov/pubs/EN-05-10536.pdf), one of the reforms introduced by the act is that older adults with substantial incomes face increasing Part B premium costs. Table 5.10 shows the standard Part B premium of $104.90 per month and monthly premiums for high-income individuals and couples. It also shows the premium amounts (paid in addition to the prescription drug plan premiums) that must be paid to obtain prescription drug coverage.

In "7.9 Million People with Medicare Have Saved over $9.9 Billion on Prescription Drugs" (March 21, 2014, http://www.cms.gov/Newsroom/MediaRelease Database/Press-releases/2014-Press-releases-items/2014-03-21.html), the CMS reported that in the four years since the ACA had been signed into law, 7.9 million Medicare beneficiaries saved $9.9 billion on prescription drugs, an average of $1,265 per beneficiary. In 2013 alone, 4.3 million seniors and people with disabilities saved $3.9 billion, or an average of $911 per beneficiary. Use of preventive services also grew. In 2013 about 37.2 million Medicare beneficiaries obtained at least one preventive service with no cost sharing, up from 34.1 million in 2012.

TABLE 5.10

Monthly Medicare premiums, 2014

Modified adjusted gross income (MAGI)	Part B monthly premium amount	Prescription drug coverage monthly premium amount
Individuals with a MAGI of $85,000 or less	2013 standard premium = $104.90	Your plan premium
Individuals with a MAGI above $85,000 up to $129,000	Standard premium + $167.80	Your plan premium + $50.20
Individuals with a MAGI above $129,000	Standard premium + $230.80	Your plan premium + $69.30

SOURCE: "Monthly Medicare Premiums for 2014," in *Medicare Premiums: Rules For Higher-Income Beneficiaries*, Social Security Administration, 2014, http://www.socialsecurity.gov/pubs/EN-05-10536.pdf (accessed May 19, 2014)

Medicaid

Medicaid was enacted by Congress in 1965 under Title XIX (Grants to States for Medical Assistance Programs) of the Social Security Act. It is a joint federal-state program that provides medical assistance to selected categories of low-income Americans: the aged, people who are blind or disabled, and financially struggling families with dependent children. Medicaid covers hospitalization, physicians' fees, laboratory and radiology fees, and long-term care in nursing homes. It is the largest source of funds for medical and health-related services for the poorest Americans and the second-largest public payer of health care costs, after Medicare.

The Deficit Reduction Act (DRA) was signed into law by President George W. Bush (1946–) in 2006. The act changed many aspects of the Medicaid program. Some of the changes are mandatory provisions that the states must enact, such as proof of citizenship and other criteria that will make it more difficult for people to qualify for or enroll in Medicaid. Other changes are optional; they allow the states to make drastic changes to the Medicaid program through state plan amendments. For example, states can choose to require anyone with a family income more than 150% of the poverty level to pay a premium of as much as 5% of their income. Before the act, the states had to provide a mandatory set of services to Medicaid recipients. As of March 31, 2006, the states could modify their Medicaid benefits such that they were comparable to those offered to federal and state employees, the benefits provided by the HMO with the largest non-Medicaid enrollment, or coverage approved by the U.S. secretary of health and human services.

In 2014 the ACA expanded coverage by establishing national Medicaid eligibility criteria. People with incomes below 133% of the poverty level became eligible for Medicaid coverage. By 2016 the CBO estimates that Medicaid, along with the Children's Health Insurance Program (CHIP), will cover an additional 17 million people, mostly low-income adults, which will significantly reduce the number of uninsured Americans. In "Total Medicaid and CHIP Enrollment, February and March 2014" (May 1, 2014, http://kff.org/health-reform/state-indicator/total-medicaid-and-chip-enrollment-february-and-march-2014), the Kaiser Family Foundation reports that in the 27 states that expanded Medicaid, average monthly enrollment increased 8.3% in March 2014 compared with pre-open enrollment monthly averages. For example, in Oregon, which expanded Medicaid, enrollment grew 43.7% in March 2014 compared with a 5.6% decrease in Wyoming, which did not expand Medicaid.

According to Robert Pear in "Law Lifts Enrollment in Medicaid by Millions" (NYTimes.com, April 4, 2014), by February 2014 Medicaid enrollment had increased by at least 3 million from September 2013, before the federal government's HealthCare.gov insurance marketplace was active. Expanded eligibility includes individuals under age 65 with incomes up to 138% of the federal poverty level (up to $16,100 for an individual and $32,900 for a family of four). Along with Oregon, the states with the largest percentage increases in enrollment were Colorado, Vermont, and West Virginia. The CBO projected that in 2014 an estimated 8 million people gained Medicaid coverage, which would increase federal spending by $19 billion

LONG-TERM HEALTH CARE

One of the most urgent health care problems facing Americans in the 21st century is the growing need for long-term care. Long-term care refers to health and social services for people with chronic illnesses or mental or physical conditions so disabling that they cannot live independently without assistance; they require care daily. Longer life spans and improved life-sustaining technologies are increasing the likelihood that more people than ever before may eventually require costly long-term care.

Limited and Expensive Options

Caring for chronically ill or elderly patients presents difficult and expensive choices for Americans: they must either provide long-term care at home or rely on a nursing home. Home health care was the fastest-growing segment of the health care industry during the first half of the 1990s. Although the rate of growth slowed during the late 1990s, the CMS projects that the home health care sector will more than double, from $77.9 billion in 2012 to $157.2 billion in 2022. (See Table 5.5.)

High Cost of Long-Term Care

The options for quality, affordable long-term care in the United States are limited but improving. The National Health Policy Forum estimates in "The Basics: National Spending for Long-Term Services and Supports (LTSS), 2012" (March 27, 2014, http://www.nhpf.org/library/the-basics/Basics_LTSS_03-27-14.pdf) that nursing home costs average more than $80,000 per year, depending on services and location. According to the Genworth 2014 Cost of Care Survey (March 2014, https://www.gen worth.com/dam/Americas/US/PDFs/Consumer/corporate/130568_032514_CostofCare_FINAL_nonsecure.pdf), in 2011 nursing home care cost an average of $240 per day for a private room, or $85,440 per year. Many nursing home residents rely on Medicaid to pay these fees. In 2014 Medicaid covered an estimated 48.8% of nursing home costs for older Americans. (See Table 5.11.) The most common sources of payment at admission were Medicare (which pays only for short-term stays after hospitalization), private insurance, and other private funds. The primary source of payment changes as a stay lengthens. After their funds are exhausted, nursing home residents on Medicare shift to Medicaid.

To be eligible for long-term-care coverage by Medicaid, an individual must have an income that is less than the cost of care in the facility at the Medicaid rate and must meet income and resource limits. Many older adults must "spend down" to deplete their life savings to qualify for Medicaid assistance. This term refers to a provision in Medicaid coverage that provides care for seniors whose income exceeds eligibility requirements. For example, if their monthly income is $100 over the state Medicaid eligibility line, they can spend $100 per month on their medical care, and Medicaid will cover the remainder.

Nursing home care may seem cost-prohibitive, but even an unskilled caregiver who makes home visits earned about $19 per hour in 2014; skilled care costs much more, and most older adults cannot afford this expense. The Genworth 2014 Cost of Care Survey reports that in 2014 the average hourly rates were $19 for homemaker services ("hands off" care that is limited to household chores rather than patient care) and $20 for home health aide services ("hands on" care that is personal, such as bathing or grooming, but not medical).

It should be noted that lifetime savings may be exhausted long before the need for care ends. The National Health Policy Forum estimates in "The Basics: National Spending for Long-Term Services and Supports (LTSS), 2012" that the total expenditure for long-term-care services in 2012 (excluding the value of donated care from relatives and friends) was $219.9 billion, an amount equal to 9.3% of total U.S. personal health care spending that year.

In The Next Four Decades: The Older Population in the United States, 2010 to 2050 (May 2010, http://www.census.gov/prod/2010pubs/p25-1138.pdf), Grayson K. Vincent and Victoria A. Velkoff of the U.S. Census

TABLE 5.11

Nursing home and continuing care expenditures, by source of funds, 2006–22

Year	Total	Out-of-pocket payments	Health insurance[a]					Other third party payers[c]
			Total	Private health insurance	Medicare	Medicaid	Other health insurance programs[b]	
Historical estimates					Amount in billions			
2006	$117.3	$33.9	$75.8	$9.4	$22.4	$41.3	$2.8	$7.6
2007	126.4	37.1	80.3	10.2	24.9	42.1	3.2	8.9
2008	132.6	38.5	85.9	10.8	27.7	43.8	3.6	8.2
2009	138.5	39.4	90.7	11.7	30.1	45.0	3.9	8.5
2010	143.0	40.0	94.0	12.2	32.3	45.5	4.0	9.0
2011	149.3	39.9	100.4	12.4	37.6	46.1	4.3	9.0
Projected								
2012	151.2	42.4	99.4	13.2	36.0	45.6	4.6	9.5
2013	156.8	44.0	102.9	13.8	37.6	46.8	4.9	9.9
2014	164.0	45.6	108.2	14.3	40.0	48.8	5.1	10.2
2015	172.2	47.1	114.5	14.8	43.1	51.2	5.4	10.6
2016	182.0	48.9	122.1	15.3	47.0	54.0	5.7	11.0
2017	193.2	50.8	130.9	15.9	51.6	57.4	6.1	11.5
2018	205.4	52.9	140.5	16.5	56.2	61.4	6.5	12.0
2019	218.1	55.3	150.4	17.2	60.7	65.6	6.9	12.5
2020	231.9	57.8	161.1	17.9	65.6	70.2	7.3	13.0
2021	246.8	60.5	172.7	18.7	71.1	75.2	7.8	13.6
2022	264.2	63.4	186.6	19.5	78.1	80.6	8.3	14.2
Historical estimates					Per capita amount			
2006	$393	$114	d	d	d	d	d	d
2007	420	123	d	d	d	d	d	d
2008	436	127	d	d	d	d	d	d
2009	452	128	d	d	d	d	d	d
2010	463	130	d	d	d	d	d	d
2011	480	128	d	d	d	d	d	d
Projected								
2012	482	135	d	d	d	d	d	d
2013	496	139	d	d	d	d	d	d
2014	514	143	d	d	d	d	d	d
2015	535	146	d	d	d	d	d	d
2016	561	151	d	d	d	d	d	d
2017	590	155	d	d	d	d	d	d
2018	622	160	d	d	d	d	d	d
2019	655	166	d	d	d	d	d	d
2020	690	172	d	d	d	d	d	d
2021	728	179	d	d	d	d	d	d
2022	773	186	d	d	d	d	d	d
Historical estimates					Percent distribution			
2006	100.0	28.9	64.7	8.0	19.1	35.2	2.4	6.4
2007	100.0	29.4	63.5	8.0	19.7	33.3	2.6	7.1
2008	100.0	29.1	64.8	8.2	20.9	33.0	2.7	6.2
2009	100.0	28.4	65.4	8.4	21.7	32.5	2.8	6.1
2010	100.0	28.0	65.7	8.6	22.6	31.8	2.8	6.3
2011	100.0	26.7	67.2	8.3	25.2	30.9	2.9	6.1
Projected								
2012	100.0	28.0	65.7	8.7	23.8	30.1	3.0	6.3
2013	100.0	28.1	65.6	8.8	24.0	29.8	3.1	6.3
2014	100.0	27.8	66.0	8.7	24.4	29.8	3.1	6.2
2015	100.0	27.4	66.5	8.6	25.0	29.7	3.2	6.2
2016	100.0	26.9	67.1	8.4	25.8	29.7	3.2	6.1
2017	100.0	26.3	67.8	8.2	26.7	29.7	3.2	5.9
2018	100.0	25.8	68.4	8.0	27.3	29.9	3.1	5.8
2019	100.0	25.3	68.9	7.9	27.8	30.1	3.2	5.7
2020	100.0	24.9	69.5	7.7	28.3	30.3	3.2	5.6
2021	100.0	24.5	70.0	7.6	28.8	30.5	3.2	5.5
2022	100.0	24.0	70.6	7.4	29.6	30.5	3.2	5.4
Historical estimates					Annual percent change from previous year shown			
2006	—	—	—	—	—	—	—	—
2007	7.8	9.6	5.9	8.4	11.2	1.9	14.9	18.1
2008	4.9	3.7	6.9	6.7	11.2	4.1	11.1	−8.5
2009	4.5	2.2	5.6	7.7	8.8	2.8	8.4	4.3
2010	3.2	1.7	3.7	4.9	7.2	1.0	3.5	5.6
2011	4.4	−0.3	6.8	1.5	16.5	1.4	6.4	0.5

TABLE 5.11

Nursing home and continuing care expenditures, by source of funds, 2006–22 [CONTINUED]

Year	Total	Out-of-pocket payments	Health insurance[a]				Other health insurance programs[b]	Other third party payers[c]
			Total	Private health insurance	Medicare	Medicaid		
Projected			Annual percent change from previous year shown					
2012	1.3	6.2	−1.0	6.2	−4.1	−1.2	6.7	5.0
2013	3.7	3.9	3.6	4.3	4.2	2.6	6.4	4.1
2014	4.6	3.5	5.1	3.7	6.4	4.5	5.6	3.8
2015	5.0	3.4	5.8	3.6	7.8	4.8	5.5	3.8
2016	5.7	3.7	6.7	3.6	9.2	5.5	5.6	3.8
2017	6.2	4.0	7.3	3.7	9.7	6.3	6.1	4.0
2018	6.3	4.2	7.3	3.9	9.0	6.9	6.3	4.1
2019	6.2	4.4	7.0	4.2	8.0	6.9	6.2	4.3
2020	6.3	4.6	7.1	4.2	8.1	7.0	6.5	4.3
2021	6.4	4.6	7.3	4.3	8.3	7.1	6.9	4.3
2022	7.0	4.8	8.0	4.5	9.9	7.3	6.6	4.4

[a]Includes private health insurance (employer sponsored insurance and other private insurance, which includes marketplace plans), Medicare, Medicaid, Children's Health Insurance Program (Titles XIX and XXI), Department of Defense, and Department of Veterans' Affairs.
[b]Children's Health Insurance Program (Titles XIX and XXI), Department of Defense, and Department of Veterans' Affairs.
[c]Includes worksite health care, other private revenues, Indian Health Service, workers' compensation, general assistance, maternal and child health, vocational rehabilitation, other federal programs, Substance Abuse and Mental Health Services Administration, other state and local programs, and school health.
[d]Calculation of per capita estimates is not applicable.
Notes: Projections include effects of the Affordable Care Act and an alternative to the sustainable growth rate.
Per capita amounts based on July 1 Census resident based population estimates. Numbers and percents may not add to totals because of rounding.

SOURCE: "Table 13. Nursing Care Facilities and Continuing Care Retirement Communities; Aggregate and per Capita Amounts, Percent Distribution and Annual Percent Change by Source of Funds: Calendar Years 2006–2022," in *National Health Expenditures Projections 2012–2022*, U.S. Department of Health and Human Services, Centers for Medicare and Medicaid Services, 2013, http://www.cms.gov/Research-Statistics-Data-and-Systems/Statistics-Trends-and-Reports/NationalHealthExpendData/downloads/proj2012.pdf (accessed May 19, 2014)

Bureau project that the population over the age of 85 years (those most likely to require long-term care) will nearly quadruple by 2050. Although disability rates among older adults have declined in recent years, reducing somewhat the need for long-term care, the CBO anticipates that the growing population of people likely to require long-term care will no doubt increase spending commensurate with this growth.

MENTAL HEALTH SPENDING

In *Projections of National Expenditures for Mental Health Services and Substance Abuse Treatment, 2004–2014* (2008, http://www.samhsa.gov), a study funded by the Substance Abuse and Mental Health Services Administration (SAMHSA), Katharine R. Levit et al. predicted that spending for mental health and substance abuse (alcohol and chemical dependency) treatment in the United States would reach $239 billion in 2014, up from $121 billion in 2003, representing 6.9% of all health care spending. Mental health and substance abuse spending was projected to increase fourfold between 1986 and 2014, less than the sixfold increase that was forecast for total health care spending. This is in part because mental health treatment does not involve the costly technology that drives overall health care costs. Figure 5.2 shows how mental health and substance abuse spending accounted for a smaller share of total health care spending by 2014.

Health care industry observers attribute the decrease in mental health inpatient services to the increased emphasis on drug treatment of mental health disorders, the increasing frequency of outpatient treatment, the closure of psychiatric hospitals, and the cost containment efforts of managed care. Despite the higher spending for psychoactive prescription drugs, some industry observers believe the increased availability of effective drug therapy actually served to contain mental health spending by enabling providers to offer drug therapy instead of more costly inpatient treatment.

In "Seizing Opportunities under the Affordable Care Act for Transforming the Mental and Behavioral Health System" (*Health Affairs*, vol. 31, no. 2, February 2012), David Mechanic of Rutgers University asserts that new forms of reimbursement for mental health services such as fixed payments per client per time period and single payment for a package of services incentivize providers to improve the coordination and continuity of care. For example, the ACA encourages state Medicaid programs to offer health homes for people with mental illness that are supported by matching federal funds for the first two years. Funds may be used to pay a "patient-designated health home provider who provides care management, makes necessary referrals, provides individual and family support, and uses health information technology to monitor and coordinate the various service providers involved."

FIGURE 5.2

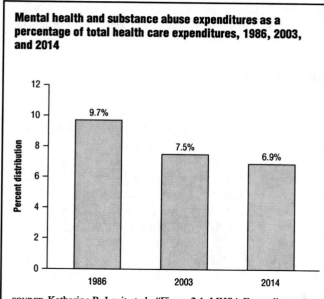

Mental health and substance abuse expenditures as a percentage of total health care expenditures, 1986, 2003, and 2014

SOURCE: Katharine R. Levit et al., "Figure 2.1. MHSA Expenditures As a Percent of Total Health Care Expenditures: 1986, 2003, and 2014," in *Projections of National Expenditures for Mental Health and Substance Abuse Treatment 2004–2014*, Substance Abuse and Mental Health Services Administration, 2008, http://store.samhsa.gov/shin/content/SMA08-4326/SMA08-4326.pdf (accessed May 19, 2014)

SAMHSA Spending

According to the U.S. Department of Health and Human Services (HHS), in *HHS Budget in Brief, Fiscal Year 2015* (2014, http://www.hhs.gov/budget/fy2015-hhs-budget-in-brief/hhs-fy2015budget-in-brief-samhsa.html), the fiscal year (FY) 2015 budget for SAMHSA was $3.6 billion, $63 million less than the FY 2014 budget. The funds were used to continue to improve access to mental health services, to prevent suicide and substance abuse and promote mental health, to integrate primary care and addiction services, and to address prescription drug abuse.

State Mental Health Agency Expenditures

A number of court rulings during the 1970s and an evolution in professional thinking prompted the release of many people with serious mental illness from institutions to community treatment programs. The census (the number of patients or occupants, which is frequently referred to as a rate) of public mental hospitals sharply declined, and increasing pressure was put on the states to deliver community-based treatment.

State mental health agencies (SMHAs) operate the public mental health system that acts as a safety net for poor, uninsured, and otherwise indigent people suffering from mental illness. In *Mental Health Financing in the United States: A Primer* (April 2011, http://www.kff.org/medicaid/upload/8182.pdf), the Kaiser Commission on Medicaid and the Uninsured explains that these public mental health systems are heavily dependent on Medicaid and "in many states, the two are jointly budgeted, with states attributing their matching funds for Medicaid to the budget of state mental health agencies." The SMHAs vary from state to state. Some state agencies purchase, regulate, administer, manage, and provide care and treatment, whereas others simply purchase care using public funds that include general state revenues and federal funds. Medicaid is also the fastest-growing component of SMHA spending; however, the share of Medicaid mental health spending that is controlled by the SMHAs varies widely by state.

Increased Medicaid financing of the SMHAs has had several beneficial effects on state systems. For example, it increased the amount of funds that are available for mental health services, catalyzed the shift to community-based treatment over institutional care, and improved access to insurance coverage and treatment for low-income people with mental health needs. Similar to the movement of privately insured people into managed care, during the 1990s state Medicaid programs turned to managed care organizations (MCOs) and behavioral health services in an effort to contain costs.

The SMHAs manage funds from the SAMHSA Mental Health Block Grant program. The program was created in 1982, and its flexible funding enables states to innovate, develop, and expand successful community-based programs. Block grants (lump sums of money) are awarded based on a formula that considers each state's population, service costs, income, and taxable resources, and the funds enable the states to finance community mental health treatment programs.

In "Strategies to Enroll Uninsured People with Mental Health Conditions under the Affordable Care Act" (National Association of State Mental Health Program Directors, January 2014, http://www.nasmhpd.org/docs/Policy/NASMHPDEnrollment%20Issue%20Paper%20__January%202014.pdf), Joel E. Miller and Robert W. Glover explain that special strategies are necessary to reach individuals with mental illness and substance use disorders who are newly eligible for coverage under the ACA. For example, Miller and Glover note that reaching homeless people with mental illness may be challenging and may require multiple contacts before they are willing to learn about and enroll in coverage. Miller and Glover identify other populations that may require special outreach efforts in order to obtain coverage and receive care, including incarcerated individuals who will need coverage after their release, uninsured veterans, and minority populations.

HIGH COSTS OF RESEARCH

Medical and pharmaceutical research, disease prevention research, and the work to develop and conduct clinical trials of new drugs are expensive. The National

Institutes of Health (NIH) reports in "Estimates of Funding for Various Research, Condition, and Disease Categories" (March 7, 2014, http://report.nih.gov/categorical _spending.aspx) that its FY 2015 budget allocated an estimated $3 billion for human immunodeficiency virus (HIV) and acquired immunodeficiency syndrome (AIDS) research, compared with $834 million to investigate obesity prevention and treatment. Pharmaceutical manufacturers also spend billions of dollars every year researching and developing new medicines. For example, according to the Pharmaceutical Research and Manufacturers of America (PhRMA; 2012 http://www.phrma.org/ about/phrma), U.S. pharmaceutical companies spent $49.5 billion in 2011. By contrast, the entire NIH FY 2011 budget was $30.7 billion.

Decisions about how much is spent to research a particular disease are not based solely on how many people develop the disease or die from it. Rightly or wrongly, economists base the societal value of an individual on his or her earning potential and productivity (the ability to contribute to society as a worker). The bulk of the people who die from heart disease, stroke, and cancer are older adults. Many have retired from the workforce, and their potential economic productivity is usually low or nonexistent. (This is not an observation about how society values older adults; instead, it is simply an economic measure of present and future financial productivity.)

In contrast, AIDS patients are often much younger and die in their 20s, 30s, and 40s. Until they develop AIDS, their potential productivity, measured in economic terms, is high. The number of work years lost when they die is considerable. Using this economic equation to determine how disease research should be funded, it may be considered economically wise to invest more money to research AIDS because the losses, which are measured in potential work years rather than in lives, are so much greater.

Once a new drug receives FDA approval, its manufacturer is ordinarily allowed to hold the patent on the drug to recoup its investment. During the life of the patent the drug is priced much higher than if other manufacturers were allowed to compete by producing generic versions of the same drug. After the patent expires, competition between pharmaceutical manufacturers generally lowers the price. For example, HIV/AIDS drugs are granted only seven years of exclusivity under legislation to encourage research and promote development of new treatments.

In *PhRMA 2014 Profile* (2014, http://www.phrma .org/sites/default/files/pdf/2014_PhRMA_PROFILE.pdf), PhRMA explains that the pharmaceutical manufacturer must cover the cost not only of research and development for the approximately three out of 10 drugs that

succeed but also for many that fail. PhRMA observes that manufacturers spend more than $1.2 billion to bring brand-name drugs to market, including the expense of 10 to 15 years of product development.

High Cost of Prescription Drugs

Spending for prescription drugs is the fastest-growing component of health care spending. In 2014 prescription drug expenditures reached $275.9 billion and were projected to rise to $455 billion by 2021. (See Table 5.9.) "Drug Prices Soar for Top-Selling Brands" (Bloomberg .com, May 1, 2014) shows that the cost of 74 top selling brand-name prescription drugs for diseases such as arthritis, cancer, diabetes and multiple sclerosis increased at least 75% between 2007 and 2014. For example, costs for the arthritis drug Celebrex increased 92% during this period, costs for the allergy drug Nasonex increased 98%, and costs for the cholesterol-lowering drug Crestor rose 103%.

To control prescription drug expenditures, many hospitals, health plans, employers, and other group purchasers have attempted to obtain discounts and rebates for bulk purchases from pharmaceutical companies. Some have developed programs to encourage health care practitioners and consumers to use less-expensive generic drugs, and others have limited, reduced, or even eliminated prescription drug coverage.

In "What the Affordable Care Act Means for Prescription Coverage" (WashingtonPost.com, March 17, 2014), CVS Caremark reports that in the four years since it was enacted, the ACA had already provided much-needed relief from prescription drug costs for more than 7.3 million Medicare beneficiaries, saving them a total of $8.9 billion.

Generic Drugs Promise Cost Savings

When patents expire on popular brand-name drugs, the entry of generic versions of these drugs to the market promises cost savings for consumers and payers. Generic drugs usually cost 10% to 30% less when they first enter the market and even less once additional generic manufacturers join in the competition. According to Pharmacy Purchasing & Products in "Major Patent Expirations for 2010–2015" (*Generic Drug Supplement*, vol. 6, no. 9, September 2009), among the drugs with patents that were set to expire in 2015 were Neulasta (to treat rheumatoid arthritis and psoriasis), Lantus (to treat diabetes), Clarinex (an antihistamine), Miacalcin (to treat osteoporosis), and Zetia (to lower cholesterol). In "Generic Drugs: The Same Medicine for Less Money" (ConsumerReports.org, 2014), Consumer Reports explains that people who pay a flat-fee co-pay can expect to pay $5 to $15 less per prescription when they opt for generic drugs rather than for brand-name drugs, and those who pay a co-pay based on the cost of the drug also save because brand-name drugs cost about three times as much as generic versions.

How Will the ACA Affect Drug Costs?

Because it mandates prescription drugs as one of 10 essential health benefits that insurance plans must offer, the ACA makes drug coverage a core part of coverage, effectively prohibiting insurers from adding on a prescription drug benefit plan to health coverage at an additional cost. In addition, prescription drug costs count toward out-of-pocket caps on medical expenses (about $6,400 for individuals and $12,800 for families).

The ACA also authorizes the FDA to approve generic versions of biologic drugs (drugs derived from living organisms that are used to prevent, diagnose, or treat diseases) and grant biologics manufacturers 12 years of exclusive use before generics can be developed. In "Medicine Use and Shifting Costs of Healthcare" (April 2014, http://www.imshealth.com/deployedfiles/imshealth/Global/Content/Corporate/IMS%20Health%20Institute/Reports/Secure/IIHI_US_Use_of_Meds_for_2013.pdf), the IMS Institute for Healthcare Informatics reports, "Out-of-pocket costs continue to rise for patients, despite generic medicines now representing 86% of prescriptions, and average out-of-pocket costs falling below $10 overall."

The institute attributes ACA provisions for the observation that in 2013 the number of prescriptions with no out-of-pocket costs, such as smoking cessation treatment and oral contraceptives, increased. These "free" prescriptions account for 23% of all prescriptions filled at pharmacies. On the other hand, the institute credits the slower growth in per capita spending in 2013 to the pattern of patent expiries, rather than the ACA and asserts, "The return to nominal spending growth in 2013 is not yet a reflection of the access expansions and insurance reforms from the Affordable Care Act."

RATIONING HEALTH CARE

When health care rationing (allocating medical resources) is defined as "all care that is expected to be beneficial is not always available to all patients," most health care practitioners, policy makers, and consumers accept that rationing has been, and will continue to be, a feature of the U.S. health care system. Most American opinion leaders and industry observers accept that even a country as wealthy as the United States cannot afford all the care that is likely to benefit its citizens. The practical considerations of allocating health care resources involve establishing priorities and determining how these resources should be rationed.

Opponents of Rationing

There is widespread agreement among Americans that rationing according to patients' ability to pay for health care services or insurance is unfair. Ideally, health care should be equitably allocated on the basis of need and the potential benefit derived from the care. Those who argue against rationing fear that society's most vulnerable populations (older adults, the poor, and people with chronic illnesses) suffer most from the rationing of health care.

Many observers believe improving the efficiency of the U.S. health care system will save enough money to supply basic health care services to all Americans. They suggest that because expenditures for the same medical procedures vary greatly in different areas of the country, standardizing fees and costs could realize great savings. They also believe money could be saved if greater emphasis is placed on preventive care and on effective strategies to prevent or reduce behaviors that increase health risk such as smoking, alcohol and drug abuse, and unsafe sexual practices. Furthermore, they insist that the high cost of administering the U.S. health care system could be streamlined with a single payer for health care as in the Canadian system.

Supporters of Rationing

Those who endorse rationing argue that the spiraling cost of the U.S. health care system stems from more than simple inefficiency. They attribute escalating costs to the aging population, rapid technological innovation, and the increasing costs of labor and supplies.

Not everyone who supports rationing thinks the U.S. health care system is working well. Some rationing supporters believe that the nation's health care system charges too much for the services it delivers and that it fails altogether to deliver to the millions of the uninsured. In fact, they point out that the United States already rations health care by not covering the uninsured. Other health care–rationing advocates argue that the problem is one of basic cultural assumptions, not the economics of the health care industry. Americans value human life, believe in the promise of health and quality health care for all, and insist that diseases can be cured. They contend the issue is not whether health care should be rationed but how care is rationed. They believe the United States spends too much on health compared with other societal needs, too much on the old rather than on the young, more on curing and not enough on caring, and too much on extending the length of life and not enough on enhancing the quality of life. Supporters of rationing argue instead for a system that guarantees a minimally acceptable level of health care for all, while reining in the expensive excesses of the current system, which often acts to prolong life at any cost.

The Oregon Health Plan: An Experiment in Rationing

In 1987 Oregon designed a new, universal health care plan that would simultaneously expand coverage and contain costs by limiting services. Unlike other states, which trimmed budgets by eliminating people from Medicaid eligibility, Oregon chose to eliminate low-priority services. Michael Janofsky reports in "Oregon Starts to Extend Health Care" (*New York Times*, February 19, 1994) that the Oregon Health Plan, which was approved in August 1993, aimed to provide Medicaid to 120,000 additional residents living below the federal poverty level. The plan also established a high-risk insurance pool for people who were refused health insurance coverage because of preexisting medical conditions, offered more insurance options for small businesses, and improved employees' abilities to retain their health insurance benefits when they changed jobs. A gradual increase in the state cigarette tax was expected to provide $45 million annually, to help fund the additional estimated $200 million needed over the next several years.

Oregon developed a table of health care services and performed a cost-benefit analysis to rank them. It was decided that Oregon Medicaid would cover the top 565 services on a list of 696 medical procedures. Janofsky notes that services that fell below the cutoff point were "not deemed to be serious enough to require treatment, like common colds, flu, mild food poisoning, sprains, cosmetic procedures and experimental treatments for diseases in advanced stages."

As the Oregon Health Services Commission (HSC) prepared to establish the priorities, it decided that disease prevention and quality of well-being (QWB) were the factors that most influenced the ranking of the treatments. QWB drew fire from those who felt that such judgments could not be decided subjectively. Active medical or surgical treatment of terminally ill patients also ranked low on the QWB scale, whereas comfort and hospice care ranked high. The HSC emphasized that its QWB judgments were not based on an individual's quality of life at a given time; such judgments were considered ethically questionable. Instead, it focused on the potential for change in an individual's life, posing questions such as: "After treatment, how much better or worse off would the patient be?"

Critics countered that the plan obtained its funding by reducing services that were currently offered to Medicaid recipients (often poor women and children) rather than by emphasizing cost control. Others objected to the ranking and the ethical questions raised by choosing to support some treatments over others.

According to Jonathan Oberlander of the University of North Carolina, Chapel Hill, in "Health Reform Interrupted: The Unraveling of the Oregon Health Plan" (*Health Affairs*, vol. 26, no. 1, January 2007), the Oregon Health Plan initially did serve to reduce the percentage of uninsured Oregonians from 18% in 1992 to 11% in 1996, but its early success proved difficult to sustain. By 2003 the Oregon plan was not even close to achieving its goal of having no uninsured people in the state. In fact, the ranks of the uninsured were growing, so much so that by 2003 they reached 17%. An economic downturn in the state and the state's strategy of explicit rationing are cited by Oberlander as reasons for the ambitious plan's failure to achieve its goals.

The Oregon HSC continued to modify the plan's covered benefits. In January 2002 the HSC began refining the list of covered services. The HSC sought to reduce the overall costs of the plan by eliminating less effective treatments and determining if any covered medical conditions could be more effectively treated using standardized clinical practice guidelines (step-by-step instructions for diagnosis and treatment of specific illnesses or disorders) while preserving basic coverage. The benefit review process is ongoing with the HSC submitting a new prioritized list of benefits on July 1 of each even-numbered year for review by the legislative assembly.

In accordance with the ACA option of expanding Medicaid, in 2014 the Oregon Health Plan coverage was extended to more low-income adults who in the past did not qualify for the plan. Prior to 2014, to be eligible people had to be at or below 100% of the federal poverty level. In 2014 coverage was offered to people who earned up to 138% of the federal poverty level, which at that time was about $16,100 a year for a single person or $32,900 a year for a family of four. In the first three months of the year, more than 200,000 Oregonians signed up for coverage, as reported by the Oregon Health Authority (2014, http://oregon.gov/oha/pages/ohp2014.aspx).

The rapid influx of newly insured patients strained the resources of the state's health care system. In "Wave of Newly Insured Patients Strains Oregon Health Plan" (NPR.com, April 8, 2014), Kristian Foden-Vencil reports that a health plan in Lane County, Oregon, that expected about 26,000 new enrollees in the first few years saw close to that number enroll immediately. Furthermore, the plan's CEO explains, "These patients who are coming onto the program—many have not seen a physician for years. We're dealing with not just a large number of patients, but also what appears to be a much sicker population of patients."

Rationing by HMOs

Until 2000 steadily increasing numbers of Americans received their health care from HMOs or other managed care systems. According to the Kaiser Family Foundation in "Total HMO Enrollment" (2014, http://kff.org/other/state-indicator/total-hmo-enrollment), by July 2012, the nation's 545 HMOs enrolled 73.6 million people, which was nearly five times the enrollment rate two decades earlier (15.1 million).

Managed care programs have sought to control costs by limiting coverage for experimental, duplicative, and unnecessary treatments. Before physicians can perform experimental procedures or prescribe new treatment plans, they must obtain prior authorization (approval from the patient's managed care plan) to ensure that the expenses will be covered.

Increasingly, patients and physicians are battling HMOs for approval to use and receive reimbursement for new technology and experimental treatments. Judges and juries, moved by the desperate situations of patients, have frequently decided cases against HMOs, regardless of whether the new treatment has been shown to be effective.

"SILENT RATIONING." Physicians and health care consumers are concerned that limiting coverage for new, high-cost technology will discourage research and development for new treatments before they have even been developed. This is called "silent rationing" because patients will never know what they have missed.

In an effort to control costs, some HMOs have discouraged physicians from informing patients about certain treatment options, including those that are extremely expensive or not covered by the HMO. This has proved to be a highly controversial issue, both politically and ethically. In December 1996 the HHS ruled that HMOs and other health plans cannot prevent physicians from telling Medicare patients about all available treatment options.

Could Less Health Care Be Better Than More?

Although health care providers and consumers fear that rationing sharply limits access to medical care and will ultimately result in poorer health among affected Americans, researchers are also concerned about the effects of too much care on the health of the nation. Several studies suggest that an oversupply of medical care may be as harmful as an undersupply.

In the landmark study *Geography and the Debate over Medicare Reform* (February 13, 2002, http://content .healthaffairs.org/cgi/reprint/hlthaff.w2.96v1), John E. Wennberg, Elliott S. Fisher, and Jonathan S. Skinner of Dartmouth Medical School find tremendous regional variation in both the utilization and the cost of health care that they believe is explained, at least in part, by the distribution of health care providers. Variations in physicians' practice styles—whether they favor outpatient treatment over hospitalization for specific procedures such as biopsies (surgical procedures to examine tissue to detect cancer cells)—greatly affect demand for hospital care.

Variation in demand for health care services in turn produces variation in health care expenditures. Wennberg, Fisher, and Skinner report wide geographic variation in Medicare spending. Medicare paid more than twice as much to care for a 65-year-old in Miami, Florida, where the supply of health care providers is overabundant, than it spent on care for a 65-year-old in Minneapolis, Minnesota, a city with an average supply of health care providers. To be certain that the differences were not simply higher fees in Miami, the researchers also compared rates of utilization. They find that older adults in Miami visited physicians and hospitals much more often than their counterparts in Minneapolis.

Wennberg, Fisher, and Skinner also wanted to be sure that the differences were not caused by the severity of illness, so they compared care during the last six months of life to control for any underlying regional differences in the health of the population. Remarkably, the widest variations were observed in care during the last six months of life, when older adults in Miami saw physician specialists six times as often as those in Minneapolis. The researchers assert that higher expenditures, particularly at the end of life, do not purchase better care. Instead, they finance generally futile interventions that are intended to prolong life rather than to improve the quality of patients' lives. Wennberg, Fisher, and Skinner conclude that areas with more medical care, higher utilization, and higher costs fared no better in terms of life expectancy, morbidity (illness), or mortality (death), and that the care that people received was no different in quality from care received by people in areas with average supplies of health care providers.

In *The Care of Patients with Severe Chronic Illness: An Online Report on the Medicare Program by the Dartmouth Atlas Project* (2006, http://www.dartmouthatlas .org/downloads/atlases/2006_Chronic_Care_Atlas.pdf), John E. Wennberg et al. detail differences in the management of Medicare patients with severe chronic illnesses. The researchers find that average utilization and health care spending varied by state, region, and even by hospital in the same region. Expenditures were not linked with rates of illness in different parts of the country; instead, they reflected how intensively selected resources (e.g., acute care hospital beds, specialist physician visits, tests, and other services) were used to care for patients who were very ill but could not be cured. Because other research demonstrates that, for these chronically ill Americans, receiving more services does not result in improved health outcomes, and because most Americans say they prefer to avoid excessively high-tech end-of-life care, the researchers conclude that Medicare spending for the care of the chronically ill could be reduced by as much as 30%, while improving quality, patient satisfaction, and outcomes. The research by Wennberg et al. and similar studies pose two important and as yet unanswered questions: How much health care is needed to deliver the best health to a population? Are Americans getting the best value for the dollars spent on health care?

In "Stemming the Tide of Overtreatment in U.S. Healthcare" (Reuters.com, February 16, 2012), Debra Sherman reports that in an effort to prevent increased government intervention, medical professional societies such as the American College of Physicians (the largest medical specialty group in the United States) are disseminating guidelines to help physicians refine screening procedures to prevent excessive testing and procedures. Industry observers also believe that economic incentives must be realigned to support this effort. Otis Brawley, the chief medical officer of the American Cancer Society, explains that patients are often given expensive tests, although cheaper ones are better, because "no one can make money off of" the less costly tests.

In "Competing with the Conventional Wisdom: Newspaper Framing of Medical Overtreatment" (*Health Communication*, vol. 29, no. 2, 2014), Kim Walsh-Childers and Jennifer Braddock observe that although overtreatment likely accounts for as much as 30% of all U.S. health care spending, a review of 98 newspaper articles about it published from January 2007 through December 2010 finds that few stories emphasized the financial burden of overtreatment. Instead, the articles focused more on legal issues and uncertainty, specifically about cancer testing and treatment as a driver of overutilization.

Economic Impact of the ACA

The CBO indicates in *Updated Estimates of the Effects of the Insurance Coverage Provisions of the Affordable Care Act, April 2014* (http://www.cbo.gov/sites/default/files/cbofiles/attachments/45231-ACA_Es timates.pdf) that the ACA will reduce federal government costs and reduce the federal deficit. From fiscal years 2013 to 2022, the ACA is predicted to reduce the deficit by $109 billion and from 2023 to 2032, the ACA is projected to reduce the deficit by an average of 0.5 percent of GDP each year, for total deficit reduction of nearly $1.6 trillion over that decade. (See Figure 5.3.)

The ACA will increase the proportion of persons under age 65 with insurance from about 80% before implementation of the ACA to about 89% by 2016. (See Table 5.12.) The CBO projects that 26 million more individuals will be insured each year from 2017 through 2024 than would have been the case without the ACA. In 2018 and beyond, an estimated 25 million people will have coverage through the exchanges, and 13 million more will be covered through Medicaid and CHIP than would have been the case without the ACA. (See Table 5.12.)

FIGURE 5.3

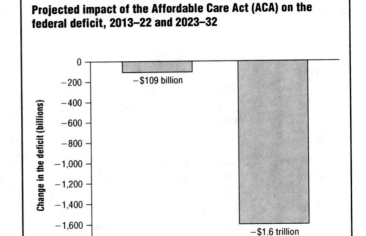

Projected impact of the Affordable Care Act (ACA) on the federal deficit, 2013–22 and 2023–32

SOURCE: Jason Furman, "The Affordable Care Act Will Dramatically Reduce Deficits over the Next Two Decades," in *Six Economic Benefits of the Affordable Care Act*, The White House Council of Economic Advisors, February 6, 2014, http://www.whitehouse.gov/blog/2014/02/06/six-economic-benefits-affordable-care-act (accessed May 20, 2014)

The ACA expenditures include subsidies for insurance purchased through the exchanges and increased costs for Medicaid expansion. These expenses will be partially offset by penalties paid by individuals and employers and by revenues from an excise tax on high-premium insurance plans. For example, the CBO reports in *Updated Estimates of the Effects of the Insurance Coverage Provisions of the Affordable Care Act, April 2014* that people who do not obtain coverage will pay the greater of two amounts: either a flat dollar penalty per adult in a family ($695 in 2016) or a percentage of a household's adjusted gross income (2.5% in 2016). These payments are forecast to total $46 billion from 2015 to 2024. Employer penalties will total $139 billion during the same period.

It is also anticipated that by enabling workers to seek new job opportunities without the fear of losing their employer-sponsored health care coverage, the legislation may stimulate business growth. In "Six Economic Benefits of the Affordable Care Act," Furman observes that ACA tax credits will make it easier for Americans to obtain health care and to meet other needs, which will increase the consumer demand throughout the economy and thereby reduce unemployment.

Workers will also benefit from the slower growth in health care spending. Furman asserts that slower growth in health care costs reduces the health insurance premiums paid by employers and some portion the premium savings are passed along to workers in the form of higher wages.

TABLE 5.12

Effects of the Affordable Care Act (ACA) on health insurance coverage, 2014–24

[Millions of nonelderly people, by calendar year]

	2014	2015	2016	2017	2018	2019	2020	2021	2022	2023	2024
Insurance coverage without the ACA[a]											
Medicaid and CHIP	35	35	34	33	33	34	34	34	35	35	35
Employment-based coverage	156	158	160	163	164	165	165	165	166	166	166
Nongroup and other coverage[b]	24	24	25	25	26	26	26	26	27	27	27
Uninsured[c]	54	55	55	55	55	56	56	56	57	57	57
Total	**270**	**272**	**274**	**277**	**278**	**280**	**281**	**282**	**283**	**284**	**285**
Change in insurance coverage under the ACA											
Insurance exchanges	6	13	24	25	25	25	25	25	25	25	25
Medicaid and CHIP	7	11	12	12	13	13	13	13	13	13	13
Employment-based coverage[d]	*	−2	−7	−7	−8	−8	−8	−8	−8	−7	−7
Nongroup and other coverage[b]	−1	−3	−4	−4	−4	−4	−4	−4	−4	−5	−5
Uninsured[c]	−12	−19	−25	−26	−26	−26	−26	−26	−26	−26	−26
Uninsured under the ACA											
Number of uninsured nonelderly people[c]	42	36	30	30	29	30	30	30	31	31	31
Insured as a percentage of the nonelderly population											
Including all U.S. residents	84	87	89	89	89	89	89	89	89	89	89
Excluding unauthorized immigrants	86	89	91	92	92	92	92	92	92	92	92
Memorandum:											
Exchange enrollees and subsidies											
Number with unaffordable offer from employer[e]	**	**	**	**	**	**	**	**	**	**	**
Number of unsubsidized exchange enrollees (millions of people)[f]	1	3	5	6	6	6	6	6	6	6	6
Average exchange subsidy per subsidized enrollee (dollars)	4,410	4,250	4,830	4,930	5,300	5,570	5,880	6,220	6,580	6,890	7,170

Notes: Figures for the nonelderly population include residents of the 50 states and the District of Columbia who are younger than 65.
CHIP = Children's Health Insurance Program.
*Between −500,000 and zero.
**Between zero and 500,000.
[a]Figures reflect average enrollment over the course of a year and include spouses and dependents covered under family policies; people reporting multiple sources of coverage are assigned a primary source.
[b]"Other" includes Medicare; the changes under the ACA are almost entirely for nongroup coverage.
[c]The uninsured population includes people who will be unauthorized immigrants and thus ineligible either for exchange subsidies or for most Medicaid benefits; people who will be ineligible for Medicaid because they live in a state that has chosen not to expand coverage; people who will be eligible for Medicaid but will choose not to enroll; and people who will not purchase insurance to which they have access through an employer, an exchange, or directly from an insurer.
[d]The change in employment-based coverage is the net result of projected increases and decreases in offers of health insurance from employers and changes in enrollment by workers and their families.
[e]Workers who would have to pay more than a specified share of their income (9.5 percent in 2014) for employment-based coverage could receive subsidies through an exchange.
[f]Excludes coverage purchased directly from insurers outside of an exchange.

SOURCE: "Table 2. Effects of the Affordable Care Act on Health Insurance Coverage," in *Updated Estimates of the Effects of the Insurance Coverage Provisions of the Affordable Care Act, April 2014*, Congressional Budget Office, 2014, http://www.cbo.gov/sites/default/files/cbofiles/attachments/45231-ACA_Estimates .pdf (accessed May 16, 2014)

Finally, ACA measures to enhance the quality and efficiency of health care delivery will serve to improve health outcomes (how patients fare as a result of treat-ment). Healthier workers will be more productive, miss fewer days of work and are less likely to become disabled.

CHAPTER 6
INSURANCE: THOSE WITH AND THOSE WITHOUT

In 1798 Congress established the U.S. Marine Hospital Services for seamen. It was the first time an employer offered health insurance in the United States. Payments for hospital services were deducted from the sailors' salary.

In the 21st century many factors affected the availability of health insurance, including the economy, employment, income, personal health status, and age. Implementation of the Patient Protection and Affordable Care Act (ACA) reduced the impact of these factors on access to health insurance coverage, extending coverage to millions of Americans who were previously unable to obtain it. By March 2014, the close of the ACA's first open enrollment period, the Urban Institute's Health Reform Monitoring Survey (April 3, 2014, http://hrms .urban.org/quicktakes/changeInUninsurance.html) estimated that about 5.4 million people who were previously uninsured had obtained coverage via the federal exchanges, and an estimated 2 million others signed up via state exchanges.

Carmen DeNavas-Walt, Bernadette D. Proctor, and Jessica C. Smith of the U.S. Census Bureau report in *Income, Poverty, and Health Insurance Coverage in the United States: 2012* (September 2013, http://www.census .gov/prod/2013pubs/p60-245.pdf) that in 2012, 63.9% of Americans were covered during all or part of the year by private health insurance, and 54.9% were covered by employment-based health insurance. (See Table 6.1.) The researchers note that the percentage of Americans covered by private and employment-based health insurance was essentially unchanged from 2011 and that the percentage of people covered by government health insurance increased only slightly. Medicare (a federal health insurance program for people aged 65 years and older and people with disabilities) covered 15.7% of Americans in 2012, and Medicaid (a state and federal health insurance program for low-income

people) covered 16.4%. For the fourth consecutive year the percentage and number of people covered by Medicaid were higher than the percentage and number covered by Medicare. Another 15.4% of Americans were without health coverage. DeNavas-Walt, Proctor, and Smith indicate that the percentage of the U.S. population without health coverage in 2012 decreased slightly from its peak in 2010. (See Figure 6.1.)

According to Michael E. Martinez and Robin A. Cohen of the National Center for Health Statistics (NCHS) in *Health Insurance Coverage: Early Release of Estimates from the 2013 National Health Interview Survey* (March 2014, http://www.cdc.gov/nchs/data/nhis/ earlyrelease/insur201403.pdf), the percentage of adults aged 18 to 64 years without health care coverage at the time of the survey interview was 20.5% in 2013, down from its peak of 22.3% in 2010. (See Figure 6.2.) In 2013 there were 56 million (18%) people of all ages who were uninsured for at least part of the 12 months preceding the interview, and 33.7 million (10.8%) had been uninsured for more than a year.

The overwhelming majority of the uninsured were adults aged 18 to 64 years. Figure 6.3 shows the percentages of children under the age of 18 years and adults aged 18 to 64 years that were uninsured at the time of the interview, by age group, and by sex. Figure 6.4 shows the percentages of people uninsured at the time of the interview, uninsured for at least part of the year, uninsured for more than a year, and those with public and private insurance.

WHO WAS UNINSURED IN 2013?

Not surprisingly, in 2013 poverty status was associated with a lack of health insurance coverage. Among people of all ages, the poor or near poor were more likely to be uninsured than those who were not poor. (The

Coverage rates by type of health insurance, 2011 and 2012

[People as of March of the following year]

Coverage type	2011	2012
Any private plan[a]	63.9	63.9
Any private plan alone[b]	52.0	52.0
Employment-based[a]	55.1	54.9
Employment-based alone[b]	45.1	44.8
Direct-purchase[a]	9.8	9.8
Direct-purchase alone[b]	3.6	3.6
Any government plan[a]	32.2	32.6
Any government plan alone[b]	20.4	20.7
Medicare[a]	15.2	15.7
Medicare alone[b]	4.9	5.4
Medicaid[a]	16.5	16.4
Medicaid alone[b]	11.5	11.3
Military health care[a, c]	4.4	4.4
Military health care alone[b, c]	1.3	1.3
Uninsured	15.7	15.4

[a]The estimates by type of coverage are *not* mutually exclusive; people can be covered by more than one type of health insurance during the year.

[b]The estimates by type of coverage are mutually exclusive; people did not have any other type of health insurance during the year.

[c]Military health care includes Tricare and CHAMPVA (Civilian Health and Medical Program of the Department of Veteran Affairs), as well as care provided by the Department of Veterans Affairs and the military.

SOURCE: Carmen DeNavas-Walt, Bernadette D. Proctor, and Jessica C. Smith, "Table 8. Coverage Rates by Type of Health Insurance: 2011 and 2012," in *Income, Poverty, and Health Insurance Coverage in the United States: 2012*, U.S. Census Bureau, September 2013, http://www.census.gov/prod/2013pubs/p60-245.pdf (accessed April 28, 2014)

Census Bureau defines "poor" people as those below the poverty threshold; "near poor" people have incomes of 100% to less than 200% of the poverty threshold; and "not poor" people have incomes equal to or greater than 200% of the poverty threshold.) For example, among people under age 65 in the 2013 National Health Interview Survey, 27.4% of those who were poor and 29.1% of those who were near poor were uninsured at the time of the interview, compared with just 9.9% of those who were not poor in 2013. (See Table 6.2.)

The proportion of people who did not have health insurance in 2013 for at least part of the year preceding the interview varied by geography. It was greatest in the South (24.4%) and West (22.9%), and less in the Midwest (16.1%) and Northeast (14.4%). (See Table 6.3.) Hispanics (40.7%) and non-Hispanic African Americans (25%) were more likely than Asian Americans (16%) and non-Hispanic whites (14.6%) to be uninsured in 2013.

The Uninsured by Age and Sex

Among people under the age of 65 years in 2013, the percentage of people without insurance at the time of the interview was highest among adults aged 25 to 34 years (26.7%) and lowest among young people under the age of 18 years (6.7%). (See Figure 6.3.) Among adults of all ages, men were more likely than women to be uninsured.

The Uninsured by Type of State Health Insurance Marketplace and Medicaid Expansion Status

Under provisions of the ACA, states had the option of expanding Medicaid coverage to cover more low-income Americans. As expected residents of states that opted to expand Medicaid were less likely to be uninsured than residents of states that had not expanded Medicaid. (See Table 6.4.)

The ACA also created online health insurance marketplaces (also known as health exchanges) in each state where people can compare and purchase government-regulated and standardized plans. The online marketplaces also provide information about programs that help people with low to moderate incomes pay for coverage. In some states, the marketplace is run by the state; in others the federal government runs it. Enrollment via the online marketplaces began in October 2013.

In the third quarter of 2013 people in states with federally operated marketplaces were more likely to be uninsured than residents of states with state-based marketplaces or states with partnership marketplaces (hybrid marketplaces in which the state runs certain functions and makes key decisions, including tailoring the marketplace to meet local needs and market conditions, but which is operated by the federal government). (See Table 6.5.)

ACA Expands Coverage despite Problematic Rollout

The ACA rollout was plagued with problems. HealthCare.gov, the website enrollment system that was intended to make shopping for and purchasing coverage easy, was plagued by problems. The website was slow, erratic, and unreliable. Many users were unable to log in or complete their applications, and the site crashed often or was inaccessible. Some of the website problems were due to the fact that multiple contractors were involved with its development, resulting in various components being incompatible.

Many state exchange websites were similarly unsuccessful, leaving consumers frustrated and angry. In "How the iPod President Crashed" (Businessweek.com, October 31, 2013), Ezra Klein asserted that "the disastrous launch of healthcare.gov ... dealt a devastating blow to Obama's vision" of health care reform. Along with the flawed website, the president's promise that all Americans could keep their existing insurance policies if they so wished proved to be untrue, as insurers stopped offering plans that did not meet ACA requirements. Despite the ill-fated launch, Klein opined that the ACA could "emerge from a troubled launch to become a wildly successful program."

Klein's words were prophetic. By December 2013 the website problems were resolving, and enrollments picked up through March and April 2014. By April 2014, 8 million Americans had signed up for private

FIGURE 6.1

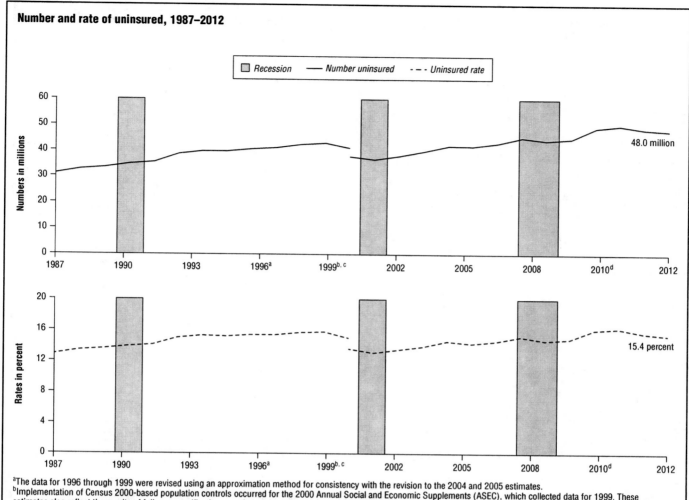

Number and rate of uninsured, 1987–2012

☐ Recession — Number uninsured - - - Uninsured rate

aThe data for 1996 through 1999 were revised using an approximation method for consistency with the revision to the 2004 and 2005 estimates.
bImplementation of Census 2000-based population controls occurred for the 2000 Annual Social and Economic Supplements (ASEC), which collected data for 1999. These estimates also reflect the results of follow-up verification questions, which were asked of people who responded "no" to all questions about specific types of health insurance coverage in order to verify whether they were actually uninsured. This change increased the number and percentage of people covered by health insurance, bringing the Current Population Survey (CPS) more in line with estimates from other national surveys.
cThe data for 1999 through 2009 were revised to reflect the results of enhancements to the editing process.
dImplementation of 2010 Census population controls.
Note: Respondents were not asked detailed health insurance questions before the 1988 CPS.
The data points are placed at the midpoints of the respective years.

SOURCE: Carmen DeNavas-Walt, Bernadette D. Proctor, and Jessica C. Smith, "Figure 8. Number Uninsured and Uninsured Rate: 1987 to 2012," in *Income, Poverty, and Health Insurance Coverage in the United States: 2012*, U.S. Census Bureau, September 2013, http://www.census.gov/prod/2013pubs/p60-245.pdf (accessed April 28, 2014).

health insurance via the exchanges created by the ACA. Countless others purchased plans directly from health insurance companies and brokers. An additional 3 million people enrolled in Medicaid between October 2013 and February 2014 in the 26 states and District of Columbia that extended Medicaid enrollment under the ACA, as reported by Robert Pear in "Law Lifts Enrollment in Medicaid by Millions" (NYTimes.com, April 4, 2014).

In April 2014 the Congressional Budget Office (CBO) released *Updated Estimates for the Insurance Coverage Provisions of the Affordable Care Act, April 2014* (http://www.cbo.gov/publication/45231), an analysis of the financial impact of the ACA. The CBO reports that ACA implementation cost the government $5 billion

less in 2014 than was previously projected and is projected to cover more individuals than previously anticipated. Nonetheless, a significant portion of the population will remain uninsured even after full implementation of the law.

LACK OF INSURANCE HAS SIGNIFICANT CONSEQUENCES

The Institute of Medicine observes in *America's Uninsured Crisis: Consequences for Health and Health Care* (February 2009, http://books.nap.edu/openbook.php?record_id=12511) that the economic downturn exacerbated Americans' health problems because more Americans are uninsured. The institute explains that

FIGURE 6.2

Percentage of persons aged 18–64 without health insurance at the time of interview, for at least part of the past year, or for more than a year, 1997–2013

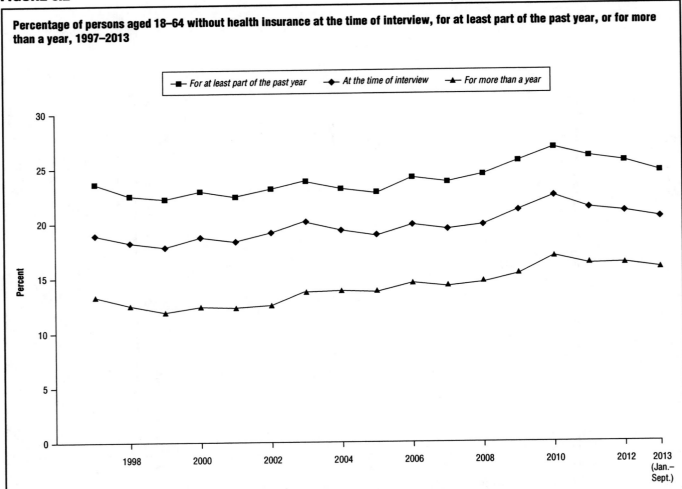

Note: Estimates for 2013 are based on data collected from January through September. Data are based on household interviews of a sample of the civilian noninstitutionalized population.

SOURCE: Michael E. Martinez and Robin A. Cohen, "Figure 2. Percentages of Adults Aged 18–64 Who Lacked Health Insurance Coverage at the Time of Interview, for at Least Part of the Past Year, or for More Than a Year: United States, 1997–September 2013," in *Health Insurance Coverage: Early Release of Estimates from the 2013 National Health Interview Survey*, National Center for Health Statistics, March 2014, http://www.cdc.gov/nchs/data/nhis/earlyrelease/insur201403.pdf (accessed April 28, 2014)

"fewer people have access to coverage at work, more people find the costs of private coverage too expensive, and others lose public coverage because of changed personal circumstances, administrative barriers, and program cutbacks." The institute also notes that rigorous research confirms that uninsurance has a profound negative effect on the health and mortality of adults and children.

Families USA, a national nonprofit, nonpartisan organization dedicated to helping all Americans obtain quality health care, finds that having health insurance is literally a matter of life or death for some Americans. In *Dying for Coverage: The Deadly Consequences of Being Uninsured* (June 2012, http://familiesusa2.org/assets/pdfs/Dying-for-Coverage.pdf), Kim Bailey of Families USA reports that 26,100 people aged 25 to 64 years "died prematurely due to a lack of health coverage in 2010." Between 2005 and 2010, 134,120 deaths were attributable to the lack of health insurance.

In "Spillover Effects of the Uninsured: Local Uninsurance Rates and Medicare Mortality from Eight Procedures and Conditions" (*Inquiry*, vol. 50, no. 1, Spring 2013), Stacey McMorrow observes that lack of insurance limits access to care, which may result in poor health outcomes and financial consequences. Low demand for services from a large uninsured population may prompt providers to stop offering specific services or may even discourage them from staffing and maintaining offices or clinics in areas with large numbers of uninsured residents.

SOURCES OF HEALTH INSURANCE
People under the Age of 65 Years

For people under the age of 65 years there are two principal sources of health insurance coverage: private

FIGURE 6.3

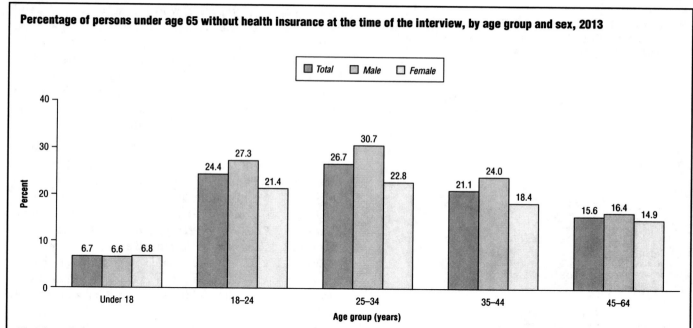

Percentage of persons under age 65 without health insurance at the time of the interview, by age group and sex, 2013

Notes: Estimates for 2013 are based on data collected from January through September. Data are based on household interviews of a sample of the civilian noninstitutionalized population.

SOURCE: Michael E. Martinez and Robin A. Cohen, "Figure 5. Percentage of Persons under Age 65 without Health Insurance Coverage at the Time of Interview, by Age Group and Sex: United States, January–September 2013," in *Health Insurance Coverage: Early Release of Estimates from the 2013 National Health Interview Survey*, National Center for Health Statistics, March 2014, http://www.cdc.gov/nchs/data/nhis/earlyrelease/insur201403.pdf (accessed April 28, 2014)

insurance (from employer or private policies) and Medicaid. The ACA created new designations for health plans and providers. Qualified health plans are private health plans that are approved for sale in the health insurance marketplace—they may, for example, be offered by insurance exchanges. As reported in the 2013 National Health Interview Survey, between 1997 and 2012 the proportion of those covered by private insurance at the time of the interview declined. (See Table 6.6.) During this same period the percentage covered by public health plans grew.

DeNavas-Walt, Proctor, and Smith report that the percentage of people covered by employment-based health insurance decreased to 54.9% in 2012 from 55.1% in 2011. (See Table 6.1.) In contrast, during the 1980s close to 70% of workers obtained private health insurance through their employers. This decline is consistent with the continuing decline in all forms of private health coverage.

Two major factors contributed to the long-term decline in private health insurance. The first is the rising cost of health care, which frequently leads to greater cost sharing between employers and employees. Some workers simply cannot afford the higher premiums and co-payments (the share of the medical bill the employee pays for each health service). The second factor is the

shift in U.S. commerce from the goods-producing sector, where health benefits have traditionally been provided, to the service sector, where many employers do not offer health insurance.

Industry observers predict that the percentage of employers offering health benefits will continue to decrease. In the book *Reinventing American Health Care* (2014), Ezekiel Emanuel, a physician, medical ethicist, and academic, predicts that under the ACA this decrease will likely accelerate. He asserts that employers will choose instead to raise salaries or offer large, defined contributions to workers. Emanuel believes that the exchanges will offer consumers many choices, and most will purchase their coverage through the exchanges. Because government-subsidized insurance is available to people earning less than 400% of the federal poverty limit, some employers may opt to save money by relying on the government to subsidize their workers' health insurance rather than doing so themselves. Emanuel predicts that by 2025 fewer than 20% of private-sector workers will have employer-sponsored health coverage.

In contrast to this view, in *The Launch of the Affordable Care Act in Selected States: Coverage Expansion and Uninsurance* (March 2014, http://www.urbaninstitute.org/UploadedPDF/413036-The-Launch-of-the-Affordable-Care-Act-in-Selected-States-Coverage-Expansion-and-Uni

FIGURE 6.4

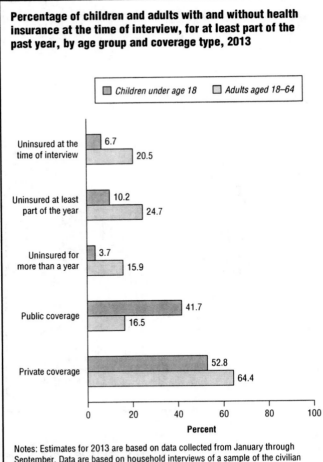

Percentage of children and adults with and without health insurance at the time of interview, for at least part of the past year, by age group and coverage type, 2013

Children under age 18 ☐ Adults aged 18–64

Uninsured at the time of interview	6.7 / 20.5
Uninsured at least part of the year	10.2 / 24.7
Uninsured for more than a year	3.7 / 15.9
Public coverage	41.7 / 16.5
Private coverage	52.8 / 64.4

Percent (0, 20, 40, 60, 80, 100)

Notes: Estimates for 2013 are based on data collected from January through September. Data are based on household interviews of a sample of the civilian noninstitutionalized population.

SOURCE: Michael E. Martinez and Robin A. Cohen, "Figure 1. Percentage of Persons without Health Insurance, by Three Measurements and Age Group and Percentage of Persons with Health Insurance at the Time of Interview, by Coverage Type and Age Group: United States, January–September 2013," in *Health Insurance Coverage: Early Release of Estimates from the 2013 National Health Interview Survey*, National Center for Health Statistics, March 2014, http://www.cdc.gov/nchs/data/nhis/earlyrelease/insur201403.pdf (accessed April 28, 2014)

nsurance.pdf), the Urban Institute asserts that employer coverage will likely increase because of the presence of the Small Business Health Options Program (SHOP) Marketplace, which makes it easier for small employers to search for and compare plans and compare premiums, generating increased competition and over time, lower premiums. Tax credits for small employers and the individual mandate also should result in small increases in employer coverage because workers required to obtain coverage are likely to choose to obtain it through their employers.

People Aged 65 Years and Older

There are three sources of health insurance for people aged 65 years and older: private insurance, Medicare, and Medicaid. Medicare is the federal government's primary health program for people who are aged 65 years and older, and all people in this age group are eligible for certain basic benefits under Medicare. Medicaid is the federal program for the poor and people with disabilities. Martinez and Cohen report in *Health Insurance Coverage* that in 2013 a scant 1.1% of adults aged 65 years and older went without some type of health insurance during at least part of the year preceding the interview.

Older adults may be covered by a combination of private health insurance and Medicare, or Medicare and Medicaid, depending on their income and level of disability. Nearly all adults over age 65 are covered by Medicare. In *Health, United States, 2013: With Special Feature on Prescription Drugs* (May 2014, http://www.cdc.gov/nchs/data/hus/hus13.pdf), the NCHS reports that in 2011, 11.5% of older adults were covered by an employer-sponsored plan, 28.4% were covered by a Medicare-risk health maintenance organization (HMO), 19.8% had Medigap insurance to supplement their Medicare coverage, 14.4% used Medicare to obtain care on a fee-for-service basis, and 8.6% were covered by Medicaid.

MEDICARE ADVANTAGE

Medicare Advantage, also known as Medicare+Choice or Medicare Part C, became available to Medicare recipients on January 1, 1999. It came about as a result of the Balanced Budget Act of 1997 and was designed to supplement Medicare Parts A and B. Medicare Advantage offers beneficiaries a wider variety of health plan options than previously available. These options include traditional (fee-for-service) Medicare, Medicare provider–sponsored organizations, preferred provider organizations (PPOs), Medicare HMOs, and medical savings accounts (MSAs).

Medicare provider–sponsored organizations are organized and operated the same way that HMOs are. However, they are administered by providers (physicians and hospitals). Patients in PPOs may seek care from any physician associated with the plan. Medicare HMOs are more like traditional Medicare, except patients may pay more out-of-pocket expenses. MSAs have two parts: an insurance policy and a savings account. Medicare pays the insurance premium and deposits a fixed amount into an MSA each year to pay for an individual's health care.

In "Medicare Advantage 2014 Spotlight: Plan Availability and Premiums" (November 25, 2013, http://kff.org/medicare/issue-brief/medicare-advantage-2014-spotlight-plan-availability-and-premiums), Marsha Gold et al. of the Kaiser Family Foundation report that more than 2,000 Medicare Advantage plans were available in 2014. In 2014 the plans covered an estimated 16 million older

TABLE 6.2

Percentage of persons under age 65 who were uninsured at the time of interview, by poverty status, 2008–13

Poverty status[a] and year	Uninsured[b] at the time of interview	Public health plan coverage[c]	Private health insurance coverage[d]
		Percent	
Poor (<100% FPL)			
2008	27.9	55.5	17.9
2009	30.2	56.7	14.1
2010	29.5	56.0	15.5
2011	28.2	56.2	16.6
2012	28.3	57.1	16.1
2013 (Jan.–Sept.)	27.4	59.1	14.4
Near-poor (≥100% and <200% FPL)			
2008	30.6	34.7	36.3
2009	29.4	36.7	35.9
2010	32.3	36.2	33.2
2011	30.4	37.7	33.5
2012	29.5	37.1	35.2
2013 (Jan.–Sept.)	29.1	38.6	34.0
Not-poor (≥200% FPL)			
2008	10.2	8.5	82.5
2009	10.7	9.0	81.6
2010	10.7	9.7	81.0
2011	10.1	9.9	81.4
2012	9.8	10.3	81.3
2013 (Jan.–Sept.)	9.9	10.4	81.0
Unknown			
2008	21.0	19.4	60.7
2009	22.3	20.8	57.9
2010	22.7	21.0	57.3
2011	21.0	26.2	53.9
2012	20.4	28.8	52.1
2013 (Jan.–Sept.)	20.1	23.8	57.8

FPL = Federal poverty level.

[a]Based on family income and family size, using the U.S. Census Bureau's poverty thresholds. "Poor" persons are defined as those below the poverty threshold; "Near-poor" persons have incomes of 100% to less than 200% of the poverty threshold; and "Not-poor" persons have incomes of 200% of the poverty threshold or greater. Estimates may differ from estimates that are based on both reported and imputed income.

[b]A person was defined as uninsured if he or she did not have any private health insurance, Medicare, Medicaid, Children's Health Insurance Program (CHIP), state-sponsored or other government-sponsored health plan, or military plan at the time of interview. A person was also defined as uninsured if he or she had only Indian Health Service coverage or had only a private plan that paid for one type of service, such as accidents or dental care.

[c]Includes Medicaid, Children's Health Insurance Program (CHIP), state-sponsored or other government-sponsored health plan, Medicare, and military plans. A small number of persons were covered by both public and private plans and were included in both categories.

[d]Includes any comprehensive private insurance plan (including health maintenance and preferred provider organizations). These plans include those obtained through an employer, purchased directly, or purchased through local or community programs. Private coverage excludes plans that pay for only one type of service, such as accidents or dental care. A small number of persons were covered by both public and private plans and were included in both categories.

Notes: Estimates for 2013 are based on data collected from January through September. Data are based on household interviews of a sample of the civilian noninstitutionalized population.

SOURCE: Michael E. Martinez and Robin A. Cohen, "Table 4. Percentage of Persons under Age 65 Who Lacked Health Insurance Coverage, Had Public Health Plan Coverage, and Had Private Health Insurance Coverage at the Time of Interview, by Poverty Status and Year: United States, 2008–September 2013," in *Health Insurance Coverage: Early Release of Estimates from the 2013 National Health Interview Survey*, National Center for Health Statistics, March 2014, http://www.cdc.gov/nchs/data/nhis/earlyrelease/insur201403.pdf (accessed April 28, 2014)

adults or 30% of Medicare beneficiaries. The average out-of-pocket limit increased to $4,797 in 2014 from $4,333 in 2013, and nearly half (41%) of plans had out-of-pocket limits of $5,000 or more. Average plan premiums in 2014 were $49 per month.

CHANGING MEDICARE REIMBURSEMENT

Medicare reimbursement varies in different parts of the country, although everyone pays the same amount to Medicare through taxes. As a result, older adults in some geographic regions have access to a more comprehensive range of services (e.g., coverage for nursing home care and eyeglasses) than older adults in other regions.

Describing this practice as unfair and outdated, legislators have repeatedly called for more equitable reimbursement formulas. For example, since 2002 the Medi-Fair Act (previously called the Medicare Fairness in Reimbursement Act; aimed to improve the provision of items and services provided to Medicare beneficiaries residing in rural areas in part by improving reimbursement) has repeatedly failed to pass. The Medicare Improvements for Patients and Providers Act of 2008 aimed to stem declining reimbursement by postponing a provision to reduce some Medicare reimbursement rates. The bill became law in July 2008.

The ACA aims to make health care financing more transparent. According to the Centers for Medicare and

TABLE 6.3

Percentage without health insurance, by selected characteristics, 2013

Selected characteristic	Uninsured[a] at the time of interview	Public health plan coverage[b]	Private health insurance coverage[c]
		Percent	
Race/ethnicity			
Hispanic or Latino	40.7	18.1	41.8
Non-Hispanic			
White, single race	14.6	14.3	72.7
Black, single race	25.0	25.9	50.6
Asian, single race	16.0	13.5	71.2
Other races and multiple races	23.0	26.4	53.1
Region			
Northeast	14.4	19.6	67.3
Midwest	16.1	15.3	70.3
South	24.4	16.3	60.7
West	22.9	15.9	62.5
Education			
Less than high school	41.2	30.0	30.0
High school diploma or GED[d]	26.3	20.4	54.9
More than high school	13.7	12.2	75.6
Employment status			
Employed	18.5	8.6	73.7
Unemployed	47.7	24.3	28.4
Not in workforce	19.4	40.1	44.5
Poverty status[e]			
<100% FPL	39.4	42.5	18.9
≥100% and ≤138% FPL	41.9	31.1	28.2
>138% and ≤250% FPL	32.6	18.5	50.5
>250% and ≤400% FPL	16.7	9.8	75.4
>400% FPL	5.4	7.1	88.9
Unknown	22.2	16.4	62.8
Marital status			
Married	15.2	12.8	73.7
Widowed	20.9	32.4	49.7
Divorced or separated	24.3	25.0	52.6
Living with partner	32.2	18.4	50.2
Never married	26.0	19.3	55.4

FPL = Federal poverty level.

[a]A person was defined as uninsured if he or she did not have any private health insurance, Medicare, Medicaid, Children's Health Insurance Program (CHIP), state-sponsored or other government-sponsored health plan, or military plan. A person was also defined as uninsured if he or she had only Indian Health Service coverage or had only a private plan that paid for one type of service, such as accidents or dental care.

[b]Includes Medicaid, Children's Health Insurance Program (CHIP), state-sponsored or other government-sponsored health plan, Medicare and military plans. A small number of persons were covered by both public and private plans and were included in both categories.

[c]Includes any comprehensive private insurance plan (including health maintenance and preferred provider organizations). These plans include those obtained through an employer, purchased directly, or purchased through local or community programs. Private coverage excludes plans that pay for only one type of service, such as accidents or dental care. A small number of persons were covered by both public and private plans and were included in both categories.

[d]GED is General Educational Development high school equivalency diploma.

[e]Based on family income and family size, using the U.S. Census Bureau's poverty thresholds. The percentage of respondents with "Unknown" poverty status for this 5-level categorization is 16.3%. This value is greater than the corresponding value for the 3-level poverty categorization because of greater uncertainty when assigning individuals to more detailed poverty groups.

Estimates may differ from estimates that are based on both reported and imputed income.

Notes: Estimates for 2013 are based on data collected from January through September. Data are based on household interviews of a sample of the civilian noninstitutionalized population.

SOURCE: Michael E. Martinez and Robin A. Cohen, "Table 9. Percentage of Adults Aged 18–64 Who Lacked Health Insurance Coverage, Had Public Health Plan Coverage, and Had Private Health Insurance Coverage at the Time of Interview, by Selected Demographic Characteristics: United States, January–September 2013," in *Health Insurance Coverage: Early Release of Estimates from the 2013 National Health Interview Survey*, National Center for Health Statistics, March 2014, http://www.cdc.gov/nchs/data/nhis/earlyrelease/insur201403.pdf (accessed April 28, 2014)

Medicaid Service (CMS) in the press release "Historic Release of Data Gives Consumers Unprecedented Transparency on the Medical Services Physicians Provide and How Much They Are Paid" (April 9, 2014, http://www .cms.gov/Newsroom/MediaReleaseDatabase/Press-releases/ 2014-Press-releases-items/2014-04-09.html), in May 2013 the CMS released hospital charge data enabling consumers to compare hospital charges for common inpatient and out-patient services across the country. In April 2014 the CMS released comparable data for physicians enabling comparisons by specialty, location, the types of medical service and procedures delivered, and Medicare payment.

Medicare Prescription Drug, Improvement, and Modernization Act

In December 2003 President George W. Bush (1946–) signed the Medicare Prescription Drug, Improvement, and Modernization Act into law. Heralded as landmark

TABLE 6.4

Percentage without health insurance, by state Medicaid expansion status, 2008–13

Age group, state Medicaid expansion status, and year	Uninsured[a] at the time of interview	Public health plan coverage[b]	Private health insurance coverage[c]
		Percent	
Under 65 years			
States moving forward with Medicaid expansion at this time[d]			
2008	14.7	19.4	67.0
2009	15.4	20.7	65.3
2010	16.4	21.8	63.1
2011	15.3	23.1	62.9
2012	15.0	23.1	63.3
2013 (Jan.–Sept.)	15.3	23.9	62.1
States not moving forward with Medicaid expansion at this time[e]			
2008	19.0	19.1	63.3
2009	20.0	21.3	60.1
2010	20.3	22.1	59.0
2011	19.6	22.7	59.1
2012	19.2	24.0	58.3
2013 (Jan.–Sept.)	18.3	23.0	60.1
0–17 years			
States moving forward with Medicaid expansion at this time[d]			
2008	7.0	33.8	60.7
2009	5.9	36.3	59.5
2010	6.7	38.2	56.5
2011	5.9	40.2	55.4
2012	5.3	40.4	55.9
2013 (Jan.–Sept.)	5.9	41.2	54.2
States not moving forward with Medicaid expansion at this time[e]			
2008	11.2	34.8	55.3
2009	10.8	39.4	51.3
2010	9.0	41.7	50.7
2011	8.3	42.0	50.9
2012	8.0	43.9	49.4
2013 (Jan.–Sept.)	7.6	42.4	51.2
18–64 years			
States moving forward with Medicaid expansion at this time[d]			
2008	17.7	13.7	69.5
2009	19.0	14.7	67.5
2010	20.1	15.5	65.6
2011	18.9	16.6	65.8
2012	18.5	16.7	66.0
2013 (Jan.–Sept.)	18.8	17.5	65.0
States not moving forward with Medicaid expansion at this time[e]			
2008	22.1	12.9	66.5
2009	23.6	14.2	63.6
2010	24.8	14.4	62.2
2011	24.1	15.1	62.3
2012	23.7	16.1	61.8
2013 (Jan.–Sept.)	22.4	15.4	63.7

[a]A person was defined as uninsured if he or she did not have any private health insurance, Medicare, Medicaid, Children's Health Insurance Program (CHIP), state-sponsored or other government-sponsored health plan, or military plan. A person was also defined as uninsured if he or she had only Indian Health Service coverage or had only a private plan that paid for one type of service, such as accidents or dental care.

[b]Includes Medicaid, Children's Health Insurance Program (CHIP), state-sponsored or other government-sponsored health plan, Medicare and military plans. A small number of persons were covered by both public and private plans and were included in both categories.

[c]Includes any comprehensive private insurance plan (including health maintenance and preferred provider organizations). These plans include those obtained through an employer, purchased directly, or purchased through local or community programs. Private coverage excludes plans that pay for only one type of service, such as accidents or dental care. A small number of persons were covered by both public and private plans and were included in both categories.

[d]States moving forward with Medicaid expansion include AZ, AR, CA, CO, CT, DE, DC, HI, IL, IA, KY, MD, MA, MI, MN, NV, NJ, NM, NY, NC, ND, OH, OR, RI, VT, WA, and WV (as of October 31, 2013).

[e]States not moving forward with Medicaid expansion include AL, AK, FL, GA, ID, IN, KS, LA, ME, MS, MO, MT, NE, NH, OK, PA, SC, SD, TN, TX, UT, VA, WI, and WY (as of October 31, 2013).

Notes: Estimates for 2013 are based on data collected from January through September. Data are based on household interviews of a sample of the civilian noninstitutionalized population.

SOURCE: Michael E. Martinez and Robin A. Cohen, "Table 12. Percentage of Persons under Age 65 Who Were Uninsured, Had Public Health Plan Coverage, and Had Private Health Insurance Coverage at the Time of Interview, by Age Group, State Medicaid Expansion Status, and Year: United States, 2008–September 2013," in *Health Insurance Coverage: Early Release of Estimates from the 2013 National Health Interview Survey*, National Center for Health Statistics, March 2014, http://www.cdc.gov/nchs/datanhis/earlyrelease/insur201403.pdf (accessed April 28, 2014)

TABLE 6.5

Percentage without health insurance by state Health Insurance Marketplace type, 2008–13

Age group, state Health Insurance Marketplace type, and year	Uninsured[a] at the time of interview	Public health plan coverage[b]	Private health insurance coverage[c]
		Percent	
Under 65 years			
State-based Marketplace states[d]			
2008	15.1	20.0	66.1
2009	16.1	20.7	64.3
2010	16.3	21.6	63.2
2011	15.9	23.6	61.8
2012	15.2	24.2	61.8
2013 (Jan.–Sept.)	15.5	25.1	60.6
Partnership Marketplace states[e]			
2008	12.5	18.6	70.3
2009	14.1	21.1	66.7
2010	14.7	22.5	64.8
2011	14.3	22.7	64.5
2012	14.1	20.8	66.7
2013 (Jan.–Sept.)	14.1	21.7	66.0
Federally Facilitated Marketplace states[f]			
2008	18.5	19.0	63.8
2009	19.0	21.2	61.2
2010	20.1	22.1	59.1
2011	18.8	22.6	60.0
2012	18.6	23.6	59.3
2013 (Jan.–Sept.)	17.9	22.9	60.6
0–17 years			
State-based Marketplace states[d]			
2008	6.9	34.7	59.7
2009	6.9	36.5	57.9
2010	6.7	38.0	56.4
2011	6.4	40.9	54.2
2012	5.4	42.2	53.9
2013 (Jan.–Sept.)	6.1	42.7	52.2
Partnership Marketplace states[e]			
2008	3.9	33.8	64.5
2009	3.1	37.7	62.0
2010	4.1	40.7	57.9
2011	4.2	39.6	58.0
2012	3.6	38.5	59.9
2013 (Jan.–Sept.)	4.2	38.4	59.3
Federally Facilitated Marketplace states[f]			
2008	11.1	34.0	56.1
2009	10.0	38.5	53.0
2010	9.2	40.7	51.3
2011	8.0	41.4	51.8
2012	7.9	42.7	50.8
2013 (Jan.–Sept.)	7.6	41.8	51.9
18–64 years			
State-based Marketplace states[d]			
2008	18.3	14.3	68.6
2009	19.6	14.6	66.8
2010	19.9	15.3	65.9
2011	19.5	17.1	64.7
2012	18.8	17.7	64.7
2013 (Jan.–Sept.)	19.0	18.5	63.8
Partnership Marketplace states[e]			
2008	15.9	12.5	72.6
2009	18.5	14.5	68.5
2010	18.9	15.3	67.6
2011	18.4	15.9	67.1
2012	18.1	13.9	69.3
2013 (Jan.–Sept.)	17.8	15.4	68.5

legislation, the act provides older adults and people with disabilities with a prescription drug benefit, more choices, and improved benefits under Medicare. On June 1, 2004, seniors and people with disabilities began using their Medicare-approved drug discount cards to obtain savings on prescription medicines. Low-income beneficiaries qualified for a $600 credit to help pay for their prescriptions. Besides providing coverage for

TABLE 6.5

Percentage without health insurance by state Health Insurance Marketplace type, 2008–13 [CONTINUED]

Age group, state Health Insurance Marketplace type, and year	Uninsured[a] at the time of interview	Public health plan coverage[b]	Private health insurance coverage[c]
Federally Facilitated Marketplace states[f]			
2008	21.4	13.0	66.9
2009	22.6	14.3	64.5
2010	24.5	14.7	62.2
2011	23.0	15.1	63.3
2012	22.8	16.1	62.7
2013 (Jan.–Sept.)	22.0	15.5	64.0

[a]A person was defined as uninsured if he or she did not have any private health insurance, Medicare, Medicaid, Children's Health Insurance Program (CHIP), state-sponsored or other government-sponsored health plan, or military plan. A person was also defined as uninsured if he or she had only Indian Health Service coverage or had only a private plan that paid for one type of service, such as accidents or dental care.
[b]Includes Medicaid, Children's Health Insurance Program (CHIP), state-sponsored or other government-sponsored health plan, Medicare and military plans. A small number of persons were covered by both public and private plans and were included in both categories.
[c]Includes any comprehensive private insurance plan (including health maintenance and preferred provider organizations). These plans include those obtained through an employer, purchased directly, or purchased through local or community programs. Private coverage excludes plans that pay for only one type of service, such as accidents or dental care. A small number of persons were covered by both public and private plans and were included in both categories.
[d]State-based Marketplace states include CA, CO, CT, DC, HI, ID, KY, MD, MA, MN, NV, NM, NY, OR, RI, VT, and WA (as of October 31, 2013).
[e]Partnership Marketplace states include AR, DE, IL, IA, MI, NH, and WV (as of October 31, 2013).
[f]Federally-facillitated Marketplace states include AL, AK, AZ, FL, GA, IN, KS, LA, ME, MS, MO, MT, NE, NJ, NC, ND, OH, OK, PA, SC, SD, TN, TX, UT, VA, WI, and WY (as of October 31, 2013).
Notes: Estimates for 2013 are based on data collected from January through September. Data are based on household interviews of a sample of the civilian noninstitutionalized population.

SOURCE: Michael E. Martinez and Robin A. Cohen, "Table 12. Percentage of Persons under Age 65 Who Were Uninsured, Had Public Health Plan Coverage, and Had Private Health Insurance Coverage at the Time of Interview, by Age Group, State Health Insurance Marketplace Type, and Year: United States, 2008–September 2013," in *Health Insurance Coverage: Early Release of Estimates from the 2013 National Health Interview Survey*, National Center for Health Statistics, March 2014, http://www.cdc.gov/nchs/data/nhis/earlyrelease/insur201403.pdf (accessed April 28, 2014).

TABLE 6.6

Percentage with public and private health insurance and without health insurance, 1997–2013

Age group and year	Uninsured at the time of interview[a]	Public health plan coverage[b]	Private health insurance coverage[c]
All ages		Percent	
1997	15.4	23.3	70.7
2005	14.2	26.4	67.3
2008	14.7	28.9	64.1
2009	15.4	30.4	61.9
2010	16.0	31.4	60.2
2011	15.1	32.4	60.1
2012	14.7	33.4	59.6
2013 (Jan.–Sept.)	14.5	33.6	59.6
Under 65 years			
1997	17.4	13.6	70.8
2005	16.0	16.8	68.4
2008	16.7	19.3	65.4
2009	17.5	21.0	62.9
2010	18.2	22.0	61.2
2011	17.3	23.0	61.2
2012	16.9	23.5	61.0
2013 (Jan.–Sept.)	16.7	23.5	61.2

[a]A person was defined as uninsured if he or she did not have any private health insurance, Medicare, Medicaid, Children's Health Insurance Program (CHIP), state-sponsored or other government-sponsored health plan, or military plan. A person was also defined as uninsured if he or she had only Indian Health Service coverage or had only a private plan that paid for one type of service, such as accidents or dental care.
[b]Includes Medicaid, Children's Health Insurance Program (CHIP), state-sponsored or other government-sponsored health plan, Medicare, and military plans. A small number of persons were covered by both public and private plans and were included in both categories.
[c]Includes any comprehensive private insurance plan (including health maintenance and preferred provider organizations). These plans include those obtained through an employer, purchased directly, or purchased through local or community programs. Private coverage excludes plans that pay for only one type of service, such as accidents or dental care. A small number of persons were covered by both public and private plans and were included in both categories.
Notes: Estimates for 2013 are based on data collected from January through September. Data are based on household interviews of a sample of the civilian noninstitutionalized population.

SOURCE: Adapted from Michael E. Martinez and Robin A. Cohen, "Table 3. Percentage of Persons Who Lacked Health Insurance, Had Public Health Plan Coverage, and Had Private Health Insurance Coverage at the Time of Interview, by Age Group and Selected Years: United States, 1997–September 2013," in *Health Insurance Coverage: Early Release of Estimates from the 2013 National Health Interview Survey*, National Center for Health Statistics, March 2014, http://www.cdc.gov/nchs/data/nhis/earlyrelease/insur201403.pdf (accessed April 28, 2014).

prescription drugs, this legislation gave seniors the opportunity to choose the coverage that best meets their needs. For example, some older adults opted for traditional Medicare coverage along with the new prescription benefit. Others obtained dental or eyeglass coverage or enrolled in plans that reduced their out-of-pocket costs.

The legislation stipulated that as of 2005 all newly enrolled Medicare beneficiaries would be covered for a complete physical examination and other preventive services, such as blood tests to screen for diabetes. The law also aimed to assist Americans to pay out-of-pocket health costs by enabling the creation of health savings accounts, which allow Americans to set aside up to $4,500 per year, tax free, to save for medical expenses.

Nonetheless, concerns about the solvency of the Medicare program and its capacity to meet the health care needs of growing numbers of Americans aging into eligibility have been increasing in recent years. The media have reported the ill effects of coverage gaps, with

multiple stories of older adults opting to forgo prescription medication because they were unable to afford it. The ACA not only extends the program's solvency but also will completely close the coverage gap (known as the donut hole) in prescription drug coverage by 2020.

CHILDREN

In 2013 nearly 7% of children under the age of 18 years were uninsured, according to the National Health Interview Survey. (See Figure 6.4.) Approximately 10.2% had been uninsured for part of the year preceding the interview, and 3.7% had been uninsured for more than a year. Martinez and Cohen report in *Health Insurance Coverage* that in 2013 poor children (8.3%) and near-poor children (10%) were much more likely to be uninsured at the time of the interview than children who were not poor (4.3%). Figure 6.5 shows that between 1997 and 2013 the percentage of poor and near-poor children who lacked health insurance coverage generally decreased. However, from 2012 to 2013 there was an increase in uninsured poor children (8.3% in 2013 compared with 7.5% in 2012).

FIGURE 6.5

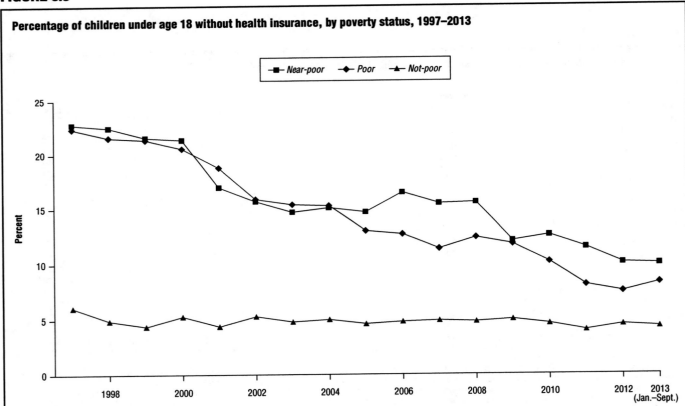

Percentage of children under age 18 without health insurance, by poverty status, 1997–2013

Note: Estimates for 2013 are based on data collected from January through September. Data are based on household interviews of a sample of the civilian noninstitutionalized population.

SOURCE: Michael E. Martinez and Robin A. Cohen, "Figure 4. Percentage of Children under Age 18 Who Were Uninsured at the Time of Interview, by Poverty Status: United States, 1997–September 2013," in *Health Insurance Coverage: Early Release of Estimates from the 2013 National Health Interview Survey, January–September 2013*, National Center for Health Statistics, March 2014, http://www.cdc.gov/nchs/data/nhis/earlyrelease/insur201403.pdf (accessed April 28, 2014)

In 2013, 52.8% of American children were insured under private health insurance plans, either privately purchased or obtained through their parents' workplace. (See Figure 6.4.) Martinez and Cohen report that the rate of private coverage of children aged 17 and under decreased to 52.8% in 2013 from 66.2% in 1997; during this period public coverage of those aged 17 and under increased to 41.7% from 21.4%.

Some industry analysts attribute the declining proportion of uninsured children and the increasing proportion of children covered by Medicaid during the late 1990s to expansion of the Children's Health Insurance Program (CHIP), which targeted children from low-income families and was instituted during the late 1990s. Medicaid enrollment growth peaked during the recession and then slowed as the economy started to recover.

The ACA increases health coverage, improves benefits, and provides insurance protections for children. It eliminates preexisting coverage exclusions for children and improves health insurance for children by expanding coverage through Medicaid and CHIP. It requires children's health insurance to provide coverage for basic dental and vision care and guarantees children access to affordable health insurance policies, regardless of whether their parents change or leave their jobs, relocate, or become ill or disabled.

According to the CMS in "Medicaid Enrollment Grows by More than 3 Million" (April 4, 2014, http://www.hhs.gov/healthcare/facts/blog/2014/04/medicaid-chip-determinations-february.html), by February 2014 an additional 3 million people enrolled in Medicaid or CHIP compared with enrollment before October 1, 2013, when the exchanges opened. Enrollment in states' expanded Medicaid coverage increased fivefold compared with states that did not expand Medicaid. Eligibility also grew. Between October 2013 and February 2014, 11.7 million people were deemed eligible for Medicaid and CHIP, up from 8.9 million reported eligible in the preceding 10 months.

HEALTH INSURANCE PORTABILITY AND ACCOUNTABILITY ACT

In August 1996 President Bill Clinton (1946–) signed the Health Insurance Portability and Accountability Act (HIPAA). This legislation aimed to provide better portability (transfer) of employer-sponsored insurance from one job to another. HIPAA ensured that people who had employer-sponsored health coverage would be able to maintain their health insurance even if they lost their job or moved to a different company. They would, of course, have to continue to pay for their insurance. However, they no longer had to fear that they would be denied coverage because of preexisting medical conditions or be forced to go without health insurance for prolonged waiting periods.

Industry observers and policy makers viewed HIPAA as an important first step in the federal initiative to significantly reduce the number of uninsured people in the United States. Besides its portability provisions, HIPAA changed tax laws to make it easier for Americans to pay for medical care and initiated a pilot program of MSAs that would grow into a significant new initiative in paying for health care.

In 2013 the Department of Health and Human Services released final regulations that reflect legislative changes made to the HIPAA's privacy and data security rules. The new regulations prohibit the sale of protected health information and the use of such information for marketing or fund-raising.

HEALTH SAVINGS ACCOUNTS

HIPAA also authorized a five-year demonstration project designed to test the concept of MSAs, which are similar to individual retirement accounts. Beginning on January 1, 1997, approximately 750,000 people with high-deductible health plans (high-deductible plans were defined as those that carried a deductible of $1,600 to $2,400 for an individual or $3,200 to $4,800 for families) could make tax-deductible contributions into interest-bearing savings accounts. The funds deposited into these accounts could be used to purchase health insurance policies and pay co-payments and deductibles. People using MSAs could also deduct any employer contributions into the accounts as tax-deductible income. Any unspent money remaining in the MSA at the end of the year was carried over to the next year, thereby allowing the account to grow.

To be eligible to create an MSA, individuals had to be younger than 65 years old, self-employed, and uninsured or had to work in firms with 50 or fewer employees that did not offer health care coverage. Withdrawals to cover out-of-pocket medical expenses were tax free, and the money invested grew on a tax-deferred basis. Using MSA funds for any purpose unrelated to medical care or disability resulted in a 15% penalty. However, when MSA users reached age 65, the money could be withdrawn for any purpose and was taxed at the same rate as ordinary income.

Supporters of MSAs believed consumers would be less likely to seek unnecessary medical care if they knew they could keep the money that was left in their accounts for themselves at the end of the year. Experience demonstrated that MSAs could simultaneously help contain health care costs, allow consumers greater control and freedom of choice of health care providers, enable consumers to save for future medical and long-term care expenses, and improve access to medical care.

In February 2001 President Bush advocated more liberal rules governing MSAs and proposed making them permanently available to all eligible Americans. Congress reviewed the president's proposed reforms and during its 2001–02 session lowered the minimum annual deductible to increase the number of eligible Americans, allowed annual MSA contributions up to 65% of the maximum deductible for individuals and 75% for families, and extended the availability of MSAs through December 31, 2003.

The Medicare Modernization Act of 2003 included provisions to establish health savings accounts (HSAs) for the general population. Like the MSA program it replaced, HSAs offer a variety of benefits, including more choice, greater control, and individual ownership. Specific features of HSAs include:

- Permanence and portability
- Availability to all individuals with a qualified high-deductible health plan
- Minimum deductible of $1,000 per individual plan and $2,000 per family plan
- Allowing annual contributions to equal 100% of the deductible
- Allowing both employer and employee contributions
- Not placing a cap on taxpayer participation
- Allowing tax-free rollover of up to $500 in unspent flexible spending accounts

For 2015, HSAs enabled individuals to deposit up to $3,350 ($6,650 for families) per year in the accounts tax free, and the funds were rolled over from one year to the next. Also, funds could be withdrawn to pay for medical bills or saved for future needs, including retirement.

Pros and Cons of HSAs

Brent Hunsberger explains in "HSAs: The Pros and Cons of Health Savings Accounts" (OregonLive.com, May 18, 2013) that the timing of contributions to an HSA is flexible (funds accrue and roll over from year to year, and contributions may be made up to the filing date of that year's tax return). For example, for 2015, contributions could be made until April 15, 2016. Others (parents, spouses or even friends) can contribute to the HSA, and its owner still takes the tax deduction for it.

Hunsberger also notes the potential pitfalls. Many HSAs have monthly maintenance and withdrawal fees, receipts and records must be kept documenting qualified health expenses, and HSA owners must be covered by a high-deductible health plan. They cannot, for example, be covered on a parent's or spouse's low-deductible plan.

Nonetheless, America's Health Insurance Plans, a national association that represents companies providing health insurance coverage to more than 200 million Americans, reports in "Health Savings Account Enrollment Reaches 15.5 Million" (June 26, 2013, http://www.ahipcoverage.com/2013/06/26/health-savings-account-enrollment-reaches-15-5-million) that as of June 2013, 15.5 million people had an HSA. This was a 15% increase over the prior year. HSA plan enrollment varied by geography, with the highest numbers in Illinois (903,000 enrollees), Texas (889,364 enrollees), California (808,019 enrollees), Ohio (686,616 enrollees), and Michigan (577,208 enrollees).

Advocates of HSAs believe that by having consumers assume an increasing burden of escalating medical care costs, HSAs will stimulate both comparison shopping for health care providers and competition that will ultimately reduce the rate at which costs are rising. In "Employer and Worker Contributions to Health Reimbursement Arrangements and Health Savings Accounts, 2006–2013" (*EBRI Notes*, vol. 35, no. 2, February 2014), Paul Fronstin of the Employee Benefit Research Institute finds a relationship between health engagement and contributions to an HSA. Consumers engaged in their health care were more likely to check whether their plans covered their care or medication and checked the cost of a visit, medication, or other service before receiving care. They also checked quality ratings of providers before seeking care, talked to their doctors about prescription costs and were more likely to use online cost-tracking tools to manage health expenses. Engaged consumers also contributed higher amounts to their HSAs than those with no engagement.

HEALTH INSURANCE COSTS CONTINUE TO SKYROCKET

According to the Kaiser Family Foundation in *Employer Health Benefits: 2013 Annual Survey* (2013, http://kaiserfamilyfoundation.files.wordpress.com/2013/08/8465-employer-health-benefits-20132.pdf), health insurance premiums increased modestly but still outpaced inflation (1.1%), with the average family premium increasing 4% between 2012 and 2013. Premiums averaged $5,884 for individual coverage and $16,351 for family coverage. Workers paid an average of 18% of the premium for individual coverage and 29% of the premium for family coverage.

The Kaiser Family Foundation explains that the percentage of workers with deductibles for individual coverage of $1,000 or more increased, as did the average co-payments for primary or specialty physician office visits. The average annual deductible for individual coverage was $1,135 up from $735 in 2008. The majority (75%) of covered workers incurred co-payments for office visits and prescription drugs. The majority (81%) of workers were enrolled in plans with co-payments or another form of cost sharing for prescription drugs.

The Kaiser Family Foundation finds that 57% of employers offered health benefits in 2013, down from 69% in 2010. The percentage of workers enrolled in grandfathered health plans (plans exempt from many provisions of the ACA) declined to 36% of covered workers in 2013 from 48% in 2012 and 56% in 2011. Because many provisions of the ACA became effective in 2014, in the 2013 survey firms were asked whether they plan to self-insure. (Self-insured plans are not required to adhere to many the health benefits rules that apply to fully insured plans.) Six percent of firms offering fully insured plans in 2013 said they planned to self-insure, and an additional 11% said they were unsure of their future strategy.

HEALTH INSURERS HAVE HEIGHTENED OVERSIGHT

The ACA established the Office of Consumer Information and Insurance Oversight (September 3, 2014, http://www.cms.gov/About-CMS/Agency-Information/ CMSLeadership/Office_CCIIO.html) to provide "national leadership in setting and enforcing standards for health insurance that promote fair and reasonable practices to ensure affordable, quality health care coverage is available to all Americans." Renamed the Center for Consumer Information and Insurance Oversight, it is a part of CMS.

The Center for Consumer Information and Insurance Oversight has ongoing responsibility for "implementing, monitoring compliance with, and enforcing the new rules governing the insurance market and the new rules regarding the Medical Loss Ratio" (the requirement that insurance companies spend at least 80% or 85% of premium dollars on medical care). It is also responsible for "rate review at the federal level and for assisting states in cracking down on unreasonable rate increases."

Impact of the ACA on Health Insurers

In *Report to Congress on the Impact on Premiums for Individuals and Families with Employer-Sponsored Health Insurance from the Guaranteed Issue, Guaranteed Renewal and Fair Health Insurance Premiums Provisions of the Affordable Care Act* (CMS Office of the Actuary, February 21, 2014, http://www.cms.gov/Research-Statistics-Data-and-Systems/Research/ActuarialStudies/Downloads/ ACA-Employer-Premium-Impact.pdf), the CMS notes that health insurance companies can only vary their premiums based on consumers' age, tobacco use, geographical location, family size, and the value of the plan. The oldest consumers cannot be charged more than three times as much as the youngest adults, and smokers may be charged no more than 1.5 times the premium for nonsmokers.

Before provisions of the ACA took effect in 2014, insurers could offer lower premiums to small employers with younger and healthier employees who presumably would have fewer health care needs, and much higher rates to small employers with older and sicker employees with more health care needs. As a result firms with older employees paid higher premiums. The sex distribution of workers also influenced premiums. Before 2014, employers with more women of childbearing age were frequently charged higher premiums.

The CMS analysis assumes that if employer premiums increase, then the employee contribution will rise as well, and if the employer premiums are reduced, then employee contributions decrease. The CMS estimated that ACA requirements resulted in premium rate increases for about 11 million people and premium rate reductions for about 6 million.

MENTAL HEALTH PARITY

In terms of mental health care, parity refers to the premise that the same range and scope of insurance benefits available for other illnesses should be provided for people with mental illness. Historically, private health insurance plans have provided less coverage for mental illness than for other medical conditions. Coverage for mental health was more restricted and often involved more cost sharing (higher co-payments and deductibles) than coverage for medical care. As a result, many patients with severe mental illness, who frequently required hospitalizations and other treatment, quickly depleted their mental health coverage.

During the 1990s there was growing interest in parity of mental health with other health services. The Mental Health Parity Act of 1996 sought to bring mental health benefits closer to other health benefits. The act amended the 1944 Public Health Service Act and the 1974 Employee Retirement Income Security Act by requiring parity for annual and lifetime dollar limits but did not place restrictions on other plan features such as hospital and office visit limits. It also imposed federal standards on the mental health coverage offered by employers through group health plans. The National Council of State Legislatures, in *State Laws Mandating or Regulating Mental Health Benefits* (January 2014, http://www .ncsl.org/research/health/mental-health-benefits-state-mandates.aspx), observes that by 2014, 49 states had laws governing mental health parity.

Legislation Establishes Mental Health Parity

The Paul Wellstone and Pete Domenici Mental Health Parity and Addiction Equity Act of 2008 expanded the Mental Health Parity Act by prohibiting group health plans and group health insurance companies from imposing treatment limitations or financial requirements for coverage of mental health that are different from those used for medical and surgical benefits. In "New Rules Promise Better Mental Health Coverage" (NYTimes.com, January 29, 2010), Robert Pear explains that eliminating disparities between physical health care and mental health care makes it easier for people to obtain care for conditions ranging from depression and anxiety to eating disorders and substance abuse. The Obama administration predicted that the parity requirement would benefit "111 million people in 446,400 group health plans offered by private employers, and 29 million people in 20,000 plans sponsored by state and local governments." The act was projected to increase insurance premiums 0.4%, which translates into $25.6 billion between 2010 and 2019.

Effects of the ACA on Mental Health Parity

According to the National Council of State Legislatures in *State Laws Mandating or Regulating Mental Health Benefits*, the ACA contains two main provisions that are aimed at improving mental health parity: expanding "the reach of the applicability of the federal mental health parity requirements" and establishing "a mandated benefit for the coverage of certain mental health and substance abuse disorder services." Furthermore, the legislation expands the reach of federal mental health parity requirements to qualified health plans as established by the ACA, to Medicaid nonmanaged care plans, and to plans offered to individuals.

Parity May Not Solve All Access Problems

According to Susan Brink in "Mental Health Now Covered under ACA, but Not for Everyone" (USNews.com, April 29, 2014), parity alone will not eliminate all obstacles to gaining access to mental health care. Brink explains that although the ACA permits young adults to remain on their parents' health plans to age 26 and prevents insurance companies from denying coverage to persons with preexisting mental health disorders, such as schizophrenia, depression or drug or alcohol dependence, shortages of mental health providers and gaps in coverage may still compromise access to care.

Some states (Colorado, Massachusetts, Minnesota, New Jersey, Oregon, and Vermont) have taken steps to improve mental health care using novel delivery systems. Accountable care organizations, patient-centered medical homes, and community care organizations use teams of health professionals to coordinate and provide mental health care. Medicaid programs in states such as Oregon also incentivize providers to keep people healthy and out of the hospital by paying a fixed amount per patient.

Brink, however, observes that mental health patients may not fare as well in the 21 states that have not opted to expand Medicaid coverage. Joel Miller, executive director of the American Mental Health Counselors Association asserts, "Nearly 4 million uninsured people with mental health conditions will be locked out of the health insurance system, and therefore lack access to timely, quality mental health services and a consistent source of care."

FINANCING THE ACA

In *Updated Estimates for the Insurance Coverage Provisions of the Affordable Care Act, April 2014*, the CBO estimates that the coverage provisions of the ACA cost $36 billion in 2014, $5 billion less than the previous projection for the year. From 2015 to 2024 the ACA will cost an estimated $1.4 billion, $104 million less than the previous projections. (See Figure 6.6.)

The CBO estimates that the ACA will reduce the number of nonelderly people without health insurance coverage by 26 million to 30 million in 2017 and subsequent years, leaving about 30 million nonelderly residents uninsured in those years. It also indicates that "fewer people are now expected to obtain health insurance coverage from their employer or in insurance exchanges; more are now expected to obtain coverage from Medicaid or CHIP or from nongroup or other sources. More are expected to be uninsured."

The ACA is financed by a combination of health care savings resulting from programs that improve efficiency and accountability, incentivize quality and cost-effective care, and reduce waste, fraud, and inefficiencies. It also contains provisions to raise revenue such as an annual fees paid by health insurers and manufacturers and importers of prescription drugs along with taxes on indoor tanning services and medical devices.

Floyd Norris indicates in "Merely Rich and Superrich: The Tax Gap Is Narrowing" (NYTimes.com, April 17, 2014) that revenues also are generated via taxes on the wealthiest Americans. Beginning in 2013 individuals who earned more than $200,000 per year and couples who earned more than $250,000 per year paid an additional 3.8% Medicare payroll tax. Americans in this tax bracket will also pay a 3.8% tax on unearned income such as dividends.

FIGURE 6.6

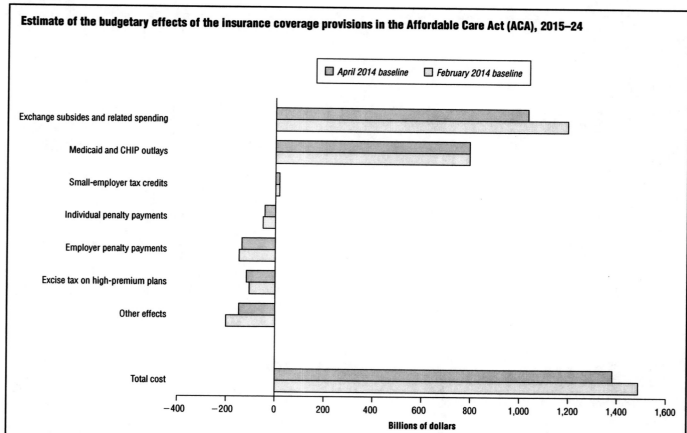

Estimate of the budgetary effects of the insurance coverage provisions in the Affordable Care Act (ACA), 2015–24

Note: CHIP = Children's Health Insurance Program.

SOURCE: "Budgetary Effects of the Insurance Coverage Provisions of the Affordable Care Act, 2015 to 2024," in *Updated Estimates of the Effects of the Insurance Coverage Provisions of the Affordable Care Act, April 2014*, Congressional Budget Office, April 2014, http://www.cbo.gov/publication/45231 (accessed May 5, 2014)

CHAPTER 7
INTERNATIONAL COMPARISONS OF HEALTH CARE

International comparisons are often difficult to interpret because the definitions of terms, the reliability of data, the cultures, and the values differ. What is important in one society may be unimportant or even nonexistent in another. A political or human right that is important in one nation may be meaningless in a neighboring nation. Evaluating the quality of health care systems is an example of the difficulties involved in comparing one culture to another.

Even within the United States there are cultural and regional variations in health care delivery. A visit to a busy urban urgent care center might begin with the patient completing a brief medical history, followed by five or 10 minutes with a nurse who measures and records the patient's vital signs (pulse, respiration, and temperature), and conclude with a 15-minute visit with a physician, who diagnoses the problem and prescribes treatment. In contrast, on the islands of Hawaii a visit with a healer may last several hours and culminate with a prayer, a song, or an embrace. Hawaiian healers, called kahunas, are unhurried and offer an array of herbal remedies, bodywork (massage, touch, and manipulative therapies), and talk therapies (counseling and guidance), because they believe that the healing quality of the encounter, independent of any treatment offered, improves health and well-being.

Although comparing the performance of health care systems and health outcomes (how people fare as a result of receiving health care services) is of benefit to health care planners, administrators, and policy makers, the subjective nature of such assessments should be duly considered.

A COMPARISON OF HEALTH CARE SPENDING, RESOURCES, AND UTILIZATION

The Organisation for Economic Co-operation and Development (OECD) provides information about 34 member countries that are governed democratically and participate in the global market economy. It collects and publishes data about a wide range of economic and social issues including health and health care policy. The OECD member nations are generally considered to be the wealthier, more developed nations in the world. The OECD (2014, http://www.oecd.org/about/membersandpartners) indicates that its member countries are Australia, Austria, Belgium, Canada, Chile, the Czech Republic, Denmark, Estonia, Finland, France, Germany, Greece, Hungary, Iceland, Ireland, Israel, Italy, Japan, Luxembourg, Mexico, the Netherlands, New Zealand, Norway, Poland, Portugal, the Slovak Republic, Slovenia, South Korea, Spain, Sweden, Switzerland, Turkey, the United Kingdom, and the United States.

Percentage of Gross Domestic Product Spent on Health Care

Although health has always been a concern for Americans, the growth in the health care industry since the mid-1970s has made it a major factor in the U.S. economy. For many years the United States has spent a larger proportion of its gross domestic product (GDP; the total market value of final goods and services produced within an economy in a given year) on health care than have other nations with similar economic development. According to the OECD, the United States spent 17.7 percent of its GDP on health care in 2011. (See Figure 7.1.) The next highest country was the Netherlands, with 11.9 percent. In most other high-income countries the share was less than 11 percent. Other nations that spent large percentages of their GDP on health care in 2011 included France (11.6%), Germany (11.3%), Canada (11.2%), Switzerland (11%), Denmark (10.9%), Austria (10.8%), and Belgium (10.5%). Of the member nations that reported health care expenditure data in 2011, Estonia (5.9%), Turkey (6.1%), Mexico (6.2%), and Luxembourg (6.6%) spent the least in the OECD.

FIGURE 7.1

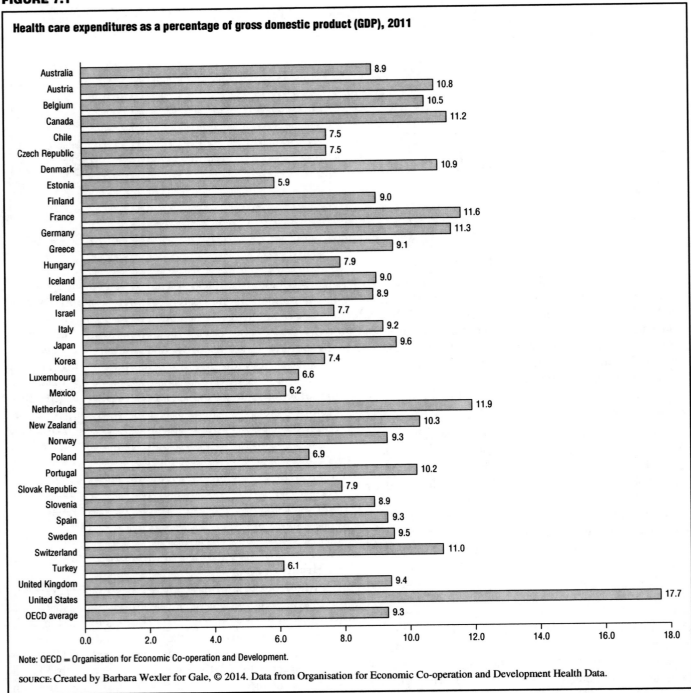

Health care expenditures as a percentage of gross domestic product (GDP), 2011

Country	Percentage
Australia	8.9
Austria	10.8
Belgium	10.5
Canada	11.2
Chile	7.5
Czech Republic	7.5
Denmark	10.9
Estonia	5.9
Finland	9.0
France	11.6
Germany	11.3
Greece	9.1
Hungary	7.9
Iceland	9.0
Ireland	8.9
Israel	7.7
Italy	9.2
Japan	9.6
Korea	7.4
Luxembourg	6.6
Mexico	6.2
Netherlands	11.9
New Zealand	10.3
Norway	9.3
Poland	6.9
Portugal	10.2
Slovak Republic	7.9
Slovenia	8.9
Spain	9.3
Sweden	9.5
Switzerland	11.0
Turkey	6.1
United Kingdom	9.4
United States	17.7
OECD average	9.3

Note: OECD = Organisation for Economic Co-operation and Development.

SOURCE: Created by Barbara Wexler for Gale, © 2014. Data from Organisation for Economic Co-operation and Development Health Data.

Per Capita Spending on Health Care

According to the OECD, in *Health at a Glance 2013: OECD Indicators* (November 21, 2013, http://www.oecd-ilibrary.org/social-issues-migration-health/health-at-a-glance-2013_health_glance-2013-en), the United States also experienced the highest per capita spending for health care services in 2011, spending an average of $8,508 per citizen. No other country came close to spending this amount per capita in 2011: Norway spent $5,669 per citizen; Switzerland, $5,643; the Netherlands, $5,099;

Austria $4,546; Canada, $4,522; Germany, $4,495; Denmark, $4,448; Luxembourg, $4,246; France, $4,118; Belgium, $4,061; and Sweden, $3,925. In 2011 Turkey ($906) spent the least per capita of any OECD member nation on health care, followed by Mexico ($977), Estonia ($1,303), Poland ($1,452), and Chile ($1,568).

Who Pays for Health Care?

Public expenditures for health care services as a percentage of GDP vary widely between the OECD member countries. In *Health at a Glance 2013*, the OECD notes that public spending on health accounted for an average of 78% of spending for medical services across OECD member countries in 2011 and that the remaining 22% of spending was paid by private sources, mainly private insurance and individuals. In the United States public funding accounted for 50% of spending for medical services. By contrast, public sources in the Netherlands and Norway accounted for 90% and 88%, respectively. Other nations with above-average contributions of public funding to medical service expenditures included Belgium (78%), Germany (79%), New Zealand (83%), France (85%), Iceland (87%), Italy (87%), Japan (87%), Sweden (87%), Denmark (89%), Estonia (90%), and the Czech Republic (92%). Public expenditures on medical services per capita were lowest in Mexico (48%) and the United States (50%).

In terms of out-of-pocket payments as a share of total health expenditures in 2011, the United States, at 12%, was below the OECD average of 20%. In France and the United Kingdom out-of-pocket payments as a share of total health expenditures were low, at 8% and 10%, respectively. In contrast, out-of-pocket spending as a share of total health care spending was highest in Chile (38%) and Mexico (49%). Out-of-pocket spending as a share of total health care spending was also high in the Slovak Republic (24%), Israel (25%), Switzerland (26%), Hungary (27%), Portugal (29%), Greece (31%), and South Korea (37%).

Because the United States does not currently have a government-funded national health care program that provides coverage for all of its citizens, U.S. private insurance expenditures cover the costs generally assumed by government programs that finance health care delivery in comparable OECD member nations. The Patient Protection and Affordable Care Act and the Health Care and Education Reconciliation Act (which are now commonly known as the ACA) aim to not only provide health insurance coverage for the overwhelming majority of Americans but also change the ways in which Americans purchase and pay for health care. When the ACA is fully implemented and previously uninsured Americans are covered by either subsidized private plans or Medicaid expansion, it is anticipated that the mix of payment sources (public, private, and out of pocket) will shift. For example, expanded Medicaid eligibility will increase the share of public expenditures, and the limits on maximum health plan deductibles may reduce out-of-pocket expenditures.

Spending on Pharmaceutical Drugs

The OECD indicates in *Health at a Glance 2013* that in 2011 the United States spent more per capita ($985) on pharmaceutical drugs than any other OECD member country. The average pharmaceutical spending was $483 per capita. Per capita pharmaceutical spending was also high in Canada ($701), Greece ($673), Ireland ($648), Japan ($648), Germany ($632), and Belgium ($627). In contrast, Chile spent $178; Mexico, $259; Denmark, $266; and Estonia, $272, per capita on pharmaceuticals.

Hospital Utilization Statistics

The number of hospital beds is a gross measure of resource availability; however, it is important to remember that it does not reflect capacity to provide emergency or outpatient hospital care. In general, it also does not measure the number of beds that are devoted to nonacute or other long-term care, although it is known that in Japan many of the beds designated as acute care are actually used for long-term care. According to the OECD, in "OECD Health Data—Frequently Requested Data" (2014, http://stats.oecd.org/Index.aspx?DataSet Code=SHA), of the OECD member countries reporting acute care hospital beds per 1,000 population, Japan (13.5) and South Korea (8.8) had the highest numbers in 2010. The United States was among the lowest, at 3.1 beds per 1,000 population, trailed only by the United Kingdom (2.9), New Zealand (2.7) Sweden (2.7), Turkey (2.5), Chile (2), and Mexico (1.6).

Hospital lengths of stay have consistently declined since 1960, in part because increasing numbers of illnesses can be treated as effectively in outpatient settings and because many countries have reduced inpatient hospitalization rates and the average length of stay (ALOS) to control health care costs. In 2012 South Korea (16.1 days) had the longest acute care ALOS of the OECD member nations, followed by Finland (11 days), the Czech Republic (9.5 days), Hungary (9.5 days), Germany (9.2 days), and Switzerland (8.6). The shortest hospital stays in 2012 were in Mexico (3.9 days), Turkey (4 days), and Ireland (5.6 days).

Medical practice, particularly the types and frequency of procedures performed, also varies from one country to another. The OECD looks at rates of cesarean section (delivery of a baby through an incision in the abdomen as opposed to vaginal delivery) per 1,000 live births and found both growth in the rates of cesarean section (as a percentage of all births) and considerable variation in the rates for this surgical procedure. In 2011 the highest rates for cesarean sections per 1,000 live births were reported in Turkey (461.6), Italy (377.1), South Korea (346.1), and Hungary (335.8). In "Searching for the Optimal Rate of Medically Necessary Cesarean Delivery" (*Birth*, vol. 41, no. 3, September 2014), Jiangfeng Ye et al. looked at 19 countries that have readily accessible cesarean delivery and low maternal and infant mortality, including countries in Europe, North America,

FIGURE 7.2

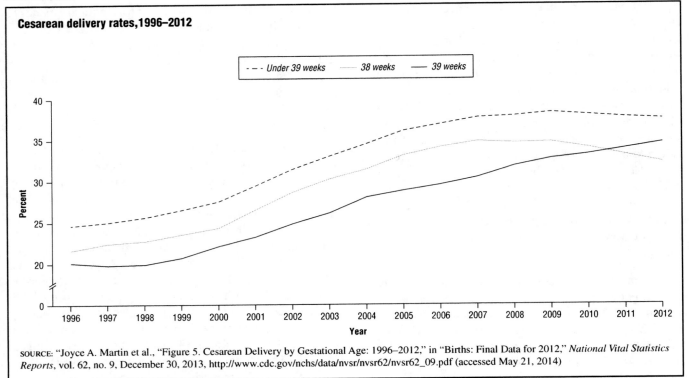

Cesarean delivery rates,1996–2012

SOURCE: "Joyce A. Martin et al., "Figure 5. Cesarean Delivery by Gestational Age: 1996–2012," in "Births: Final Data for 2012," *National Vital Statistics Reports*, vol. 62, no. 9, December 30, 2013, http://www.cdc.gov/nchs/data/nvsr/nvsr62/nvsr62_09.pdf (accessed May 21, 2014)

Australia, New Zealand, and Japan. The researchers find that although most countries have seen sharp increases in cesarean delivery rates, the higher rates do not improve maternal or infant mortality rates. Figure 7.2 shows the dramatic rise in cesarean sections among mothers of all ages between 1996 and 2012 in the United States. Because cesarean section is performed in the hospital and involves at least an overnight stay, the frequency with which it and other surgical procedures are performed contributes to hospitalization rates and expenditures.

Physicians' Numbers Are Increasing

Since 1960 the OECD member nations have all enjoyed growing physician populations. In *Health at a Glance 2013*, the OECD reports that in 2011 Greece reported the highest ratio of practicing physicians, 6.1 per 1,000 population, with most countries ranging between 2 and 4 physicians per 1,000 population. The OECD countries that had the fewest practicing physicians were Chile (1.6 per 1,000 population), Turkey (1.7), South Korea (2), Japan (2.2), Mexico (2.2), and Poland (2.2). At 2.5 physicians per 1,000 population, the United States was also below the OECD average of 3.2.

The ratio of physicians to population is a limited measure of health care quality, because many other factors, such as the availability of other health care providers as well as the accessibility and affordability of health care services, also influence the quality of health care

systems. Furthermore, during the last 25 years research has shown that more medical care, in terms of numbers and concentration of health care providers, is not necessarily linked to better health status for the population. For example, the Dartmouth Institute for Health Policy and Clinical Practice indicates in "The Physician Workforce" (2014, http://www.dartmouthatlas.org/keyissues/issue.aspx?con=2940) that increasing the physician population will make the U.S. health care system worse rather than better. The institute contends that "first, unfettered growth is likely to exacerbate regional inequities in supply and spending; our research has shown that physicians generally do not choose to practice where the need is greatest. Second, expansion of graduate medical education would most likely further undermine primary care and reinforce trends toward a fragmented, specialist-oriented health care system."

OVERVIEWS OF SELECTED HEALTH CARE SYSTEMS

David Squires of the Commonwealth Fund uses data collected by the OECD and other agencies to compare health care systems and performance in industrialized countries in *Multinational Comparisons of Health Systems Data, 2013* (November 2013, http://www.commonwealthfund.org) and in *Explaining High Health Care Spending in the United States: An International Comparison of Supply, Utilization, Prices, and Quality* (May 2012, http://www.commonwealthfund.org). This section also presents the results of a study conducted by the International Federation of Health Plans, *2013 Comparative Price Report* (April 2014, http://static.squarespace .com), that analyzes health plan data from 28 countries and shows variation in medical and hospital prices by country.

Squires looks at OECD data for 13 industrialized countries: Australia, Canada, Denmark, France, Germany, Japan, the Netherlands, New Zealand, Norway, Sweden, Switzerland, the United Kingdom, and the United States. He finds that the United States outspends other industrialized countries; however, the quality of U.S. health care, in terms of measures such as cervical cancer screening rates, flu immunization, and breast cancer survival rates and the percentage of the population that smokes, is not significantly superior to other less costly health care systems.

Another significant difference between the United States and other OECD countries is the lack of universal health insurance coverage. This gap in coverage explains why Americans go without needed health care more often than people in other OECD countries and why, in comparison to the other industrialized countries, the United States does not fare well in measures of access to care and equity in health care between high- and low-income populations. As the provisions of the ACA take effect, and the majority of Americans obtain health care coverage, these disparities will likely diminish, but not disappear entirely. According to Jeffrey Young, in "More Proof That American Health Care Prices Are Sky-High" (HuffingtonPost.com, April 17, 2014), industry observers predict that even 10 years after full implementation of the ACA millions of Americans will still lack health coverage.

Squires notes other key findings by the OECD, including:

- Spending growth slowed in many OECD member countries between 2000 and 2011. The average annual rate of spending growth was 4%.

- The United States reported the highest prevalence of obesity among adults in 2011, at 36.5%. Australia (28.3%) and New Zealand (27.8%) also reported high rates of obesity.

- Japan and the United States have more diagnostic imaging equipment—magnetic resonance imaging (MRI)—than any other OECD member. For example, in 2009 Australia had 5.9 MRI units per million population, compared with the United States, at 25.9, and Japan, at 43.1.

The United States

The U.S. health care financing system is based on the private insurance model. Employer-based health insurance is tax subsidized—that is, health insurance premiums are a tax-deductible business expense and are not generally taxed as employee compensation. Premiums for individual policies purchased by self-employed Americans became fully tax deductible in 2003. Benefits, premiums, and provider reimbursement methods differ among private insurance plans and among public programs as well.

Most physicians who provide both ambulatory care (hospital outpatient service and office visits) and inpatient hospital care are reimbursed on either a fee-for-service or per capita basis (literally, per head, but in managed care frequently per member per month), and payment rates vary among insurers. Increasing numbers of physicians are salaried; they are employees of the government, hospital, and health care delivery systems, universities, and private industry.

The nation's hospitals are paid on the basis of charges, costs, negotiated rates, or diagnosis-related groups (fixed payments for a specific diagnosis), depending on the insurer. There are no overall global budgets or expenditure limits. Nevertheless, managed care (oversight by some group or authority to verify the medical necessity of treatments and to control the cost of health care) has assumed an expanding role. Managed care plans and payers (government and private health insurance) now exert greater control over the practices of individual health care providers in an effort to control costs. To the extent that they govern reimbursement, managed care organizations are viewed by many industry observers as dictating the methods, terms, and quality of health care delivery.

IS THE UNITED STATES SPENDING MORE AND GETTING LESS? A primary indicator of the quality of health care delivery in any nation is the health status of its people. Many factors affect the health of individuals and populations: heredity, race and ethnicity, gender, income, education, geography, violent crime, environmental agents, and exposure to infectious diseases, as well as access to and availability of health care services.

Still, in the nation that spends the most on the health of its citizens, it seems reasonable to expect to see tangible benefits of expenditures for health care—that is, measurable gains in health status. This section considers three health outcomes (measures used to assess the health of a population)—life expectancy at birth, infant mortality (death), and health care costs—and selected aspects of health care delivery such as access and quality to determine the extent to which U.S. citizens derive health benefits from record-high outlays for medical care.

Overall, life expectancy at birth consistently increased in all the OECD member countries since 1960; however, historically, U.S. life expectancy has remained slightly below the OECD average. For example, Table 7.1 shows that in 2010 U.S. life expectancy for women (81 years)

TABLE 7.1

Life expectancy at birth, Organisation for Economic Co-operation and Development (OECD) countries, selected years 1980–2011

[Data are based on reporting by OECD countries]

Country	Male					Female				
	1980	1990	2000	2010	2011	1980	1990	2000	2010	2011
At birth					Life expectancy, in years					
Australia	71.0	73.9	76.6	79.5	†79.7	78.1	80.1	82.0	84.0	†84.2
Austria	69.0	72.3	75.2	77.9	78.3	76.1	79.0	81.2	83.5	†83.9
Belgium	69.9	72.7	74.6	77.6	†77.8	76.7	79.5	81.0	83.0	83.2
Canada	71.7	74.4	76.3	—	—	78.9	80.8	81.7	—	—
Chile	—	69.4	73.7	75.9	†75.7	—	76.5	80.0	82.0	†81.0
Czech Republic[a]	66.9	67.6	71.7	74.5	††74.8	74.0	75.5	78.5	80.9	††81.1
Denmark	71.2	72.0	74.5	77.2	77.8	77.3	77.8	79.2	81.4	81.9
Estonia	64.2	64.7	65.2	70.6	71.2	74.2	74.9	76.2	80.8	81.3
Finland	69.3	71.0	74.2	76.9	77.3	78.0	79.0	81.2	83.5	83.8
France	70.2	72.8	75.3	78.2	78.7	78.4	80.9	83.0	85.3	85.7
Germany[b]	69.6	72.0	75.1	78.0	78.4	76.2	78.5	81.2	83.0	83.2
Greece	73.0	74.7	75.5	78.4	78.5	77.5	79.5	80.6	82.8	83.1
Hungary	65.5	65.2	67.5	70.7	71.2	72.8	73.8	76.2	78.6	78.7
Iceland	73.5	75.5	77.8	79.8	80.7	80.4	80.7	81.6	84.1	84.1
Ireland	70.1	72.1	74.0	78.7	††78.3	75.6	77.7	79.2	83.2	††82.8
Israel[c]	72.1	74.9	76.7	79.7	79.9	75.7	78.4	80.9	83.6	83.6
Italy	70.6	73.8	76.9	79.8	†80.1	77.4	80.3	82.8	85.0	†85.3
Japan	73.4	75.9	77.7	79.6	79.4	78.8	81.9	84.6	86.3	85.9
Korea	61.8	67.3	72.3	77.2	77.7	70.0	75.5	79.6	84.1	84.5
Luxembourg	70.0	72.4	74.6	77.9	78.5	75.6	78.7	81.3	83.5	83.6
Mexico	64.1	67.0	70.5	71.1	71.2	70.2	74.0	76.1	77.0	77.2
Netherlands	72.5	73.8	75.6	78.9	79.4	79.2	80.3	80.7	83.0	83.1
New Zealand	70.1	72.5	75.9	79.1	79.4	76.2	78.4	80.8	82.8	83.0
Norway	72.4	73.5	76.0	79.0	79.1	79.3	79.9	81.5	83.3	83.6
Poland	66.0	66.3	69.6	72.1	††72.6	74.4	75.3	78.0	80.7	††81.1
Portugal	67.9	70.6	73.2	76.7	††77.6	74.9	77.5	80.2	82.8	††84.0
Slovak Republic[a]	66.8	66.7	69.2	71.7	††72.3	74.4	75.7	77.5	79.3	††79.8
Slovenia	—	69.8	72.2	76.4	76.8	—	77.8	79.9	83.1	83.3
Spain	72.3	73.4	75.8	79.1	79.4	78.5	80.6	82.9	85.3	85.4
Sweden	72.8	74.8	77.4	79.6	79.9	79.0	80.6	82.0	83.6	83.8
Switzerland	72.3	74.0	77.0	80.3	††80.5	79.0	80.9	82.8	84.9	††85.0
Turkey	55.8	††65.4	69.0	71.8	72.0	60.3	††69.5	73.1	76.8	77.1
United Kingdom	70.2	72.9	75.5	78.7	79.1	76.2	78.5	80.3	82.6	83.1
United States	70.0	71.8	74.1	76.2	—	77.4	78.8	79.3	81.0	—

—Data not available.

†Data are estimated.

††Break in series.

[a]In 1993, Czechoslovakia was divided into two nations, the Czech Republic and Slovakia. Data for years prior to 1993 are from the Czech and Slovak regions of Czechoslovakia.

[b]Until 1990, estimates refer to the Federal Republic of Germany; from 1995 onward data refer to Germany after reunification.

[c]Statistical data for Israel are supplied by, and under the responsibility of, the relevant Israeli authorities. The use of such data by OECD is without prejudice to the status of the Golan Heights, East Jerusalem, and Israeli settlements in the West Bank under the terms of international law.

Notes: Because calculation of life expectancy estimates varies among countries, ranks are not presented. Therefore, comparisons among countries and their interpretation should be made with caution. Some estimates for selected countries and selected years were revised and differ from previous editions of *Health, United States*.

SOURCE: Adapted from "Table 17. Life Expectancy at Birth and at Age 65, by Sex: Organisation for Economic Co-operation and Development (OECD) Countries, Selected Years 1980–2011," in *Health, United States, 2013: With Special Feature on Prescription Drugs*, U.S. Department of Health and Human Services, Centers for Disease Control and Prevention, National Center for Health Statistics, May 2014, http://www.cdc.gov/nchs/data/hus/hus13.pdf (accessed May 23, 2014). Data from Organisation for Economic Co-operation and Development Health Data.

was surpassed by all OECD member countries except the Czech Republic (80.9 years), Estonia (80.8), Poland (80.7), the Slovak Republic (79.3 years), Hungary (78.6), Mexico (77 years), and Turkey (76.8 years). Infant mortality also declined sharply during this period, but the United States fared far worse than most OECD member countries—in 2010 the United States ranked number 26 with an infant mortality rate of 6.1 deaths per 1,000 live births. (See Table 7.2.)

Ida Hellender of Physicians for a National Health Program observes in "The Deepening Crisis in U.S. Health Care: A Review of Data" (*International Journal of Health Services*, vol. 41, no. 3, 2011) that the United States ranks 49th in life expectancy and 42nd globally in deaths among children under the age of five years, trailing every country in western Europe and many other nations. The U.S. child mortality rate has declined by more than 40% since 1990, but it remains higher than many other nations.

Hellender also notes that although the United States spends twice as much per capita on health care as other developed countries, it ranked last in quality, efficiency, and equity when compared with Australia, Canada, Germany, the Netherlands, New Zealand, and the United Kingdom. The United Kingdom was named first in quality and the Netherlands was ranked first in all the other measures. In measures of access, efficiency,

TABLE 7.2

Infant mortality and international rankings, Organisation for Economic Co-operation and Development (OECD) countries, selected years 1960–2010

[Data are based on reporting by OECD countries]

Country[b]	1960	1970	1980	1990	2000	2008	2009	2010	International rankings[a] 1960	2010
					Infant[c] deaths per 1,000 live births					
Australia	20.2	17.9	10.7	8.2	5.2	4.1	4.3	4.1	5	20
Austria	37.5	25.9	14.3	7.8	4.8	3.7	3.8	3.9	19	19
Belgium	31.4	21.1	12.1	8.0	4.8	3.7	3.5	3.6	17	12
Canada	27.3	18.8	10.4	6.8	5.3	5.1	4.9	—	12	—
Chile	120.3	79.3	33.0	16.0	8.9	7.8	7.9	7.4	27	27
Czech Republic	20.0	20.2	16.9	10.8	4.1	2.8	2.9	2.7	4	5
Denmark	21.5	14.2	8.4	7.5	5.3	4.0	3.1	3.4	8	9
Finland	21.0	13.2	7.6	5.6	3.8	2.6	2.6	2.3	6	1
France	27.7	18.2	10.0	7.3	4.5	3.8	3.9	†3.6	13	12
Germany	35.0	22.5	12.4	7.0	4.4	3.5	3.5	3.4	18	9
Greece	40.1	29.6	17.9	9.7	5.9	2.7	3.1	3.8	20	15
Hungary	47.6	35.9	23.2	14.8	9.2	5.6	5.1	5.3	23	23
Ireland	29.3	19.5	11.1	8.2	6.2	3.8	3.3	3.8	15	15
Israel[d]	—	24.2	15.6	9.9	5.5	3.8	3.8	3.7	—	14
Italy	43.9	29.6	14.6	8.1	4.3	3.3	3.9	3.4	22	9
Japan	30.7	13.1	7.5	4.6	3.2	2.6	2.4	2.3	16	1
Korea	—	45.0	—	—	—	3.5	3.2	3.2	—	7
Mexico	92.3	—	52.6	—	19.4	15.2	14.6	14.1	26	29
Netherlands	16.5	12.7	8.6	7.1	5.1	3.8	3.8	3.8	2	15
New Zealand	22.6	16.7	13.0	8.4	6.3	5.0	5.2	5.5	10	24
Norway	16.0	11.3	8.1	6.9	3.8	2.7	3.1	2.8	1	6
Poland	56.1	36.4	25.4	19.4	8.1	5.6	5.6	5.0	24	22
Portugal	77.5	55.5	24.3	10.9	5.5	3.3	3.6	2.5	25	3
Slovak Republic	28.6	25.7	20.9	12.0	8.6	5.9	5.7	5.7	14	25
Spain	43.7	28.1	††12.3	7.6	4.3	3.3	3.2	3.2	21	7
Sweden	16.6	11.0	6.9	6.0	3.4	2.5	2.5	2.5	3	3
Switzerland	21.1	15.1	9.1	6.8	4.9	4.0	4.3	3.8	7	15
Turkey	189.5	145.0	117.5	††51.5	31.6	12.1	10.2	7.8	28	28
United Kingdom	22.5	18.5	12.1	7.9	5.6	4.7	4.6	4.2	9	21
United States	26.0	20.0	12.6	9.2	6.9	6.6	6.4	6.1	11	26

—Data not available.
†Data are estimated.
††Break in series.
[a]Rankings are from lowest to highest infant mortality rates (IMR). Countries with the same IMR receive the same rank. The country with the next highest IMR is assigned the rank it would have received had the lower-ranked countries not been tied, i.e., skip a rank. The latest year's international rankings are based on 2010 data because that is the most current data year for which most countries have reported their final data to OECD. Countries without an estimate in the OECD database are omitted from this table. Relative rankings for individual countries may be affected if not all countries have reported data to OECD.
[b]Refers to countries, territories, cities, or geographic areas with at least 2.5 million population in 2000 and with complete counts of live births and infant deaths according to the United Nations Demographic Yearbook.
[c]Under 1 year of age.
[d]Statistical data for Israel are supplied by, and under the responsibility of, the relevant Israeli authorities. The use of such data by the OECD is without prejudice to the status of the Golan Heights, East Jerusalem, and Israeli settlements in the West Bank under the terms of international law.
Notes: Some rates for selected countries and selected years were revised and differ from previous editions of *Health, United States*.

SOURCE: "Table 16. Infant Mortality Rates and International Rankings: Organisation for Economic Co-operation and Development (OECD) Countries, Selected Years 1960–2010," in *Health, United States, 2013: With Special Feature on Prescription Drugs*, U.S. Department of Health and Human Services, Centers for Disease Control and Prevention, National Center for Health Statistics, May 2014, http://www.cdc.gov/nchs/data/hus/hus13.pdf (accessed May 23, 2014). Data from Organisation for Economic Co-operation and Development Health Data.

equity, premature deaths, infant mortality, and healthy life expectancy among older adults, the United States trailed the other countries, coming in last or next to last. Table 7.3 shows that in 2010 the life expectancy of a man aged 65 was 17.7 years in the United States, compared with about 19 years in Australia, France, Israel, Japan, New Zealand, and Switzerland. For a woman of the same age, the life expectancy in the United States was 20.3 years, compared with between 22 and 24 years in France, Italy, Japan, Spain, and Switzerland.

Compared with the systems of other industrialized countries, the U.S. health care system is not only more costly but also less affordable and accessible. In "Access, Affordability, and Insurance Complexity Are Often Worse in the United States Compared to 10 Other Countries" (*Health Affairs*, vol. 32, no. 12, November 13, 2013), a survey of 11 countries conducted by the Commonwealth Fund, Cathy Schoen et al. cite examples of disparities. For example, the researches note that 37% of U.S. adults went without recommended care in 2013, compared with just 4% to 6% in the United Kingdom and Sweden. Likewise, 23% of U.S. adults had difficulty paying medical bills, compared with less than 13% of adults in France and 6% or less in the United Kingdom, Sweden, and Norway.

TABLE 7.3

Life expectancy at age 65, Organisation for Economic Co-operation and Development (OECD) countries, selected years 1980–2011

[Data are based on reporting by OECD countries]

Country	Male					Female				
	1980	1990	2000	2010	2011	1980	1990	2000	2010	2011
At 65 years					Life expectancy, in years					
Australia	13.7	15.2	16.9	18.9	19.1[†]	17.9	19.0	20.4	21.8	22.0[†]
Austria	12.9	14.4	16.0	17.9	18.1	16.3	18.1	19.6	21.4	21.7
Belgium	12.9	14.3	15.6	17.6	17.8[†]	16.8	18.8	19.7	21.3	21.5[†]
Canada	14.5	15.7	16.5	—	—	18.9	19.9	20.2	—	—
Chile	—	13.7	15.5	17.1	16.6[†]	—	17.2	19.3	20.8	19.6[†]
Czech Republic[a]	11.2	11.7	13.8	15.5	15.6[††]	14.4	15.3	17.3	19.0	19.2[††]
Denmark	13.6	14.0	15.2	17.0	17.3	17.7	17.9	18.3	19.7	—
Estonia	—	12.0	12.6	14.2	14.7	—	15.8	17.0	19.4	20.0
Finland	12.6	13.8	15.5	17.5	17.7	17.0	17.8	19.5	21.5	21.7
France	13.6	15.5	16.8	18.9	19.3	18.2	19.8	21.4	23.4	23.8
Germany[b]	12.8	14.0	15.8	17.8	18.2	16.3	17.7	19.6	20.9	21.2
Greece	15.2	15.7	16.1	18.5	18.5	17.0	18.0	18.4	20.4	20.6
Hungary	11.6	12.1	13.0	14.1	14.3	14.7	15.4	16.7	18.2	18.3
Iceland	15.7	16.4	17.8	18.3	18.9	19.3	19.8	19.8	21.5	21.5
Ireland	12.6	13.3	14.6	18.1	17.9[††]	15.7	17.0	18.0	21.1	20.7[††]
Israel[c]	—	15.7	17.0	18.9	19.0	—	17.8	19.0	21.2	21.2
Italy	13.3	15.2	16.7	18.6	18.8[††]	17.1	19.0	20.7	22.4	22.6[†]
Japan	14.6	16.2	17.5	18.7	18.7	17.7	20.0	22.4	23.8	23.7
Korea	10.5	12.4	14.3	17.2	17.4	15.1	16.3	18.2	21.6	21.9
Luxembourg	12.6	14.3	15.5	17.3	17.8	16.5	18.5	20.1	21.6	21.6
Mexico	15.4	16.0	16.5	16.6	16.7	17.0	18.0	18.4	18.5	18.5
Netherlands	13.7	14.4	15.4	17.7	18.1	18.0	19.1	19.3	21.0	21.2
New Zealand	13.2	14.6	16.5	18.8	19.0	17.0	18.3	19.8	21.2	21.3
Norway	14.3	14.6	16.1	18.0	18.2	18.2	18.7	19.9	21.2	21.4
Poland	12.0	12.4	13.5	15.1	15.4[††]	15.5	16.2	17.5	19.5	19.9[††]
Portugal	13.1	14.0	15.4	17.1	18.1[††]	16.1	17.1	18.9	20.6	21.8[††]
Slovak Republic[a]	12.1	12.3	12.9	14.0	14.5[††]	15.3	16.0	16.7	18.0	18.4[††]
Slovenia	—	13.4	14.2	16.8	16.9	—	17.1	18.7	21.0	21.1
Spain	14.6	15.5	16.7	18.6	18.7	17.8	19.3	20.8	22.7	22.8
Sweden	14.3	15.4	16.7	18.3	18.5	18.1	19.2	20.2	21.2	21.3
Switzerland	14.3	15.3	17.0	19.0	19.2[††]	18.2	19.7	20.9	22.5	22.6[†]
Turkey	11.7	12.8[††]	13.4	14.0	14.1	12.8	14.3[††]	15.1	16.0	16.1
United Kingdom	12.6	14.0	15.8	18.3	18.3	16.6	17.9	19.0	20.9	21.2
United States	14.1	15.1	16.0	17.7	—	18.3	18.9	19.0	20.3	—

—Data not available.

[†]Data are estimated.

[††]Break in series.

[a]In 1993, Czechoslovakia was divided into two nations, the Czech Republic and Slovakia. Data for years prior to 1993 are from the Czech and Slovak regions of Czechoslovakia.

[b]Until 1990, estimates refer to the Federal Republic of Germany; from 1995 onward data refer to Germany after reunification.

[c]Statistical data for Israel are supplied by, and under the responsibility of, the relevant Israeli authorities. The use of such data by OECD is without prejudice to the status of the Golan Heights, East Jerusalem, and Israeli settlements in the West Bank under the terms of international law.

Notes: Because calculation of life expectancy estimates varies among countries, ranks are not presented. Therefore, comparisons among countries and their interpretation should be made with caution. Some estimates for selected countries and selected years were revised and differ from previous editions of *Health, United States*.

SOURCE: Adapted from "Table 17. Life Expectancy at Birth and at Age 65 Years, by Sex: Organisation for Economic Co-operation and Development (OECD) Countries, Selected Years 1980–2011," in *Health, United States, 2013: With Special Feature on Prescription Drugs*, U.S. Department of Health and Human Services, Centers for Disease Control and Prevention, National Center for Health Statistics, May 2014, http://www.cdc.gov/nchs/data/hus/hus13.pdf (accessed May 23, 2014). Data from Organisation for Economic Co-operation and Development Health Data.

Schoen et al. report that 75% of Americans feel the U.S. health care system "needs to undergo fundamental changes." The researchers attribute Americans' dissatisfaction to access and affordability as well as to the complexity of navigating the health care system, especially insurance paperwork.

Germany

The German health care system is based on the social insurance model. Statutory sickness funds and private insurance cover the entire population. In "The German Health Care System, 2011" (Sarah Thomson et al., eds., *International Profiles of Health Care Systems, 2013*, November 2013, http://www.commonwealthfund.org), Miriam Blümel of the Berlin University of Technology states that since 2009 health insurance has been mandatory for all citizens and permanent residents. Coverage is provided by competing, nonprofit, nongovernmental health insurance funds in the statutory health insurance scheme (SHI) or by voluntary private health insurance.

During the late 1990s Germany was the second highest among the OECD member countries in health expenditures per capita, but the OECD notes in *Health at a Glance 2013* that by 2011 Germany ranked 15th in health expenditures per capita. Public funds, a combination of social insurance and general government funds, paid for more than three-quarters (77%) of total expenditures for health care in 2011, which was nearly the OECD average of 72%.

Ambulatory (outpatient) and inpatient care operate separately in the German health care system. German hospitals are public and private, operate for profit and not for profit, and generally do not have outpatient departments. About half of all hospital beds are not for profit, but the number of private, for-profit hospitals has increased in recent years and accounts for about one-sixth of all beds. Since 2004 inpatient care has been paid for via diagnosis-related groups based on 1,187 categories. Ambulatory care physicians are paid on the basis of fee schedules that are negotiated between the organizations of sickness funds and the organizations of physicians. A separate fee schedule for private patients uses a similar scale.

In 1993 Germany's Health Care Reform Law went into effect. It tied increases in physician, dental, and hospital expenditures to the income growth rate of members of the sickness funds. It also limited the licensing of new ambulatory care physicians (based on the number of physicians already in an area) and set a cap for overall pharmaceutical outlays. Still, according to the OECD, Germany boasted 3.8 practicing physicians per 1,000 population in 2011, a ratio that was higher than the OECD average of 3.2.

The health care reforms were not, however, successful at containing health care costs. Growth in health care spending was attributed to the comparatively high level of health care activity and resources, along with rising pharmaceutical expenditures and efforts to meet the health care needs of an aging population.

Between 2010 and 2012 more health reforms were instituted. In 2010 the SHI Financing Act, which pays a flat per capita rate for SHI, was enacted into law. The SHI Reform Act of 2010 and the Pharmaceuticals Market Reform Act of 2011 required pharmaceutical manufacturers to increase their discount from 6% to 16%, and the SHI Care Structure Act aimed to improve services nationwide by addressing problems of under- and oversupply. The General Law on Patients' Rights was implemented 2013 to strengthen patients' rights. It incorporates the treatment agreement into the civil code, establishing the rights, duties, and forms of etiquette for the relationship between provider and patient and requires that patient requests for information and documentation be fulfilled.

Canada

The Canadian system is characterized as a provincial government health insurance model, in which each of the provinces operates its own health system under general federal rules and with a fixed federal contribution. All provinces are required to offer insurance coverage for all medically necessary services, including hospital care and physician services. However, additional services and benefits may be offered at the discretion of each province. Most cover preventive services, routine dental care for children, and outpatient drugs for older adults (with a co-payment) and the poor.

Canadian citizens have equal access to medical care, regardless of their ability to pay. Entitlement to benefits is linked to residency, and the system is financed through general taxation. Private insurance is prohibited from covering the same benefits that are covered by the public system, yet a majority of Canadians are covered by private supplemental insurance policies. These policies generally cover services such as adult dental care, cosmetic surgery, and private or semiprivate hospital rooms. The OECD reports in *Health at a Glance 2013* that Canada's total health expenditures accounted for 11.2% of the GDP in 2011.

The delivery system consists mostly of community hospitals and self-employed physicians. Nearly all of Canadian hospital beds are public; private hospitals do not participate in the public insurance program. Most hospitals are not for profit and are funded on the basis of global institution-specific or regional budgets. (A global institution-specific budget allocates a lump sum of money to a large department or area; then all the groups in that department or area must negotiate to see how much of the total money each group receives.) Physicians in both inpatient and outpatient settings are paid on a negotiated, fee-for-service basis. Sara Allin and David Rudoler of the University of Toronto report in "The Canadian Health Care System, 2013" (Sarah Thomson et al., eds., *International Profiles of Health Care Systems, 2013*, November 2013, http://www.com monwealthfund.org) that 70% of total health expenditures were publicly funded in 2012, and 30% of total health expenditures were from private sources (private insurance and out-of-pocket payments). About two-thirds of Canadians have supplementary private insurance coverage, which many obtain through their employers. These supplemental plans cover services such as vision and dental care, prescription drugs, rehabilitation services, home care, and private rooms in hospitals.

CONTROLLING COSTS. According to Allin and Rudoler, cost containment is achieved through single-payer purchasing power and that increases in health care expenditures generally occur in response to government investment decisions. Actions to control costs include "mandatory annual global budgets for hospitals and regional health authorities, negotiated fee schedules for health care providers, drug formularies, and reviews of the diffusion of technology." The federal Patented Medicine Prices Review Board, an independent body, regulates the prices of newly patented prescription medications. It guarantees "that patented drug prices are not 'excessive,' on the basis of their 'degree of innovation,'" and compares the prices of existing prescription drugs in Canada with the prices of these drugs in other countries, including the United States.

Allin and Rudoler report that recent cost-containment efforts include reducing the prices of generic drugs. In 2013 all provinces/territories except Quebec started bulk purchasing six of the highest-selling generic drugs. Other provinces/territories, such as Saskatchewan and Manitoba, have taken steps to reduce waste and add value to the process of health care delivery, consistent with the principles of lean management advocated by the Institute for Healthcare Improvement.

Between 2008 and 2013 Canada's health care spending outpaced the rate of inflation by nearly 4%. In "Sustainability of the Canadian Health Care System and Impact of the 2014 Revision to the Canada Health Transfer" (September 2013, http://www.soa.org/Canadian-Health-Care-Sustainability), an analysis of the system, Stéphane Levert asserts that without government intervention to limit health care expenditures, provincial/territorial spending for health care is projected to increase 5.1% per year, growing from 44% in 2013 to 103% of total provincial/territorial revenues by 2037. Levert also finds that the country does not have an adequate physician supply to meet the needs of the population in the coming decades and concludes, "that without significant government intervention, the Canadian health care system in its current form is not sustainable."

According to Trudy Lieberman, in "U.S., Canadian Health Care Systems Share Some Challenges" (HealthJournalism.org, January 15, 2014), in 2011 Canada had the third-highest per capita health spending of OECD-developed nations. Lieberman observes that Canadians "report long waits for primary care and high use of emergency rooms compared to other countries such as Germany, France and the United Kingdom." Older adults admitted to acute care hospitals may have longer lengths of stay than are necessary because there is a lack of long-term care facilities.

Europe

In "The Political Economy of Austerity and Healthcare: Cross-National Analysis of Expenditure Changes in 27 European Nations 1995–2011" (*Health Policy*, vol. 115, no. 1, March 2014), Aaron Reeves et al. look at political, economic, and health system factors that influenced health care expenditures in 27 European Union countries between 1995 and 2011. The researchers point out that although nearly all European countries experienced economic recessions since 2007, not all responded by cutting health care spending. For example, Austria and Germany suffered comparable recessions between 2008 and 2009; Austria reduced per capita government spending on health care, whereas Germany increased its per capita spending.

Reeves et al. observe that some countries allowed total spending to increase to meet growing needs, despite rising debts and deficits; some allowed health care spending to rise, based on the assumption that improved quality and accessibility of health services would stimulate economic growth; and some slowed or reduced government health spending. The researchers note that changes in health care spending were not "determined by the ideology of the governing party," but that countries that received International Monetary Fund (IMF) loans were more likely to have cut health care expenditures. The IMF explains in the fact sheet "IMF Lending" (September 5, 2014, http://www.imf.org/external/np/exr/facts/howlend.htm) that its loans enable countries to "rebuild their international reserves, stabilize their currencies, continue paying for imports, and restore conditions for strong economic growth." Reeves et al. call for future research to assess the health effects of reduced spending.

ENGLAND. England employs the National Health Service (NHS), or Beveridge, model to finance and deliver health care. The entire population is covered under a system that is financed primarily from general taxation. There is minimal cost sharing. In 2011, 83% of all health spending was from public funds. Anthony Harrison of the King's Fund in London explains in "The English Health Care System, 2013" (Sarah Thomson et al., eds., *International Profiles of Health Care Systems, 2013*, November 2013, http://www.commonwealthfund.org) that the NHS "provides or pays for: preventive services, including screening, immunization, and vaccination programs; inpatient and outpatient hospital care; physician services; inpatient and outpatient drugs; some dental care; some eye care; mental health care, including some care for those with learning disabilities; palliative care; some long-term care; rehabilitation, including physiotherapy (e.g., after-stroke care); and home visits by community-based nurses."

England's hospital beds are public and generally owned by the NHS. The OECD reports in "OECD Health Data—Frequently Requested Data" that in 2010 there were 2.9 beds per 1,000 population, which was comparable to the United States (3.1 beds), but fewer than other European nations, such as France (6.4) and Germany (8.3).

Parliament and the Department of Health share the responsibility for health legislation and policy matters. Health services are organized and managed by regional and local public authorities. General practitioners serve as primary care physicians and are reimbursed on the basis of a combination of capitation payments (payments for each person served), fee for service, and other allowances. Hospitals receive overall budget allotments from district health authorities, and hospital-based physicians are salaried. Harrison notes that private insurance reimburses both physicians and hospitals on a fee-for-service basis. Approximately 11% of the population had private health insurance in 2011.

Most general practitioners, who are the frontline of health care delivery, are either self-employed or salaried hospital-based physicians. According to Harrison, in 2012 there were 8,088 general practices—1,480 solo practices and 3,525 practices with five or more general practitioners—and each practice saw an average of 6,891 patients.

Michael Ybarra notes in "Healthcare around the World" (*American Academy of Emergency Medicine*, vol. 16, no. 6, 2009) that the NHS pioneered many cost-containment measures that are currently used by the United States and other countries seeking to slow health care expenditures. These approaches include:

- Cost-effective analysis—calculated as a ratio, and often expressed as the cost per year per life saved, the cost-effectiveness analysis of a drug or procedure relates the cost of the drug or procedure to the health benefits it produces. This analysis enables delivery of clinically efficient, cost-effective care.

- Cost-minimization analysis—primarily applied to the pharmaceutical industry, this technique identifies the lowest cost among pharmaceutical alternatives that provide clinically comparable health outcomes.

- Cost-utility analysis—this measures the costs of therapy or treatment. Economists use the term *utility* to describe the amount of satisfaction a consumer receives from a given product or service. This analysis measures outcomes in terms of patient preference and is generally expressed as quality-adjusted life years. For example, an analysis of cancer chemotherapy drugs considers the various adverse side effects of these drugs because some patients may prefer a shorter duration of symptom-free survival rather than a longer life span marked by pain, suffering, and dependence on others for care.

Harrison reports that the NHS aimed to save $32 billion between 2011 and 2015 by strictly limiting pay increases, economical purchasing of NHS supplies, increased use of generic drugs, reductions in payments for hospitals, and other measures intended to improve operational efficiency.

England's health care system faces access challenges and disparities in health outcomes. For example, in "Over the Rainbow: Delivering on the Promise of England's New Public Health System" (*Journal of Epidemiology and Community Health*, vol. 68, no.1, 2014), David Conrad of Public Health England cites the gap in life expectancy between the general population and residents of "deprived areas" as a glaring example of persistent health inequality. Conrad hopes that England's new public health system, which began in April 2014, will be able to effectively address these kinds inequalities.

FRANCE. The French health care system is based on the social insurance, or Bismarck, model. Virtually the entire population is covered by a legislated, compulsory health insurance plan that is financed by the social security system. The system is funded through employer and employee payroll taxes (43%), a national income tax (33%), revenue from taxes on tobacco and alcohol (8%), state subsidies (2%), and funds from other branches of social security (8%). The OECD notes in *Health at a Glance 2013* that the total expenditure for health in France was 11.6% of the GDP in 2011.

According to the OECD, the public share of total health spending in 2011 was 70%, and 16% of expenditures represented direct, out-of-pocket payments. Physicians practicing in municipal health centers and public hospitals are salaried, but physicians in private hospitals and ambulatory care settings are typically paid on a negotiated, fee-for-service basis. The government establishes the reimbursement schedule for physicians and for other health care goods and services including pharmaceutical drugs. Public hospitals are granted lump-sum budgets, and private hospitals are paid on the basis of negotiated per diem payment rates. In "OECD Health Data—Frequently Requested Data," the OECD reports that the number of hospital beds per 1,000 population declined from 8 in 2000 to 6.3 in 2012.

Isabelle Durand-Zaleski of Assistance Publique, Hôpitaux de Paris, explains in "The French Health Care System, 2013" (Sarah Thomson et al., eds., *International Profiles of Health Care Systems, 2013*, November 2013, http://www.commonwealthfund.org) that in 2004 health financing reform laws introduced a gatekeeping system for adults. Although the system is voluntary, strong financial incentives, such as higher co-payments for visits and prescriptions without referral from the gatekeeper, encourage participation. By 2011 85% of the population had registered with a gatekeeper and physicians and hospitals were generally accepting of moderate fee schedules, cost-sharing arrangements, and global budgeting to control costs.

In 2012 the government moved to reduce excessive billing. Physicians who agreed to limit their extra billing to just $95 above their conventional reimbursement were granted reduced social insurance premiums and higher fees for procedures. Durand-Zaleski reports that the move was decidedly unpopular among physicians. By May 2013 just 3,000 of the 25,000 eligible physicians had signed the agreement. A more successful cost-containment measure introduced that same year offers patients who accept generic as opposed to brand-name prescription drugs essentially free medication. The rate of substitution of generic drugs for brand-name drugs rose from 71% to 84% in one year, yielding cost savings of more than $270 million.

Like other countries, the French health care system has problems with access and inequalities. In "Disparities in Access to Health Care in Three French Regions" (*Health Policy*, vol. 114, no 1, January 2014), Michael K. Gusmano et al. compare access to primary and specialty care in three metropolitan regions of France and identify the factors that contribute to disparities in access to care in these regions. Not surprisingly, the researchers find that residents in low-income areas and patients treated in public hospitals had poorer access to primary and specialty care. Gusmano et al. conclude, "Even within a national health insurance system that minimizes the financial barriers to health care and has one of the highest rates of spending on health care in Europe, the challenge of minimizing these disparities remains."

Japan

Japan's health care financing is based on the social insurance model. According to the OECD, in *Health at a Glance 2013*, 82% of health expenditures were from public funds in 2011. Ryozo Matsuda of Ritsumeikan University notes in "The Japanese Health Care System, 2013" (Sarah Thomson et al., eds., *International Profiles of Health Care Systems, 2013*, November 2013, http://www.commonwealthfund.org) that the universal public health insurance system involves coverage from 3,500 insurers.

The OECD indicates that the health care system, which cost 9.6% of Japan's GDP in 2011, is financed through employer and employee income-related premiums. Limited private insurance exists for supplemental coverage and is purchased by about one-third of the population. In 2011 out-of-pocket expenses accounted for 15% of health expenditures.

Physicians and hospitals are paid on the basis of national, negotiated fee schedules. Japan manages with fewer physicians per capita than most OECD member countries—just 2.2 physicians per 1,000 population in 2011. Physicians practicing in public hospitals are salaried, whereas those practicing in physician-owned clinics and private hospitals are reimbursed on a fee-for-service basis, with financial incentives for taking better care of patients with chronic diseases. Physicians not only diagnose, treat, and manage illnesses but also prescribe and dispense pharmaceuticals.

According to Matsuda, about 55% of Japan's hospitals are nonprofit and privately operated. Although hospital admissions are less frequent, hospital stays in Japan are typically far longer than in the United States or in any other OECD member nation, allowing hospitals and physicians to overcome the limitations of the fee schedules.

The health status of the Japanese is one of the best in the world. Japanese men and women are among the longest living in all of the OECD member countries. In 2011 life expectancy at birth was 79.4 years for men and 85.9 years for women. (See Table 7.1.) The Japanese infant mortality rate in 2010, at 2.3 deaths per 1,000 live births, was the lowest of the OECD countries. (See Table 7.2.) These two sets statistics are usually considered to be reliable indicators of a successful health care system. It should be noted, however, that Japan does not have a large impoverished class, as the United States does, and its diet is considered to be among the most healthful in the world.

Matsuda explains that the disasters that beset Japan in 2011—the destructive earthquake, tsunami, and nuclear emergency—destroyed a significant portion of the health care infrastructure. Restoring vital health services to the affected region has been a national priority, and Matsuda observes that "rebuilding is a primary focus of the current government." In "Planning Innovation and Post-disaster Reconstruction: The Case of Tohoku, Japan" (*Planning Theory and Practice*, vol. 15, no. 2, 2014), Kayo Murakamia et al. observe that in many areas such as Tohoku, Japan, recovery and rebuilding were still under way in 2014, three years after the disasters. This is in part because Tohoku was already in decline before the disasters—its rural industries had collapsed and its aging population was unable to reinvigorate the local economy. In areas such as Tohoku, populations are predicted to decline in the coming two decades. As a result, tax revenues will decline, whereas maintenance and operational costs and health and welfare-related expenditures will increase. Furthermore, reconstruction requires annual budgets that are 10 times greater than required before the disasters. There is growing concern that the costs of new facilities are going to be prohibitive and could even trigger a national financial collapse.

CHAPTER 8
CHANGE, CHALLENGES, AND INNOVATION IN HEALTH CARE DELIVERY

Since the 1970s the U.S. health care system has experienced rapid and unprecedented change. The sites where health care is delivered have shifted from acute inpatient hospitals to outpatient settings, such as ambulatory care and surgical centers, clinics, physicians' offices, and long-term care and rehabilitation facilities. Patterns of disease have changed from acute infectious diseases that require episodic care to chronic conditions that require ongoing care. Even threats to U.S. public health have changed—for example, epidemics of infectious diseases have largely been replaced by epidemics of chronic conditions such as obesity, diabetes, and mental illness. At the end of 2001 the threat of bioterrorism became an urgent concern of health care planners, providers, policy makers, and the American public; between 2009 and 2010 the nation was mobilized to mitigate the effects of the H1N1 pandemic influenza; and in 2010 the government took historic action by passing the Patient Protection and Affordable Care Act and the Health Care and Education Reconciliation Act (which are now commonly known as the ACA), which aim to provide health care coverage to nearly all of the nation's people. In 2014 the health care system organized a response to the Ebola virus outbreak in West Africa and treated cases of the disease that were diagnosed in the United States.

There are new health care providers—midlevel practitioners (advanced practice nurses, certified nurse midwives, physician assistants, and medical technologists)—and new modes of diagnosis such as genetic testing. Furthermore, the rise of managed care, the explosion of biotechnology, and the availability of information on the Internet have dramatically changed how health care is delivered.

The ACA emphasizes the use of health information technology (IT), especially the adoption of electronic health records (EHRs). The act promotes the use of EHRs and other IT not only to help achieve the objectives of health care reform, including intensifying efforts to assess, monitor, and improve patient safety and quality of service delivery, but also to simplify the administration of health services, ensure cost-effective health service delivery, and reduce the growth of health care expenditures.

In "Does the Accountable Care Act Aim to Promote Quality, Health, and Control Costs or Has It Missed the Mark? Comment on 'Health System Reform in the United States'" (*International Journal of Health Policy and Management*, vol. 2, no. 2, February 2014), Carol Molinari of the University of Baltimore explains that the ACA contains financial incentives and penalties that are aimed at improving the quality and coordination of care and reducing health care costs. For example, accountable care organizations and medical homes are incentivized to provide a continuum of health services to manage and coordinate care. Hospitals are penalized for hospital-acquired infections and readmission of Medicare patients.

Some health care industry observers suggest the speed at which these changes have occurred has further harmed an already complicated and uncoordinated health care system. There is concern that the present health care system cannot keep pace with scientific and technological advances. Many worry that the health care system is already unable to deliver quality care to all Americans and that it is so disorganized that it will be unable to meet the needs of the growing population of older Americans and the estimated 30 million previously uninsured Americans who will gain health care coverage, or to respond to the threat of a pandemic or an act of bioterrorism.

This chapter considers several of the most pressing challenges and opportunities faced by the U.S. health care system, including:

- Safety—ensuring safety by protecting patients from harm or injury inflicted by the health care system (e.g., preventing medical errors, reducing hospital-acquired infections, and safeguarding consumers from medical fraud). Besides actions to reduce problems caused by the health care system, safety and quality may be ensured by providers' use of clinical practice guidelines (standardized plans for diagnosis and treatment of disease and the effective application of technology to information and communication systems).

- Information management—IT, including the Internet, can provide health care providers and consumers with timely access to medical data, patient information, and the clinical expertise of specialists. For example, in "The Impact of EHR and HIE on Reducing Avoidable Admissions: Controlling Main Differential Diagnoses" (*BMC Medical Informatics and Decision Making*, vol. 13, April 2013), Ofir Ben-Assuli, Itamar Shabtai, and Moshe Leshno analyze emergency department data to determine whether EHR use resulted in more accurate and informed admission decisions. The researchers find that EHR use resulted in fewer seven-day readmissions and fewer single-day admissions. Besides reducing readmissions, EHR systems are credited with improving the timeliness and accuracy of communication and coordination among providers and with patients, creating shorter lengths of stay, and making it easier to pinpoint the causes of errors and take action to prevent them.

SAFETY

Patient safety is a critical component of health care quality. Although the United States is generally viewed as providing quality health care services to its citizens, the Institute of Medicine (IOM) estimates in the landmark report *To Err Is Human: Building a Safer Health System* (1999, http://www.nap.edu/books/0309068371/html) that as many as 98,000 American deaths per year are the result of preventable medical errors. More than 7,000 of these deaths are estimated to be due to preventable medication errors.

In 2013 HealthGrades, Inc., an independent health care quality research organization that grades hospitals based on a range of criteria and provides hospital ratings to health plans and other payers, issued its 10th update of the 1999 IOM report. In *Patient Safety and Satisfaction: The State of American Hospitals* (April 2013), HealthGrades finds that hospitals that received the highest patient safety ratings were very different from those in the bottom 5% for patient safety. Specifically, in the hospitals that were noted for safety, patients were 81% less likely to suffer a hip fracture following surgery, 80% less likely to acquire pressure ulcers (bedsores), and 70% less likely to acquire a catheter-related bloodstream infection in the hospital.

AHRQ Patient Safety Indicators

The Agency for Healthcare Research and Quality (AHRQ) has identified qualities and characteristics of organizational culture that contribute to or detract from patient safety in hospitals. Figure 8.1 lists and defines the 10 composites that are used to assess the safety culture in hospitals.

In *Hospital Survey on Patient Safety Culture: 2014 User Comparative Database Report* (March 2014, http://www.ahrq.gov/professionals/quality-patient-safety/patientsafetyculture/hospital/2014/hsops14pt1.pdf), Joann Sorra et al. report the results of a survey of 653 hospitals with a total of 405,281 hospital staff respondents that was conducted between 2007 and October 2012. The composite scores, which give each hospital equal weight rather than favoring larger hospitals with more survey respondents, show how hospitals fared on these indicators in 2014. The survey items with the highest average percent positive response (86%) were from the patient safety culture characteristic Teamwork within Units: "People support one another in this unit" and "When a lot of work needs to be done quickly, we work together as a team to get the work done." The item with the lowest average percent positive response (35%) was from the patient safety culture characteristic Nonpunitive Response to Error: "Staff worry that mistakes they make are kept in their personnel file."

Figure 8.2 shows how survey respondents view their hospital work area or unit in terms of its overall patient safety. On average, most respondents were positive, with three-quarters (76%) awarding their work area or unit a patient safety grade of A (33%) or B (43%). More than half (56%) of the survey respondents said the number of events reported during the past 12 months had not changed. (See Figure 8.3.) Over a quarter (28%) of hospitals reported a 5% or greater decrease in the number of events reported. The frequency of patient safety event reporting was deemed an area for improvement for most hospitals because the underreporting of events suggests that potential patient safety problems may go undetected and, as a result, may not be addressed.

Strengthening Safety Measures

In response to a request from the U.S. Department of Health and Human Services (HHS), the IOM's Committee on Data Standards for Patient Safety created a detailed plan to develop standards for the collection, coding, and classification of patient safety information. The 550-page plan, *Patient Safety: Achieving a New Standard for Care* (2004), called on the HHS to assume the lead in establishing a national health information infrastructure that would provide immediate access to complete patient information and decision support tools, such as clinical practice guidelines, and capture patient

FIGURE 8.1

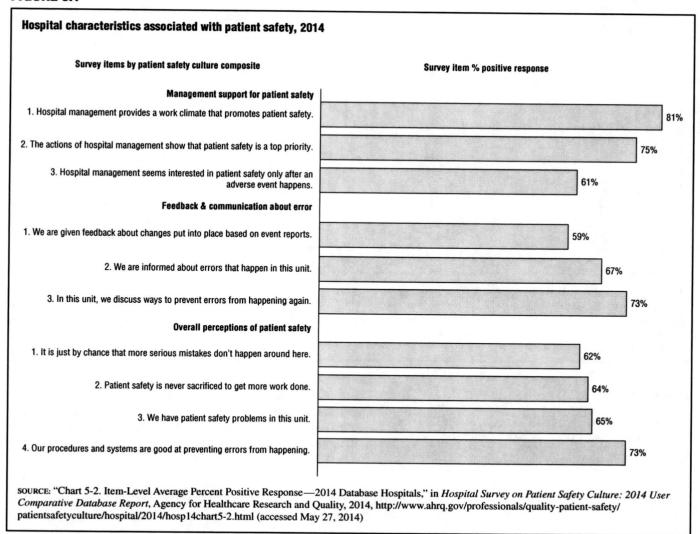

Hospital characteristics associated with patient safety, 2014

Survey items by patient safety culture composite | Survey item % positive response

Management support for patient safety

1. Hospital management provides a work climate that promotes patient safety. — 81%

2. The actions of hospital management show that patient safety is a top priority. — 75%

3. Hospital management seems interested in patient safety only after an adverse event happens. — 61%

Feedback & communication about error

1. We are given feedback about changes put into place based on event reports. — 59%

2. We are informed about errors that happen in this unit. — 67%

3. In this unit, we discuss ways to prevent errors from happening again. — 73%

Overall perceptions of patient safety

1. It is just by chance that more serious mistakes don't happen around here. — 62%

2. Patient safety is never sacrificed to get more work done. — 64%

3. We have patient safety problems in this unit. — 65%

4. Our procedures and systems are good at preventing errors from happening. — 73%

SOURCE: "Chart 5-2. Item-Level Average Percent Positive Response—2014 Database Hospitals," in *Hospital Survey on Patient Safety Culture: 2014 User Comparative Database Report*, Agency for Healthcare Research and Quality, 2014, http://www.ahrq.gov/professionals/quality-patient-safety/patientsafetyculture/hospital/2014/hosp14chart5-2.html (accessed May 27, 2014)

safety data for use in designing constantly improving and safer health care delivery systems.

The IOM plan exhorted all health care settings to develop and implement comprehensive patient safety programs and recommended that the federal government launch patient safety research initiatives aimed at increasing knowledge, developing tools, and disseminating results to maximize the effectiveness of patient safety systems. The plan also advised the designation of a standardized format and terminology for identifying and reporting data related to medical errors.

In July 2005 President George W. Bush (1946–) signed into law the Patient Safety and Quality Improvement Act. Angela S. Mattie and Rosalyn Ben-Chitrit surmise in "Patient Safety Legislation: A Look at Health Policy Development" (*Policy, Politics, and Nursing Practice*, vol. 8, no. 4, November 2007) that the IOM call for action to improve patient safety in *To Err Is Human* prompted Congress to pass legislation.

How Will the ACA Improve Patient Safety?

Barry R. Furrow of Drexel University states in "Regulating Patient Safety: The Patient Protection and Affordable Care Act" (*University of Pennsylvania Law Review*, vol. 159, May 10, 2011) that "ten years after the IOM report, the level of adverse events in hospitals has not improved in any major way." He explains that the ACA has a range of provisions that are aimed at improving the quality of the health care system by reducing errors and promoting patient safety. The act mandates and funds continuous, data-driven testing of the performance of health care professionals and facilities. It also funds demonstration projects of novel health care delivery systems and requires that their performance be measured and analyzed to determine whether they merit wider adoption. Furrow concludes that the ACA "offers a strong regulatory push toward the goal of 'flawless execution,' the health care equivalent of zero defects in industrial production."

The ACA also aims to improve health care quality and safety by supporting patient safety organizations. In

FIGURE 8.2

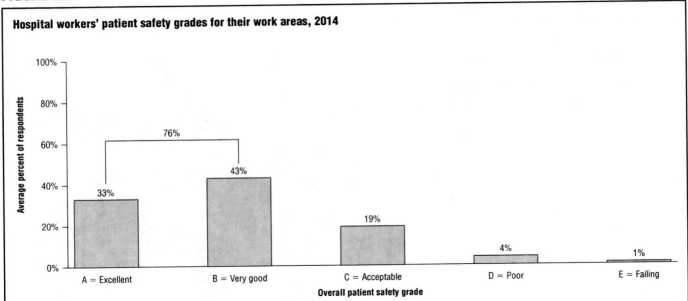

Hospital workers' patient safety grades for their work areas, 2014

SOURCE: Joann Sorra et al., "Chart 5-3. Average Percentage of 2014 Database Respondents Giving Their Work Area/Unit a Patient Safety Grade," in *Hospital Survey on Patient Safety Culture: 2014 User Comparative Database Report*, Agency for Healthcare Research and Quality, 2014, http://www.ahrq .gov/professionals/quality-patient-safety/patientsafetyculture/hospital/2014/hosp14chart5-3.html (accessed May 27, 2014)

FIGURE 8.3

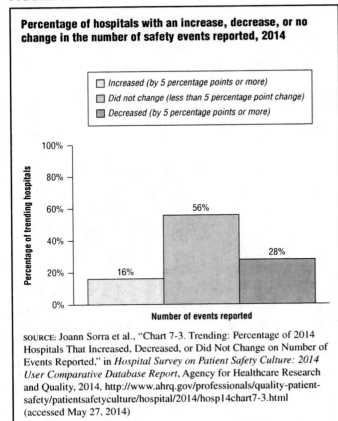

Percentage of hospitals with an increase, decrease, or no change in the number of safety events reported, 2014

SOURCE: Joann Sorra et al., "Chart 7-3. Trending: Percentage of 2014 Hospitals That Increased, Decreased, or Did Not Change on Number of Events Reported," in *Hospital Survey on Patient Safety Culture: 2014 User Comparative Database Report*, Agency for Healthcare Research and Quality, 2014, http://www.ahrq.gov/professionals/quality-patient-safety/patientsafetyculture/hospital/2014/hosp14chart7-3.html (accessed May 27, 2014)

"Common Formats" (2014, http://www.pso.ahrq.gov/ common), the AHRQ explains that patient safety organizations collect information about three kinds of safety events: incidents (safety events that reached the patient, independent of whether they caused harm), near misses (safety events that did not reach the patient), and unsafe conditions (situations that increase the likelihood of a patient safety event).

Who Is Responsible for Patient Safety?

Many federal, state, and private-sector organizations work together to reduce medical errors and improve patient safety. The Centers for Disease Control and Prevention (CDC) and the U.S. Food and Drug Administration are the leading federal agencies that conduct surveillance and collect information about adverse events resulting from treatment or the use of medical devices, drugs, or other products. In April 2011 the HHS formed the Partnership for Patients Initiative. Funded by the ACA, this public-private partnership's goal was to reduce preventable harm by 40% by the end of 2013. Table 8.1 shows improvement in selected hospital-acquired conditions between 2010 and 2013. For example, from 2010 through the end of 2013 the occurrence of pressure ulcers (bed sores) decreased 25.2% and falls decreased 14.7%.

The U.S. Departments of Defense and Veterans Affairs (VA), which are responsible for health care services for U.S. military personnel, their families, and veterans, have instituted computerized systems that have reduced medical errors. The VA established the Centers of Inquiry for Patient Safety, and its hospitals also use bar-code technology and computerized medical records to prevent medical errors.

TABLE 8.1

Percentage improvement in selected hospital-acquired conditions, 2010–13

	Ventilator-associated pneumonia (VAP)	Early elective delivery (EED)	Obstetric trauma rate (OB)[a]	Venous thromboembolic complications (VTE)	Falls and trauma	Pressure ulcers
Results to date	53.2%↓	64.5%↓	15.8%↓	12.9%↓	14.7%↓	25.2%↓
Source[b]	NDNQI	HENs	HENs	CMS	NDNQI	NDNQI

[a]Vaginal delivery without instrument.
[b]National Database of Nursing Quality Indicators (NDNQI), Centers for Medicare & Medicaid Services (CMS), and Hospital Engagement Network (HEN) submitted April 2014 data. In HEN-reported data, baseline and current periods vary across HENs.

SOURCE: "Table 2. Improvement in Select Hospital-Acquired Conditions from 2010 Baseline through 4th Quarter 2013," in *New HHS Data Shows Major Strides Made in Patient Safety, Leading to Improved Care and Savings*, U.S. Department of Health & Human Services, May 7, 2014, http://innovation.cms.gov/Files/reports/patient-safety-results.pdf (accessed May 27, 2014)

Safe medical care is also a top priority of the states and the private sector. In 2000 some of the nation's largest corporations, including General Motors and General Electric, joined together to address health care safety and efficacy (the ability of an intervention to produce the intended diagnostic or therapeutic effect in optimal circumstances) and to help direct their workers to health care providers (hospitals and physicians) with the best performance records. Called the Leapfrog Group (http://www.leapfroggroup.org), this business coalition was founded by the Business Roundtable, a national association of Fortune 500 chief executive officers, to leverage employer purchasing power that initiates innovation and improves the safety of health care.

The Leapfrog Group publishes hospital quality and safety data to assist consumers in making informed hospital choices. Hospitals provide information to the Leapfrog Group through a voluntary survey that requests information about hospital performance across four quality and safety practices with the potential to reduce preventable medical mistakes and improve health care quality. In "Hospital Safety Score Reveals Hospitals Becoming Safer, but Dangers to Patients Lurk" (April 29, 2014, http://www.leapfroggroup.org/policy_leadership/leapfrog_news/5186996), the Leapfrog Group notes that it issued safety scores to 2,522 hospitals. Of the hospitals evaluated, 804 earned an A, 668 earned a B, 878 earned a C, 150 earned a D, and 22 earned an F. Hospital safety scores are available to the public online at http://hospitalsafetyscore.org. Website visitors can search for hospital scores for free; the site also offers information on how patients can protect themselves during a hospital stay.

PREVENTING MEDICAL ERRORS AND IMPROVING PATIENT SAFETY. TeamSTEPPS (http://teamstepps.ahrq.gov/abouttoolsmaterials.htm), a program developed jointly by the Department of Defense and the AHRQ, aims to optimize patient outcomes by improving communication and other teamwork skills among health care professionals. TeamSTEPPS applies team training principles that were developed in military aviation and private industry to health care delivery. Figure 8.4 shows the four competency areas that lead to improved team performance, attitude, and knowledge. TeamSTEPPS helps improve team performance by teaching:

- Leadership—how to direct, coordinate, assign tasks, motivate team members, and facilitate optimal performance

- Situation monitoring—how to develop common understandings of team environment, apply strategies to monitor teammate performance, and maintain a shared mental model

- Mutual support—how to anticipate other team members' needs through accurate knowledge and shift workload to achieve balance during periods of high workload or stress

- Communication—how to effectively exchange information among team members, regardless of how it is communicated

Professional societies are also concerned with patient safety. Over half of all the Joint Commission's hospital standards pertain to patient safety. Since 2002 hospitals seeking accreditation from the Joint Commission have been required to adhere to stringent patient safety standards to prevent medical errors. The Joint Commission standards also require hospitals and individual health care providers to inform patients when they have been harmed in the course of treatment. The goal of these standards is to prevent medical errors by identifying actions and systems that are likely to produce problems before they occur. An example of this type of preventive measure, which is called prospective review, is close scrutiny of hospital pharmacies to be certain that the ordering, preparation, and dispensing of medications is accurate. Similar standards have been developed for Joint Commission–accredited nursing homes, outpatient clinics, laboratories, and managed care organizations.

FIGURE 8.4

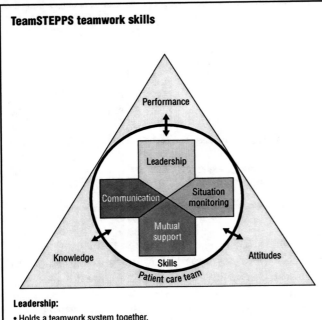

TeamSTEPPS teamwork skills

Performance

Leadership

Communication

Situation monitoring

Mutual support

Knowledge

Skills

Attitudes

Patient care team

Leadership:
• Holds a teamwork system together.
• Ensures a plan is conveyed, reviewed, and updated.
• Facilitated through communication, continuous monitoring of the situation, and fostering of an environment of mutual support.

SOURCE: "Slide 4. TeamSTEPPS Teamwork Skills," in *TeamSTEPPS Fundamentals Course: Module 4. Leading Teams*, Agency for Healthcare Research and Quality, March 2014, http://www.ahrq.gov/professionals/education/curriculum-tools/teamstepps/instructor/fundamentals/module4/slleadership.html#im1 (accessed May 27, 2014)

On January 1, 2004, the Joint Commission began surveying and evaluating health care organizations using new medication management standards. The revised standards placed greater emphasis on medication safety by increasing the pharmacists' role in managing safe, appropriate medication use and strengthening their authority to implement organization-wide improvements in medication safety.

In "2014 National Patient Safety Goals" (2014, http://www.jointcommission.org/standards_information/npsgs.aspx), the Joint Commission describes new national patient safety goals. For example, by January 2016 hospitals will be expected to develop and implement clinical alarm safety policies to address alarms from equipment such as cardiac monitors, intravenous machines, and ventilators as well as procedures and educate staff in the organization about alarm system management. Other goals include improving the accuracy of patient identification by using at least two patient identifiers when providing care and improving medication safety and communication among caregivers.

HOSPITALS DESIGNED FOR SAFETY. The AHRQ describes in "Scale Up & Spread" (2014, https://innovations.ahrq.gov/scale-up-and-spread) initiatives and strategies that hospitals and other health service providers can

implement to improve patient safety. Service delivery innovations that were evaluated and presented in 2014 include a program that involves at least weekly rounds by physician-nurse infection prevention teams, which produced a 70% decrease in hospital-associated infections; enhanced pathology reports that supplement traditional laboratory results, which have "reduced ordering errors by clinicians"; and a program using patient safety rounds and practice guidelines to "help establish a culture of safety within the organization. During these rounds, hospital management and frontline staff work together to identify hazards and take actions to reduce or eliminate them."

In "'The National Surgery Quality Improvement Project (NSQIP)': A New Tool to Increase Patient Safety and Cost Efficiency in a Surgical Intensive Care Unit" (*Patient Safety in Surgery*, vol. 8, no. 19, April 2014), John McNelis and Maria Castaldi discuss a hospital's surgical outcomes before and after interventions—such as elevating the head of the bed and prompt extubation (the weaning and removal from the ventilator)—were implemented to address high rates of pneumonia and prolonged intubation (as indicated by days on a ventilator). Over the two-year study period there was progressive improvement—an estimated 32 episodes of pneumonia and 160 episodes of days on the ventilator after 48 hours were prevented.

CLINICAL PRACTICE GUIDELINES

Clinical practice guidelines (CPGs) are evidence-based protocols—documents that advise health care providers about how to diagnose and treat specific medical conditions and diseases. CPGs offer physicians, nurses, other health care practitioners, health plans, and institutions objective, detailed, and condition- or disease-specific action plans.

Widespread dissemination and use of CPGs began during the 1990s in an effort to improve the quality of health care delivery by giving health care professionals access to current scientific information on which to base clinical decisions. The use of guidelines also aimed to enhance quality by standardizing care and treatment throughout a health care delivery system such as a managed care plan or hospital and throughout the nation.

Early attempts to encourage physicians and other health professionals to use CPGs was met with resistance, because many physicians rejected CPGs as formulaic "cookbook medicine" and believed they interfered with physician-patient relationships. Over time, however, physicians were educated about the quality problems that resulted from variations in medical practice, and opinions about CPGs gradually changed. Physician willingness to use CPGs also increased when they learned that adherence to CPGs offered some protection from medical malpractice and other liability. Nurses and other health professionals more readily adopted CPGs, presumably because their training and practice was oriented more toward following instructions than physicians' practices had been.

The National Guideline Clearinghouse (http://www.guideline.gov) is a database of CPGs that have been produced by the AHRQ in conjunction with the American Medical Association (AMA) and the American Association of Health Plans. The clearinghouse offers guideline summaries and comparisons of guidelines covering the same disease or condition prepared by different sources and serves as a resource for the exchange of guidelines between practitioners and health care organizations.

CPGs vary depending on their source. All recovery and treatment plans, however, are intended to generate the most favorable health outcomes. Federal agencies such as the U.S. Public Health Service and the CDC, as well as professional societies, managed care plans, hospitals, academic medical centers, and health care consulting firms, have produced their own versions of CPGs.

Practically all guidelines assume that treatment and healing will occur without complications. Because CPGs represent an optimistic approach to treatment, they are not used as the sole resource for development or evaluation of treatment plans for specific patients. CPGs are intended for use in conjunction with evaluation by qualified health professionals able to determine the applicability of a specific CPG to the specific circumstances involved. Modification of the CPGs is often required and advisable to meet specific, organizational objectives of health care providers and payers.

It is unrealistic to expect that all patients will obtain ideal health outcomes as a result of health care providers' use of CPGs. Guidelines may have greater utility as quality indicators. Evaluating health care delivery against CPGs enables providers, payers, and policy makers to identify and evaluate care that deviates from CPGs as part of a concerted program of continuous improvement of health care quality.

COMMUNICATION AND INFORMATION MANAGEMENT TECHNOLOGIES

The explosion of communication and information management technologies has already revolutionized health care delivery and holds great promise for the future. Health care data can be easily and securely collected, shared, stored, and used to promote research and development over great geographic distances and across traditionally isolated industries. Online distance learning programs for health professionals and the widespread availability of reliable consumer health information on the Internet have increased understanding and awareness of the causes and treatment of illness. This section describes several recent applications of technology to the health care system.

Telemedicine and Telehealth

The terms *telemedicine* (healing at a distance) and *telehealth* (the remote exchange of data between a patient and a clinician as part of health care management) describe a variety of technology-enhanced interactions that occur by way of telephone lines, videoconferencing, iPads, and smartphone applications. Telemedicine may be as simple and commonplace as a phone conversation between a patient and a health professional in the same town or as sophisticated as surgery directed via satellite and video technology from one continent to another.

Advocates of telemedicine opine that it can effectively address health care workforce shortages; save patients time, money, and travel; reduce unnecessary emergency department and hospital visits; and improve the management of chronic conditions. However, widespread adoption of telemedicine faces ongoing challenges. Physicians must be licensed in each state where they treat patients, even when treating them remotely. Most health care professionals have not been trained in telemedicine and concerns about security of sensitive health-related information persist.

Cynthia LeRouge and Monica J. Garfield describe in "Crossing the Telemedicine Chasm: Have the U.S. Barriers to Widespread Adoption of Telemedicine Been Significantly Reduced?" (*International Journal of Environmental Research and Public Health*, vol. 10, no. 12, December 2013) the benefits of telemedicine, including:

- Reduced health care costs
- Increased patient access to providers, especially in medically underserved areas
- Improved quality, integration, and continuity of care
- Faster and more convenient treatment resulting in reduction of lost work time and travel costs for patients

LeRouge and Garfield explain that there have been financial, technological, and legal barriers to widespread adoption of telemedicine—such as lack of broadband infrastructure, perceived inconvenience, provider resistance, and reimbursement issues—but observe that the ACA focus on coordinating care using health IT provides an opportunity to establish it as an accepted method of health care delivery. Because telemedicine can ensure that patients receive the appropriate care at the appropriate site by a suitable provider while avoiding duplication and waste, it can serve to improve access and reduce the cost of care.

In "Use of Telemedicine Can Reduce Hospitalizations of Nursing Home Residents and Generate Savings for Medicare" (*Health Affairs*, vol. 33, no. 2, February 2014), David C. Grabowski and A. James O'Malley find that telemedicine can reduce hospitalization of nursing home patients because it provides access to physicians during off hours, which many nursing homes lack. The researchers conclude that when nursing homes adopt telemedicine instead of relying on on-call physicians, hospitalizations and the costs—which are estimated at $1 billion per year—decrease.

Bruce Japsen opines in "ObamaCare, Doctor Shortage to Spur $2 Billion Telehealth Market" (Forbes.com, December 23, 2013) that as barriers (e.g., low reimbursement, lack of physician support, and ineffective implementation) to telemedicine fall, its use will rapidly increase. Expansion of telehealth will be largely fueled by the ACA, which emphasizes provider accountability reimbursement based on the value of care provided rather than on traditional fee-for-service reimbursement. Japsen reports that the telemedicine market is forecast to grow from $240 million in 2013 to $1.9 billion in 2018.

Besides improving access and reducing costs, telemedicine augments patient outcomes. For example, in "Telemedicine Intervention Improves ICU Outcomes" (*Critical Care Research and Practice*, 2013), Farid Sadaka et al. examine mortality and length of stay rates in a hospital intensive care unit (ICU) before and after the use of telemedicine, which delivered the expertise of ICU intensivists and critical care nurses to assist bedside caregivers in monitoring and managing critically ill patients. The researchers find that the use of telemedicine significantly improved ICU mortality and length of stay rates.

Telemedicine has been used in schools to improve access to care, treat middle ear infections, improve management of diabetes, and increase appropriate referral to specialists. It has also helped school-aged children and their parents gain access to psychiatric treatment. Alison Knopf notes in "School-Based Telehealth Brings Psychiatry to Rural Georgia" (*Behavioral Healthcare*, vol. 33, no. 1, January–February 2013) that telemedicine makes psychiatry available to children who otherwise would have no access to care from child and adolescent psychiatrists. Knopf observes that a school-based telemedicine program reduced emergency department utilization, resulting in savings of more than $350,000 in one year.

Telemedicine has also proven to be a cost-effective alternative to psychiatric hospitalization. Caroline Cassels reports in "Telemental Health Dramatically Cuts Psychiatric Hospitalization Rates" (Medscape.com, May 9, 2012) the results of a study that was presented at the American Psychiatric Association's 2012 annual meeting. The large-scale study, which analyzed four years of data on 98,609 mental health patients between 2006 and 2010, showed that delivering telemental health services

via high-definition video transmission to patients in rural areas dramatically reduced psychiatric hospitalization rates.

Although telemedicine may lower costs by reducing hospitalization, other research reports improved patient outcomes using telehealth with only modest cost savings. In "Effect of Telehealth on Use of Secondary Care and Mortality: Findings from the Whole System Demonstrator Cluster Randomised Trial" (*BMJ*, vol. 344, no. 3874, June 21, 2012), Adam Steventon et al. analyzed the records of 3,230 patients with chronic health conditions (diabetes, chronic obstructive pulmonary disease, and heart failure), some of whom received telehealth services and some of whom did not. The researchers find that patients who received telehealth services had lower mortality rates and fewer emergency hospital admissions than those who did not receive telehealth care. The modest cost savings observed were attributed to lower utilization of hospital services.

Joseph Kvedar, Molly Joel Coye, and Wendy Everett emphasize in "Connected Health: A Review of Technologies and Strategies to Improve Patient Care with Telemedicine and Telehealth" (*Health Affairs*, vol. 33, no. 2, February 2014) that telemedicine is one of the keys to achieving the ACA goal of expanded access to health care for millions of Americans. The researchers assert, "When properly implemented, the broad adoption of connected health has the potential to extend care across populations of both acute and chronically ill patients and help achieve the important policy goals of improving access to high-quality and efficient health care." Kvedar, Coye, and Everett explain that health care can be more effective and efficient when clinicians are electronically connected to other clinicians, patients to clinicians, and patients to other patients. They opine that these technologies will be even more useful as "devices become smaller; are powered by longer-lasting sources of energy; and are connected more effectively to other devices and to repositories of data, such as electronic health records."

Online Patient-Physician Consultations and Communication

In 2012 Accenture conducted a survey and reported the results in "The Accenture Connected Health Pulse Survey" (2013, http://www.accenture.com/SiteCollection Documents/PDF/Accenture-Is-Healthcare-Self-Service-Online-Enough-to-Satisfy-Patients.pdf). It finds that 90% of Americans said they want to access their health information online. The majority (88%) want to receive e-mail reminders for preventive or follow-up care, 83% want access to personal health information, 76% want to communicate with their doctors via e-mail, 73% want to refill prescriptions online, and 72% want to schedule appointments online.

Physician use of health IT and online communication is growing. Anne-Marie J. Audet, David Squires, and Michelle M. Doty compare in "Where Are We on the Diffusion Curve? Trends and Drivers of Primary Care Physicians' Use of Health Information Technology" (*Health Services Research*, vol. 49, no. 1, February 2014) physician use of technology in 2009 and 2012. The researchers find that primary care physicians' use of health IT significantly increased since 2009. For example, 40% of physicians prescribed medication electronically in 2009, compared with 64% in 2012, and adoption of EHRs rose from 46% to 69% during the same period. In 2012, 30% of primary care practices allowed patients to request appointments online, 34% of patients could e-mail physicians, and 36% of patients could request prescription refills online.

Brett Keller et al. surveyed public health professionals to find out about their use of social media, including blogs, Facebook, Twitter (a microblogging medium), and YouTube, and reported their findings in "Mind the Gap: Social Media Engagement by Public Health Researchers" (*Journal of the Medical Internet Research*, vol. 16, no. 1, January 2014). The researchers note that despite the public health professionals' belief that social media has the potential to advance public health objectives, only a small minority of them use it professionally. The majority of respondents were either disinterested or actively opposed to professional engagement in the social media space, opining that it is too time consuming or that an activity such as blogging might compromise their academic credibility.

In "Tips for Telephone and Electronic Medical Consultation" (*Indian Journal of Pediatrics*, vol. 80, no. 11, November 2013), Sailesh G. Gupta of Ashna Children's Hospital in Mumbai, India, reports that although patients expect telephone and e-mail consultations, these electronic consultations may not provide adequate information for diagnosis. Gupta asserts that telephone consults should be offered only after a prior face-to-face meeting and should be followed by a face-to-face visit as soon as possible. He notes that concerns about e-mail and other online encounters center on the privacy and security of patient information exchanged and physician reimbursement for time spent in electronic exchanges with patients. Besides legal and privacy issues, some industry observers suggest that guidelines should be developed for e-encounters to ensure that they are clinically appropriate and are not used as substitutes for needed, but more costly, face-to-face visits.

Disseminating Health Information via Twitter

Ranit Mishori et al. describe in "Mapping Physician Twitter Networks: Describing How They Work as a First Step in Understanding Connectivity, Information Flow, and Message Diffusion" (*Journal of Medical Internet Research*, vol. 16, no. 4, April 2014) the growing use of Twitter in medicine. The researchers list the characteristics of four medical networks—the AMA, the American Academy of Family Physicians (AAFP), the American Academy of Pediatrics (AAP), and the American College of Physicians (ACP)—and analyze their dissemination potential and their actual dissemination of health and medical information. For each network, tweets sent between July 1, 2012, and September 12, 2012, were counted, along with the number of retweets and the details of their dissemination.

Mishori et al. find that "the AMA had the largest number of followers—and thus, information diffusion potential—and was trailed by the AAP, AAFP, and ACP, respectively." The researchers conclude that although having a large number of followers promotes dissemination, small networks can achieve high levels of dissemination if they have a community that actively retweets. They also counsel that "the content of the messages is of course of utmost importance. Even with strong channels for dissemination, tweets must be timely and engaging in order to provide the hook for followers to retweet and begin to reach the vast potential audience."

TECHNOLOGY MAY HELP EDUCATE MORE NURSES. One key factor limiting the supply of nurses is a shortage of nursing faculty, which restricts class size and ultimately the numbers of nurses graduating each year. According to the American Association of Colleges of Nursing, in "Nursing Faculty Shortage" (August 18, 2014, http://www.aacn.nche.edu/media-relations/fact-sheets/nursing-faculty-shortage), in 2012–13 approximately 78,089 qualified applicants were turned away from nursing schools because of a lack of faculty. One way to remedy this situation may be to offer some nursing courses online. In "Transforming a RN to BSN Program to an On-line Delivery Format" (*Kentucky Nurse*, vol. 60, no. 1, 2012), Cathy H. Abell, Deborah Williams, and M. Susan Jones of Western Kentucky University describe the transformation of a registered nurse (RN) program that uses a combination of traditional classes and online learning to a bachelor of science in nursing (BSN) program that is completely online. They deem the transformation a success and conclude, "The RN to BSN faculty perceive the on-line program as essential for the seamless transition toward a higher academic degree. They are committed to offering this program as a means for nurses who are place bound to achieve the BSN."

MORE STAFF, RATHER THAN TECHNOLOGY, IS KEY TO IMPROVING PATIENT SAFETY AND QUALITY OF CARE. Despite rapid advances in technology, many industry observers feel that it is not sufficient to solve the projected nursing shortage reported by the U.S. Bureau of Labor Statistics in "The 30 Occupations with the Largest

Projected Number of Total Job Openings Due to Growth and Replacements, 2010–20" (February 1, 2012, http://www.bls.gov/news.release/ecopro.t10.htm). The report notes that the United States will require over 1.1 million replacement nurses by 2020. In "The Recent Surge in Nurse Employment: Causes and Implications" (*Health Affairs*, vol. 28, no. 4, July–August 2009), Peter I. Buerhaus, David I. Auerbach, and Douglas O. Staiger observe that although the nursing shortage slowed as a result of the economic recession, it is still forecast to reach 260,000 RNs by 2025—twice as large as any U.S. nursing shortage since the mid-1960s. The researchers identify the retirement of older nurses as the key contributor to the anticipated shortfall.

According to Kathleen J. H. Sparbel et al., who gave the presentation "Interprofessional Education: Building Collaborations in Didactic and Clinical Nurse Practitioner Education for Improved Patient Outcomes" (April 5, 2014, https://nonpf.confex.com/nonpf/2014co/webprogram/Session3794.html) at the National Organization of Nurse Practitioner Faculties' 40th annual meeting, collaboration of diverse and varied disciplines—nursing, physical therapy, social services, pharmacy, and others—is necessary to decrease health care errors, improve patient safety, and enhance patient outcomes. Collaboration is enhanced by education and communication and practiced in the classroom and clinical settings.

Promise of Robotics

One technological advance that promises to reduce hospital operating costs and enable hospital workers to spend more time caring for patients is the use of robots. Once relegated to the realm of science fiction, automated machines such as self-guided robots to perform many routine hospital functions have seen a resurgence in the 21st century.

In "Robots Get to Work" (*Modern Healthcare*, vol. 43, no. 21, May 2013), Rachel Landen and Jaimy Lee describe the growing use of robotics in hospitals: robots that deliver linens and lab results and dispense medication; that enable physicians to perform remote, real-time consultations and communicate with patients at a distance; and that monitor critically ill patients in the ICU. Robots in hospitals either replace tasks formerly performed by employees such as packaging drugs or delivering surgical tools or enhance those that use telemedicine to connect clinicians and patients. Many academic medical centers have invested in robotic technology, but the cost—often more than $1 million—has impeded adoption by smaller hospitals. Landen and Lee note that although robotic automation can improve safety by reducing errors and "help reduce costs, make operations more efficient and serve as a marketing tool to position hospitals as early adopters of cutting-edge technology,"

it is still not known whether this costly technology delivers on its promise.

Landen and Lee describe novel uses of robotic technology, including a system that "replicates a person in a distant location" by using a camera, microphones, and video display. The system enables the remote user to "travel" throughout a facility and may be used by family members to "virtually visit" hospital and nursing home patients. Also in development is a system that uses robotics, radio frequency identification technology, and computer vision to locate, sort, deliver, and sterilize surgical tools.

Some robots are involved in more than simply routine, menial tasks. Ada T. Ng and P. C. Tam assert in "Current Status of Robot-Assisted Surgery" (*Hong Kong Medical Journal*, vol. 20, no. 3, June 2014) that "the introduction of robot-assisted surgery, and specifically the da Vinci Surgical System, is one of the biggest breakthroughs in surgery since the introduction of anaesthesia, and represents the most significant advancement in minimally invasive surgery of this decade." The researchers observe that although robotics was first used in orthopedics, neurosurgery, and cardiac surgery, its use in urology, especially prostate surgery, led to its widespread adoption. They also note that studies show that robotic surgery patients fare as well as those who receive unassisted surgery; however, additional research is needed to fully determine the clinical value and cost-effectiveness of robots in surgical procedures.

Some surgical robots are miniature versions that can be inserted through a laparoscope, whereas others may be small enough to be inserted without incisions through the body's naturally occurring openings, such as the mouth, vagina, or rectum. Apollon Zygomalas et al. describe in "Miniature Surgical Robots in the Era of NOTES and LESS: Dream or Reality?" (*Surgical Innovations*, May 14, 2014) the potential application of inserting microrobots through natural orifices to perform specific tasks in the abdomen, including minimally invasive surgery.

However, some researchers feel the effectiveness of robotic surgery has been adopted without the necessary evaluation of its clinical utility and cost-effectiveness. For example, in "Localised Prostate Cancer: Clinical and Cost-Effectiveness of New and Emerging Technologies" (*Journal of Clinical Urology*, vol. 7, no. 4, July 2014), Yiannis Philippou et al. assert that adoption of techniques such as robotic prostatectomy may be driven by economic incentives rather than by rigorous clinical evidence. The researchers also opine, "Treatment decisions should be driven by cancer risk and patient preference rather than by financial incentives or availability of technology."

Other applications of robotic surgery have demonstrated cost-effectiveness. J. Kenneth Byrd et al. report in "Transoral Robotic Surgery and the Unknown Primary: A Cost-Effectiveness Analysis" (*Otorhinolaryngology—Head and Neck Surgery*, vol. 150, no. 6, March 11, 2014) the results of a study of the cost-effectiveness of transoral robotic surgery for the diagnosis and treatment of head and neck cancer. The researchers find that this type surgery is cost-effective when compared with traditional examination under anesthesia.

Similarly, an economic assessment of robot-assisted surgical training finds that it is cost-effective. In "Simulation-Based Robot-Assisted Surgical Training: A Health Economic Evaluation" (*International Journal of Surgery*, vol. 11, no. 9, November 2013), Shabnam Rehman et al. note that robotic simulation is a useful and efficient way to teach technical skills.

INNOVATION SUPPORTS QUALITY HEALTH CARE DELIVERY

The health care industry is awash in wave after wave of new technologies, models of service delivery, reimbursement formulae, legislative and regulatory changes, and increasingly specialized personnel ranks. Creating change in hospitals and in other health care organizations requires an understanding of diffusion (the process and channels by which new ideas are communicated, spread, and adopted throughout institutions and organizations). Diffusion of technology involves all the stakeholders in the health care system: policy makers and regulatory agencies establish safety and efficacy, government and private payers determine reimbursement, vendors of the technology are compared and one is selected, hospitals and health professionals adopt the technology and are trained in its use, and consumers are informed about the benefits of the new technology.

The decision to adopt new technology involves a five-stage process beginning with knowledge about the innovation. The second stage is persuasion, the period when decision makers form opinions based on experience and knowledge. Decision is the third phase, when commitment is made to a trial or pilot program, and is followed by implementation, the stage during which the new technology is put in place. The process concludes with the confirmation stage, the period during which the decision makers seek reinforcement for their decision to adopt and implement the new technology.

Communicating Quality

As all of the provisions of the ACA are implemented, industry observers hope that consumers armed with data about comparative costs and quality will be better able to make informed health care purchases—choosing providers that offer quality care and competitive fees. Jill

Mathews Yegian et al. explain in "Engaged Patients Will Need Comparative Physician-Level Quality Data and Information about Their Out-of-Pocket Costs" (*Health Affairs*, vol. 32, no. 2, February 2013) that patients need comparable and meaningful information about the quality and cost of health care to choose health care providers. The researchers look at various ways to deliver this information to consumers and find two overarching models. The first model highlights public reporting of information and is produced or supported by philanthropic or government institutions that aim to improve provider quality and efficiency. Examples of this model include the Robert Wood Johnson Foundation's Aligning Forces for Quality website and the AHRQ's Chartered Value Exchanges. The second model encompasses private-sector, for-profit "one-stop-shopping" websites that provide personalized information about cost and quality to support consumers' health purchasing decisions. Examples of this model include Castlight, Change Healthcare, UnitedHealthcare, Aetna, and Anthem. Yegian et al. assert that "state and federal policy makers can spur the creation and use of consumer-oriented information by supporting all-payer claims databases to facilitate sharing of cost data, standards for EHRs to facilitate sharing of quality data, and a unified approach to presenting information that prioritizes the consumer over competing agency agendas."

In "Evidence-Based Health Information from the Users' Perspective—A Qualitative Analysis" (*BMC Health Services Research*, vol. 13, October 10, 2013), Irene Hirschberg et al. look at how consumers understand and respond to evidence-based health care, which consists of unbiased and reliable information based on the current state of medical knowledge and encompasses a range of actions, including use of medical practice guidelines, shared decision making, comparative effectiveness research, and transparency of cost and quality information. Consumer attitudes, assumptions, and beliefs about evidence-based health care are of increasing importance because the ACA emphasizes its use.

Hirschberg et al. find that many consumers are unused to understanding and interpreting evidence-based health information. The researchers observe that there is a broad range of reactions to evidence-based health information and that health literacy (the ability to process and understand health information needed to make appropriate health decisions) varies widely among consumers. Because there are gaps in knowledge about the characteristics of quality care, considerable consumer education will likely be required before consumers can become fully engaged in evidence-based decision making. Hirschberg et al. recommend involving consumers in the development of evidence-based health information messages to identify effective ways to convey the information. The researchers conclude that "a clearer presentation of the basis of scientific research, e.g. on data acquisition and study quality, as well as the limits and possibilities, may help improve consumers' understanding."

MAKING THE GRADE: HEALTH CARE REPORT CARDS. The publication of medical outcomes report cards and disease- and procedure-specific morbidity rates (the degree of disability caused by disease) and mortality rates (the number of deaths caused by disease) has attracted widespread media attention and sparked controversy. Advocates for the public release of clinical outcomes and other performance measures contend that despite some essential limitations, these studies offer consumers, employers, and payers the means for comparing health care providers.

Some skeptics question the clinical credibility of scales such as surgical mortality, which they claim are incomplete indicators of quality. Others cite problems with data collection or speculate that data are readily manipulated by providers to enhance marketing opportunities sufficient to compromise the utility and validity of published reports. Long term, the effects of published comparative evaluation of health care providers on network establishment, contracting, and exclusion from existing health plans are uncertain and in many instances may be punitive (damaging). Hospitals and medical groups may be forced to compete for network inclusion on the basis of standardized performance measures.

The number of websites that rate physicians and hospitals continues to grow, with Angie's List and Vitals .com joining more established sites such as Health.org and HealthGrades.com and the Centers for Medicare and Medicaid Services' Hospital Compare and Physician Compare websites, which compare hospital and physician costs, outcomes, and patient satisfaction data. The sites describe physicians' training, experience, certification, and any disciplinary actions taken against them, as well as patient ratings. They also encourage physicians to respond to patient comments. Some industry observers contend that the sites, especially those that use anonymous ratings, have the potential to further erode patient-physician relationships by prompting physicians to behave defensively.

Aleksandra Zgierska, David Rabago, and Michael M. Miller assess in "Impact of Patient Satisfaction Ratings on Physicians and Clinical Care" (*Patient Preference and Adherence*, no. 8, April 2014) physicians' perceptions about the impact of patient surveys on their job satisfaction and clinical practice. Not unexpectedly, the researchers find that if physicians view patient satisfaction survey data as potentially punitive, then the data are more likely to have an extremely unfavorable impact on physician satisfaction. Some physicians even reported that the use of patient satisfaction surveys prompted them to consider leaving medical practice. More concerning, however, is the finding that "the use of patient satisfaction surveys may promote, at least among some clinicians and under certain circumstances, a culture of care that can be partially driven by satisfaction score rather than evidence based; this can potentially compromise healthcare outcomes as well as violate clinicians' sense of professional integrity, contributing, in turn, to job dissatisfaction." Physicians were concerned that aiming to score well on such surveys might promote inappropriate treatment, such as prescribing unnecessary antibiotics or ordering unnecessary tests.

Zgierska, Rabago, and Miller conclude that their findings are troubling, especially in view of "the widespread and progressive utilization of patient satisfaction ratings as an integral metric of quality-of-care assessment, and call for a more rigorous evaluation of the use of patient satisfaction surveys and the linkage of data from such surveys to other variables (such as physician compensation, job retention, or job promotion)."

Despite legitimate concern about the objectivity, reliability, validity, and potential for manipulating data, there is consensus that scrutiny and dissemination of quality data will escalate. Business groups and employers continue to request physician, hospital, and health plan data to design their health benefit programs. When choosing between health plans involving the same group of participating hospitals and physicians, employers request plan-specific information to guide their decisions. Companies and employer-driven health care coalitions seeking to assemble their own provider networks rely on physician- and hospital-specific data, such as the quality data provided by HealthGrades, during the selection process.

The most beneficial use of the data is to inspire providers to improve health care delivery systematically. When evidence of quality problems is identified, health plans and providers must be prepared to launch a variety of interventions to address and promptly resolve problems.

CHAPTER 9
PUBLIC OPINION ABOUT THE HEALTH CARE SYSTEM

As with many other social issues, public opinion about health care systems, providers, plans, coverage, and benefits varies in response to a variety of personal, political, and economic forces. Personal experience and the experience of friends, family, and community opinion leaders (trusted sources of information such as clergy, prominent physicians, and local business and civic leaders) exert powerful influences on public opinion. Health care marketing executives have known for years that the most potent advertising any hospital, medical group, or managed care plan can have is not a full-page newspaper advertisement or prime-time television advertising campaign. It is positive word-of-mouth publicity.

The influence of the news media, advertising, and other attempts to sway health care consumers' attitudes and purchasing behaviors cannot be overlooked. A single story about a miraculous medical breakthrough or life-saving procedure can reflect favorably on an entire hospital or health care delivery system. Similarly, a lone mistake, an adverse reaction to a drug, or a misstep by a single health care practitioner can impugn (attack as lacking integrity) a hospital, managed care plan, or pharmaceutical company for months or even years, prompting intense media scrutiny of every action taken by the practitioner, facility, or organization.

Political events, the economy, and pending legislation can focus public attention on a particular health care concern, supplant one health-related issue with another, or eclipse health care from public view altogether. For example, during the period prior to the March 2010 passage of the Patient Protection and Affordable Care Act and the Health Care and Education Reconciliation Act (which are now commonly known as the ACA), there was heated debate about the scope and provisions of the legislation, which continued to persist throughout 2014.

In fact, opposition to the ACA mounted with questions about the constitutionality of many of its provisions, such as requiring individuals to obtain health insurance coverage (called the individual mandate) and officials from 26 states filed a lawsuit against the act. The case eventually went before the U.S. Supreme Court and was argued in March 2012. In June 2012 the Supreme Court surprised many observers when it ruled in *National Federation of Independent Business v. Sebelius, Secretary of Health and Human Services* (No. 11-393) that the ACA is constitutional. Chief Justice John G. Roberts (1955–) joined the majority in affirming the ACA. Roberts ruled that the individual mandate, which would impose a fine on Americans opting to forgo health insurance coverage, was a tax that the government had the authority to impose and that the mandate was not unconstitutional. The court did, however, significantly restrict the expansion of Medicaid by affording the states some leeway: they could choose not to expand their Medicaid programs without incurring the financial penalties the ACA would have imposed.

Besides government funding of entitlement programs and other public policy issues that are frequently divisive, some industry observers believe health care providers, policy makers, biomedical technology and research firms, and academic medical centers have fanned the flames of consumer dissatisfaction with the U.S. health care system by overselling the promise and the progress of modern medicine. They fear that the overzealous promotion of every scientific discovery with a potential clinical application has created unrealistic expectations of modern medicine. Health care consumers who believe there should be "one pill for every ill" or feel all technology should be made widely available even before its efficacy (the ability of an intervention to produce the intended diagnostic or therapeutic effect in optimal circumstances) has been demonstrated are more likely to be dissatisfied with the present health care system.

AMERICANS FEEL THE U.S. HEALTH SYSTEM WORKS

Most Americans feel the U.S. health care system is working. In *In U.S., 66% Satisfied Health System Works for Them* (March 17, 2014, http://www.gallup.com/poll/167951/satisfied-health-system-works.aspx), Frank Newport of the Gallup Organization asserts, "Most Americans do not believe the healthcare system in this country is in crisis." In a March 2014 poll two-thirds (66%) of respondents said the health care system is working for them. (See Table 9.1.) Not unexpectedly, more people with health insurance were satisfied with the system (72%), but even among the uninsured, one-third (33%) were satisfied with the system.

Young adults aged 18 to 29 years (73%) and adults aged 65 years and older (80%) were the most likely to be satisfied with the health care system in 2014. (See Table 9.2.) Newport opines that young adults, who are generally healthy, typically make fewer demands of the system and as such are likely to be satisfied. They may also not be paying insurance premiums because they may be covered by their parents' policy (the ACA extended coverage to age 26) or may pay lower premiums based on their age and lack of dependents in need of coverage. Medicare beneficiaries have historically reported high levels of satisfaction with the health care system.

Satisfaction with the health care system varies with political party affiliation. More Democrats (78%) were satisfied with the system than Republicans (61%) or independents (59%) in 2014. (See Table 9.3.) Newport attributes this difference to the fact that Democrats are more likely to support the ACA, and this support may translate into higher levels of satisfaction with the current health care system.

AMERICANS' CHANGING VIEWS ABOUT HEALTH CARE REFORM

Frank Newport, Jeffrey M. Jones, and Lydia Saad of the Gallup Organization observe in *State of the Union: The Public Weighs In on 10 Key Issues* (January 31, 2014, http://www.gallup.com/poll/167162/state-union-public-weighs-key-issues.aspx) that "Americans cite the Affordable Care Act ... as the single greatest achievement, as well as the single biggest failure, so far in the president's administration." Americans' support for the ACA did not increase after the law was passed—in fact, their views were relatively unchanged or were more negative than they were before the law passed. Figure 9.1 shows that disapproval of the ACA rose from 45% in November 2012 to 54% in January 2014. During the same period the percentage of people who approve of the ACA fell from 48% to 38%.

In *Number of Americans Saying ACA Has Hurt Them Inches Up* (March 6, 2014, http://www.gallup.com/poll/167756/number-americans-saying-aca-hurt-inches.aspx), Justin McCarthy of the Gallup Organization notes that in 2014, 63% of Americans said the ACA has not affected them yet, 23% felt the law has hurt them or their families, and 10% said it has helped. (See Figure 9.2.) Figure 9.3 shows that although Americans' views about the long-term impact of the ACA have fluctuated, they have not changed appreciably since 2012. Nearly twice as many Americans said in 2014 the ACA will make their health care situations worse (40%) instead of better (21%), and 36% expected it will make no difference.

Mary Agnes Carey of the Kaiser Family Foundation notes in "Most Americans Say the Health Law Has Not Affected Their Families: Poll" (May 30, 2014, http://capsules.kaiserhealthnews.org/index.php/2014/05/most-americans-say-the-health-law-has-not-affected-their-families-poll/#more-28564) that in a May 2014 poll six out 10

TABLE 9.1

Satisfaction with U.S. health care system by insurance status, 2014

ARE YOU SATISFIED OR DISSATISFIED WITH HOW THE HEALTHCARE SYSTEM IS WORKING FOR YOU?

	Satisfied	Dissatisfied	No opinion
	%	%	%
National adults	66	32	3
Have health insurance	72	26	2
Do not have health insurance	33	59	8

SOURCE: Frank Newport, "Are You Satisfied or Dissatisfied with How the Healthcare System Is Working for You?" in *U.S., 66% Satisfied Health System Works for Them*, The Gallup Organization, March 17, 2014, http://www.gallup.com/poll/167951/satisfied-health-system-works.aspx (accessed June 2, 2014). Copyright © 2014 Gallup, Inc. All rights reserved. The content is used with permission; however, Gallup retains all rights of republication.

TABLE 9.2

Satisfaction with U.S. health care system by age group, 2014

ARE YOU SATISFIED OR DISSATISFIED WITH HOW THE HEALTHCARE SYSTEM IS WORKING FOR YOU?

[By age]

	Satisfied	Dissatisfied	No opinion
	%	%	%
18 to 29	73	26	1
30 to 49	60	38	2
50 to 64	56	39	4
65+	80	17	4

SOURCE: Frank Newport, "Are You Satisfied or Dissatisfied with How the Healthcare System Is Working for You? By Age," in *U.S., 66% Satisfied Health System Works for Them*, The Gallup Organization, March 17, 2014, http://www.gallup.com/poll/167951/satisfied-health-system-works.aspx (accessed June 2, 2014). Copyright © 2014 Gallup, Inc. All rights reserved. The content is used with permission; however, Gallup retains all rights of republication.

Americans said they feel unaffected by the ACA. Slightly more than one-third (38%) of respondents favored the law and 45% opposed it. Despite this low level of support, Carey reports that consistent with previous polls, the majority (59%) of Americans, including majorities of Democrats and independents, said "they want their congressional representative to improve the law rather than repeal it and replace it."

TABLE 9.3

Satisfaction with U.S. health care system by political party affiliation, 2014

ARE YOU SATISFIED OR DISSATISFIED WITH HOW THE HEALTHCARE SYSTEM IS WORKING FOR YOU?

[By party ID]

	Satisfied	Dissatisfied	No opinion
	%	%	%
Republicans	61	38	1
Independents	59	36	5
Democrats	78	20	2

Interestingly, Americans' familiarity with the ACA has not increased, even though many of its provisions have been implemented. In *Americans' Familiarity with Healthcare Law Unchanged* (February 6, 2014, http://www.gallup.com/poll/167351/americans-familiarity-healthcare-law-unchanged.aspx), Andrew Dugan of the Gallup Organization reports that in February 2014, 68% of Americans were very or somewhat familiar with the ACA and 32% were not too or not at all familiar with the law. (See Figure 9.4.) Gallup polls from August 2013 through February 2014 indicate that the percentages of those familiar and not familiar with the ACA have not changed.

Political Party Affiliation Predicts ACA Support

Andrew Dugan and Frank Newport of the Gallup Organization indicate in *Politics Are Biggest Factor in Views of Healthcare Law* (April 1, 2014, http://www.gallup.com/poll/168170/politics-biggest-factor-views-healthcare-law.aspx) that political party affiliation is the strongest predictor of whether Americans disapprove of the ACA. Table 9.4 shows the odds of an individual disapproving of the ACA based on an analysis of Gallup poll data collected between August 2013 and March 2014. Dugan and Newport note that additional factors, such as race and ideology, influence support for the law but do not exert as strong an influence. Other characteristics, such as income and employment, which seem of consequence in terms of support for legislation intended to help the uninsured obtain insurance, are not significant predictors.

FIGURE 9.1

Percentage of Americans that approve and disapprove of the Affordable Care Act (ACA), November 2012–January 2014

DO YOU GENERALLY APPROVE OR DISAPPROVE OF THE 2010 AFFORDABLE CARE ACT, SIGNED INTO LAW BY PRESIDENT OBAMA THAT RESTRUCTURED THE U.S. HEALTHCARE SYSTEM?

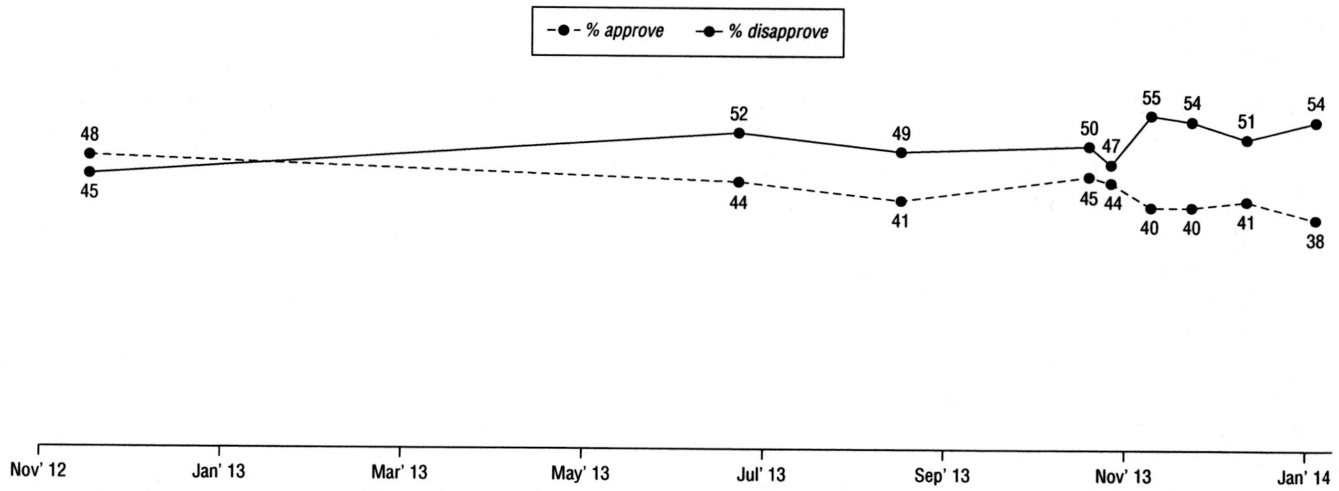

November 2012 wording: Do you generally approve or disapprove of the 2010 affordable care act, also known as "Obama-care" that restructured the U.S. healthcare system?

FIGURE 9.2

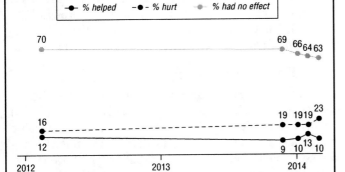

Percentage of Americans that feel the Affordable Care Act (ACA) has helped or hurt them, or had no effect, 2012–14

AS YOU MAY KNOW, A FEW OF THE PROVISIONS OF THE HEALTHCARE LAW HAVE ALREADY GONE INTO EFFECT. SO FAR, HAS THE NEW LAW HELPED YOU AND YOUR FAMILY, NOT HAD AN EFFECT, OR HAS IT HURT YOU AND YOUR FAMILY?

FIGURE 9.3

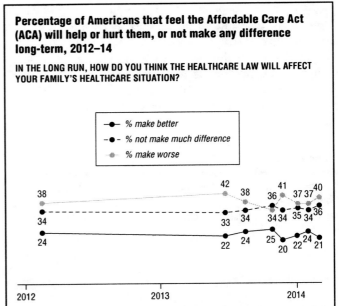

Percentage of Americans that feel the Affordable Care Act (ACA) will help or hurt them, or not make any difference long-term, 2012–14

IN THE LONG RUN, HOW DO YOU THINK THE HEALTHCARE LAW WILL AFFECT YOUR FAMILY'S HEALTHCARE SITUATION?

Interestingly, although Republicans generally oppose the ACA, they are more likely to say they are familiar with the law than are Democrats or independents. In 2014 more than three-quarters (78%) of Republicans said they are very or somewhat familiar with the law, compared with 64% of Democrats and 65% of independents. (See Table 9.5.) Dugan asserts in *Americans' Familiarity with Healthcare Law Unchanged* that familiarity with the law seems to increase opposition to it. More than half (58%) of Americans who are familiar with the law disapprove of it, whereas just 35% of those unfamiliar with the law oppose it.

Carey also finds a partisan divide. Overall, about 30% of Americans said they know someone who gained access to health insurance because of the ACA, while 23% know someone who lost a job and 19% know someone who had work hours cut as a result of the law. Democrats (46%) were more likely to know someone who obtained coverage than were Republicans (19%). In contrast, more Republicans than Democrats were likely to know of someone who lost a job (34% versus 23%) or had work hours reduced (34% versus 19%) because of the ACA.

AMERICANS ARE STILL CONCERNED ABOUT HEALTH CARE COSTS

In view of the fact that health care spending accounts for nearly one-fifth of the U.S. gross domestic product (the total market value of final goods and services produced within an economy in a given year) and that health care costs and out-of-pocket expenses are escalating, it is understandable that Americans are extremely concerned about health care costs. Gallup surveys have repeatedly found that health care costs often top the list of health problems Americans believe beset the nation and are perceived as more urgent than threats of specific diseases.

According to Dugan, in *Retirement Remains Americans' Top Financial Worry* (April 22, 2014, http://www.gallup.com/poll/168626/retirement-remains-americans-top-financial-worry.aspx), concerns about medical care costs reached a record high in 2012, when 62% of Americans said they worry about being able to pay for needed care. Dugan notes that although not having enough money in retirement topped the list of Americans' financial concerns in April 2014, with 59% of Americans expressing this concern, not being able to pay medical costs in the event of a serious illness or accident was a close second—more than half (53%) of Americans said they are very or moderately worried about this possibility. (See Table 9.6.)

Dugan observes that people of all ages are worried about medical care costs. Adults aged 18 to 29 years (52%) worry about not being able to pay medical costs in the event of a serious illness or accident, possibly because they are more likely than other age groups to be uninsured and to have little savings. (See Table 9.7.)

FIGURE 9.4

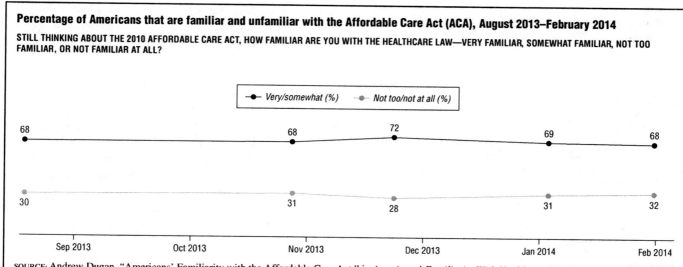

Percentage of Americans that are familiar and unfamiliar with the Affordable Care Act (ACA), August 2013–February 2014

STILL THINKING ABOUT THE 2010 AFFORDABLE CARE ACT, HOW FAMILIAR ARE YOU WITH THE HEALTHCARE LAW—VERY FAMILIAR, SOMEWHAT FAMILIAR, NOT TOO FAMILIAR, OR NOT FAMILIAR AT ALL?

● Very/somewhat (%)   ● Not too/not at all (%)

68   68   72   69   68

30   31   28   31   32

Sep 2013   Oct 2013   Nov 2013   Dec 2013   Jan 2014   Feb 2014

TABLE 9.4

Odds of disapproving of the Affordable Care Act (ACA) by political party affiliation, ideology and race, 2013–14

Republicans are as much as **17 times** more likely to disapprove than Democrats
Independents are as much as **5 times** more likely to disapprove than Democrats
Whites are as much as **4 times** more likely to disapprove than nonwhites
Conservatives are as much as **6 times** more likely to disapprove than liberals
Moderates are as much as **2 times** more likely to disapprove than liberals

Adults aged 65 years and older also worry about not being able to pay the bills associated with a serious illness or accident, even though the overwhelming majority have health insurance. Dugan opines that "given the formidable cost of protracted, continual medical care that often characterizes older Americans' later years, many senior citizens may feel their health insurance alone cannot handle such a financial burden."

CONSUMER SATISFACTION WITH HEALTH CARE FACILITIES

Despite the problems that continue to plague hospitals, such as shortages of nurses and other key personnel, diminished reimbursement, shorter inpatient lengths of stay, sicker patients, and excessively long waiting times for patients in emergency and other hospital departments, consumer satisfaction with many aspects of hospital service has remained relatively high.

For example, in "Survey of Patients' Hospital Experiences (HCAHPS)—National Average" (2014, https://data.medicare.gov/Hospital-Compare/Survey-of-Patients-Hospital-Experiences-HCAHPS-Nat/89u8-shx4), the Centers for Medicare and Medicaid Services provides data from the Hospital Consumer Assessment of Healthcare Providers and Systems (HCAHPS). These data find high levels of patient satisfaction with communication with nurses (79% said nurses always communicated well) and physicians (82% said doctors always communicated well). (See Figure 9.5.) They also indicate high levels of patient satisfaction with pain control (71%), room cleanliness (73%), and information given them about what to do during their recovery at home (85%).

In "Patient Complaints in Healthcare Systems: A Systematic Review and Coding Taxonomy" (*BMJ Quality and Safety*, vol. 23, 2014), Tom W. Reader, Alex Gillespie, and Jane Roberts of the London School of Economics review 59 studies describing more than 88,000 patient complaints and analyze the issues underlying the complaints. The most common issues that triggered patient complaints concerned how they were treated (15.6%) and communication (13.7%).

Lise M. Verhoef et al. observe in "Social Media and Rating Sites as Tools to Understanding Quality of Care: A Scoping Review" (*Journal of Medical Internet Research*, vol. 16, no. 2, February 20, 2014) that increasing numbers of consumers share health care experiences online, at social networking sites, or at sites where they rate the quality of their health care providers. The researchers looked at research considering the relationship between the information shared on social media and the quality of care. They assert that social media could

TABLE 9.5

Percentage of Americans that are familiar and unfamiliar with the Affordable Care Act (ACA), by political party affiliation, 2014

	Republican (%)	Independent (%)	Democrat (%)
Very familiar	25	15	19
Somewhat familiar	53	50	45
Not too familiar	18	21	19
Not familiar at all	3	13	16

SOURCE: Andrew Dugan, "Americans' Familiarity with the Healthcare Law, by Self-Identified Party Affiliation," in *Americans' Familiarity With Healthcare Law Unchanged*, The Gallup Organization, February 6, 2014, http://www.gallup.com/poll/167351/americans-familiarity-healthcare-law-unchanged.aspx (accessed June 4, 2014). Copyright © 2014 Gallup, Inc. All rights reserved. The content is used with permission; however, Gallup retains all rights of republication.

TABLE 9.6

Americans' top financial concerns, April 2014

NEXT, PLEASE TELL ME HOW CONCERNED YOU ARE RIGHT NOW ABOUT EACH OF THE FOLLOWING FINANCIAL MATTERS, BASED ON YOUR CURRENT FINANCIAL SITUATION—ARE YOU VERY WORRIED, MODERATELY WORRIED, NOT TOO WORRIED, OR NOT WORRIED AT ALL?

	Very worried/ moderately worried	Not too worried/not at all worried
	%	%
Not having enough money for retirement	59	35
Not being able to pay medical costs in the event of a serious illness or accident	53	45
Not being able to maintain the standard of living you enjoy	48	52
Not having enough money to pay off your debt	40	48
Not being able to pay medical costs for normal healthcare	39	57
Not having enough to pay your normal monthly bills	36	62
Not having enough money to pay for your children's college	35	31
Not being able to pay your rent, mortgage, or other housing costs	31	64
Not being able to make the minimum payments on your credit cards	16	65

Ranked by percentage very worried/moderately worried.

SOURCE: Andrew Dugan, "Americans' Top Financial Concerns," in *Retirement Remains Americans' Top Financial Worry*, The Gallup Organization, April 22, 2014, http://www.gallup.com/poll/168626/retirement-remains-americans-top-financial-worry.aspx (accessed June 5, 2014). Copyright © 2014 Gallup, Inc. All rights reserved. The content is used with permission; however, Gallup retains all rights of republication.

foster transparency in the quality of health care from the consumer's perspective. They also note that hospital ratings on online sites such as Yelp (a commercial rating website) correlate well with more traditional ratings, such as the HCAHPS scores at government websites. However, Verhoef et al. caution that people using social media are not representative of the population because, for example, older adults and ethnic minorities are underrepresented. Nonetheless, they conclude that "social media, and especially rating sites, could be a fast and efficient way to gather information about quality of care" and "might make expensive, traditional measures of patient experiences unnecessary in the future."

Government Website Posts Patient Satisfaction Survey Data

Industry observers attribute some of the improvement in inpatient hospital care satisfaction to the fact that the federal government posts the results of the HCAHPS survey on the website "Hospital Compare" (http://www.hospitalcompare.hhs.gov), which enables consumers to compare up to three hospitals. The website is a public-private venture led by organizations that represent the hospital industry, providers, and consumers with coordination and oversight from government agencies.

The website aims to help consumers choose the best hospital for selected surgical procedures by detailing how often hospitals give recommended treatments that are known to get the best results for patients with certain medical conditions. It includes mortality rates and hospital readmission rates for each hospital as well as other information such as whether the hospital uses electronic health records and the waiting times for selected emergency departments. It also provides information about a hospital's quality of care, as measured by patient surveys.

The Joint Commission conducted research to determine how consumers understand and use the data available at "Hospital Compare" and reported the results in "Exploring Consumer Understanding and Use of Electronic Hospital Quality Information" (February 2013, http://www.jointcommission.org/assets/1/6/Exploring_Consumer_Understanding_and_Use_of_Electronic_Hospital_Quality_Information.pdf). The commission finds that consumers:

- Ask to view all data they feel are related to quality of care, such as how clinicians, hospitals, and other health care providers perform

- Want data specific to their medical conditions, in addition to patient care data and performance evaluations

- Prefer how numerical data are presented, such that higher numbers correspond to better performance

- Prefer data that are presented in simpler and more easily understood formats, such as tables and figures that clearly display whether the data met or failed to meet a threshold

- Want to view summary displays that list information, such as mortality rates, infection rates, medical errors, and hospital ranking/success rate

In "Public Reporting on Quality and Costs" (HealthAffairs.org, March 8, 2012), Julia James concurs that "much remains to be done to make public reports

TABLE 9.7

Americans' top financial concerns, by age group, April 2014

% Very/Moderately worried

	18 to 29	30 to 49	50 to 64	65+
	%	%	%	%
Not having enough money for retirement	50	70	68	37
Not having enough money to pay for your children's college	46	55	23	8
Not being able to pay medical costs in the event of a serious illness or accident	52	54	58	43
Not having enough money to pay off your debt	47	45	42	20
Not being able to maintain the standard of living you enjoy	52	44	52	41
Not being able to pay medical costs for normal healthcare	35	37	46	33
Not having enough to pay your normal monthly bills	40	33	38	29
Not being able to pay your rent, mortgage, or other housing costs	40	30	31	20
Not being able to make the minimum payments on your credit cards	14	17	18	15

Ranked by percentage very/moderately worried among 30- to 49-year-olds.

SOURCE: Andrew Dugan, "Americans' Top Financial Concerns, by Age," in *Retirement Remains Americans' Top Financial Worry*, The Gallup Organization, April 22, 2014, http://www.gallup.com/poll/168626/retirement-remains-americans-top-financial-worry.aspx (accessed June 5, 2014). Copyright © 2014 Gallup, Inc. All rights reserved. The content is used with permission; however, Gallup retains all rights of republication.

accessible, understandable, and relevant." She also looks at whether report cards and other public performance data serve to improve the quality of health care and reduce costs. James notes that studies have produced conflicting conclusions about the extent to which consumers use public reports, whether providers modify their behavior in response to the results of survey data, and whether reporting changes outcomes.

For example, one study found that reporting outcome data on the "Hospital Compare" website did not reduce mortality in acute care hospitals. However, another study indicated that medical groups that publicly reported their performance on diabetes care were more likely to adopt diabetes improvement interventions than those that did not report their performance.

A GROWING NUMBER LOOK FOR HEALTH INFORMATION ONLINE

Although public trust in hospitals and personal physicians remains relatively high, and many people seek and receive health education from physicians, nurses, and other health professionals, a growing number of Americans are seeking health information online.

Man Hung et al. note in "Uncovering Patterns of Technology Use in Consumer Health Informatics" (*Wiley Interdisciplinary Reviews: Computational Statistics*, vol. 5, no. 6, November–December 2013) that Internet access and use have grown rapidly and that health information technology available via the Internet is considered an important way to encourage personal health management. The most frequently used health information technologies

are searching for information online, mobile health technologies, and personal health records. The key issues that have not yet been completely resolved are confidentiality, privacy, and security concerns and ensuring that consumers have access to accurate and reliable health information.

In *Health Online 2013* (January 15, 2013, http://www.pewinternet.org/files/old-media/Files/Reports/PIP_HealthOnline.pdf), Susannah Fox and Maeve Duggan of the Pew Research Center report that in 2012 nearly three-quarters (72%) of Internet users said they looked for health information online during the past year. The majority (77%) started with a search engine such as Google, Bing, or Yahoo. Thirteen percent began at sites that were dedicated to health information, such as WebMD, whereas as smaller percentages began their searches at general sites (2%), such as Wikipedia, or at social networking sites (1%), such as Facebook. Nearly one-third (31%) of cell phone users and more than half (52%) of smartphone users used their phones to find health or medical information.

According to Fox and Duggan, more women than men looked for health information online in 2012, and Internet users with higher levels of educational attainment were more likely to search for medical information online. Most searched for information about diseases or conditions, treatments or procedures, and health care providers. About a quarter (26%) of people seeking health information online in 2012 were asked to pay to view information, but just 2% indicated they paid to access that information.

FIGURE 9.5

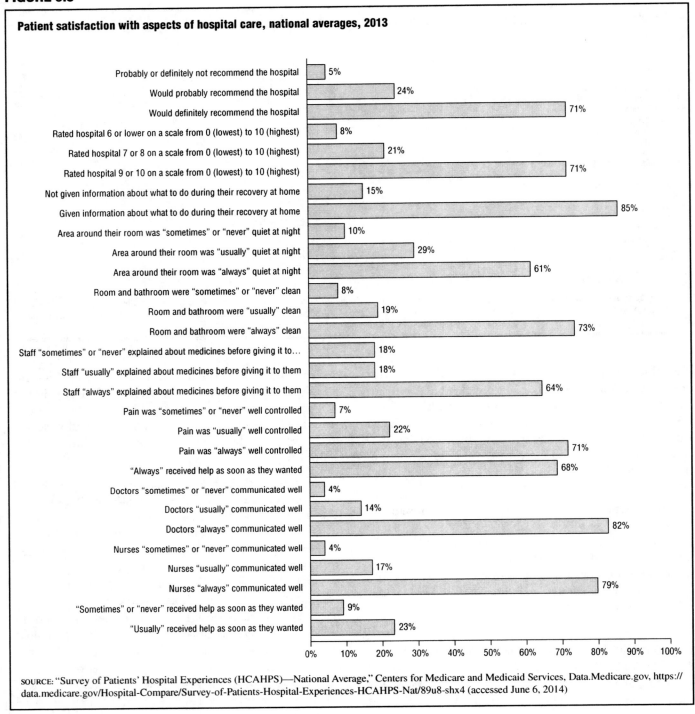

Patient satisfaction with aspects of hospital care, national averages, 2013

SOURCE: "Survey of Patients' Hospital Experiences (HCAHPS)—National Average," Centers for Medicare and Medicaid Services, Data.Medicare.gov, https://data.medicare.gov/Hospital-Compare/Survey-of-Patients-Hospital-Experiences-HCAHPS-Nat/89u8-shx4 (accessed June 6, 2014)

Fox and Duggan indicate that nearly six out of 10 (59%) people who looked for health information online in 2012 used online resources to try to diagnose their own condition or someone else's. When asked if the information found online led them to think they needed to seek medical care or could take care of the condition at home, nearly half (46%) said the condition needed the attention of a physician, whereas 38% said it could be cared for at home. More than half (53%) of people attempting to diagnose their condition using information obtained online said they talked with a medical professional about the information they found.

Finding Accurate, Reliable Health Information Online

Reliable public sources of consumer and provider health information on the Internet include the National Institutes of Health, the Centers for Disease Control and Prevention, and MEDLINE, as well as websites that are produced by medical professional organizations such as the American Medical Association, the American Heart

Association, and the Cancer Society. Health plans, hospitals, and other providers also post accurate, reliable information online. There is also an abundance of unreliable information, from companies marketing "cures" for medical problems to health-related user-generated content that contains incorrect or misleading information. All but the savviest of consumers may have trouble distinguishing accurate, credible sources of health information from those that are not trustworthy.

Kenneth Lee et al. assert in "Interventions to Assist Health Consumers to Find Reliable Online Health Information: A Comprehensive Review" (*PLoS ONE*, vol. 9, no. 4, 2014) that "there appears to be a need for initiatives to assist health consumers to develop their capacity to find reliable health information on the Internet." They evaluate a variety of interventions, including face to face, online, and other types of instruction, designed to help consumers find reliable online information about chronic health conditions. Lee et al. note that various student-centered educational approaches help consumers learn to find credible information online and observe that a contributing factor to the positive results reported by workshop-based training may be due to engagement between the trainers and the participants.

In "What Young People Want from Health-Related Online Resources: A Focus Group Study" (*Journal of Youth Studies*, vol. 16, no. 5, August 2013), Gillian Fergie, Kate Hunt, and Shona Hilton assert that for young people especially, user-generated content on social media websites is a frequently used source of health information. The researchers examined the perceptions and experiences of young people aged 14 to 18 years with health-related content online, particularly through social media, and their strategies for determining the reliability of online health-related information. Fergie, Hunt, and Hilton find that although young people are active consumers of health-related content online and value both expert-generated and user-generated content, they are concerned about the reliability of information and take a knowledgeable and cautious approach when viewing information posted on social media websites. The researchers conclude that young people use different criteria when assessing the reliability of health information on expert, fact-based websites and on social media sites.

Using Social Media to Communicate Health Information

Social media have the potential to serve as an important platform for health education, information, and intervention. David Grande et al. observe in "Translating Research for Health Policy: Researchers' Perceptions and Use of Social Media" (*Health Affairs*, vol. 33, no. 7, July 2014) that a growing number of medical journals, public health agencies, and health care organizations are increasingly using social media to communicate health information. Grande et al. surveyed health policy researchers about using social media, traditional media, and direct outreach to distribute research findings to policy makers. Although the survey respondents deemed all three approaches effective, during the preceding year only 14% had tweeted and 21% had blogged about health research or related health policy. Health policy researchers described social media as potentially risky professionally because it could be mistaken for self-promotion. They also worry that they do not know how to use social media effectively because it is unfamiliar technology. Furthermore, respondents indicated they "will need evidence-based strategies, training, and institutional resources to use social media to communicate evidence." Grande et al. conclude, "Social media are a new and relatively untested tool, but they have the potential to create new communication channels between researchers and policy makers that can help narrow that gap."

Heather J. Hether, Sheila T. Murphy, and Thomas W. Valente report in "It's Better to Give Than to Receive: The Role of Social Support, Trust, and Participation on Health-Related Social Networking Sites" (*Journal of Health Communication: International Perspectives*, April 25, 2014) that Internet users are no longer just consumers of online health content; many produce online health content as well. Social networking sites and peer-to-peer support communities are increasingly used as venues for the exchange of health-related information and advice. The positive impacts of social support on health outcomes have been observed in both offline, face-to-face encounters and online interactions.

Hether, Murphy, and Valente surveyed more than 100 pregnant members of popular pregnancy-related sites. They find that time spent at the sites was less likely to predict health-related outcomes, such as having a positive attitude toward living healthfully while pregnant and following recommendations posted on the sites, than users' assessments of qualities such as trust in the sites. The perception of providing, rather than receiving, social support from the sites was associated with the most positive outcomes, including seeking more information from additional sources and following recommendations posted on the sites. The researchers explain, "This suggests that highly supportive community members may act as information bridges, seeking information from other sources and relaying it back to the online community."

Physician Use of Digital Communication

Physician use of e-mail, patient portals, and texting to communicate with patients is growing. According to the press release "Stethoscopes and Smartphones: Physicians Turn to Digital Tools to Boost Patient Outcomes"

(May 29, 2014, http://www.prnewswire.com/news-releases/stethoscopes-and-smartphones-physicians-turn-to-digital-tools-to-boost-patient-outcomes-261089461.html), Manhattan Research conducted the survey Taking the Pulse in 2014 and found that 40% of physicians feel such digital communication improves outcomes. Nearly half (47%) had used mobile devices such as smartphones or tablets to show patients images or videos, about a quarter communicated with patients through a portal, more than one-third had recommended that patients use health applications, and about 20% had communicated with patients using secure messaging platforms.

MARKETING PRESCRIPTION DRUGS TO CONSUMERS

Although health care consumers continue to receive much of their information from health professionals and the Internet, many also learn about health care services and products from reports in the news media and from advertising. Media advertising (the promotion of hospitals, health insurance, managed care plans, medical groups, and related health services and products) has been a mainstay of health care marketing efforts since the 1970s. During the early 1990s pharmaceutical companies made their first forays into advertising of prescription drugs directly to consumers. Before the 1990s pharmaceutical companies' promotion efforts had focused almost exclusively on physicians, the health professionals who prescribe their products.

Since the mid-1990s spending on prescription drugs has escalated. In 1997 the U.S. Food and Drug Administration (FDA) released guidelines governing direct-to-consumer (DTC) advertising and seemingly opened a floodgate of print, radio, and television advertisements promoting prescription drugs. Industry observers wondered if this upsurge of DTC advertising had resulted in more, and possibly inappropriate, prescribing and higher costs.

Spending for DTC Advertising Slows

It stands to reason that pharmaceutical companies must be receiving significant returns on their DTC advertising investments to justify increasing budgets for consumer advertising, but it is difficult to measure the precise impact of consumer advertising on drug sales. In the press release "IMS Health Study: Spending Growth Returns for U.S. Medicines" (April 15, 2014, http://www.imshealth.com), the IMS Institute for Healthcare Informatics reports that after a 1% decline in 2012, prescription drug sales grew 3.2% to $329.2 billion in 2013. Rachel Kornfield et al. report in "Promotion of Prescription Drugs to Consumers and Providers, 2001–2010" (*PLoS ONE*, vol. 8, no. 3, 2013) that spending on DTC prescription drug advertising peaked at $36.1 billion (13.4% of sales) in 2004 and then declined to $27.7

billion (9% of sales) in 2010. The researchers note that advertising not only influences demand for prescription drugs and physician prescribing but also increases physician visits for disorders treated by advertised drugs.

Kornfield et al. attribute the decline in prescription drug advertising to the fact that there have been fewer new drugs introduced to the market in the past decade and that more of the recent market entrants are biologics (drugs used by a smaller number of patients, administered by injection, and sold at higher prices), which are promoted differently from patients who can self-administer. An example of such a biologic is bevacizumab, a drug used to treat cancer that is delivered intravenously and costs more than $100,000 for a one-year supply.

According to Kevin M. Fain and Alexander G. Caleb, in "Mind the Gap: Understanding the Effects of Pharmaceutical Direct-to-Consumer Advertising" (*Medical Care*, vol. 52, no. 4, April 2014), DTC advertising resurged in 2012, accounting for about 13% of promotional spending. Advocates of DTC advertising contend that it empowers consumers and increases treatment rates. Detractors worry that consumers are not knowledgeable enough to evaluate the advertising and that growing consumer demand may prompt physicians to overprescribe.

Fain and Caleb note that since 1997, when the FDA relaxed its policy on prescription drug advertising, DTC advertisements have increased consumer awareness of available treatments but have also created confusion about a drug's relative risks and benefits. Similarly, some research finds that DTC advertisements help patients ask good questions during physician visits, but other evidence questions whether DTC advertising benefits or hampers patient-physician interactions. Fain and Caleb suggest that because pharmaceutical companies benefit from DTC advertising, they should share the results of their research on its influence in terms of public health outcomes.

Is DTC Advertising of Psychoactive Drugs Helpful or Harmful?

In "Statistics" (2014, http://www.nimh.nih.gov/health/statistics/index.shtml), the National Institute of Mental Health estimates that in 2012, 18.6% of Americans aged 18 years and older were affected by a mental disorder and 4.1% suffered from a serious mental illness. Other surveys find that as many as 30% of adults in the United States suffer from mental disorders. For example, the Harvard School of Medicine's National Comorbidity Survey (July 2007, http://www.hcp.med.harvard.edu/ncs) finds that in any given year 32.4% of all Americans meet the criteria for having a mental illness and that the lifetime prevalence of any diagnosable mental disorder is 57.4%.

Although these studies rely primarily on self-reporting, they suggest that the United States is in the throes of an epidemic of mental illness. However, some researchers argue that Americans' mental health is no worse than it was in past decades. They contend that the availability and aggressive marketing of psychopharmacological agents (prescription drugs that are used to treat mental health problems such as nervousness, anxiety, panic, and shyness) have prompted the overdiagnosis of mental health problems and conditions motivated primarily by the desire to increase drug sales.

According to Rosemary J. Avery, Matthew Eisenberg, and Kosali I. Simon, in "The Impact of Direct-to-Consumer Television and Magazine Advertising on Antidepressant Use" (*Journal of Health Economics*, vol. 31, no. 5, September 2012), DTC advertising of antidepressant drugs affects the use of these drugs. The researchers estimate that television advertising produces an increase of between 6% and 10% in antidepressant drug use.

In "How Does Direct to Consumer Advertising Affect the Stigma of Mental Illness?" (*Community Mental Health Journal*, vol. 50, no. 7, October 2014), Patrick W. Corrigan et al. examine the effect of DTC advertising of psychiatric medication on people who self-identify as having mental illness and on the population at large. The researchers showed an advertisement for Cymbalta, an antidepressant, to both groups of consumers. After viewing the advertisement, people who self-identified as having mental illness said they felt "less blame, less dangerousness, less social avoidance, more pity, and greater willingness to help." By contrast, the attitude of the general public worsened—they "were less likely to offer help, endorse recovery, and agree with self-determination attitudes towards people with mental illness." Corrigan et al. conclude that DTC advertisements for psychiatric drugs "may increase the public's stigma towards people with mental illness but reduce stigma among individuals who identify as having a mental illness."

Nathan P. Greenslit and Ted J. Kaptchuk explain in "Antidepressants and Advertising: Psychopharmaceuticals in Crisis" (*Yale Journal of Biology and Medicine*, vol. 85, no. 1, March 2012) that "psychopharmaceuticals are currently in crisis [because] the science of depression has become a contest between scientists, pharmaceutical marketing, physicians, professional medical organizations, regulatory agencies, and patients." The mechanisms of action (how the drugs work) and the efficacy of antidepressant drugs have been called into question by rigorous population studies that find them no more effective than placebo (an inactive compound; the placebo effect is a health benefit, such as pain relief, that arises from the patient's expectation that the placebo will provide relief, rather than from the placebo itself). Greenslit and Kaptchuk note that "despite such broad uncertainty over both the scientific explanations and efficacy of antidepressants, DTC advertising is still a nearly 5 billion dollar per year industry (and practically unique to the United States, as no other country except New Zealand allows it)."

Greenslit and Kaptchuk observe that since 1997, when the FDA approved DTC advertising, pharmaceutical companies have been accused of overstating claims of drug efficacy, minimizing the health risks that are associated with antidepressant use, and increasing consumer demand for the drugs by characterizing everyday experiences such as sadness, anxiety, and shyness as symptoms of mental illness. In contrast, advocates contend that DTC advertising reduces the stigmas that are associated with mental illness, educates consumers, promotes patient participation in clinical decision making, and improves patient adherence to medication and other treatment. Critics counter that advertising is intended to persuade, not educate, and that it promotes inappropriate use of prescription drugs or diverts consumers from safer, less costly alternatives.

Opponents contend that DTC advertising is primarily intended to drive sales and that it:

- Increases prescription drug costs

- Does not provide the impartial, objective information that would enable consumers to make informed health choices

- Increases risk because, unlike other consumer goods, prescription drugs, even when administered properly, may cause serious adverse reactions

- Takes unfair advantage of vulnerable people facing difficult treatment choices, especially people who suffer from mental illness

- Aims to increase awareness and utilization of newer products to gain market share and recoup development costs (new drugs are not necessarily safer or more effective but are usually costlier, and often little is known about their long-term risks)

- Does not enhance consumer awareness or public health because there is no evidence that advertising helps patients make better choices about prescription drug use

- May unduly influence physician-prescribing practices; physicians often rely on manufacturers for information about drugs, rather than on independent sources, and many studies show that the physicians most influenced by pharmaceutical advertising tend to prescribe less judiciously

Regardless, many mental health professionals and consumers favor DTC advertising because they believe it informs consumers that there is effective treatment for potentially debilitating mental disorders and helps them overcome reluctance to seek needed treatment. For example, Kaitlin P. Gallo, Jonathan S. Comer, and David H. Barlow assert in "Direct-to-Consumer Marketing of Psychological Treatments for Anxiety Disorders" (*Journal of Anxiety Disorders*, vol. 27, no. 8, December 2013) that DTC advertising increases consumer awareness and utilization of evidence-based psychological treatment.

IMPORTANT NAMES
AND ADDRESSES

**Accreditation Association for
Ambulatory Health Care**
5250 Old Orchard Rd., Ste. 200
Skokie, IL 60077
(847) 853-6060
FAX: (847) 853-9028
E-mail: info@aaahc.org
URL: http://www.aaahc.org/

Administration for Community Living
One Massachusetts Ave. NW
Washington, DC 20001
(202) 619-0724
FAX: (202) 357-3555
E-mail: aclinfo@acl.hhs.gov
URL: http://www.acl.gov/

**Agency for Healthcare Research
and Quality
Office of Communications and
Knowledge Transfer**
540 Gaither Rd., Ste. 2000
Rockville, MD 20850
(301) 427-1104
URL: http://www.ahrq.gov/

America's Essential Hospitals
1301 Pennsylvania Ave. NW, Ste. 950
Washington, DC 20004-1712
(202) 585-0100
FAX: (202) 585-0101
E-mail: info@essentialhospitals.org
URL: http://essentialhospitals.org/

**American Academy of Child and
Adolescent Psychiatry**
3615 Wisconsin Ave. NW
Washington, DC 20016-3007
(202) 966-7300
FAX: (202) 966-2891
URL: http://www.aacap.org/

American Academy of Family Physicians
11400 Tomahawk Creek Pkwy.
Leawood, KS 66211-2680
(913) 906-6000

1-800-274-2237
FAX: (913) 906-6075
URL: http://www.aafp.org/

**American Academy of Physician
Assistants**
2318 Mill Rd., Ste. 1300
Alexandria, VA 22314
(703) 836-2272
E-mail: aapa@aapa.org
URL: http://www.aapa.org/

**American Association for Geriatric
Psychiatry**
6728 Old McLean Village Dr.
McLean, VA 22101
(703) 556-9222
FAX: (703) 556-8729
URL: http://www.aagponline.org/

**American Association for Marriage
and Family Therapy**
112 S. Alfred St.
Alexandria, VA 22314-3061
(703) 838-9808
FAX: (703) 838-9805
URL: http://www.aamft.org/

**American Association of Pastoral
Counselors**
9504A Lee Hwy.
Fairfax, VA 22031-2303
(703) 385-6967
FAX: (703) 352-7725
E-mail: info@aapc.org
URL: http://www.aapc.org/

American Cancer Society
250 Williams St. NW
Atlanta, GA 30303
1-800-227-2345
URL: http://www.cancer.org/

American Chiropractic Association
1701 Clarendon Blvd.
Arlington, VA 22209

(703) 276-8800
FAX: (703) 243-2593
E-mail: memberinfo@acatoday.org
URL: http://www.acatoday.org/index.cfm/

American College of Nurse Practitioners
225 Reinekers Lane, Ste. 525
Alexandria, VA 22314
(703) 740-2529
FAX: (703) 740-2533
URL: https://acnp.enpnetwork.com/

American Counseling Association
5999 Stevenson Ave.
Alexandria, VA 22304
1-800-347-6647
FAX: 1-800-473-2329
URL: http://www.counseling.org/

American Dental Association
211 E. Chicago Ave.
Chicago, IL 60611-2678
(312) 440-2500
URL: http://www.ada.org/

American Diabetes Association
1701 N. Beauregard St.
Alexandria, VA 22311
1-800-342-2383
URL: http://www.diabetes.org/

American Geriatrics Society
40 Fulton St., 18th Floor
New York, NY 10038
(212) 308-1414
FAX: (212) 832-8646
E-mail: info.amger@americangeriatrics.org
URL: http://www.americangeriatrics.org/

American Heart Association
7272 Greenville Ave.
Dallas, TX 75231
1-800-242-8721
URL: http://www.americanheart.org/

American Hospital Association
155 N. Wacker Dr.
Chicago, IL 60606
(312) 422-3000
URL: http://www.aha.org/

American Medical Association
AMA Plaza
330 N. Wabash Ave., Ste. 39300
Chicago, IL 60611-5885
1-800-262-3211
URL: http://www.ama-assn.org/

**American Osteopathic
Association**
142 E. Ontario St.
Chicago, IL 60611-2864
(312) 202-8000
1-800-621-1773
FAX: (312) 202-8200
URL: http://www.osteopathic.org/

**American Pharmacists
Association**
2215 Constitution Ave. NW
Washington, DC 20037
(202) 628-4410
1-800-237-2742
FAX: (202) 783-2351
URL: http://www.pharmacist.com/

**American Physical Therapy
Association**
1111 N. Fairfax St.
Alexandria, VA 22314-1488
(703) 684-2782
1-800-999-2782
FAX: (703) 706-8536
URL: http://www.apta.org/

American Psychiatric Association
1000 Wilson Blvd., Ste. 1825
Arlington, VA 22209
(703) 907-7300
1-888-357-7924
E-mail: apa@psych.org
URL: http://www.psych.org/

**American Psychiatric Nurses
Association**
3141 Fairview Park Dr., Ste. 625
Falls Church, VA 22042
(571) 533-1919
1-855-863-2762
FAX: 1-855-883-2762
URL: http://www.apna.org/

**American Psychological
Association**
750 First St. NE
Washington, DC 20002-4242
(202) 336-5500
1-800-374-2721
URL: http://www.apa.org/

Association of American Medical Colleges
655 K St. NW, Ste. 100
Washington, DC 20001-2399

(202) 828-0400
URL: http://www.aamc.org/

Association for Psychological Science
1133 15th St. NW, Ste. 1000
Washington, DC 20005
(202) 293-9300
FAX: (202) 293-9350
URL: http://www.psychological
science.org/

**Center for Mental Health Services
Substance Abuse and Mental Health
Services Administration**
Room 6-1057
1 Choke Cherry Rd.
Rockville, MD 20857
(240) 276-1310
URL: http://www.samhsa.gov/about-us/
who-we-are/offices-centers/cmhs

**Center for Studying Health System
Change**
1100 First St. NE, 12th Floor
Washington, DC 20002
(202) 484-5261
FAX: (202) 863-1763
URL: http://www.hschange.org/

**Centers for Disease Control and
Prevention**
1600 Clifton Rd.
Atlanta, GA 30333-4027
1-800-232-4636
E-mail: cdcinfo@cdc.gov
URL: http://www.cdc.gov/

**Centers for Medicare and Medicaid
Services**
7500 Security Blvd.
Baltimore, MD 21244
(410) 786-3000
1-877-267-2323
URL: http://www.cms.gov/

Children's Defense Fund
25 E St. NW
Washington, DC 20001
1-800-233-1200
E-mail: cdfinfo@childrensdefense.org
URL: http://www.childrensdefense.org/
 ʼ

Families USA
1201 New York Ave. NW, Ste. 1100
Washington, DC 20005
(202) 628-3030
FAX: (202) 347-2417
E-mail: info@familiesusa.org
URL: http://www.familiesusa.org/

**Health Coalition on Liability
and Access**
PO Box 78096
Washington, DC 20013-8096
URL: http://www.hcla.org/

**Health Resources and Services
Administration
U.S. Department of Health and Human
Services**
5600 Fishers Lane
Rockville, MD 20857
1-888-275-4772
URL: http://www.hrsa.gov/index.html/

Hospice Association of America
228 Seventh St. SE
Washington, DC 20003
(202) 546-4759
FAX: (202) 547-9559
URL: http://www.nahc.org/HAA/

The Joint Commission
One Renaissance Blvd.
Oakbrook Terrace, IL 60181
(630) 792-5800
FAX: (630) 792-5005
URL: http://www.jointcommission.org/

**March of Dimes Birth Defects
Foundation**
1275 Mamaroneck Ave.
White Plains, NY 10605
(914) 997-4488
URL: http://www.marchofdimes.com/

**Medical Group Management
Association**
104 Inverness Terrace East
Englewood, CO 80112-5306
(303) 799-1111
1-877-275-6462
E-mail: support@mgma.com
URL: http://www.mgma.com/

Mental Health Association
2000 N. Beauregard St., Sixth Floor
Alexandria, VA 22311
(703) 684-7722
1-800-969-6642
FAX: (703) 684-5968
URL: http://www.nmha.org/

**National Association of Community
Health Centers**
7501 Wisconsin Ave., Ste. 1100W
Bethesda, MD 20814
(301) 347-0400
URL: http://www.nachc.com/

**National Association of School
Psychologists**
4340 East West Hwy., Ste. 402
Bethesda, MD 20814
(301) 657-0270
1-866-331-NASP
FAX: (301) 657-0275
URL: http://www.nasponline.org/

National Association of Social Workers
750 First St. NE, Ste. 700
Washington, DC 20002
(202) 408-8600
URL: http://www.socialworkers.org/

National Center for Health Statistics
U.S. Department of Health and Human
Services
3311 Toledo Rd.
Hyattsville, MD 20782
1-800-232-4636
URL: http://www.cdc.gov/nchs/

National Committee for Quality
Assurance
1100 13th St. NW, Ste. 1000
Washington, DC 20005
(202) 955-3500
1-888-275-7585

FAX: (202) 955-3599
URL: http://www.ncqa.org/

National Institute of Mental
Health
Science Writing, Press, and Dissemination
Branch
6001 Executive Blvd.
Rm. 6200, MSC 9663
Bethesda, MD 20892-9663
1-866-615-6464
FAX: (301) 443-4279
E-mail: nimhinfo@nih.gov
URL: http://www.nimh.nih.gov/

United Network for Organ Sharing
700 N. Fourth St.
Richmond, VA 23219
(804) 782-4800
1-888-894-6361
FAX: (804) 782-4817
URL: http://www.unos.org/

World Health Organization
Avenue Appia 20
Geneva 27, 1211Switzerland
(011-41) 22-791-2111
FAX: (011-41) 22-791-3111
URL: http://www.who.int/

RESOURCES

Agencies of the U.S. Department of Health and Human Services collect, analyze, and publish a wide variety of health statistics that describe and measure the operation and effectiveness of the U.S. health care system. The Centers for Disease Control and Prevention tracks nationwide health trends and reports its findings in several periodicals, especially its *Advance Data* series, *National Ambulatory Medical Care Survey*, *HIV Surveillance Reports*, and *Morbidity and Mortality Weekly Reports*. The National Center for Health Statistics provides a complete statistical overview of the nation's health in its annual *Health, United States*.

The National Institutes of Health provides definitions, epidemiological data, and research findings about a comprehensive range of medical and public health subjects. The Centers for Medicare and Medicaid Services monitors the nation's health spending. The agency's quarterly *Health Care Financing Review* and annual *Data Compendium* provide complete information on health care spending, particularly on allocations for Medicare and Medicaid. The Administration for Community Living provides information about the health, welfare, and services available for older Americans.

The Agency for Healthcare Research and Quality researches and documents access to health care, quality of care, and efforts to control health care costs. It also examines the safety of health care services and ways to prevent medical errors. The Joint Commission and the National Committee for Quality Assurance are accrediting organizations that focus attention on institutional health care providers, including the managed care industry.

The U.S. Census Bureau, in its *Current Population Reports* series, details the status of insurance among selected U.S. households.

Medical, public health, and nursing journals offer a wealth of health care system information and research findings. The studies cited in this edition are drawn from a range of professional publications, including *American Academy of Emergency Medicine*, *American Journal of Nursing*, *Annals of Emergency Medicine*, *Birth*, *BMC Health Services Research*, *BMJ*, *Health Affairs*, *Health Policy*, *International Journal of Health Services*, *Journal of Epidemiology and Community Health*, *Journal of the American Medical Association*, *Journal of Hospital Medicine*, and *Policy, Politics, and Nursing Practice*.

Gale, Cengage Learning thanks the Gallup Organization for the use of its public opinion research about health care costs, quality, and concerns. It would also like to thank the many professional associations, voluntary medical organizations, and foundations dedicated to research, education, and advocacy about the efforts to reform and improve the health care system that were included in this edition.

INDEX

Page references in italics refer to photographs. References with the letter t following them indicate the presence of a table. The letter f indicates a figure. If more than one table or figure appears on a particular page, the exact item number for the table or figure being referenced is provided.

A

AAAHC (Accreditation Association for Ambulatory Health Care), 75–76

AAFP (American Academy of Family Physicians), 147

AAMC (Association of American Medical Colleges), 18

AAP (American Academy of Pediatrics), 49, 147

"AAP Principles Concerning Retail-Based Clinics" (AAP), 49–50

AARP, 14

Abell, Cathy H., 147

"About Chiropractic" (American Chiropractic Association), 38

"About HHS" (HHS), 63

"About Psychiatric-Mental Health Nurses" (American Psychiatric Nurses Association), 34

"About the National Institutes of Health" (NIH), 71

ACA. *See* Patient Protection and Affordable Care Act

"The ACA's Cuts to Medicare Threaten Home Health Care Jobs, Patients" (Dolin), 56

Accenture, 146

"The Accenture Connected Health Pulse Survey" (Accenture), 146

"Access, Affordability, and Insurance Complexity Are Often Worse in the United States Compared to 10 Other Countries" (Schoen et al.), 133–134

Access Is the Answer (NACHC), 6

Access to health care
    ACA reform for improved access, 13–14
    in Canada, 135
    for children, 7–8
    children, age-adjusted percentages of selected measures of health care access for children under age 18, 10t–11t
    consumer access to care, 4
    in France, 137
    mental health care, 12–13
    race/ethnicity and regular sources of medical care, 6
    reduction of disparities in, 8–9, 12
    regular source of health care improves access, 5–6
    as right or privilege, 14–15
    supply/distribution of needed services, 4–5
    telemedicine for, 145–146
    women, obstacles of, 6–7
    See also Health care system, U.S.

Accountable care organizations (ACOs), 61

Accreditation
    Accreditation Association for Ambulatory Health Care, 75–76
    description of, 73
    of health care providers, 73–76
    Joint Commission, 73–74
    National Committee for Quality Assurance, 74–75
    National Quality Forum, 76
    for nurse practitioners/physician assistants, 28

Accreditation Association for Ambulatory Health Care (AAAHC), 75–76

Accreditation Council for Graduate Medical Education (ACGME), 18

ACF (Administration for Children and Families), 64, 66

ACGME Common Program Requirements, 18

ACL (Administration for Community Living), 64

ACOs (accountable care organizations), 61

Acquired immunodeficiency syndrome (AIDS)
    CDC partnerships for battle against, 70
    identification of, 64
    NIH research budget for, 102

ACS (American Cancer Society), 77–78, 159

Acupuncture, 37

Administration for Children and Families (ACF), 64, 66

Administration for Community Living (ACL), 64

Administration on Aging, 66

Advanced practice nurses
    description of, 27
    psychiatric nurses, 34
    training for, 28

Advertising
    influence on public opinion, 151
    marketing prescription drugs to consumers, 160–162

Affordable Care Act. *See* Patient Protection and Affordable Care Act

"The Affordable Care Act & Medicare" (CMS), 97

"Affordable Care Act's Role in Slowing Health Costs Debated" (Persaud), 85

African Americans
    access to mental health care, 13
    children's access to health care, 7
    disparities in access to health care, 9, 12
    regular source of health care for, 6
    uninsured, 110

Age
    aging population as factor of health care boom, 38–39
    concern about health care costs by, 154–155
    financial concerns, Americans' top, by age group, 157t

hospital ED patients with, 45–46
hospital emergency department visits and, 44
Medicaid, 97–98
Medicaid for public hospitals, 43
Medicare, 92–94, 96–97
Medicare Advantage, 114–115
Medicare reimbursement, changes to, 115–116, 118, 120
mental health parity, 123–124
Oregon Health Plan and, 104
overview of, 109
percentage of children/adults with/ without health insurance at time of interview, for at least part of past year, by age group/coverage type, 114*f*
percentage of persons aged 18–64 without health insurance at time of interview, for at least part of past year, or for more than a year, 112*f*
percentage of persons under age 65 who were uninsured at time of interview, by poverty status, 115*f*
percentage of persons under age 65 without health insurance at time of interview, by age group/sex, 113*f*
percentage with public/private health insurance, without health insurance, 119(*t*6.6)
percentage without health insurance, by selected characteristics, 116*t*
percentage without health insurance, by state Health Insurance Marketplace type, 118*t*–119*t*
percentage without health insurance, by state Medicaid status, 117*t*
PPOs, 60–61
projected growth in health care spending, 79–81
projected spending growth, 83
satisfaction with U.S. health care system by insurance status, 152(*t*9.1)
sources of, 112–114
uninsured, 109–111
uninsured, number/rate of, 111*f*
U.S. *vs.* other OECD countries regarding, 131
for women with ACA, 7
"Health Insurance & Managed Care" (Kaiser Family Foundation), 59–60
Health Insurance Coverage: Early Release of Estimates from the 2013 National Health Interview Survey (Martinez & Cohen)
on children and health insurance, 120–121
on older adults without health insurance, 114
on uninsured, 109
Health Insurance Marketplace
with ACA, 2–3
CMS management of, 65

health insurance enrollment via, 110–111
NCQA accreditation of, 74–75
percentage without health insurance by type of state health insurance marketplace, 110, 118*t*–119*t*
Health Insurance Portability and Accountability Act (HIPAA), 121
Health insurers, oversight for, 123
Health maintenance organizations (HMOs)
fans/critics of, 60
Medicare Advantage, 114–115
Medicare-risk HMOs, control of costs, 93–94
NCQA accreditation of, 75
overview of, 59–60
rationing by, 104–105
Health Online 2013 (Fox & Duggan), 157–158
Health psychologists, 33
Health Reform: Implications for Women's Access to Coverage and Care (Kaiser Family Foundation), 6–7
"Health Reform Interrupted: The Unraveling of the Oregon Health Plan" (Oberlander), 104
Health Resources and Services Administration (HRSA)
on demand for intensivists, 19
on number of advanced practice nurses, 28
work of, budget of, 65
"Health Savings Account Enrollment Reaches 15.5 Million" (America's Health Insurance Plans), 122
Health savings accounts (HSAs)
eligibility requirements, 121
features of, 122
Health status, of U.S. citizens, 131–133
Health technologies. *See* Technologies, health
"Healthcare around the World" (Ybarra), 137
Healthcare Effectiveness Data and Information Set (HEDIS), 75
HealthCare.gov, 2, 110
HealthGrades, Inc., 140, 150
Health.org, 150
Healthy People initiative, 54–55
Heart disease, 77
"Heart Health as Young Adult Linked to Mental Function in Mid-life" (American Heart Association), 77
HEDIS (Healthcare Effectiveness Data and Information Set), 75
Hellender, Ida, 132
Heritage Foundation, 15
Hether, Heather J., 159
HHS. *See* U.S. Department of Health and Human Services

HHS Budget in Brief, Fiscal Year 2015 (HHS), 101
High blood pressure, 77
"High-Reliability Health Care: Getting There from Here" (Chassin & Loeb), 74
Hilton, Shona, 159
HIPAA (Health Insurance Portability and Accountability Act), 121
Hirschberg, Irene, 149–150
Hispanics
access to mental health care, 13
children's access to health care, 7
regular source of health care for, 6
uninsured, 110
"Historic Release of Data Gives Consumers Unprecedented Transparency on the Medical Services Physicians Provide and How Much They Are Paid" (CMS), 115–116
"Historical Highlights" (HHS), 63–64
"History of the American Heart Association" (American Heart Association), 77
HIV. *See* Human immunodeficiency virus
HMO Act, 59
HMOs. *See* Health maintenance organizations
Home health care
development of, 55
growth of, 98
Medicare spending for, 56
nursing home occupancy and, 50
"Home Health Care" (*Family Economics and Nutrition Review*), 55
Homeless people
access to mental health care and, 12, 55
with mental illness, 53, 101
Homeopathic medicine, 36–37
Hospice care
concept/philosophy of, 56–57
increased use of, 58
in Oregon Health Plan, 104
Hospital Compare website, 150, 156–157
Hospital Consumer Assessment of Healthcare Providers and Systems (HCAHPS)
consumer satisfaction with hospitals, 155
results posted on Hospital Compare, 156–157
Hospital emergency departments (EDs)
catering to older people, 46
patients with health insurance, 45–46
visits to, 44
visits within past 12 months among adults, 47*t*–48*t*
visits within past 12 months among children under age 18, 45*t*–46*t*

health care reform with ACA, 2–3

on mental health parity, 124

National Commission on Fiscal Responsibility and Reform, 96

"ObamaCare, Doctor Shortage to Spur $2 Billion Telehealth Market" (Japsen), 146

"Obamacare's 'Cadillac Tax' Could Help Reduce the Cost of Health Care" (Frist), 90

Oberlander, Jonathan, 104

Obesity

international comparisons of, 131

NIH research budget for, 102

Obstetrician-gynecologist, 19

Occupancy rates

hospitals, beds, occupancy rates, by type of ownership/size of hospital, 42t

of hospitals, decline of, 41

nursing home beds, residents, occupancy rates, 51t

of nursing homes, 50

Occupational Outlook Handbook (BLS)

on chiropractors, 38

on counselors, 35

on employment of RNs, 26

on number of dentists, 28

on occupational therapists, 31

on pharmacists, 33

on physician working conditions/ earnings, 21–23

on wages for mental health professionals, 34

Occupational therapists (OTs), 31

"Occupational Therapy's Role in Health Care Reform" (American Occupational Therapy Association), 31

"OECD Health Data—Frequently Requested Data" (OECD)

on health care in England, 136

on health care in France, 137

hospital utilization statistics, 129–130

Older people

cost of Medicaid for, 97–98

cost of Medicare for, 92–94, 96–97

as factor of health care boom, 38–39

home health care for, 55–56

hospital emergency departments for, 46

long-term health care, cost of, 98, 100

long-term-care facilities for, 50–53

sources of health insurance for, 114

spending on disease research and, 102

O'Malley, A. James, 145–146

"On Breaking One's Neck" (Relman), 2

Oncologist, 19

OPTN ("Organ Procurement and Transplantation Network"), 47–48

OPTN Policies (UNOS), 49

Oregon

health care rationing, 104

Medicaid expansion in, 46

Oregon Health Authority, 104

Oregon Health Plan, 104

Oregon Health Services Commission, 104

"Oregon Starts to Extend Health Care" (Janofsky), 104

"Organ Procurement and Transplantation Network" (OPTN), 47–48

Organ transplants

donor-recipient matching, 48–49

number performed, 47–48

Organisation for Economic Co-operation and Development (OECD)

on Canadian health care system, 135

on French health care system, 137

on German health care system, 134–135

on health care in England, 136

on health care in Japan, 137

international comparison of health care spending, resources, utilization, 127–130

See also International comparisons of health care

Orthodontists, 29

Osler, William, 17

Osteopathy, 17

Otolaryngologist, 19

OTs (occupational therapists), 31

"Outlook 2014: Public Hospitals" (Johnson), 43–44

Out-of-pocket spending

impact of ACA on, 83

international comparisons of, 129

with Medicare Advantage, 114, 115

Medicare Prescription Drug, Improvement, and Modernization Act and, 120

percentage of nation's health costs paid by, 84

on prescription drugs, 90, 92, 103

Outpatient clinics

AAAHC accreditation of, 75–76

mental health, 53

shift to health care delivery at, 139

"Over the Rainbow: Delivering on the Promise of England's New Public Health System" (Conrad), 137

Oversight, of health insurers, 123

Overtreatment, 105–106

P

PacifiCare of Oklahoma, Inc. v. Burrage, 60

Pain

hospice care for, 57

painkiller overdoses, 70

Palliative care, 56–58

Parkinson, John, 3

Partnership for Patients Initiative, 142

PAs. *See* Physician assistants

Pastoral counselors, 35

Patent

cost of prescription drugs, ACA and, 103

for new drug, 102

Patented Medicine Prices Review Board, 135–136

Pathologist, 19

"Patient Complaints in Healthcare Systems: A Systematic Review and Coding Taxonomy" (Reader, Gillespie, & Roberts), 155

Patient portals, physician use of, 159–160

Patient Protection and Affordable Care Act (ACA)

access to health insurance coverage with, 109

accountable care organizations and, 61

changes to health care delivery with, 139

children, health insurance for, 121

constitutionality of, 151

designed to address key issues of health care system, 1

disproportionate share hospitals and, 44

economic impact of, 106–107

effects of insurance coverage provisions on federal deficit, 94t

effects on health insurance coverage, 107t

estimate of budgetary effects of insurance coverage provisions in, 125f

expanding role of NPs with, 28

as factor of health care boom, 39–40

financing, 124

health care reform with, 2–3

health care spending, impact on, 85, 90

health insurance coverage, expansion of, 110–111

in HHS milestones, 64

home health care funding and, 56

hospital emergency department use and, 46

impact on cost of health care, 106–107

impact on managed care plans, 61

impact on Medicare, 97

impact on national health expenditures, 87t–88t

for improved access to health care, 13–14

Joint Commission and, 74

Medicaid changes with, 97–98

Medicare Part D spending, 90, 92

Medicare reimbursement, changes to, 115–116

mental health parity and, 124

mental health spending and, 100

odds of disapproving of by political party affiliation, ideology, race, 155t

Oregon Health Plan and, 104

out-of-pocket spending and, 83

oversight of health insurers, 123

patient safety improvements with, 141–142

"What the Affordable Care Act Means for Prescription Coverage" (CVS Caremark), 102

"What Young People Want from Health-Related Online Resources: A Focus Group Study" (Fergie, Hunt, & Hilton), 159

"What's the First Step in Transforming American Health Care?" (Pear), 1–2

"Where Are We on the Diffusion Curve? Trends and Drivers of Primary Care Physicians' Use of Health Information Technology" (Audet, Squires, & Doty), 147

Whites
children's access to health care, 7
disparities in access to health care, 12
regular source of health care for, 6
uninsured, 110

"Who Are the Innovators? Nursing Homes Implementing Culture Change" (Grabowski et al.), 52–53

Williams, Deborah, 147

Wishnov, Frappier Estate v., 60

Women, 6–7
See also Gender

Word-of-mouth publicity, 151

Working conditions
of physicians, 21
of residency training, 18

Overdue charge is 10 cents per day,
Including Saturdays, Sundays and holidays.

14 DAY LOANS
NO RENEWALS

CPSIA information can be obtained
at www.ICGtesting.com
Printed in the USA
FFOW05n0214040615